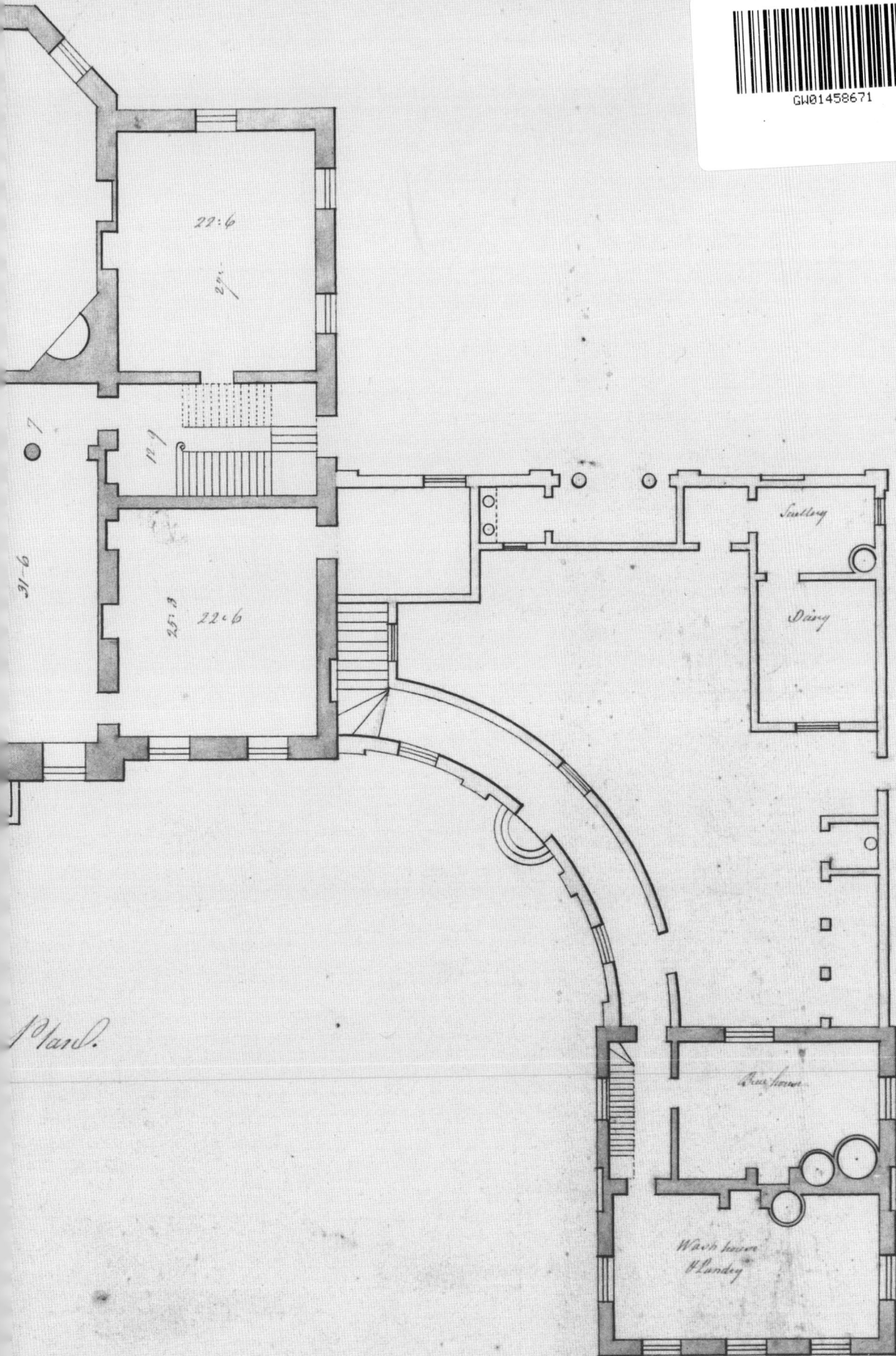

22:6

2":6

7

17:9

31:6

26:9   22:6

Plan.

Scullery

Dairy

Brew house

Wash house
& Laundry

11   60   70   00

THE LIFE AND WORKS OF

John Carr
of York

Portrait of John Carr by George Dance

By courtesy of the British Library

THE LIFE AND WORKS OF

John Carr of York

———

BRIAN WRAGG

EDITED BY

GILES WORSLEY

OBLONG

YORK · 2000

First published in 2000 by
Oblong Creative Ltd
The Annexe
Wharfebank Business Centre
Ilkley Road
Otley
LS21 3JP
UK

PAPERBACK ISBN 0 9536574 1 8
HARDBACK ISBN 0 9536574 2 6

COVER/JACKET ILLUSTRATIONS
front Portrait of John Carr by Sir William Beechey,
with a drawing of Buxton Crescent and the spire
of Horbury Church in the background
By courtesy of the National Portrait Gallery, London

back The staircase, Norton Place, Lincolnshire
Crown copyright. National Monuments Record

ENDPAPERS
front Design by John Carr for the ground floor
of Wiganthorpe Hall, Yorkshire
Mrs Mary Wragg

back Design by John Carr for the ground floor
of Leventhorpe Hall, Yorkshire
Mrs Mary Wragg

DESIGNED AND TYPESET BY OBLONG CREATIVE LTD, OTLEY, UK
PRINTED AND BOUND BY SMITH SETTLE LTD, OTLEY, UK

CONTENTS

―――――――

ACKNOWLEDGEMENTS

AUTHOR'S ACKNOWLEDGEMENTS

FIRST, I THANK MY WIFE for the pleasure of her company on many of my Carr excursions. I acknowledge a grant from Sheffield University Grants Committee which enabled a start to be made on this study.

My grateful thanks are also due to many others whose aid was essential particularly in the early days when family documents and Carr records had made only a limited appearance in libraries and record offices. Although the list which follows is lengthy, the names of several collaborators may have been omitted; if so, then to these friends I offer my sincere apologies: Canon G. W. C. Addleshaw; Col. R. A. Alec-Smith; Dr Mary Andrews; Mr R. L. Arundale; Mr M. Y. Ashcroft; Father Hugh Aveling; Miss Rosemary Ashbee; Lord Airedale; Mrs Janet Ball; Mr J. Barnfather; Mr Geoffrey Beard; Sir Hugh Bell; Major Bell; Mr A. Betteridge; Mr H. Bilton; Mr J. O. Blair-Cunynghame; Mr A. Bleasby; Mr Alfred Booth; Mr Charles Bramley; Mr R. Bretton; Mr H. Brook; Mr James Brown; Mr W. C. Brown; Miss Elizabeth Brunskill; Professor L. B. Budden; Mr R. J. A. Bunnett; Lady Alice Burne-Murdoch; Mr D. R. Buttress; Lord Chesham; Brigadier R. C. Chichester-Constable; Mr Hugh Chomely; Dr G. Kitson Clark; Mr Richard Clegg; Lt. Col. P. T. Clifton; Lady Evelyn Collins, Mr J. M. Collinson; Mr H. M. Colvin; Mr Francis J. Cooper; Abbess Kathleen Cooper; Mr A. B. Craven; Mr C. K. Croft-Andrew; Mr J. N. St. G. Curwen; Mrs G. Dent; Mr R. F. Dell; Mr F. M. Doyne; Mr A. R. Duffy; Mr W. A. Eden; Mr W. Ryle Elliot; Mr Ellis Flack; Mr John Fleming; Earl Fitzwilliam; Father James Forbes; Mr R. N. Forbes; Miss Amy G. Foster; Mr C. H. Fox; Col. F. G. W. Lane-Fox; Mr Frank Fordham; Mr R. Sharpe France; Mr S. Clayton Fryers; Milnes Gaskell; Dr E. A. Gee; Mr David Gerard; Mr Christopher Gilbert; Mr A. E. Gilfillan; Mr Chrisopher Gotch; Mr W. A. Grace; Mr Irvine E. Gray; Miss Dorothy Greene; Mr Graham Greenfield; Lord Grimesthorpe; Mr L. R. A. Grove; Mr W. E. Gundill; Mr Rupert Gunnis; Mr J. M. Guthrie; Lord Halifax; Mr K. M. Hamilton; Mr T. W. Hanson; Mr Dudley Harbron; Lord Harcourt; Mr John B. Harper; Mr John Harris; Mr A. N. Harrison; Mr R. G. Heape; Mr L. A. J. Heywood; Mr N. Higson; Mr M. Thoroton Hildyard; Mrs Eleanor Hill; Sir J. W. F. Hill; Mr Hugh Honour; Maj. Le G. G. W. Horton Fawkes; Major George Howard; Dr Christopher Hussey; Mr F. G. B. Hutchings; Lord Iliffe; Sir Joslan Ingilby; Maj. T. L. Ingram; Mr M. E. Ingram; Mr John Jacob; Mrs R. B. Jennings; Mr F. F. Johnson; Mr C. Jones; Mr B. C. Jones; Miss J. M. Kennedy; Sir Bernard Kenyon; Mr P. I. King; Mr James Laver; Lt. Col. J. L. B. Leicester Warren; Mr James Lees-Milne; Mrs Susan Lowndes Marques; Lord Macintosh; Mr C. E. Makepeace; Mr Henry Marshall; Lady Vera Matthews; Miss R. Meredith; Mr D. J. H. Michelmore; Mr G. R. Micklewright; Lord Middleton; Sir Owen Morshead; Mrs Mary Nattress; Mr James Needham; Lady Nelson; Duke of Norfolk; Mr Charles Ogden; Maj. G. G. Pace; Col. Robert Parker; Mr T. G. F. Paterson; Lt. Col. J. B. W. Pennyman; Mr L. Petch; Miss I. P. Pressly; Canon J. S. Purvis; Mr H. V. Radcliffe; Revd A. C. Rees; Mr Christopher Riley; Mr P. Roach; Mrs J.R. Ropner; Mr Thomas Salvin; Mr C. R. S. Sandford; Mr G. A. Selby; Mr R. S. Shapley; Mr Derek R. Sherborn; Mr G. N. G. Smith; Venerable C. J. Stranks; Lady Constance Stuart; Mrs Spencer Stanhope; Sir John Summerson; Mr Cyril Sunderland; Revd H. C. Sutton; Sir Richard Sykes; Mr J. Stuart Syme; Mr A. C. Taylor; Mr Rene Taylor; Mr John Nest-Taylor; Mr F. C. Tighe; Mrs Joan Varley; Major R. W. Verelst; Miss Marjorie Vernon; Mr Peter Walne; Miss Mary Walton; Mrs M. A. Welch; Mr John R. W. Whitfield; Mr J. E. Williams; Captain Withers; Mr T. S. Wragg; Mr W. H. Wormald; Lord Zetland.

My first thanks must be to Mrs Wragg for asking me to edit her husband's work and for accepting the inevitable editorial interventions and also to my publisher, Derek Brown. I must also thank Dr Patrick Nuttgens for persuading me to take on the project when discretion, the tight schedule and existing commitments argued that the task should be left for another.

I was determined that a book on Carr must be well illustrated and that would not have been possible without the generous support of the Paul Mellon Foundation for British Art, the Marc Fitch Fund, the Society of Architectural Historians of Great Britain, who provided a Dorothy Stroud Bursary towards the cost of this publication, and the Oliver Sheldon Fund. The help of National Monuments Record, in particular Anna Eavis, and of Camilla Costello at the Country Life Picture Library has been invaluable. To all of them I am extremely grateful.

My warmest thanks, however, must go to my wife Joanna for tolerating a year and a half of evenings, weekends and holidays given over to Carr which she, understandably, felt could have been otherwise employed.

Mine has been a task of months, not years, but it would not have been possible without the help of many individuals, in particular the staff of the various record offices, libraries and museums which hold so much Carr material. In particular, Barclays Bank Archives, the Borthwick Institute, Buckinghamshire County Records and Local Studies Service, Coutts and Co.'s Archives, East Riding of Yorkshire Record Office, Hertfordshire County Record Office, Hoare's Bank Archives, the National Library of Scotland Manuscripts Division, North Yorkshire County Record Office, Royal Bank of Scotland's Archives, Sir John Soane's Museum, Sheffield Archives, West Yorkshire Archive Service, Leeds, West Yorkshire Archive Service, Wakefield, York Archives, York Central Library and York Minster Library.

I am grateful for permission to quote from documents in their possession and in particular to S. W. Fraser Esq. for permission to quote from the Spencer-Stanhope Papers and the Trustees of the Right Hon. Olive Countess Fitzwilliam's Chattels Settlement and the Milton (Peterborough) Estates Company for permission to quote from the Wentworth Woodhouse Muniments.

Many people have helped or shared information on Carr and I am grateful to them all, particularly John Bell, Anthea Bickley, Sir Howard Colvin, Dr David Connell, Peter Day, The Lord Derwent, Tom Faulkener, The Lord Feversham, Dr Terry Friedman, Dr Ian Goodall, John Goodchild, Brett Harrison, Dr Deborah Howard, Simon Jervis, Dr Derek Linstrum, Andrew Martindale, Anthony Munford, David Neave, Patrick Nuttgens, Hugh Pagan, Mrs Diana Parker, David Pickersgill, Pete Smith, Sam Taylor, Patty Temple, John Thorp, Dr Richard Wilson, Professor John Wilton-Ely, and Lucy Worsley.

EDITOR'S INTRODUCTION

JOHN CARR'S CURRENT OBSCURITY would have surprised his contemporaries who did not suffer from the twentieth-century architectural historian's obsession with innovation, novelty and genius. Despite the fact that he worked from York and practised almost exclusively in the North, Carr's national standing was fully acknowledged by his fellow architects when he was elected as the only provincial member of the exclusive Architects Club. Founded in 1791 this consisted of fifteen of the foremost architects in London, who had to be a Royal Academician, Associate of the Royal Academy, gold medallist, or member of academies of Rome, Parma, Bologna or Paris. Carr was one of three honorary members along with Thomas Sandby, first Professor of Architecture at the Royal Academy, and Nicholas Revett, co-author of the highly influential *The Antiquities of Athens*.

Both Sir William Chambers and James Paine had sufficient respect for Carr, despite losing commissions to him, to commend his work and to the poet William Mason he was quite simply 'a greater master in Architectural ways and means than Lord North, or even Sir Gray Cooper is in political'.[1] He was also one of only a handful of architects included in the handsome folio volume *Sketches drawn from the life by George Dance, R.A. and engraved by William Daniell, A.R.A.*, which illustrated some of the most significant intellectual and military figures at the turn of the eighteenth century (Frontispiece).

Carr's work was certainly well known in his day. In volume five of *Vitruvius Britannicus*, published in 1771, more plates were given to Carr than to any other architect. William Kent has twelve, Robert Adam nine and Sir William Chambers three. Carr has fifteen. In the two volumes of *New Vitruvius Britannicus*, published in 1802 and 1808, only Robert Adam with ten plates was given more space in the first volume than Carr with nine (but then the author, George Richardson, had worked in Adam's office). No other architect was given more than five plates. In the second volume Carr's York Assize Courts took pride of place, an honour given in previous volumes to St Paul's Cathedral, Greenwich Hospital and the Horse Guards. Only Thomas Leverton had more plates.

Looking back nearly twenty years after his death Joseph Gwilt ranked Carr among the country's finest architects. In a footnote to the 1825 edition of Sir William Chambers's *Civil Architecture* he commented that it was to Palladio that 'this country is especially indebted for its progress in architecture, and for the formation of a school which has done it honor, and given it character of the first class, in the opinion of its continental neighbours. Among the names which that school enrols are those of Inigo Jones, Sir Christopher Wren, Nicholas Hawksmoor, James Gibbs, Lord Burlington, Carr of York, Sir Robert Taylor, our author himself [i.e. Chambers], and a long list whose works reflect a lustre on the name of Palladio'. Jones, Wren, Hawksmoor, Gibbs, Burlington, Chambers, even Taylor, are today firmly established among the pantheon of British architects. It is time Carr was too.

That he has rested in relative obscurity owes much to his misfortune with biographers. Many have started to work upon him. Few have seen their labours published. Robert Davies's early memoir, published in the *Yorkshire Archaeological Journal* in 1877, appeared posthumously.[2] A century later the *Ancient Monuments Society Transactions* published another posthumous tribute to Carr in 1979–80, 'John Carr, Stonecutter Extraordinary, and the Architectural Virtuosi'. It had been begun by W. A. Eden, head of the School of Architecture at Leeds, but, like Davies, Eden died before his work was published. His *John Carr: An Unpublished Monograph* is held by the University of Liverpool. The article was completed after his death by Brian Wragg. It was only one of numerous papers from the 1950s onwards in which Dr Wragg laid the foundations of modern Carr studies. But sadly, though Dr Wragg completed his doctoral thesis on Carr, his death in 1995 meant that he never pulled his researches together into the long-planned monograph on the architect.

It was with the knowledge of this frustrating history, and in the belief as a Yorkshireman that Carr had never received his due, that I agreed with Mrs Mary Wragg, Dr Wragg's widow, to take on the task of editing his work for publication. Turning the work of another author into publishable form has not been an easy task. The extent of Carr's practice means that it is hard to draw a line under research into him, as my predecessors have learnt to their cost. But I resolved not to be waylaid by the tempting goal of finality, in the firm belief that what Carr needed was a published book.

The scale of Carr's practice, spread over sixty years and hundreds of commissions, stretching from Scotland to Portugal, and as likely to include the design of a water closet as a great mansion, can seem protean. Establishing exactly what he designed and when has often proved elusive. Unlike better known contemporaries such as James Gibbs, James Paine and Robert Adam Carr never felt the need to publish his buildings in books. Nor is there a convenient central corpus of letters and drawings, as there is for the Adam brothers, for Sir William Chambers and for Sir John Soane. As well as the four volumes of drawings last sighted in 1825 others, which almost certainly survived in his office and were probably used by J. B. Atkinson and R. Davies in compiling lists of Carr's works in the 1870s, have also disappeared. Carr's bank account at Messrs Raper Clough and Swann's Bank in York, which would be the most informative source of information about his finances, does not survive and his account at Goslings is of only limited value.[3]

However, because of the nature of Carr's practice very large numbers of letters from him do survive, along with many drawings. The most important group of letters are those to the stewards at Harewood House and Wentworth Woodhouse as these stretch over many years and deal not only with the commissions in question but also shed broader light on Carr's career. Together the letters and drawings allow a remarkably full picture of Carr and of the world that he inhabited to emerge.

Perhaps no other figure gives us a fuller flavour of the world of eighteenth-century English architecture. Through studying Carr we get a vivid picture of the relationship between patronage, politics and architecture in the period. We also probably get a fuller picture of the mechanics of architectural practice than with any architect before Soane, together with an intimate study of the way Georgian architectural taste was disseminated from London to the provinces as Carr develops from the opulent richness of the Rococo to the elegant ornament of the Adamesque manner to the spare simplicity of neo-Classicism. Above all, Carr mastered the subtleties of the Georgian language of architecture. Never showy, always verging on the side of restraint, his buildings show an effortless ability to develop and vary a theme, seamlessly elaborating the same motifs so that they work as well for a humble gate lodge as for a nobleman's mansion. Others may claim the limelight, but Carr has good reason to be described as the archetypal Georgian architect.

For reasons of time editing has had to be a paper exercise. Original sources, both primary and secondary, have been extensively examined but no attempt has been made to search out Carr's buildings on the ground. Full cognisance has also been made of the substantial body of recent published material on and related to Carr and this, together with newly available primary material, has been integrated into the text. A significant number of new works have come to light during the course of the work.

There are still tantalizing mysteries to be resolved. Where, for instance, in Lincolnshire did Carr go for a fortnight at a critical moment in his early career in 1754?[4] And what was it that called him so urgently and for so long to London in 1768?[5] Do the four volumes of his drawings sold in 1825 sit in some dusty library, forgotten and uncatalogued? Does a catalogue of his library, apparently sold in 1822, survive unnoticed? Demolished buildings could prove an equally fruitful field of investigation. Edward Waterson and Peter Meadows's volumes on the lost houses of the North of England include numerous examples such as Ackton Hall, Elmsall Lodge, Horton Hall, Bradford, Finningley Hall, Healaugh Manor, Heaton Hall, in Yorkshire, and Biddlestone Hall, Northumberland, that could be by Carr. The great majority of these were in the West Riding where the scale of industrialization and urbanization meant that there was a much greater density of large houses and an equally higher risk of their demolition. We know too little about them both because of their early demolition and because many were built for merchants and industrialists, whose papers survive much less frequently than those of landed families.

But the publication of the key facts in Carr's career, together with a full, illustrated catalogue of his works, means that a solid foundation has been laid on which others can build. This book should at last place the familiar but elusive name of 'Carr of York' in firm focus.

CHAPTER ONE

YOUTH

FAMILY BACKGROUND

THE 'RAGS TO RICHES' STORY of John Carr, so reminiscent of Dick Whittington, has always had popular appeal — at any rate in Yorkshire. Rising from humble origins he was twice Lord Mayor of York, a long-standing Justice of the Peace for both the North and West Ridings, and owned his own country house. He built an impressive church for his native town of Horbury — surely, for an architect, a unique gesture — and died worth a reputed £150,000.[1] The noted antiquary Thomas Whitaker, writing in 1816, praised Carr and his achievements but concluded in rather pained surprise that one 'though born a common mason' had risen so far.[2] However, the image of the lucky labourer is misleading, perhaps as misleading as Carr's own attempts in prosperous old age to burnish the social standing of his parents and their families. For a Georgian architect his origins are both solid and unsurprising. He was born on 28 April 1723 at Horbury near Wakefield in the West Riding of Yorkshire into a well-established family of masons prosperous enough to own two quarries. The entry in the Parish Register reads: 'John Son of Robert Carr, Mason, Bapt'd ye 15th day and recieved ye 3d day of June'.

Carrs can be found in the Horbury Parish Registers from the 1620s.[3] The architect's great-grandfather, Robert Carr (1644–89), is the first to be described as a mason, or in his case a rough mason.[4] Robert's elder son, John, (1668–1736), is entered as mason in the parish registers, and so is John's eldest son, Carr's father Robert, (1697–1760).[5]

The extent of the Carrs' work and their prosperity is difficult to assess, although the family bible of John Carr the Elder (1668–1736), now at Browsholme Hall, with its annotations in Latin and Greek indicates a certain standing. The only known reference to John Carr the Elder's work is in the accounts of Wakefield Grammar School for 1717: 'to Carr of Horbury for making two round holes at the ends of the school and mending a window at the end 5/4d'.

As an old man applying for a coat of arms in 1805 Carr claimed that John Carr the Elder's father Robert 'purchased

Estates at Horbury for his residence'.[6] However, the impression of wealth suffers somewhat from an examination of the family papers, now in the Lancashire Record Office. These indicate, and confirmation is provided in the Wakefield Court Rolls, that 'Estates' was too grand a description of Robert's limited holdings. Deeds show that in 1679 he and his wife Edith bought a 'House at the Bottom of Town' together with an acre of land, the witness being John Carr who appended his mark. In 1685 he bought two roods in West Field and, in 1688, one acre for £40 in Stonebrigg. His son extended the family holding and in his will of 1736, where he was described as John Carr the Elder of Horbury, Mason, left among other things, a dwelling house with barns and two little crofts and four pieces of land in Stonebrigg fields. Significantly, he also left 'a stone quarry lying in the West Field lately purchased from Mr Smythe, also a quarry lying near the quarry last mentioned containing one rood purchased of Mr Thornton'.[7]

In his will, made in 1756, Carr's father described himself as 'Robert Carr of Horbury in the County of York Mason'.[8] Carr promoted a rather different impression, describing his father as 'architect' in the *North Riding Book of Bridges*[9] and again in the Latin panegyric which served as his father's monument in Horbury church. Translated this reads:

Here lies the body of Robert Carr, architect, a man distinguished, not by transitory ancestral titles nor by artificial splendour of wealth, but truly worthy of immortality on account of the more important gifts of mind and character. For, from an early age, fixed with an incredible love of the noblest arts he developed his great natural powers so successfully that he would undertake any problem. He devoted himself to architecture and the many sided science of mathematics. His knowledge was extraordinary being enhanced by the remarkable blamelessness of his character his gentleness and his genuine piety, throughout the whole course of his life. He died on the 3rd day of December, in the Year of Our Lord 1760.

Robert Carr was well versed in building matters, could write a good letter and, undoubtedly, designed small works. Whether these justified the title of architect is doubtful. The earliest support for that title, and the only proof of Robert

Carr's ability to draw, is contained in an entry of 1739, concerning old Horbury Church, in which Thomas Goodall and Robert Carr were ordered to draw a plan of the chapel and of proposed new additions.[10] The Order Books of the West Riding provide further illumination. On 13 January 1742 it is recorded that 'This Court refers it to John Watson and Robert Carr Masons able and Experienced Workmen to take a View at the most seasonable Times ... of all the Bridges ... belonging to the said Riding ...'.[11] The two men were to be paid seven shillings a day, more than the weekly wage of a common mason. The following year their appointment was renewed on a salary basis and they were now called Surveyors of the Riding Bridges,[12] positions they continued to hold until their deaths.

A similar example of posthumous aggrandizement can also be found in the inscription to Carr's mother Rose (1698–1774) in Horbury Church, where she is described as the daughter of John Lascelles 'Armigeri', or gentleman. Hunter's *Yorkshire Pedigrees* gives Anne as the name of Rose's mother. 'The Genealogy of the Carrs of Carr Lodge, Horbury',[13] tells us that her family were from Norton-le-Clay near Boroughbridge.[14] This all promises well: a connection with the wealthy Lascelles family with whom Carr was to be so intimately acquainted at Harewood seems about to emerge. But no reference to John Lascelles, nor to his daughter, appears in the published genealogy of the Lascelles of Harewood. There is no record of a John Lascelles having owned land or property of value in the vicinity of Norton-le-Clay. A connection with the Lascelles family would therefore seem unlikely. However, the family clearly believed in the connection, as a letter in the correspondence concerning Carr's application for arms from the architect's niece, Maria Elizabeth Carr, whose brother had been christened pointedly Lascelles Carr, makes clear: 'I suppose of the particulars of his relationships to the family of Lascelles my Uncle has acquainted Mr Radclyffe ... my Uncle no doubt has mentioned to Mr Radclyffe his mothers descent from them.'[15]

In the same correspondence Carr claims descent from Thomas Carr of Ford Castle, Sheriff of Northumberland in 1630. But as he instructed the herald to trace the detailed pedigree back only to his great-grandfather Robert Carr (1644–89), not to the Carrs of Ford Castle, his reasons (if any) for this claim are unknown. Another Northumbrian connection is provided by the seal, in black wax, used by John Carr on a letter addressed to Lord Fairfax. This bears the arms of the Carrs of Cocken. The family, related to the wealthy merchant family of the Carrs of Newcastle, were extremely well known in the North. One of them, Sir Ralph Carr MP, was three times Mayor of Newcastle. But no connection with the Northumbrian Carrs has been traced.[16]

John Carr was the eldest of nine children, yet outlived them all. His parents, listed as Robert Carr of Wakefield and Rose Lascels of Cundall, had been married in South Kilvington church (eight miles from Norton-le-Clay) on 13 November 1721.[17] His brothers and sisters were Robert, mason/architect (1724–77); Joseph (1727–33); David (1731–94); James of Burnstall, mason, but sometimes described as 'gent' (1733–1804); Samuel, a cleric, who rose to be Vicar of Finchley and Prebend of St Paul's Cathedral, (1736–94);[18] Ursula, who married, as second husband, Richard Heaton, 'gent' of Barlow Hall (1729–99); Elizabeth (1738–41) and Rose (1740–41).

Local tradition has it that Carr was born in the old stone house, with flagged roof, standing at the Northfield Lane end of Cluntergate, opposite Daw Lane, in Horbury. For its date the house is substantial with two storeys, each of four rooms. Over the doorway, in stylish carving, is the date 1739, a sundial and the combined initials of Carr's parents 'RCR'.

Samuel, twelve years Carr's younger, is understood to have attended Wakefield Grammar School but we do not know where Carr was educated, most probably it was at Horbury Town School, founded in 1710. In a letter, dated 1787, he mentions that he had been upwards of fifty years in the building trade so that he must have left school at about the age of fourteen to assist his father.[19] Nevertheless, he always produced an impressive looking letter complete with fine flowing flourishes and although the content was not always entirely grammatical it was at least up to the standard of the average eighteenth-century gentleman.

Knowledge of Carr's boyhood is limited to a few anecdotes, which should perhaps be taken with a small pinch of salt. We are told that while watching the building of Horbury Church as an old (and prosperous) man bystanders often heard him remark that he was not ashamed of it being known that he had once been so poor that on occasions he had to lie abed while his breeches were being repaired.[20] Another story, indicating early talent, is set at Bretton Hall, five or six miles from Horbury. Workmen were trying unsuccessfully to design a small building when Robert Carr called out 'Let my lad try'. No sooner said than done: Carr solved the problem and his plan was adopted.[21]

We are also told that Carr was one of the masons building a new park wall at Chevet for Sir Lionel Pilkington, going the four miles from Horbury to his work in a morning and returning in the evening. On more distant jobs, where he was absent from home for a week, he would divide a large meat pie of circular shape into six equal parts with his compasses so that he might secure one part for each day's dinner.[22] Frugality, a love of order and

1 Portrait in pastel of Carr in middle age by John Russell

YOUTH

symmetry, essential to a Palladian architect, could all be deduced from this story. The possession of compasses might also suggest that he was already more than a common labourer.

Another anecdote reflecting less credit is said to have been related gleefully by the architect in later years. Two boys on their way to school on a hot summer's day strayed in search of birds' nests into the quarry near Horbury, where the youthful Carr was working. Carr, noticing where they had hidden their lunch took the opportunity of augmenting his own dinner from their basket.[23]

Apart from these stories details are lacking of Carr's youth and we know little about the family practice before he set up as an architect, although Robert Carr was paid £13 5s in 1746 from the estate of John Smith of Newland for work done at Birthwaite.[24] But it is implicit that the association with his father, only broken with the latter's death in 1760, was particularly close in the formative years. It seems reasonable, therefore, to suppose that John acquired not only his solid understanding of materials and construction but an early knowledge of draughtsmanship from his father. Similarly, Carr must have been indebted to the father for his introduction to architectural design. There is nothing to show that anyone other than his father acted as Carr's tutor.

On 31 August 1746 Carr, aged twenty-three and apparently still no more than a mason, married Sarah, daughter of Thomas and Mary Hinchliffe of Cold Hiendley at Featherstone, about eight miles from Horbury.[25] Ten years older than her husband,[26] she is said to have been one of the domestics at Bretton Hall where Carr was then working.[27] John Carr, her nephew, sought to present a different impression when he wrote to ask the College of Heralds on 3 March 1807, for permission for 'the arms of Hinchliffe the maiden name of the wife deceased of my late Uncle to quarter with those of Carr in the Hatchment, my late Aunt was of a reputable familly (sic) of the name of Hinchliffe of Cold Hiendly, in the parish of Felkirk ...'.[28]

Very much a background figure, Sarah Carr seldom appears in Carr's letters and was not reported in the newspapers as accompanying Carr at the York Assemblies. They had no children and when she died on 19 January 1787 she was buried at Felkirk, where she had been baptized, thirty miles from York. All of this, coupled with Carr's long tours of inspection away from home, might lead one to suppose that the marriage was not all that it might have been. However, Sarah did assist in the practice by opening and answering the mail when he was away from home and there are two of her letters to Samuel Popplewell, steward at Harewood, which prove that in 1758 and 1762 she was living in York with her husband, referring to him affectionately as 'Jacki'.[29] The letters were obviously penned with difficulty.

Lack of children inclined Carr to his brothers' children, one of whom, William, he virtually adopted, eventually making him his right-hand man in the practice. Affectionate regard for his nieces, who accompanied him on many of his 'grand tours' — and their daughters — is a well-recorded facet of his character. Clark, for example, elaborates on this and describes the daughters of Ann Clark, Carr's niece, as '... the beauties of the County', adding that 'as their great uncle had no children, he took them under his guidance and patronage, and introduced them to the best society in the County. They all married rich husbands, had numerous families, and died at a good old age.'[30] Tangible recognition of concern for both nieces and nephews was finally expressed by Carr in his will.

THE FIRST BUILDINGS

Bretton and Chevet were both close to Horbury. Carr's first recorded house, suggests he was beginning to look further afield. J. B. Atkinson (grandson of Peter Atkinson, Carr's assistant and one of the successors of Carr's practice in York) lists Carr's first building as a 'house at Huckwaite built for H. M. Cookschutts in 1748'.[31] There is no town, village or hamlet called Huckwaite, but there is a Huthwaite Hall near Thurgoland fifteen miles from Horbury, which was owned by the Cockshutt family (Fig. 2). Carr's client was probably John Cockshutt, who succeeded to the property in 1739.[32]

The introduction of Carr to John Cockshutt may have come about through business connections as the Cockshutts ran the ironworks at Wortley, near Thurgoland. When Carr was working as a mason at Bretton Hall, pig iron was being supplied from blast furnaces at Bretton for the Wortley forges. A closer connection and a more likely link is that the Carrs, father and son, needing cramps and other iron objects for their building work, bought them from Cockshutt. Certainly some later vouchers in the Harewood Estate Office include one for iron plate supplied by Cockshutt on the order of Robert Carr, who was then acting as the clerk of works.

The plan of Huthwaite Hall is L-shaped. The long arm at the rear, an earlier survival with hood moulds over door and windows, contained the kitchens and servants' quarters. At right-angles to it and facing down the valley is the main building, two and a half storeys high with a gabled roof. The rooms are symmetrical about the main entrance in the middle of both main and garden elevation. The Gibbsian surround of the ground floor windows is similar to the detailing of the quoins at Arncliffe Hall of 1753, believed to be by Carr. The treatment of the interior is plain, sound and simple.

2 Huthwaite Hall, Yorkshire, built in 1748 for John Cockshutt; the entrance front

Two features of the design were particularly character-istic of the architect and occur in many of his subsequent houses: the reuse of part of the old house as kitchens and servants' quarters without any attempt at linking the two styles of architecture; and the economy of concentrating all the elevational features on one face of the building. It is evident that the embryo architect, at the age of twenty-five, was already a competent designer.

1748 was obviously a key year for Carr. It was also an opportune moment for a young architect to set up practice as the end of the eight-year-long War of the Austrian Succession set off a wave of new country house building which proved the making of a new generation of young architects.[33] In May that year Stephen Thompson, a wealthy London merchant whose family and estate were in Yorkshire, wrote to Thomas Grimston, a fellow Yorkshire squire, mentioning that he was going 'to Meet my New Overseer to put him in a way of going on with my Workmen …'. Grimston had been forced to dismiss his previous steward and overseer after he had quarrelled with one of his father's servants.[34] A subsequent letter noted that 'I have got a clever Young Fellow of a Mason at the Head of my Works.' This was Carr, who was to build Kirby Hall for Thompson.[35]

Huthwaite Hall had been a relatively small house for a client of only local significance. Kirby Hall at Little Ouse-burn, twelve miles north-west of York, was a much more impressive affair, and for a much more influential client. Indeed, it was considered of sufficient importance to justify inclusion in volume five of *Vitruvius Britannicus*, where the Earl of Burlington and Roger Morris are named as the architects. Carr's status is shown in an engraving of the mansion published by Thompson after its completion (Fig. 3), inscribed 'Elevation by Ro. Morris, Archt. and the Earl of Burlington: Executed, and the inside finishings, by J. Carr, Architect, Plans by the Owner, S.T.'

Carr's inclusion in such honourable company is perhaps due to a quirk of good fortune. Morris died in 1749, and Burlington in 1753; thus responsibility was thrown onto the shoulders of the young man. It was an opportunity not to be missed. That Carr took on the burden successfully is evinced by Thompson's acknowledgement in the engraving.

YOUTH

7

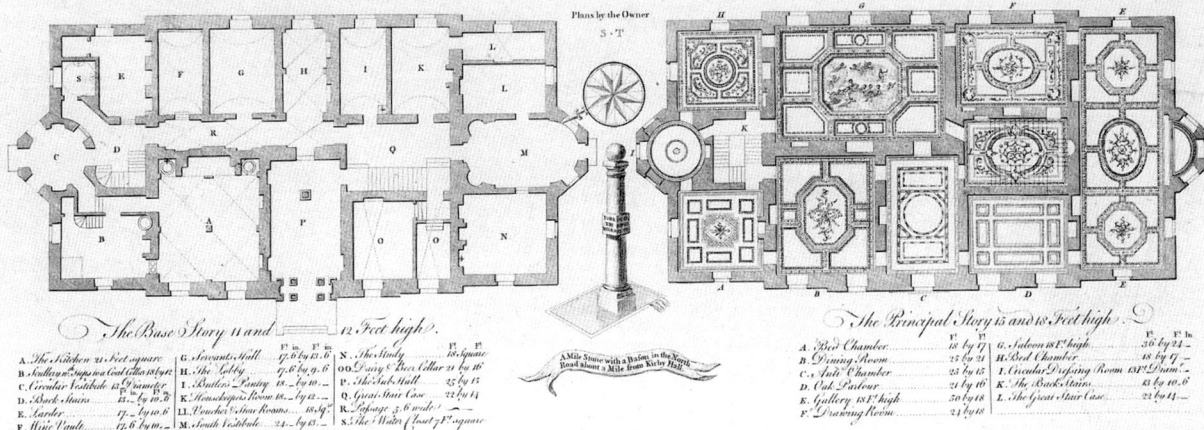

3 Kirby Hall, Yorkshire. Designed by Lord Burlington and Roger Morris. Carr supervised its erection and designed the interiors between 1748 and 1755; engraving of the entrance front

4 *opposite* Thorp Arch Hall, Yorkshire, built for William Gossip in 1749–56; the entrance front

Kirby Hall made a lasting impression on the young man. It was slightly top-heavy with a shallow rustic storey for the offices, a first floor — the *piano nobile* — containing the main rooms, an attic storey for the lesser bedrooms and the whole surmounted with a great pyramidal roof. The main windows were obviously double squares but, less obviously, if a circle were described to touch apex and ground, it would cut through the cornice to give the position of the extremities of the projecting centre. Carr later used these simple guides in several of his buildings.

The plainness and masculinity of Kirby Hall were to be the characteristics of Carr's designs. The square plinths and string courses marking floor and window cill levels were reproduced time after time, as were the hipped roofs and particularly the canted bays rising the full height of the

building. Other details were taken up though not so enthusiastically: for example, the sweeping architrave, so redolent of Burlingtonian design, to the window over the front entrance appeared in the 1750s at Arncliffe Hall, Heath Hall and Kirkleatham Church. It was subsequently dropped from the vocabulary. The plan, the simple, square shape of the central block; the internal top-lit staircase, and the varied shapes of the rooms — square, rectangular, circular and apsidal — were especially noted. As Thompson's print reveals, the interiors were designed by Carr and it interesting to see that they appeared to be of the Rococo type distinctive of the York school.

Thompson originally expected completion as early as 1752 but did not occupy the house until 1755.[36] In the meantime Carr had acquired other commissions and firmly established himself as Yorkshire's up-and-coming architect. Another very early work must have been begun at this time. Much later, at the very end of his life in 1805 Carr reminisced to Miss Heaton that the house he was then living in, Askham Hall near York, had been one of his first commissions fifty-five years earlier. Carr recalled that he had added a dining room, drawing room and 'a train of offices as long as any lady's gown in the Kingdom' to the house for Edmund Garforth, member of a much-respected York banking family.[37] The project was almost certainly a family one. Carr's nephew William was born in Askham Richard in 1749, suggesting that his mason brother Robert was probably also involved, perhaps living near the site and acting as clerk of works.

Nothing is known of Carr's work at Askham as the house was replaced by the present Tudoresque mansion in the nineteenth century. Much better documented is Thorp Arch Hall (Fig. 4), built for a friend of both Thompson and Garforth, William Gossip, the son of a West Riding mercer who was keen to establish himself as a country gentleman. Carr and his father first visited the proposed site of the new house on 8 August 1749 and finalized designs that month. Carr produced all the plans. Work progressed rapidly, the cellars were turned by February 1750 and the house was roofed in August 1751. Carr's involvement was intense. Between August 1749 and September 1750 he visited twenty-six times. Even after the roof was on he was a regular visitor, attending the site eleven times between

December 1751 and August 1752. By the end of 1753 construction was largely complete and the attention was focused on fitting up the interior, where Carr provided the hearths and mantelpieces. The house was eventually completed in 1756, at a cost of about £2,035.

Thorp Arch Hall is a simple, unadorned house of five bays and two storeys with a three-bay pediment. Its two wings, but not the body of the house, have pyramidal roofs like that at Kirby Hall. Campsmount Hall (Fig. 5), near Doncaster, is similarly plain, and again five bays wide with wings, although half a storey higher. Here Carr was paid five guineas on 8 January 1751 'for making a Design of Plans and Elevations of a house proposed to be built at Campsall by Thomas Yarborough' and a further three guineas for four journeys he had made. Yarborough, who had been toying with the idea of building a new house since about 1728, also sought designs from the young James Paine, who was rapidly establishing himself as a successful architect around Doncaster. It must have been particularly satisfying for Carr when he received the commission. His father signed a memorandum of agreement to construct the house in January 1752, which was occupied in February 1756.

Arncliffe Hall (Fig. 6), his next new house must have been begun about the same time as the rainwater heads are dated 1753, as is the pediment. Although documentation has not survived, the house, which sits above the village of Ingleby Arncliffe more than thirty miles north of York, is

5 *above* Campsmount Hall, Yorkshire, built for Thomas Yarborough in 1751–56; the entrance front
6 *below* Arncliffe Hall, Yorkshire, built for Thomas Mauleverer in about 1753; the entrance front

YOUTH

7 Arncliffe Hall, Yorkshire; the drawing room

firmly attributed to Carr. This was a more ambitious project. The south-facing garden elevation five bays wide, with a central pedimented projection, and pyramidal roof — the existing flat topped one is a replacement after fire — all bear testimony to Carr's experiences at Kirby. The unusual quoins match those at Huthwaite. The balusters (the profile of which Carr reproduced without change until the end of his days) and, particularly, the theme of a simple variation of detail on each elevation can be recognized in virtually all of Carr's buildings. Handsome stables (Fig. 8), among the first in what was to be a distinguished series, introduced two characteristic features, the use of round-headed windows, sometimes set within shallow relieving arches, linked by a running cill, and compositions with a double accent instead of a single, central accent, in this case slightly projecting bays marked by pediments.

Internally, the design is bold and elaborate with carved door casings, fine chimneypieces with and without over-mantels and scrolled brackets for busts between doorways. The most remarkable internal features are two fine ceilings, both of vigorous Rococo moulding, in the drawing room (Fig. 7) and stairwell. The centrepiece in each is of a low-relief allegorical scene. That over the staircase consists of a plump, winged young lady, said to be the Goddess of

8 Arncliffe Hall, Yorkshire; the stables

9 84 High Street, Northallerton, Yorkshire, built for Daniel Mitford in about 1755-58

Plenty, flying across the rays of a sun rising behind Rosebery Topping, one of the nearby hills in the Cleveland range. The plasterwork is patently of the York School and we can discern similar points of detail occurring not only in buildings with which Carr was associated in York, Fairfax House, for instance, but in his houses farther afield, as for example Lytham Hall, in Lancashire, where the plasterer was Joseph Cortese.

A nearby blood brother to Arncliffe Hall, five bays wide, in similar grey stone and detailing is No. 84 High Street, Northallerton (Fig. 9). Attributed to Carr, the house was built for Daniel Mitford soon after Arncliffe Hall. A document in the North Yorkshire County Record Office written in 1758, mentions that the site was leased from Edwin and Daniel Lascelles, both new clients of Carr, and notes 'This House is at present unoccupied but Mr Mitford intends shortly to remove into it'. Well-mannered, it too has the internal characteristics, though on a more modest scale, of those at Arncliffe. Like Thorp Arch Hall and Arncliffe Hall, Mitford's house had a pyramidal roof, a characteristic it shared with No. 47 Bootham in York, which was built for Mrs Mary Thompson and finished in 1752. After this date Carr reverted to more conventional roof forms.

By the early 1750s Carr was clearly beginning to establish himself as a rising young Yorkshire architect. Unlike his father and brothers Robert and James he was not prepared to remain a mason or contractor. It was not surprising, therefore, that he abandoned his native village of Horbury for York. There were good reasons for the change. York was the leading social centre in the North of England, providing an obvious potential for clients and, though lacking industry, a market centre attracting and distributing goods from and over a wide area.

Perhaps the most interesting explanation for the architect's migration to York was the one put forward by Sidney Kitson.[38] The young man, he suggested, joined a relative, a speculative builder, who in partnership with Charles Mitley, had demolished old Davy Hall in New Street replacing it with a terrace of six houses named Cumberland Row after the royal duke who quelled the rebellion of 1745. The City House Books show that the speculator, William Carr, by trade a joiner, was granted the sharing of the lease of Davy Hall with Mitley in 1747. Further, the Register of Apprentices' Indentures lists the man, apprenticed in 1735, as the son of an ostler, John Carr of York, who, in the matter of dates could just have been Carr's uncle John (1702–57). However, the uncle's occupation is recorded mason, not ostler; there is no record of his having lived in York and none of his having a joiner son.

The precise date when Carr took up residence in the City is uncertain, but in October 1751 'John Carr of the City of York, Mason' bought a house in Skeldergate, on the south side of the River Ouse, for £180.[39] The following year he applied to be made a freeman of the city, which would have been necessary if he was to practice there. The Corporation's House Books records an entry on 9 July 1752 which reads: 'And now Mr Carr who is to undertake the Building for Ornamenting Pikeing Well applied for his freedom of this City which he is Ordered to have on his Allowing Twenty five Pounds out of the sum of Eighty Eight pounds and Thirteen Shillings to be paid him for the Building.'[40] The Freedom could be obtained for nothing by patrimony, but outsiders were required to pay the substantial sum of £25. Carr, an unfranchised man working for the Corporation, could hardly evade the issue.

The Corporation was always keen on improvements. Walks along the bank of the River Ouse had been developed and Pikeing Well, whose water was thought to be beneficial to sore eyes, lay adjacent to the New Walk promenade. Charles Mitley, builder of Cumberland Row and designated at various times, carver, gilder, mason and statuary, was paid three guineas in June 1753 'for taking the Situation of the Spring of Pikeing Well and Drawing several

10 Pikeing Well, York, built for the Corporation of York in 1752–56 to enclose a medicinal spring

plans for Erecting a Grotto over the same'. Whether these plans were alternatives to Carr's earlier proposals is unclear but payment for Carr was authorized in October 1756. The Chamberlains' Accounts for 16 May 1757 register the payment to him of £88 13s, the original contract figure, less, of course, the deduction of £25 for the grant of the Freedom. Forthwith he was entered in the freemen's rolls as 'Mr John Carr, Stonecutter by order'.[41] The designation is surprising for Carr at this stage could have claimed architect or surveyor as his profession and, most certainly, the craft of mason. Possibly stonecutter — particularly making chimneypieces — was his trade when he first came to York. He certainly, continued with it as a second string even when successful as an architect.

The design of the Pikeing Well (Fig. 10) was typical of the small jobs Carr was soon undertaking in York. The chamberlain's accounts show that in 1753 he was involved in the construction of a footway through Micklegate Bar, which was built 'according to the plan with Two Arches drawn by Mr Carr'.[42] He was paid £55 11s 8d for this, £10 14s for work done to the ramparts over the Bar, £1 1s 9d to its walls and £28 16s 6d for 'stops pillars and Flagges'. He was also paid for a much smaller unspecified item: 'To Mr John Carr for work done in ye Mansion House as per Bill … 18s-6d'.[43] Even later, having achieved success as an architect, he was still prepared to accept the odd trifle: we read in the same accounts of a payment of £4 6s on 19 January 1766, for repairs to the Mansion House and on 24 January 1782, the sum of £1 1s for measuring the painting of the same building.

A similar job is recorded for 6 March 1752 in the minute books of the directors of the York Assembly Rooms: 'Ordered Mr Barstow be desired to send to Mr Carr and

11 *above* 47 Bootham, York, built for Mary Thompson in 1752
12 *opposite* Garforth House, 54 Micklegate, York, built for the Revd Edmund Garforth in about 1753–57.
Carr also worked for Garforth at Askham Hall

give him Instruction to View the Roofs of all the Assembly Rooms for raising the Pitch and giving an Estimate thereof to be laid before a Meeting of the Directors before the General Court of the 19th instant.' Within a fortnight, Carr had submitted not one but two estimates and, the lesser having been accepted, had been authorized to 'Execute the same in the best manner he is able and adhere as near to the scheme and Estimate refer'd to as the Safety and Sufficient repairing of the said Buildings will Admit and that he

deliver in the Bills of the several Workmen (he shall think proper to Employ in Executing the said repairs) to the Directors of the said Assembly Room'. Carr continued to be consulted throughout his life by the directors of the Assembly Rooms, often on matters of a menial nature. In 1753 and 1754, for example, he was asked to arrange the supply of six stoves from Mr J. Durne, stove-gratemaker of Jermyn Street, London, in order to ensure warmth in the Great Room in the winter. In October 1754, there is the

YOUTH

14

entry, 'Ordered that Mr John Carr do make three pifsing places Two without Doors and one within Doors'.[44]

Here Carr for the second time is intimately connected with a Burlington creation. Carr, whose training had been completely practical, was again confronted with a fundamental, academic theory applied in its entirety to a complete building.

Carr also soon established a comfortable practice designing town houses in York. That for Mrs Thompson in Bootham (Fig. 11), which was completed in 1752, was probably the first. This was followed by Petergate House in 1755. Carr was also probably responsible for Garforth House in Micklegate (Fig. 12), built by Carr's client at Askham Hall, Edmund Garforth and completed in 1757. Other York houses which have been attributed to Carr from this date include 39–45 Bootham, advertised for sale in the *York Courant* on 25 June 1751; 53/55 Micklegate, *c.*1752; Peasholme House, 1752; and Micklegate House for John Bourchier, completed in 1753. However, Carr's greatest York houses were to be in the 1760s, Castlegate House of 1762, and the fitting up of Fairfax House between 1761 and 1765 with some of his most sumptuous interiors.

As if Carr were not busy enough establishing his career in York, in 1752 he was called upon to help his father carry out the massive task of surveying the West Riding's bridges. That May the magistrates ordered the two bridge surveyors 'to draw plans, Representations or figures of all the said Bridges upon Vellum in a near exact and descriptive manner'. The survey was completed in the latter part of 1753. Watson's contribution was separately bound and is the smaller of the two volumes.[45] Carr's work comprised ninety-two sheets of vellum, magnificently bound in calf and ornamented with raised bands and brass clips. The title page is signed 'J. Carr' and so are thirty-seven of the plates, all of which are excellently drawn in John Carr's hand; the remainder, indifferently done, are probably by his father, Watson or subsequent surveyors. The labour of surveying and recording nearly sixty bridges was a test of draughtsmanship for the young architect, but it was also a valuable initiation, under the practical guidance of his father, in the fundamentals of bridge design and construction.

THE STANDHOUSE ON THE KNAVESMIRE

By 1753 Carr had firmly established the foundations of his future success. He had been responsible for the erection of one major country house and the design and supervision of three others, together with major alterations to a fourth. He had designed at least one town house in York, another in Northallerton and a third, for Jeremiah Dixon, in Leeds and had successfully established himself in the county capital. But it was the commission for the grandstand for York races (Fig. 13) that placed Carr's feet firmly on the road to success. The stand has long since been demolished, though part of its attractive arcade, re-erected a little way behind the conglomeration of stands that replaced it, serves as a gentle reminder of the important part it once played as a venue of Yorkshire society.

In 1730, the Ouse, overflowing its banks, flooded the racecourse, then sited on Clifton and Rawcliffe Ings, in the Forest of Galtres, necessitating a move to the present site on the Knavesmire, about a mile south of York. It was not until twenty years later that action was taken to erect a grandstand. The driving force was the Marquis of Rockingham, destined to be Carr's principal patron. Young, wealthy and one of the most influential men in the county, he was already embarking on the political career which led to his twice being Prime Minister. His interest in racing and York's political importance encouraged his enthusiastic participation in the project.

A site survey dated 1753 survives among the marquis's estate papers, subscriptions were sought and on 7 December 1753 the corporation granted a lease of the site. Four

13 Knavesmire Grandstand, York, built under the patronage of the 2nd Marquis of Rockingham in 1754–57; engraving by William Lindley

architects put forward designs in 1753 and 1754, Sir Thomas Robinson, James Paine, John Carr and Robert Dingley. Sir Thomas was early off the mark but his design, a simple affair with a rectangular room at ground level, a similar but loftier one on the first floor, and a flat roof for viewing 'in very serene weather', was rejected.

The second competitor, James Paine, was the most successful architect in the North at the time. His designs, elegant in plan with apsidal-ended main rooms and circular stair, and columned and elliptically-arched openings in the elevation were characteristic of his Paine's work. But it was probably their elegance or preciousness, redolent of the boudoir or of the garden loggia, which invited the suspicion of the hard-riding gentry. They were turned down in favour of designs by the up-and-coming John Carr.

Direct and simple — deceptively simple — Carr's was not a design that any mason or builder could have lifted out of a pattern book. Sotheron's *York Guide* of 1796 gives the accommodation: 'On the ground floor are convenient offices, and rooms for the entertainment of company to meet in, which is surrounded by a projecting miranda (with a balustrade before it) upwards of 200 feet in length, supported by a rusticated arcade 15 feet high above ground, from which miranda the company can command a prospect of the whole race-ground.' Many of the design features can

be recognized as those used repeatedly by Carr throughout his life: the plan, square plinth and string course of the arcade, the rustication, the Venetian window and the typical profile of the balusters cornice.

Lord Rockingham and the promoters now had a design, which was subsequently engraved. On the 12 August 1755 that the *York Courant* announced:

This day is published, Price 1s Sold by the Booksellers of York, and also by John Carr, Architect, in Skeldergate, Plans and Elevation of the Grand Stand erected upon Knavesmire, near York for the conveniency of seeing the Horse Races. N.B. The above Print is on a Sheet of Imperial Paper, and curiously engrav'd by Fourdrinier.

Copies of the print can often be found in the archives of northern gentry. Another and more popular print was of the perspective drawn by Carr's assistant, William Lindley (Fig. 13).

A venture supported by so many gentlemen — there were over 140 subscribers — with the means to build placed the reasonably successful local building practitioner at one stroke on the road to becoming an architect of national repute. The subscribers, entered in Rockingham's Cash Book, make an impressive list. The first half dozen, all paying £21 were the Marquis of Rockingham, the Duke of

Ancaster, Lord Fauconberg, the Earl of Holderness, the Earl of Northumberland and the Marquess of Hartington. Also included were Lord Strafford, Lord Irwin, Lord Scarborough, Lord Downe, Sir Thomas Robinson, Sir James Lowther, Sir George Savile, Sir John Ramsden, Sir Rowland Wynne, Sir Conyers Darcy, Sir Robert Hildyard. Among the squirearchy, were Daniel and Edwin Lascelles, Charles Turner, John Bourchier, Marmaduke Langdale, William Reade, Walter Hawksworth (all to be clients of Carr). Towards the end, among the plain misters — small gentry and successful tradesmen — and indicative of rising social status we see 'Mr John Carr £5 5s 0d'.

No longer did Carr act as superintendent or head of the works. Thomas Terry, was paid £20 'for Overseeing the whole for two years'. But the cash book, a large tome which almost seems to be a presentation copy judging from the beauty of the copperplate hand and the generally broad view taken of the accounts, makes it clear that Carr's control was tight as entries such as 'by Matthew Kendal for going to Hooton Roberts by Carr's Order' or 'by Richard Rassin for Carpenters' Work by Carr's Order' reveal. Total expenditure was £1,896 0s 7d, with Carr paid fees of £160 10s, although the subscriptions had raised only £1,323. The balance was met by Rockingham, who also reduced costs by providing the stone.

Clearly Carr would have achieved success without the York grandstand commission in 1755. But it was this which set the seal on his securing the attention of the Yorkshire aristocracy and gentry. Without Rockingham, without Rockingham's promotion of the stand, without Rockingham's bountiful financial support, Carr might never have received his chance. To Rockingham Carr would remain eternally grateful. The marquis was clearly satisfied with the architect's work for in due course he was appointed architect to the Rockingham estates, a post he would hold till his death.

HAREWOOD HOUSE

The grandstand on the Knavesmire at York was a critical moment in the architect's career. Harewood House is equally important. It was not only his first great house, the moment when he turned from a local, aspiring architect to one worthy of national notice, but it was also at Harewood that Carr assimilated, at first hand and early in his career, the style of Robert Adam. Together with his work at Wentworth Woodhouse, Harewood proved his longest commission and through its excellent documentation, particularly the survival of numerous letters, an invaluable insight into Carr's work is provided.

Henry Lascelles, whose wealth largely derived from the sugar plantations of the West Indies, bought the Harewood estates in about 1739. On his death in 1753, he was succeeded by his son, Edwin (1712–95), an imperious and ambitious man, Member of Parliament variously for Scarborough, Northallerton and Yorkshire. He and his brother, Daniel, acquired the estates of Gawthorpe, Goldsbrough and Plompton dominating the area between Knaresborough and Leeds. Their cousin Edward bought an estate at Stapleton near Pontefract.

Control of the considerable building work necessary for the development of the estates was beyond the range of the hard-worked steward, Samuel Popplewell. John and his father, Robert Carr, were soon at work for both Edwin and Daniel Lascelles.

By 1753 Carr may not have needed a specific introduction, but one connection could have come through Carr's early patron William Gossip who advised Edwin Lascelles's mother-in-law, Lady Dawes, on the building of her house in 1751 and provided Lascelles with information about slate prices in 1755.[46] Daniel Lascelles, primarily responsible for the Lascelles's West India merchant house in London, had a sharp temper similar to that of his brother but he was by no means as decisive. He seems to have followed in the steps of Edwin. The latter had an estate that he was improving, Daniel would do the same. After vacillating over Popplewell's carefully presented advice, he bought the Plompton estate about 1755. The lake and rocks at Plompton were renowned and formed an excellent nucleus for the fashionable pursuit of creating a romantic situation with views, hills and serpentine walks all in 'a kind of agreeable Disorder or Artful confusion'. Daniel proceeded on work for a new dam head where 'The little murmuring Rills of water, trickling down in disorder'd Streams, would create a kind of melancholy musical Tone, not altogether unpleasant'.

On purchase of the estate, John Carr had made a survey of the old mansion — according to Leland 'a fair house of stone with two towers' — and suggested renovations. These were eventually accepted by Daniel, in 1757, who tersely put it to the Steward 'I would now execute what I have paid him [Carr] for'.

Alterations were carried out and various estate buildings were started with Carr acting as architect. His father also worked as a visiting building consultant at a salary of 10s 6d a day, for instance setting out two farmhouses in 1757. His work included for some designing for on one occasion Daniel wrote 'I might perhaps misunderstand Old Carr in his design for the little House, if not, he has Ordered it to be an octagon within and to appear square without'.

Undoubtedly, the most remarkable surviving building at Plompton is the two-storeyed stable block started about 1757 (Fig. 14). Entrance to the courtyard is through a great rusticated archway surmounted by an octagonal cupola reminiscent of that of William Kent's stables at Houghton Hall, Norfolk (and to Carr's stables at Kirby Hall), as are the quoins, the engaged arcading and the ball-ornamented parapet. The cupola was not what Lascelles wanted and communications went awry. When Daniel discovered that it had been made large enough for an unwanted bell, his fury at the Carrs knew no bounds: 'Lett a stop be putt to this turrett, it is Just as I conjectured a vy Expensive Joke Ornament, and much too great for such a Building.' He was too late and the tower was finished giving a most distinctive Burlingtonian flavour to the stables.

Daniel, possibly with an eye on his brother's activities at Harewood, decided that the old manor house was unsuitable after all. Carr embarked on a replacement in 1761 (Fig. 15) but, long before the new mansion was finished, Daniel's attention had wandered to other estates. After again asking for advice from Popplewell, who recommended the purchase of the Lupsett estate, Daniel bought Goldsborough in 1762, a few miles away on the other side of the River Nidd. Now the ever-vacillating Lascelles decided to make Goldsborough Hall, a red brick gabled mansion of the early seventeenth century his home. Carr was called into to modernize it, Georgianizing several of the mullioned windows, adding a plain, Classical doorway leading into the garden and remodelling parts of the interior with such delicate detail as for it to have since been mistaken for the work of Adam. As a result work work was abandoned on Plompton Hall, explaining the mystery, mentioned in guide books, of the half-finished mansion and the curiously isolated stables in the great park.

Carr's work for Edwin Lascelles at Harewood, then known as Gawthorpe, started in 1753. It began with general advice, designs for gateways, a barn, a garden house and a portico for the old mansion house of the Gascoignes. He was already much in demand, and in September 1754 had to excuse himself for not producing drawings on account of his visiting Lincolnshire and the Marquis of Rockingham.[47]

A close friendship developed between the Carrs and the steward and the letters between the men provide good indication as to the general employment of the Carrs. Both John and Robert were very much in evidence giving of advice on materials, construction and labour in a similar manner to that offered at Plompton. They advised against the digging of a foundation before the stone footings had been prepared, otherwise the excavation, filling with water, would tumble in. In 1756 they were consulted over raising the dam head. Both objected to the inadequacy of the proposals and they submitted a method of construction that was adopted. Their advice on costs was sought though, when given, was subject to the usual queries from the keen and impatient Lascelles. On one occasion when there was some difficulty in settling prices, Lascelles remarked, 'I should think that people so well versed as Messieurs Carrs in building, would be able readily to give a satisfactory answer to every question'.

In 1755 Edwin Lascelles commissioned William Chambers to design a house and stables for him. Lascelles was obviously impressed by the reputation of the bright young man. However, Chambers's designs were rejected in favour of those of the more experienced Carrs. The executed stable-block (Fig. 16) is unusual in that it does not resemble Carr's other stables and, unusually for Carr, the stone is badly cut which has led to severe erosion, much worse, since the stables are in a hollow, than on the house on its exposed position on the hill.[48] Nevertheless, proof that Carr was the architect comes in an engraving in Wakefield City Art Gallery inscribed 'A Perspective of the Stables at Gawthorpe. Built by Edwin Lascelles Esqr 1748. J. Carr Architect. W. Lindley Sculpt.'[49] Certainly the accounts show John supplied drawings to Lascelles's requirements and added a colonnade in 1757. At Lascelles's insistence he took off some of the ball treatment. His father gave more continuous attendance, attending 197 days at 7s 6d a day between April 1755, when the foundations were dug, and January 1758.[50] The mason was a well-known local man John Muschamp, who was paid £1,359. James Rothwell was the plasterer and William Rigge supplied the slate. The total cost came to £4,500.[51]

In 1755 Lascelles, standing on a scaffold, hinted to Carr of the shape of a plan for a new house by a Mr Jones.[52] Carr, feeling a competitor breathing down his neck, fell over himself in anxiety to present the merits of his own design to Popplewell:

you will be pleased to represent mine as a rough sketch I made about a month ago not intending to show it till I had made my improvements upon it the Dimensions of the rooms are all figured and an easy access to every Room, the Area of my Plan is not greater than Mr Jones dimensions you gave me nor so big I think and I am pretty sure I have as little waste Room consequently must have as Good Rooms, I get into the Gallery, Bedchamber Dressing Room without going thro any other Room which seldom can be in such a large house and have two spacious Back Stairs of 10 feet Diamr.[53]

In February 1756 Popplewell noted that the gale 'has torn down all the scaffold where the new house is intended to stand'.

According to John Hall Stevenson of Skelton Castle, friend of Lawrence Sterne and eccentric author of *Crazy Tales*,[54] Lascelles had obtained 'plans from Everybody in England' at least as early as 1755, but he did not name the architects. Lancelot Brown may have submitted plans.[55] He was consulted in 1758, a year before the foundations were dug, but he was not employed again until 1772. So too may Matthew Brettingham. Popplewell's cash book (1749–63) records a payment on 1 September, 1757, to 'Mr Brettingham on Acct of New House £10'. Chambers's plan for the house, as for the stables, was also rejected. (Chambers does

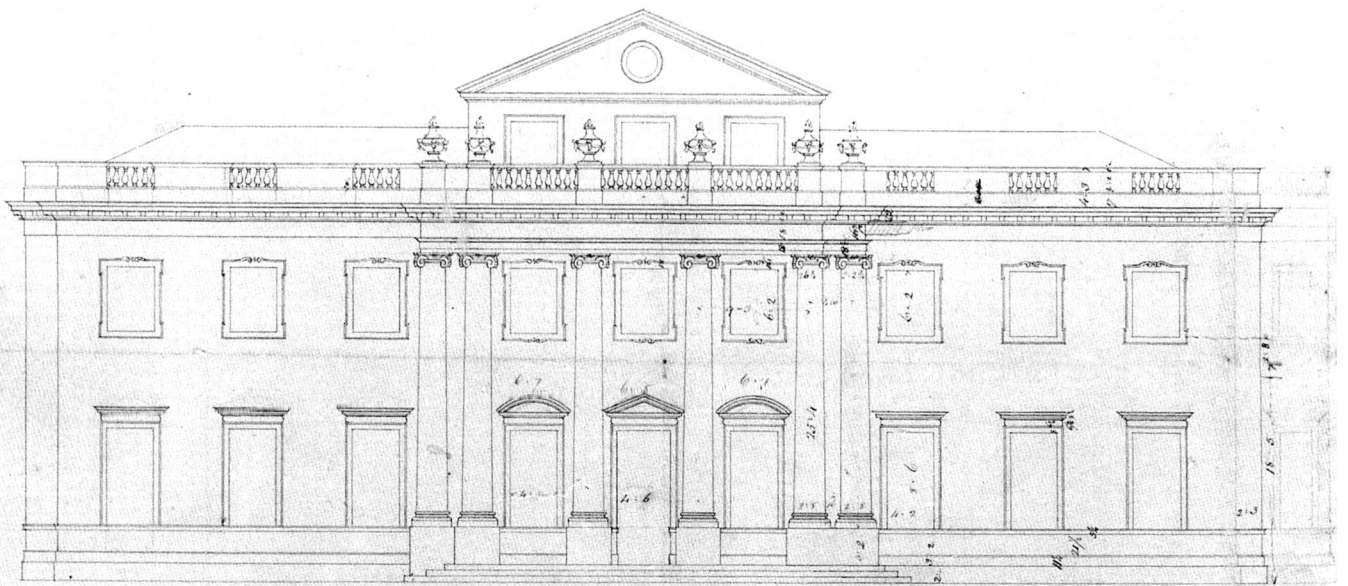

14 *above* Plompton Hall, Yorkshire; the stables and farmhouse, built for Daniel Lascelles in 1755–65

15 *below* Plompton Hall, Yorkshire, Carr's unexecuted design of 1761 for a new house for Daniel Lascelles

YOUTH

YOUTH

20

not seem to have held this against Carr for in 1774 he was happy to recommend Carr 'who would I think shine' to Thomas Scrope of Coleby Hall, Lincolnshire, for a job which he did not have time to take on.[56]

Carr was still working on a preliminary scheme, as a letter of 9 January 1758 from Robert Carr to Popplewell reveals: 'My Son has a mind to make another plan, before he comes, and by going home he will set the lad to it.' The Earl of Leicester was also involved as Lascelles clearly sought his advice. In March 1758 Lascelles wrote to Popplewell 'let Mr Carr Junr. know that if he proposes it this Spring to visit Lord Leicesters and make London on his return I wish he would do it before I left Town for I think many things might as well [be] settled here [i.e. London] if not better than in the Country'. It is not known if Carr did in fact visit Lord Leicester's house, Holkham Hall in Norfolk. Plans turned to estimates and later in 1758 Carr wrote: 'I am now with my Father in calculating the expence of your house and proposes being with you about Tuesday or Wednesday next as we hope by that time to have finished. If you have an opportunity of mentioning this to Mr Lascelles, perhaps it may not be amiss, lest he should think us negligent.'[57] Craftsmen had to be consulted. William Rigge, who invariably supplied slate to Carr's jobs, wrote in April 1758 'I shall be Extremely glad to Serve Mr Lascelles with Slate for his New Hall'.

In the end it was Carr who received the commission. The fifth volume of *Vitruvius Britannicus*, published in 1771, lists John Carr as architect of Harewood House (Fig. 17) and states: 'The Seat of Edwin Lascelles, Esquire, in Yorkshire, which was erected in 1760, in a very agreeable spot, from the designs made by Mr Carr, of York', adding 'The worthy owner has spared no expense in decorating the principal apartments, from designs made by Mr Adam'. From a study of the accounts and letters this seems a relatively fair account of the division of labour. They give the clear impression that John Carr, at first with his father and then alone, proceeded to organize and develop the building of the mansion until Robert Adam was brought in to decorate the state rooms.

Adam had arrived back in England in January 1758, and within months achieved a commission from Edwin Lascelles. On 17 June Adam wrote to his brother James:[58]

Lascelles house is now well advanced. I have made some alterations on it, but as the plan did not admit of a great many changes that has prevented the fronts from being much changed likewise. The portico I make projecting and bold dressings round the windows the pavilion fronts are quite different and the collonnades, with columns also and look well, statues, etc. adorn

16 Harewood House, Yorkshire; the stables built for Edwin Lascelles in 1755–58

the whole, and enriched freize and being done to a large scale, it is magnificent ... I have thrown in large semi-circular back courts with columns betwixt the house and wings.

The description by Robert tallies with the Harewood drawings in the Sir John Soane Museum and shows that Adam was altering and improving an earlier design. In fact, the titling on the Soane drawings, 'A New Design for Gawthorpe' suggests he hoped to start afresh. But the enthusiasm of Adam's earlier correspondence changed to despair: 'not one scrap from Lascelles so I begin to suspect him I hope he'll pay me for the plan at any rate.' Payment for £200 to a 'Mr A' in the agent's book for 16th September 1758 may refer to Adam.

It seems that this intermediate plan was the one on which construction was started. 'New House begun 6th Day of Jan 1759' declares the disbursements in the steward's accounts. Two days later, Carr discussed with Popplewell the purchase of timbering for the excavations which had already been commenced. On 22 January, after working on the dimensioned drawings and finding it necessary to extend the building by 1ft 6in, Carr asked Popplewell to excavate beyond the stakes which 'we put down ... to prevent Mr Lascelles finding fault'. He also reported delightedly great improvements in the plan, approved the previous day by Lascelles, particularly the addition of a circular room, 30ft in diameter. On 24 January Carr was still making alterations to the plan 'for the execution' and preparing to brief his father, who was to act as surveyor of works, with the method 'for proceeding with the cellars'. The foundation stone was ceremoniously laid on 23 March by Edwin Lascelles, and by July the construction of the cellars had sufficiently advanced for a query to arise as to the suitability of backing the arches with brick or stone. Carr preferred stone.

In early December 1760, Popplewell received news from Jos. Carr:

Sir, My cousin desired I would acquaint you with the death of his father and at the same time invite you to his funeral, which will be to Morrow in the Afternoon; if opportunity will permits shoud be very glad if you would come ... P.S. My cousin expects you will be a bearer.

Robert Carr had died on 3 December 1760. There was some difficulty in getting a surveyor to replace him. The only suitably qualified professional in the county known to Carr wanted '50 per annum and accommodation for himself and horse'. The man appointed, Wilkinson, was presumably the one who later supervised the building of Leeds Infirmary for Carr. He was later replaced by William Belwood, on a salary of £54 12s (52 guineas). When Belwood eventually set up in practice as an architect in York after the mansion was finished he continued to do minor works about Harewood rather to the exclusion of Carr whose charges were appreci-ably higher. Belwood, together with the assistant surveyor, John Riley, appointed in 1766 at a salary of £30 per year, gave constant supervision. Carr visited as necessary. His fees 'for drawings and attendance', variable at first, stabilized at a steady £60 a year, the last payment occurring on 5 March 1772.

Responsibility for labour and the supply of materials rested with the steward who took particular care to consult with Carr. Lascelles was keen to get his moneysworth, a point illustrated in one of his many asides to long-suffering Popplewell: 'I have no doubt of your having vouchers for every article but as I have often told it was a maxim of my Fathers that little regard should be payd to them, unless it cou'd be proved you had yr pennyworth for yr penny.' In March 1762, Popplewell informed Lascelles that 'I am for Hull tomorrow, shall then see Mr Carr and will speak to him about the blue slates'. Together, the steward and the architect, visited the port where four days were spent purchasing materials including 'Tar Glue, and Dutch Latts but no iron'. They found 'everything scarce and dear but met with all we wanted', the Seven Years War having caused a rise in building prices.

Building progressed but not without continual queries from Lascelles. Questions were asked as to how Carr proposed to drain the house, why the general works moved so slowly, and how and why the cost. In 1762, Lascelles had second thoughts about Adam's circular courts and the amateur architect Sir Thomas Robinson was brought in to give his opinion, to Carr's irritation. The accounts of the bricklayer and mason show that a certain amount of work in both courts was taken down and rebuilt with both links filled in with accommodation apart from two small rectangular courts. In 1763, when there was difficulty in getting the right timber, Lascelles agreed to sending a man to Holland with the proviso that 'It is Mr Carr's province to specify the quality, quantity and dimensions of the boards'. The timber arrived, but Lascelles, quickly finding fault with the charges, paid only after argument.

On one occasion the liaison between architect and steward went astray and a boat-load of slate ordered by Carr was left at the docks without consignment instructions. Lascelles's comments were acid. Later he asked about the frequency of the architect's visits but Popplewell was able to reply favourably: 'Indeed I do not remember how often Mr Carr has been here since you left Gawthorpe but I know he has been often. Mr Wilkinson says he has never been awanting upon any occasion.'

By 1764 work was sufficiently advanced for the portico to be erected. In March the Steward reported that the quarry mason 'Joshua Craven has cut three of the best columns you ever had and also the Capital wanted from Tinker Quarry' and, in May, 'the South Columns are all up so are the Capitals and part of the Cornish and we shall

17 Harewood House, Yorkshire, built for Edwin Lascelles in 1759–71; the south front illustrated by George Malton in 1788

begin putting up the roof next week'. The main roof was completed in September, the roofs over the east and west wings having been finished in June and October the previous year. The fabric of the building was generally completed in 1764, although it was not until 31 January 1766 that the accounts of John Muschamp, mason, and John Dodgson, bricklayer, were 'Settled and ballanced' by Carr.

In June 1765 Lascelles was not only concerned over the lack of plastering but demanding details of the house. The Steward, having already sent him an elevation, promised, 'I shall send by the York Fly tomorrow morning the Principal Plan of the floor as it now stands after all amendments, which I hope you will receive safe on Friday evening. Mr Carr came here (very luckily) yesterday, and is just now finishing it.' Presumably, the information was required to assist Robert Adam in completing his designs for the decoration of the state rooms. Shortly afterwards, Popplewell, writing to Lascelles, and acknowledging the receipt of two drawings by Adam, pointed out that the architect had misapprehended certain dimensions. He also promised to send drawings of the Music Room and Drawing Room to Adam.

These are the earliest mentions of the Scotsman in the estate correspondence.

A series of drawings from 1765 onwards (although one for a chimneypiece is dated 1762) onwards reveal Adam's involvement with the interior. His superintendence of his own designs is likely to have been limited, although in September, 1769, Thomas Sunderland and assistants were 'painting in the Hall, the Music Room and laying on specimen on Colours for Mr Adam's approbation'.

Of all the hundreds of vouchers and bills only one survives which had been checked and signed by Adam. It was the lengthy bill of £2,829 17s, submitted by Joseph Rose, the plasterer, for work done from 24 January 1766 to 10 March 1770. It lists the rooms for which Adam had produced designs: 'great Dining room, musickroom, Library, great hall, great staircase, four rooms in the private apartments, Mr L's dressing room and bed chamber, Ladys dressing room, study, portico ceiling, occasional dressing or lodging room, circular room, state bedchamber, principal dressing room, saloon, Drawing room next to the Saloon, second or Great drawing room and the great Gallery'.

Virtually the whole of the accommodation on the *piano nobile* was included. Painting started in 1767 and continued until 1772 by which time the house was occupied. Carving, as opposed to plastering, on the main floor and elsewhere was done by northern craftsmen, Richardson, Butler, Theakston and Shillito, all normally employed by Carr. Their work was measured and their accounts checked not by Adam but by Carr, his clerk, Peter Atkinson, or by the superintendent of works.

Not only Carr but those with whom he usually worked could hardly have had a closer connection with the novel Adam detail. The conversion of Rothwell and Henderson, Carr's plasterers, was rapid judging from their work in the rest of the house and in the attic storey for which incidentally, Carr supplied twelve marble chimneypieces. Carr never attempted — or never had the chance — to emulate Adam in completeness of interior design but he quickly accepted the new style for the interiors of his buildings to such effect that some of his efforts were mistaken for those of Adam. For Carr Harewood was the great house that made his reputation as a country house architect and his introduction to metropolitan fashion.

CHAPTER TWO

MATURITY

CIVIC DIGNITARY

INCREASING WEALTH would have made it difficult for Carr as a prominent inhabitant of York to escape involvement in the city's affairs. The measure of a man's success was indicated by election to civic office and appointment could only be avoided by payment of a fine. Indeed, Carr may have had some association with York's government at a relatively early date. Two drawings in the City House Books for 1756, concerning a revision of the building line in St Saviour Gate near its junction with Peasholme Green and the siting of a proposed house for Mr Dawson in Bishophill, though not signed, are apparently in his hand.[1] In 1758 his father wrote to the steward at Harewood that a proposed visit by Carr had to be postponed as 'he was obliged to go to York to attend the Lord Mayor'.[2] It is possible that Carr was a common councilman for one of the wards. This was the most junior of the city's politicians, which included the Lord Mayor, twelve aldermen, two sheriffs, the twenty-four members of the upper house, the relatively unimportant common council of seventy-two members and six chamberlains.

Carr's increasing status and wealth was demonstrated and reinforced by the erection of a substantial town house in Skeldergate in 1765–66 (Fig. 18). Carr had bought a house in Skeldergate, a main street on the west bank of the River Ouse, running down from Ouse Bridge parallel with the river, in October 1751.[3] The position had advantages if he wanted to combine architecture with trade for the navigable river skirting the district provided easy embarkation and disembarkation of materials from Queen's Staith on the west bank of the Ouse. The street remained his home for the rest of his working life. This was the address he gave in 1755 when advertising the sale of prints of the grandstand on the Knavesmire in the *York Courant* and the entries in the Poor Book of St Mary Bishophill Senior show him established there in 1759. By 1764–65 he was sufficiently prosperous to buy two adjoining properties and redevelop the whole site for his new house.[4]

In the early years, the Overseers of the Poor assessed Carr for a house, for Duke's Hall and for 'Mr Atkinson's Close' (or for a property in it). But Carr's success was rapid. In 1769, that is after his occupation of the new house and just prior to his first mayoralty, he was being assessed at 17½d per week for nine separate properties. As well as his own house, Duke's Hall and Yard and Atkinson's house these included Rodwell's house, Kipling's house, late Newton's, late Harrison's, Fairfax Close and the New House, the latter being the most expensive at 3½d per week.[5]

18 Skeldergate House, York, built by Carr for himself in 1765–66

25

After the lapse of years, it is difficult to define the use of the different properties. No doubt, some were rented out. Duke's Hall and Yard seem to have been the most likely address for any building activity. It may also have been that of the practice but as the accepted custom of the time, even for wealthy merchants, was to live at the place of work, Carr probably conducted his business from home. Certainly his letters were stamped Skeldergate and his address in advertisements asking for tenders was simply 'Mr Carr's' implying a residence. Occasionally, in his absence, his wife answered his mail. Eventually, disposing of the other properties, Carr left himself by 1789 with simply the mansion, a garden and Davy Close.

The house was a solid, plain brick building, three storeys high, and five bays wide with a central projecting porch. The *York Courant* provides more information. The house was advertised for sale after his death, with particulars available from the office of Atkinson and Phillips, architects, successors to Carr's practice. Delightful views over the River Ouse were reported from the principal floor, suggesting Carr had his drawing room there. The walls of the dining room were covered in rich tapestry acquired from Lord Holderness, a client of Carr, presumably from Hornby Castle (or perhaps Aston Hall), and the drawing room was singled out as having a splendid statuary chimneypiece. The advertisement also tells us that the building was 'calculated for the reception of a large genteel family' but gives no details as to the accommodation.[6]

Presumably, the house was not sold as, in the following year, the materials of its construction were offered for sale. From the list given, it is clear that the house was extremely commodious. There were marble flagged floors, nine statuary and other marble chimneypieces, thirteen mahogany doors to the best rooms and, elsewhere twenty-five fir doors, four columns and two handsome staircases. (The demolition sale was not a success as the house survived till after the Second World War.) The yard with outbuildings, coach houses and stabling for six horses was flanked on one side by Carr Lane rising up to the church of St Mary Bishophill Senior.

In 1766, Carr also took a lease from the corporation of a piece of ground on the other side of Skeldergate adjacent to the river.[7] This was apparently not used for business as the York maps of 1772 and 1785[8] show it laid out as a formal garden, giving the mansion house uninterrupted views of the river, New Walk, the Castle and the towering bulk of the Minster. The adjacent plot, about four hundred square yards, was also occupied by Carr and was probably used for trading, along with Duke's Hall and Yard.

On 15 January 1766 Carr was elected a city chamberlain, nominally one of the custodians of the city's income.[9] It was a position given to successful young tradesmen who, according to Drake, were expected 'rather to pay their

money than receive any'.[10] Often it was the first important step on the civic ladder, and so it was with Carr. The following year he was chosen sheriff. By now his practice was exceedingly busy and the duty would have been a nuisance. Appearing before the Bar, he offered to pay the usual fine of £70 which, being accepted, gave him exemption from the office 'for ever'. Carr's reluctance availed him little for soon he was chosen as alderman and justice of the peace, and, as the fine was so much greater, £200 or more, he took the oath on 7 June 1769.[11] The following year he was elected Lord Mayor[12] and on 3 February he was installed and took up official residence in the Mansion House. The mayor received a salary — in 1766 it was £400 — most of which disappeared on public entertainment and on the feeding of the household staff, the town clerk, his men, numerous petty officers and servants. Addressed as 'My Lord' and now fully entitled to put esquire after his name, he had reached the pinnacle of civic success which, incidentally, brought him to the notice of a still wider field of potential clients.

He soon found his civic role onerous and interfering with his practice. On 21 June 1770 he apologized to John Grimston for being unable to visit him at Kilnwick: 'we are reduced to so few Magistrates here at present that the business cannot be done without me: For want of Commissioners yesterday we cou'd not hear the Appeals for the Land Tax. We meet again in the Ainsty to day in hopes of having more Commissioners. When I shall have the pleasure of waiting of you I cannot at present determine, but I propose taking the first opportunity I have.'[13]

Minutes are usually impersonal affairs and the City House Books are no exception. We do not get the impression that Carr dominated proceedings. Nor, for that matter, that anyone else did so. The membership of committees shows that he contributed his fair share of effort. His architectural knowledge was drawn upon from time to time and for this reason his name appears more often than any other. In 1770, for example, he was authorized to purchase a row of houses in Petergate at the corner with Goodramgate for a sum not exceeding £750, the object being to improve and beautify the street by demolishing part of the row. In the same year he was appointed one of a committee of four to investigate a petition for the building of a new water wall at Skeldergate. Again, the explanatory drawing appears to be in his hand. In 1773, he was 'desired in the name of this House to view and examine the Charity School and House of Correction in this City and report his opinion' and he was again authorized to purchase a house so that the adjoining pavement could be improved and enlarged. In 1774 a lease was granted of a property near to St Leonard's Landings provided that the lessee reconstructed 'the said Building according to Mr Alderman Carr's plan'; repairs to Ouse Bridge and improvements to the

19 Portrait of Carr as Lord Mayor of York by Sir William Beechey, given by him to the York Corporation in 1803

MATURITY

nearby staith, the focal point of river activity, were also to be executed to Carr's approval.[14] In 1778, the lessee of Castle Mills was to be admitted to the freedom provided that he widened the adjoining bridge 'to the satisfaction of Mr Alderman Carr'.[15] In 1783, Carr was involved in the alterations to the cellars of the Mansion House for the proper keeping of malt liquor and with repairs to the Mansion House itself. In 1784 the wardens of Monk Ward were authorized to alter and re-roof the Cross in Thursday Market 'with the assistance of Mr Alderman Carr and Mr Leonard Terry', a master carpenter. The following year, a house was to be built 'in such a manner as the wardens of Bootham Ward and Mr Alderman Carr shall approve'.

In 1784 Carr was again shortlisted for Lord Mayor and the following year was elected a second time in place of the deceased incumbent.[16] His term of office was seemingly uneventful but it was with relief that he wrote to the steward at Wentworth Woodhouse on 30 January 1786, 'I have the pleasure to acquaint you that on fryday next I get quit of my honours and shall return quietly to my own habitation'.[17] Writing to Samuel Shore on 4 February he was more outspoken, noting that 'today I quit the troublesome office which has impeded my business exceedingly'.[18]

Thereafter Carr's active involvement with control of the city's buildings declined. Peter Atkinson, Carr's assistant, was appointed to the part-time post of City Steward in 1786 and increasingly instead of Carr's approval being sought, the minutes read 'to the satisfaction of the City Steward'. However, Carr continued to serve on committees and report on various matters. In 1791 his main interest was Selby Bridge. In 1793 and 1794, he was concerned with the city rents and leases, the purchase of properties on Ouse bridge, for general 'improvements' and treating with the Foss Navigation for the rebuilding of Monk Bridge. Later, in 1796, he helped to prepare a report on the Ouse Bridge resulting in the appointment as architect of Peter Atkinson who, on making a survey, recommended, together with a 'disinterested' London engineer, the replacement of the bridge by one of iron.

Indicative of impending retirement was his wish to be remembered. He gave to the City £666 13s 4d in thirty-five annuities to be used as he should so later direct.[19] He also presented 'a silver soup tureen and a silver tea urn of very chaste and graceful design' to the Corporation in 1796,[20] and in 1803 he offered a half length portrait by Sir William Beechey for the Mansion House (Fig. 19).[21]

As late as July 1798 Carr had the distressing but important task of heading a committee investigating the action of a colleague, Alderman Richard Hobson, accused of converting the greater part of the materials from the demolition of buildings on Ouse bridge to his own use. The last record of his attendance occurred on the 10 December 1798 when he served on a committee to determine the right of the authority to take down 'the City Walls and Bars or any part of them.' The topic was a highly controversial one.

Carr's official positions were not confined solely to York for, in 1785, he was made a Justice of the Peace of the West Riding. He also served as a magistrate in the North Riding, frequently writing to the steward at Wentworth Woodhouse that he was about to set out for Northallerton, as on 25 March 1802 when he wrote that 'I cannot come before the second Sunday after easter as I must be at Northallerton the first whole week after easter'.[22]

POLITICIAN

On the night of 28 January 1754, the heads of two of the rebels of the 1745 uprising were surreptitiously removed from Micklegate Bar. At the time Carr was organizing the repair of the gate and his scaffolding and ladders may have been used in the removal of the grisly objects. The outcry was enormous: an insult was obviously intended to His Majesty, King George II, and amid protestations of loyalty to the Crown the Lord Mayor and Commonalty offering a reward of £10 for the apprehension of the culprit.[23]

The newly formed Rockingham Club went much further. Showing 'a just Abhorrence of so infamous a Crime, an honest Resentment for such an Insult upon our Laws, a True Sense of the Happiness we enjoy under his present Majesty, and to prevent all Imputations upon his Loyal Subjects of this City' it advertised a reward of no less than fifty guineas in the York Courant. And what, may be asked, was the Rockingham Club?[24]

In the political estimation of the times, the City of York had a high standing. Representation of its many citizens had an importance which could not be claimed for pocket boroughs such as Malton, Aldborough or Boroughbridge. The city's two seats in Parliament, the choice of the two thousand resident freemen who formed the electorate, were a prize almost as much sought after as that of the county itself.

Having completed the Grand Tour, the young Marquis of Rockingham, extending his view beyond the bounds of his vast estates to politics, cast a speculative eye on the political possibilities of the City of York. Early moves were his participation in horse racing, in particular the erection of Carr's Standhouse on the Knavesmire, for which plans were afoot in 1753, and his encouragement of the formation of the Rockingham Club, to support his Whig policies. The club first met at the George Inn — the choice of which may have had some significance — on 23 December the same year.

The nominal roll of original members is missing but there is a list of 133 members attending a meeting on 3 June 1754 in the Wentworth Woodhouse papers. From this it would appear that the Club was essentially a local organization of influential York citizens, tradesmen, civic and ecclesiastical leaders together with neighbouring country gentlemen including Sir William Milner, Sir Rowland Winn and Sir Geoffrey Savile. Among those listed is 'Mr Carr'. Thus we have early evidence of the architect's political leanings and of the connection with Rockingham which was to prove such an important background to his career.

In 1755 the club started to use the Assembly Rooms for club nights and by 1763 was so well established there as to arrange for the hanging of its pictures of King William III and King George II. Eleven or twelve meetings were held each year and the club undoubtedly formed a powerful Whig interest in what Canon William Mason described to Horace Walpole as a Tory town.[25] When Rockingham, the president, exceptionally took the chair, numbers mounted to well over a hundred. Normally, attendance varied between forty and fifty with conduct of proceedings in the hands of the vice-president, a member newly elected for each meeting. As time went on, interest waned and the number of meetings dropped to two or three a year.

Carr frequently expressed his disgust to Rockingham's steward at the lack of local support and from time to time the marquis had to help the club financially. He also supplied venison for club suppers from his estates. On the occasion of his vice-presidency in January 1779 Carr took the precaution of asking the steward for a gift of venison, as the allowance for supper and malt liquor had been reduced to 15d per head — 'in order if possible to get the Club out of debt and free us from the disgrace of Lord Rockinghams discharging it as he has done, which in my opinion is a great reflection upon us, but we have a great many worthless members'.[26] By then, Carr must have been prosperous so that his request, it would seem, was a reflection not only on the members but on his own parsimony. Perhaps consciously, or sub-consciously, conforming to the attitude of his fellow freemen accustomed to being paid for their votes, he looked upon the club as a political whim of his revered marquis and therefore to be subsidized by the latter if only in terms of victuals.

The Club vigorously supported the Rockingham interest in the 1754 election. The nobleman's agent was pushed into the office of Clerk of the Peace against corporation opposition and Rockingham's nominee, Sir John Armitage, was also elected as one of the two Members of Parliament, although the corporation managed to ensure the election of the Tory, George Lane Fox, as Lord Mayor in 1757. In the bitter election of 1758 the marquis, at a cost of £12,000, was again successful in getting his man, William Thornton, elected. Similarly, he succeeded in 1761 with Sir George Armytage and 'permitted' the election of Robert Lane Fox as a sop to the opposition. In 1768, when Sir George stood down, Rockingham managed to replace him with Charles

Turner of Kirkleatham, and Lane Fox with Lord John Cavendish. Turner and Cavendish were re-elected in 1774 and 1780.

The political papers of Christopher Wyvill shed light on Carr's political activities, particularly his involvement in the Yorkshire Association which (led by Wyvill) was concerned 'at the increasing and unconstitutional influence of the Crown' and came out strongly for Parliamentary reform. The association had been formed to express independent opinion free from aristocratic influence. Not unnaturally, strong support was forthcoming from the lesser gentry and from the corporation. For Rockingham the issue was a delicate one. He too favoured reform, though not as radical as that proposed by the association, which many of his friends and local political allies supported. Perhaps his strongest concern was that it established a rival opposition powerbase in Yorkshire to his own.

Rockingham had welcomed the idea of a county meeting to discuss a petition to Parliament and attended the first meeting in December 1779 but he had been apprehensive of its contents. He hoped these would reinforce the line his party was taking in Parliament but feared would frighten off other counties from making petitions and disunite the opposition. He soon found that with the MPs excluded and an organization set up he could not control the association.

The importance of the Yorkshire Association was at its height in the 1780 election. The county seats were not problematic. Rockingham's great friend and key political ally in Yorkshire, Sir George Savile, declared his support for the association, and the other candidate, Henry Duncombe, proved acceptable to Rockingham and the association. In York Rockingham was more directly challenged when the association tried to obtain a pledge of support from Rockingham's candidates Charles Turner and Lord John Cavendish. Turner agreed but Cavendish refused and the association threatened to run a candidate against him. In the end, the association's threat did not materialize and Rockingham's candidates were returned unopposed.

Carr's name appears among the 152 signatories convening the initial meeting on 14 December 1779. He did not attend the first meeting, which, nevertheless, elected him to a committee of sixty-one to promote the petition to Parliament, along with most of Rockingham's chief supporters in the city. He again missed the second meeting, but he did attend the third and though unmentioned in the minutes appended his signature to them. Thereafter, the record of Carr's participation ceases. Rockingham had sent Carr a long letter, ostensibly enquiring after his health but also letting him know in the most courteous fashion of his doubts about the association. It was suggested that the letter should be shown to friends. Carr, who held the marquis in deep respect, doubtless took the hint and laid low.

Rockingham died in 1782 and the club paid its respects to the founder by meeting, as Carr explained, 'the remains of our deceased friend 4 miles on the Road on horseback ...' and attending 'the corps in regular procession through the City' to the Minster.[27] The club's presidency was taken over by Earl Fitzwilliam, Rockingham's nephew. At his first meeting on 9 October 1782 123 members attended. Carr was present, wisely affirming his support for Rockingham's successor who continued to employ him as architectural consultant on the former Rockingham estates.

But Fitzwilliam lacked the status and dedication of the marquis, and the generosity, for he ordered his steward to inform the club that there would be no more gifts of venison. Although meetings persisted to the end of the century, the club had lost much of its power. Fitzwilliam also lacked Rockingham's political influence and after 1782 the Yorkshire Association became increasingly radicalized and a direct threat to Fitzwilliam's leadership in the county. It is therefore curious to find Carr's name still on the 'Alphabetical list of the Members of the Committee of Association for the County of York' at a time when he was assisting what we would take to be the 'aristocratic' elements in the county election of 1784. Carelessness in revising an earlier list could have been the reason but in the *York Courant* for 15 February 1785, the year of his second mayoralty, Carr was reported as acting as chairman of a meeting of citizens called to prepare a petition to Parliament asking for reforms — and being thanked for his care and attention to business.

Confirmation of Carr's continuing Whig sympathies and of his active involvement in politics is provided in a letter which he sent to Earl Fitzwilliam in March 1784, informing him about affairs prefacing the county election. After giving a progress report on the work at Wentworth Woodhouse, he described disdainfully William Mason's manoeuvring in organizing the requisition to the High Sheriff for a County Meeting to nominate candidates. Bluntly, he stated that more than half the names in the document — most of them from the West Riding towns, Leeds, Wakefield, Sheffield and Rotherham, as well as Hull — were 'never before heard of'. He was all for what he called 'a confrontation'. Some of those mentioned, for example, the Milneses of Wakefield, the Walkers of Rotherham and Mason himself, were his clients. Carr continued, 'I wish we had a good paragraph put in the York and Leeds papers previous to the meeting, to state the dispute betwixt the K and parliament properly, for it is amazing to think how ignorant people are on the subject, they have no idea but that Mr Fox wants to get the better of the K and be the Lord Protector and therefore he and all his abettors ought to be opposed'.[28]

The requisition for a County meeting being successful, Mason's 'gentlemen' produced an address to the Crown from the York Tavern, which was hotly opposed by sixty-six other gentlemen who set up headquarters in Bluitt's

Tavern. All were affluent and their number included noblemen such as the Duke of Devonshire, the Earl of Surrey, the Earl of Carlisle, Earl Fitzwilliam and Lord Stourton. Carr came three-quarters way down the list. Wyvill and the majority of the Associators backed Henry Duncombe and William Wilberforce. The sixty-six, former members of the Yorkshire Association who had seceded (and in doing so had wrecked the Association), resolved to support Messrs Foljambe and Weddell.

The Rockingham Club was active in soliciting votes and came under abusive attack from an anonymous writer in the *York Courant*, calling them 'those despicable Tyrants'. The reply, no less spirited, was fired by the Rockingham Committee of twelve, of which Carr was a member. The Carr family were heavily involved. Both Carr's nephews, John Carr, attorney of Wakefield, and William Carr, the architect's right-hand man, acted as agents and, the 'Election Bundle' in the Wentworth Woodhouse Muniments, contains a note that 'Mr Carr returns his Compliments to the Committee and is very sorry he cannot spare a Clerk at present as he has only one left at home, and he is engaged in collecting Votes in Town'.[29] Despite these efforts Foljambe and Weddell were not elected — a considerable blow to the aspirations of the Whig aristocracy. But Carr was now firmly identified not only with the tradesmen of York but, more particularly, with the nobility. Indeed, the following year he was elected a member of the York Club, a most select gathering of noblemen and gentry which dined at Ringroses.

Carr's political opinions remained strong into old age. Writing to the steward at Wentworth Woodhouse in April 1794 he sandwiches a diatribe against Pitt between one paragraph dilating on his infirmities and another on professional matters: 'That deceitful scoundrel Pitt, instead of regarding Lord Fitzwilliam for joining of him, has made use of every means in his power to disgrace and dishonour him: but I have no doubt but my Lord's superior merit and conduct will rise superior to the diabolical intrigues of a Minister, who I hope to live to see tumble headlong over the Tarpoein Rock.'[30] Strong words for Carr.

By 1797 Carr was tired and in a despondent frame of mind. On 9 May he proposed a petition at a general meeting of York's inhabitants calling on the King to dismiss his ministers and restore trade and public credit by obtaining peace.[31] Later that month replying to a letter from Wyvill he agreed to support a requisition to the High Sheriff and despaired of the war, the apathy of the people, the corrupt Parliament and the arrogance of the Prime Minister:

20 *opposite* Lytham Hall, Lancashire, built for
Thomas Clifton in 1757–61; the staircase

21 Everingham Hall, Yorkshire, built for William Constable in 1758–61; the entrance front

I am exceeding glad to find you are now well in health, as to be able once more to step forward in defence of our much injured Country and Constitution, which from the misconduct and maladministration of the present Ministry, have brought this country, in the space of five years into much greater calamity & distress, than the history of any one Century in the British annals can exhibit, and without having obtained any one object for which they pretended it was necessary for us to go to war; notwithstanding which this Country seems to me to be in such a state of apathy and supineness, that I am in doubt whether a general petition can be obtained for the purpose of removing from his Majesties Councils the objects who have brought this Kingdom into so lamentable a situation, and without which I think it impossible to make a permanent peace or save Ireland or perhaps this Country.

The great body of the people in the West Riding have so long supported the present Minister, who have so lately sent him a Coadjutor, will be unwilling I fear to come forward and retract their Errors, though I believe the Merchants as well as the manufacturers now suffer very much from the long continuance of the war & the want of public credit — You woud be glad to see our petition from York, notwithstanding which I am afraid you will receive very little assistance from the inhabitants of this City, we have nobody of sufficient weight or consequence among us, those who once had, are like myself grown old & indifferent as well as hopeless of success, against the present corrupted house of commons, & arbitrary power and arrogant Minister. Permit me however Worthy Sir, to respect and admire you for your inflexible and unshaken perseverance, your admirable abilities, & your manly exertion of them for the good of your Country.

In spite of his concern Carr would not be attending the subsequent meeting: for health reasons he would be on his customary tour.[32]

Carr remained committed to the Whig cause and even in old age his opinion was valued as can be seen in a letter, dated 1802, from Robert Sinclair to Fitzwilliam concerning the election of a Member of Parliament for York 'I have had a conversation with Hartley, Ellis, Townend & Carr and they are unanimous in thinking that we must have some man with your Whig blood in his veins to represent us, and that Mr Dundas answers that character'. Mr Dundas was elected.

Carr's political links were critical to his success as an architect, but he never lacked work. He had no need to advertise in the papers, dedicate books to potential patrons or produce elegant volumes of his designs. The nearest approach to self-announcement was the inclusion of some of his designs in *Vitruvius Britannicus*. He was fortunate in having a father of ability, already well established, when first he started building. Apart from his obvious competence and enthusiasm, Carr probably owed his initial success to the scarcity of competent surveyors at a time of dramatically increasing building activity, but it should not be forgotten that his connection with Kirby Hall, designed by the much-admired Lord Burlington, Lord Lieutenant of the North and West Ridings, gave Carr acceptable professional status at a very early date. He was also successful — this cannot be over-emphasized — because of his incredible dedication and ability to travel. Carr also believed in maintaining his contacts. Thus, in one of the Harewood accounts, he wrote, 'For the year 1773, nothing, I only waited on Mr Lascelles as a visitor.'

The extent of his success is evident in the letter he wrote to John Grimston on 26 March 1764: 'It is with the utmost difficulty I can perform my business so to oblige the Gentlemen I am concern'd for, the Spirit of Building rages so much at present'.[33] That year saw him finishing work on Lytham Hall, Lancashire (Fig. 20), begun in 1757 and Everingham Hall, Yorkshire (Fig. 21), begun in 1758 as well as alterations to Campsall Hall, Yorkshire. New commissions in hand included Wentworth Woodhouse near Rotherham, Heath Hall near Wakefield, Fairfax House in York (Fig. 22), Harewood House near Leeds, Hornby Castle and Constable Burton Hall (Fig. 23) near Richmond and Tabley Hall in Cheshire. He was also carrying out major alterations to Aske Hall, Escrick Park, Goldsborough Hall, Cannon Hall, Swinton Park, Stapleton Park, Kirkleatham Hall and Newby Hall in Yorkshire and Welbeck Abbey in Nottinghamshire. He widened Wentbridge in the West Riding, was still at work on the estate at Plompton, may have been at work at Everingham church and certainly altered St John's church in Leeds. He also made an unsuccessful design for Wetherby Grange. No wonder he felt the spirit of building was raging.

Things were no calmer in 1769. Writing to Don Antonio do Lancastre about his design for the Hospital of San Antonio in Oporto (Fig. 24) Carr subtly let it be known how fortunate he was in getting a design for a hospital 'at a time when I am conducting so many Magnificent Structures for several Noblemen and others in the Kingdom'.[34] As he explained to the committee for the Leeds hospital that year he was too busy to execute the building. In October 1771 he had to apologize to John Grimston again, explaining that

22 Fairfax House, York; fitted out for Viscount Fairfax in 1761–65; the staircase

he 'shoud have great pleasure in waiting of you at Kilnwick if it was in my Power, but I have so many considerable Buildings committed to my care and of such consequence to the owners thereof, that I cannot avoid paying a proper attention to them'.[35] Nothing had changed in 1778 when William Mason explained to Lord Harcourt that Carr 'has so much employment abroad that he is seldom at York'.

By now Carr had moved beyond simple country-house work to public commissions. The start had been slow. After the Assembly Rooms at Beverley in 1761 he had no public buildings until the House of Correction in Wakefield in 1766. Then things began to speed up with the General Infirmary, Leeds, 1768 (Fig. 25) and the Hospital of San Antonio in Oporto, 1769. They became positively frenetic in the middle years of the 1770s with the York Assize Courts in 1772, Newark Town Hall, and the Bootham Park Hospital in York in 1774, Lincoln County Hospital and Doncaster racecourse grandstand in 1776, Nottingham racecourse grandstand in 1777, the Assembly Rooms in

23 Constable Burton, Yorkshire, built for Sir Marmaduke Wyvill in 1762–68; the entrance front

Nottingham in 1778 and the Female Prison in York in 1779. After that date Carr's only public commissions in England were the Court House and House of Correction in Northallerton in 1784 and Chesterfield Town Hall in 1787, both relatively simple buildings and nothing to compare with the grandeurs of the York Assize Court, Newark Town Hall or the Doncaster grandstand.

24 Hospital do San Antonio, Oporto, Portugal, designed by Carr in 1769 and built between then and 1843; the entrance front

The 1770s saw over ninety identifiable commissions. As well as the public buildings just mentioned these included nine new country houses begun in that decade, some of them, such as Denton Park, and Basildon Park among his finest houses. 1774 was perhaps the peak year with thirteen commissions in hand. That year saw him start work on the Town Hall at Newark, the Bootham Park Hospital at York, Leventhorpe Hall, the stables at Castle Howard, stables and the state rooms at Welbeck Abbey, design new bridges at Carlton Ferry and Kilvington, design the menagerie and rotunda at Harewood … No wonder he did not have time to provide advice on Durham Cathedral.

Carr's practice was not just designing new country houses and public buildings. Much of his work was pragmatic improvements. At Welbeck Abbey he began with new kitchens and offices, as he did at Aske Hall. When Earl Fitzwilliam succeeded at Wentworth Woodhouse his first task was to rebuild the kitchens there. Throughout his career, even at its busiest Carr can be found doing relatively minor repairs and alterations to houses and churches, as in 1772, one of his most frantic years, when he designed a vestry room for St Peter's church in Leeds and repaired John Nost's monument to Viscount Irwin.

Often his work was straightforward repair and conservation. In 1782 he drew up a detailed report on the condition

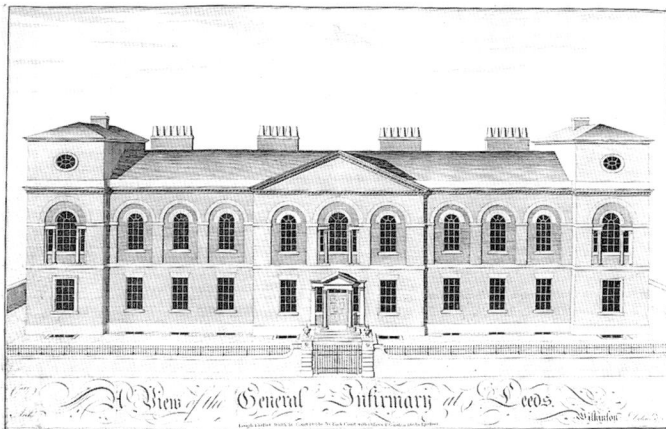

25 Leeds General Infirmary, built in 1768–71; engraving

of Lord George Cavendish's house at Latimers in Buckinghamshire. The condition of the house was appalling:

All the West side of the old part of the house is in so ruinous a state, that it ought to be taken down; The keeping that infirm part in repair would be endless & expensive, and it is at present so inconveniently disposed both on the ground floor and Chamber story, that if it shoud stand, many alterations must be made therein, and the Roof thereof is in so ruinous and complicated a state that it must undergo an expensive alteration to repair it properly. I therefore recommend the whole of the West side of the old building be taken down, and to rebuild again only so much of that space, as will be absolutely necessary for the servants Offices …

Carr's pragmatic estimate of the necessary repairs, improvements and demolition totalled £4,640.

Carr's suggested repairs at Latimers were fairly ruthless but at Hardwick Hall, Derbyshire, where £1,226 was spent between 1785 and 1791, they were so sensitive that their extent has only recently been appreciated. Here the roof was strengthened, new stonework carved for the rooftop and the chimneys rebuilt. Floors and ceilings were strengthened and plasterwork repaired in the long gallery, dining room, state room and great hall. The servants' rooms were greatly improved, replastered, provided with new fireplaces, shelves, cupboards and doors. A new water closet was also installed on the first floor.

A similar sensitivity is evident at Raby Castle, County Durham, where there was much restoration among the extensive improvements. Here Carr generally made the masons copy new details from existing models at the castle and reused medieval elements such as coping stones moved when the kitchen. Again at St Peter's church, Sheffield, where he was brought in to repair decaying stonework Carr replaced the south window on the east front with a new window copied from its neighbour. His sympathetic repairs could easily be accepted as authentic Decorated work but for the plain necking at the top of the mullions and the return of the hood moulds on to Classical imposts.

Much of Carr's church work was restoration or repair, as at All Saints church, Dewsbury, where he rebuilt the tower and aisles. Nothing, however, compared with the massive nineteen-page survey Carr produced on York Minster in 1770. Some of this was carried out at the time but Carr returned from 1794 to 1797 on a salary of £100 a year to carry out repairs to the roof.

BRIDGES

Robert Carr continued to hold the surveyorship of the West Riding bridges until his death in 1760. He was also responsible for building Masham Bridge over the River Ure, one of the finest bridges in Yorkshire and a private commission for Robert Carr from the North Riding magistrates, whose features can frequently be seen in bridges designed by his son.[36] In Horbury Church his memorial records that he was skilled as a mathematician, perhaps referring to his prowess in calculating the stresses and strains in bridge structures. John Carr was appointed surveyor 'in the room of his father' in 1761,[37] along with John Watson, who had similarly succeeded his father in 1757. It was Carr's first official appointment, bringing a salary of £30 a year.

Carr regularly attended the Sessions to make his reports. He effected repairs — the principal bridges widened or rebuilt during his surveyorship were Sheffield (1760), a three-arch pointed bridge at Cold Coniston (1763), Ferrybridge (1765) and Rotherham (1768) — and made additions to the Book of Bridges. A glance at his surveys, and those of his father, establishes a salient fact. The existing bridges, often with pointed arches and elevations plain right up to the coping, were essentially medieval in conception. Bridges designed by the Carrs, while remaining simple in treatment, were discernibly Classical. Rounded arches were used and the parapet was clearly defined on elevation by a string course marking the level of the road.

In 1772 Carr was appointed surveyor of bridges in the North Riding, the entry in the North Riding Quarter Sessions Order Book for 16 July 1772 reading: 'Mr John Carr Architect appointed principal Surveyor of the Bridges belonging to the North Riding with a Salary of One Hundred Pounds p.annum.' To hold two surveyorships of such enormous counties, both of which involved attendance at Sessions at similar times, would have taxed the resource even of John Carr. So Carr solicited those in authority to have his brother Robert appointed in his place, writing for example, on 28 October 1772 to Bacon Frank, a magistrate, for his support: 'My Bror wishes to succeed me, and I am certain he is more Capable of doing that business than any one that will offer for it, on which account I beg your Interest, and as I have not yet made my resignation publick, I think he may secure the place by a Timely

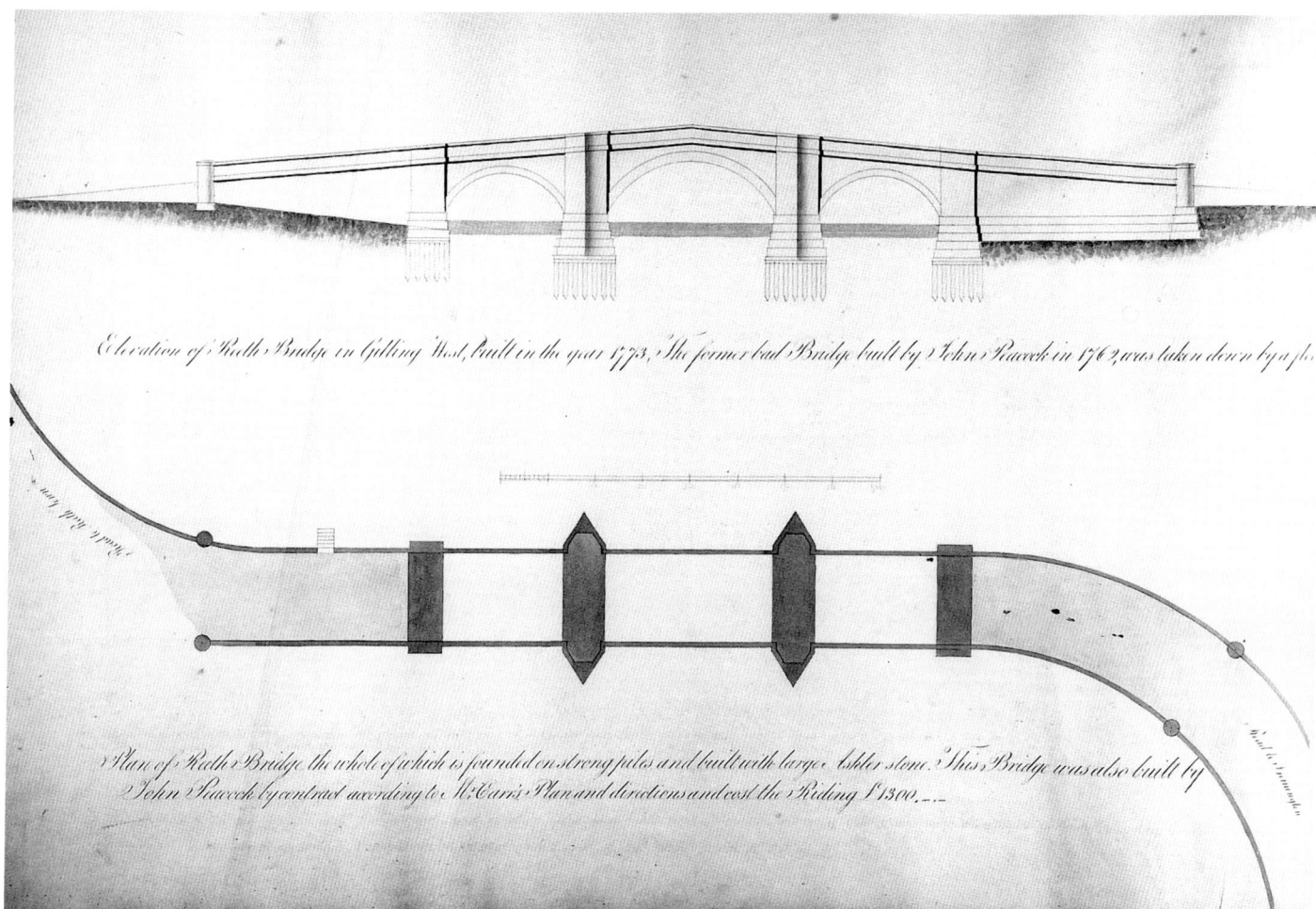

Elevation of Reeth Bridge in Gilling West, Built in the year 1773, The former bad Bridge built by John Peacock in 1762, was taken down by a fl...

Plan of Reeth Bridge the whole of which is founded on strong piles and built with large Ashler stone. This Bridge was also built by John Peacock by contract according to Mr Carr's Plan and directions and cost the Riding £1300.___

26 *above* Reeth bridge, Yorkshire, built for the North Riding Magistrates in 1773; drawing by Carr
27 *opposite above* Rutherford bridge, Yorkshire, built for the North Riding Magistrates in 1773; drawing by Carr
28 *opposite below* Greta bridge, Yorkshire, built for the North Riding Magistrates in 1773

application to Mr Zouch & some other Justices with yours & Mr Hervey's assistance.'[38] Robert was appointed on 14 January 1773 to officiate for his brother as a Surveyor of the Riding bridges. On 1 April his appointment was made permanent. When this was assured Carr resigned the lesser (and less well remunerated) position.

The North Riding appointment was an innovation. Previously the bridges had been the responsibility of the individual High Constables. Now they were brought under the care of one man with expert knowledge. Carr was required to report on all the bridges once a year, design new bridges and any additions to the existing ones, give directions for building work, examine the disbursements and assist the justices in making contracts. A deputy, Henry King, was engaged at a salary of £50 a year, 'to superintend the Execution of all Bridge Contracts under the direction of Mr Carr'.

Carr was soon at work. In October 1772 the treasurer was ordered to 'pay unto Mr Carr Fifty Pounds and Eight Shillings for viewing Barnard Castle, Reeth, Rutherford, Marske, Ayton and Greta Bridges and making plans and Elevations and directions for Rebuilding them in a proper manner and Estimates of their several Experiences and attending the Gentlemen at North Allerton when said Bridges were contracted for' (Figs 26 and 27). Four of these bridges were completed the following year at a total cost of nearly £4,000. Carr took his responsibilities seriously, setting off regularly for a fortnight's survey. On 24 March 1779, when work on the Buxton Crescent was starting, he wrote cheerfully that he was 'just setting out for a fortnight on my Bridge survey'.[39] From time to time advertisements appeared in the York papers soliciting proposals for the building and rebuilding of bridges, for which plans could be seen at 'Mr Carr's office in York'.

Many of his bridge projects were widening schemes, limited in design to the lines of the old bridge. Others, such as Appersett Bridge, obscurely sited in the wilds of the dales, distant from skilled labour, were patched rather than

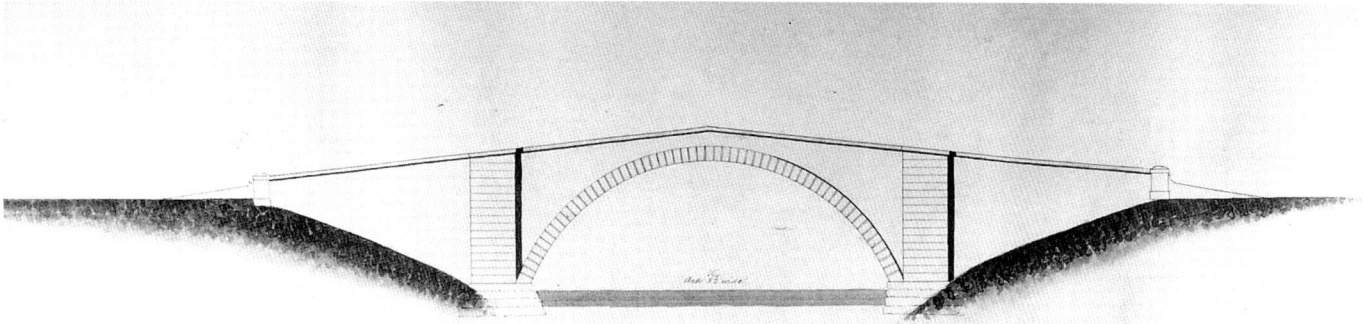

Elevation of Rutherford Bridge in the Wapentake of Gilling West

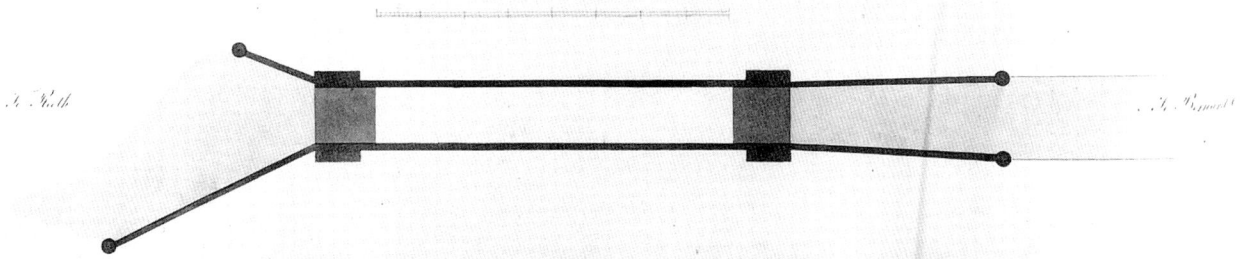

Plan of Rutherford new Bridge which was built in the year 1773, Soon after the other Bridge with two Arches was taken down by a flood, the whole of this Bridge is built with good stone got in the neighbourhood and founded upon a Rock, the building of which cost the Riding only £400 and Raising and making the 100 yards of road at each end thereof cost £100.

This Bridge was executed by Robt. Shout Junior of Helmsley according to the plan and directions given by Mr. Carr

29 Richmond bridge, Yorkshire, built for the North Riding Magistrates in 1789

completely rebuilt. For new work, Carr produced designs of simple but distinctive character such as the one at Strensall. When the occasion warranted it, he was quite capable of turning out a very architectural conception, such as Morton Bridge, near Northallerton which has ashlar and rustication in profusion and cost the substantial sum of £8,240 10*s* or the great seven-arch bridge over the Tees at Croft which he widened. One of his most elegant creations was the famous structure which arches across a leafy gorge of the River Greta in a single span (Fig. 28). Its precursor had been washed away in exceptional floods in 1771. Although Greta Bridge carried a main road it was on the edge of the Rokeby estate, and was approved and partly paid for by its owner J. B. Morritt. It thus comes into the category of a landscape feature. That certainly is how Carr treated it. Turning aside from the masculinity of his official creations, he gave the bridge a graceful curve, roundels (economically only on the park side), niches in the abutments, and a balustraded parapet. A simple, yet elegant design, it is Carr's most charming creation.

Ignoring alterations, about twenty bridges were newly built to Carr's designs. He used a limited repertoire of details, yet no two of his bridges were exactly alike. Cutwaters were sometimes V-shaped, as at Grinton, sometimes three-sided, sometimes square, even rounded as at Rich-

mond (Fig. 29), Thirsk and Skipton, and usually plain faced. Arches, rarely elliptical, were sometimes semi-circular, sometimes segmental. The voussoir ring, occasionally rubble but usually ashlar, was often rusticated and sometimes the extrados was defined by a bold torus moulding. The number of arches varied from one to seven. By necessity, many had to be well elevated: the record of bridges flooded and washed away in the North Riding is surprisingly high. In February 1772 an advertisement in the *York Courant* asked for tenders for the rebuilding of no fewer than six bridges — Rutherford, Barnard Castle, Marske, Reeth, Balder and Lune — all damaged by floods.

Carr's bridges were always of stone, either squared rubble in courses or ashlar in courses, depending on the importance of the structure. The soffit of the arch was continuous throughout and not formed of distinct ribs supporting intermediate slabs — except at Croft, where the rebuilding followed the construction of the medieval work. Foundations in normal ground were of stone. Where the support was poor, tapered oak piles, tipped with cast iron, were driven down to support a platform of fir planks on which the bridge was erected.

In Carr's private work the touch is markedly lighter, particularly those bridges designed as features in the landscape. Perhaps the best illustration of his abilities as a

MATURITY

30 The bridge at Norton Place, Lincolnshire, built for John Harrison in about 1776

designer is provided by almost a dozen different schemes — varying in completeness from rough pencil sketches to carefully drawn ink and wash drawings — for bridges across the weir separating two of the great lakes below Wentworth Woodhouse.[40] Among the collection of drawings is an engraving of the Ponte Sta Trinita in Florence designed by Bartolomeo Ammanati in 1558. This was presumably acquired by the young Marquis of Rockingham during his Grand Tour. He must have instructed Carr to produce something similar for in 1760 the architect offered on a single sheet of paper two alternative designs. The first design, closely following Ammanati, has elliptical arches, but the second shows the more usual segmental ones rather as though Carr had felt that sophistication was all very fine but that the cheaper and easier arrangement would do just as well. Rockingham's bridge was not built, but one of the rejected drawings found a use when, about 1776, a graceful balustraded bridge, similar in design, was constructed across the weir separating the lakes in front of Norton Place, a house designed by Carr in Lincolnshire (Fig. 30).

Frustrated at Wentworth Woodhouse Carr had hopes of an equally impressive bridge at Welbeck, writing in March 1763 Carr to the Duke of Portland 'if Your Grace thinks of Erecting the Bridge soon it would be proper to give directions for a quarry to be opened'.[41] The commission went

instead to Robert Mylne, fashionable architect of Westminster Bridge, but the last laugh was with Carr.[42] Twenty years later, William Bray described the action of the Duke: 'he made an extensive lake, and threw over it a magnificent bridge of three arches, the centre arch being a span of ninety feet, the side ones seventy five each, but it fell down almost as soon as compleated and has not been rebuilt'.[43]

PATRONAGE

Central to Carr's network of clients was his intimate association with the Marquis of Rockingham and the Rockingham Whigs whom he led. Rockingham introduced him to his friends, among them the Dukes of Devonshire, Portland and Kingston who all utilized the architect's services (Figs 31 and 32). (The one leading local member of the Rockingham connection who got away was the Duke of Newcastle, for whose family Stephen Wright, a clerk of William Kent's, acted as house architect.) It may have been his friendship with the marquis which brought a request from the King himself, in 1769, to see Carr's plan for the enormous hospital at Oporto which, to use the architect's own words, 'he saw with admiration and approbation'.

MATURITY

39

31 Wentworth Woodhouse, Yorkshire, the stables built for the 2nd Marquis of Rockingham in 1766–83; interior

While it is true that Carr did work for the occasional Tory, analysis of the Members of Parliament for whom he worked repeatedly reveals (where their political affiliation is clear) their Whig connections. Sir George Armytage (Kirklees) was returned unopposed as the Rockingham candidate for York in 1761. The Marquess of Titchfield (Welbeck), MP for Titchfield in 1761–62 and subsequently 3rd Duke of Portland, was a prominent member of the Rockingham group, close to Rockingham and trusted by him. The two Cavendish brothers Lord George (Holker and Latimers) and Lord John (Billing), like their nephew the Duke of Devonshire (Chatsworth, Hardwick, Buxton), were key members of the Rockingham party. Nathaniel Cholmley (Howsham, attrib.) was recommended by Rockingham to the Duke of Newcastle as member for Aldborough in 1768. Henry Curwen (Workington) was connected with the Duke of Portland and voted with the Rockingham party. His son-in-law John Christian Curwen (Workington, Belle Isle) was

supported by Portland in applying for the Carlisle seat in 1786. Sir Gilbert Elliott (Minto Racecourse, unbuilt) supported the Rockingham administration in 1782 and was frequently consulted by Portland during the Regency crisis. Anthony Eyre (Grove Hall) was returned for Borough-bridge on the interest of the Duke of Newcastle. Sir Thomas Gascoigne (Parlington, unbuilt, and Grimston Park, attrib.) was returned as member for Thirsk probably by arrangement with Rockingham, in 1780, and sat for Fitzwilliam's Malton seat in 1784. He remained one of the leading supporters of Fitzwilliam and the Opposition in Yorkshire. John Harrison (Norton Place, Fig. 33) voted consistently with the Opposition until the fall of Lord North. Sir Robert Hildyard (Winestead, attrib.) was firmly opposed to the American war and was one of the original members of the Yorkshire Association, as was Henry Duncombe (Langford), who was one of Rockingham's successful candidates for Yorkshire in 1780. Sir Charles Turner,

The Principal Front of Thoresby Lodge.

Elevation principal de la Maison de Thoresby.

32 Thoresby Lodge, Nottinghamshire, for the 2nd Duke of Kingston in 1767–71, elevation from *Vitruvius Britannicus*

MP for York from 1768 to 1783 liked to maintain his independence but was supported by Rockingham. Daniel Lascelles (Plompton, Goldsborough) and Edward Lascelles (Stapleton) both followed Edwin Lascelles (Harewood) who was chosen with Lord Rockingham's support to stand for Yorkshire in 1761 and remained an ally until, on the outbreak of the war with America, it moved over to the government, whereupon Rockingham blocked his attempt to sit again for Yorkshire. Sir James Pennyman (Ormesby and Lairgate, attribs.) was described by Rockingham in 1768 as 'a very good sort of man … with a thumping landed property, who is exceeding anxious to get into Parliament'. With Rockingham's help he secured a seat at Scarborough and voted steadily with his party. Rockingham, who married his half-sister, arranged for the election of Sir John Ramsden (Byram) for Grampound, after which he voted regularly with the Rockinghams. John Savile, Earl of Mexborough (Methley, attrib.) was classed as a pro by

Rockingham under whose administration he was granted an Irish earldom. John Smyth (Heath Hall) took an active part in the petitioning movement of 1779 and was one of the committee of seven to consider Wyvill's draft petition and help circulate it in the West Riding. Rockingham arranged for Beilby Thompson (Escrick and Wetherby Grange) to stand for Hedon in 1768, whereafter he voted regularly with the Rockinghams. Sir Charles Turner (Clints and Kirkleatham, Fig. 34), though prickly in asserting his independence, was seen as a Whig candidate for York in 1768, voted regularly with Rockingham and accepted a baronetcy from his administration. Sir William Wake (Courteenhall), though very independent, voted with the Opposition between 1774 and 1780, opposed the American war and was listed by Rockingham as a friend. William Weddell (Newby Hall) was recommended by Rockingham for Hull in 1766 and consistently followed Rockingham.

MATURITY

41

33 Norton Place, Lincolnshire, built for John Harrison in about 1776; the staircase

MATURITY

34 Kirkleatham Hall, Yorkshire, remodelled for Sir Charles Turner in 1764–67

Given the scale of Carr's practice it would be surprising if his patrons were exclusively Whig. Thus Sir Lawrence Dundas (Aske, Fig. 35) and his son Thomas (Upleatham) supported the Government; George Lane Fox, Lord Bingley, (Bramham) was always considered a Tory; Sir John Goodricke (Ribston, Fig. 36) supported the Administration on the American War; Viscount Harcourt (Nuneham, unbuilt) was an avid monarchist; Sir Francis Sykes (Basildon) voted consistently with Lord North. But these are exceptions. It is clear from Carr's close involvement with the Rockingham Club and his surviving letters that he was an avowed Whig. It cannot be coincidence that his clientele is so strongly Whig, nor that his most consistent high aristocratic patrons, Devonshire, Portland, Rockingham and Fitzwilliam should have been the leaders of that party.

Quite apart from the gregariousness of the landed gentry in attending assemblies and race meetings so that everyone knew everyone else, there were the astonishingly extensive family connections. Thus, an architect producing a design successfully for a client would presently be introduced to friends and relatives with snowball effect. Carr, employed by Edwin Lascelles, was soon engaged by the latter's brother and his cousins. Lascelles was also connected with the Roundell family who, in turn, were connected with the Beilby Thompsons and Lane Foxs, all of whom consulted with Carr. There are numerous other illustrations. Sir John

Ramsden's half-sister, for instance, was married to Lord Rockingham. His full sister to William Weddell. Thomas Dundas was married to Lord Fitzwilliam's sister. The Duke of Portland was married to the Duke of Devonshire's sister. The number of fathers and sons or successive owners of country houses employing Carr is too numerous to mention.

Carr was at home with the great landowners, but equally active among the newly prosperous businessmen of the West Riding — some of them keen to establish themselves as gentry, with the essential prerequisite of a country house, others still busily making money, but all with the finances to build. George Green, a wealthy Leeds grocer, for whom Carr built a new house; Sir Henry Ibbetson, one of the West Riding's leading merchants, whose house in Kirkgate he extended and his nephew Sir James Ibbetson, for whom Carr built Denton Park and church; Jeremiah Dixon, a Leeds merchant, who probably employed Carr both on his Leeds house and Gledhow Hall; the Denisons of Leeds, Yorkshire's leading cloth exporters, who employed Carr on the estate they bought at Ossington in Nottinghamshire; the Milnes family, the most prosperous merchants in Wakefield for whom Carr certainly built Thornes House and possibly other houses; the Walkers of Rotherham, great ironmasters, for whom Carr built Clifton Hall and Eastwood House; Christopher Rawson, a prominent Halifax

35 Aske Hall, Yorkshire; the former stables built for Sir Lawrence Dundas in 1763–69

clothier, for whom Carr built a new house in George Street; John Edwards of Pye Nest, a rich Halifax merchant; John Priestley of White Windows, Sowerby Bridge (Fig. 37), a prosperous clothier; Samuel Shore of Norton Hall in Sheffield; the Spencers and Spencer-Stanhopes of Cannon Hall, early ironmasters.

It was these contacts that brought him the Hollis Hospital in Sheffield (through Samuel Shore's recommendation), the Leeds General Infirmary, where the committee included Jeremiah Dixon, and repairs to St John's church in Leeds, where Dixon was a churchwarden.

The geographical pattern of Carr's work is revealing. It is overwhelmingly Yorkshire-based, with a particular concentration on the West Riding from Leeds down to Sheffield. He only carried out limited work west of the Pennines in Lancashire (Lytham Hall, Towneley Hall, Kirkland Hall, the Preston Guild Hall, Holker Hall — for Lord George Cavendish), Cheshire (Tabley Hall, Fig. 38), and Cumberland and Westmorland (Workington Hall, for Henry Curwen, active political supporter of the Duke of Portland, Belle Isle for his daughter, and Belle Vue). To the north he had some success in County Durham, particularly at Raby

Castle and for the Bishops of Durham, but did not penetrate the industrial or coalmining classes as he did in the West Riding. Similarly he seems to have made little if any inroad into the prosperous inhabitants of Newcastle and had only a handful of houses in Northumberland. In Scotland he had only three abortive projects.

Looking south, Carr's projects in the south of England were exceptions, explained by his northern links: work at Burlington House, Lord Rockingham's house in Grosvenor Square and Cleveland House for the Earl of Darlington; a survey of Latimers in Buckinghamshire for Lord George Cavendish; Basildon Park for Sir Francis Sykes, a Yorkshire-born nabob; plans for extending Nuneham Park near Oxford bought by William Mason, for whom Carr had built a rectory in Yorkshire; work at Milton House near Peterborough for Earl Fitzwilliam; a new rectory at Alderton in Suffolk for the brother of Bacon Frank of Campsall; designs for a rectory at Whitchurch in Shropshire, for

36 *opposite* Ribston Hall, Yorkshire, built for Sir John Goodricke in about 1773; the drawing room

MATURITY

45

37 *left* White Windows, Yorkshire, built for John Priestley in 1767–68

38 *opposite* Tabley Hall, Cheshire, built for Sir Peter Leicester in 1760–67; the entrance hall

Francis Egerton, nephew of John Egerton, Bishop of Durham, and Carr's patron at Bishop Auckland; Fawley Court for his friend Strickland Freeman, who had family links with Yorkshire; Billing Hall in Northamptonshire for Lord John Cavendish; stables at Courteenhall (Fig. 39) for Sir William Wake whose mother and wife came both from Yorkshire.

Carr was more active in the counties immediately south of Yorkshire. Lincolnshire provided a number of commissions, as did Derbyshire. But it was in Nottinghamshire that Carr was more prolific, thanks in particular to the patronage of the Duke of Portland who commissioned him to carry out extensive alterations at Welbeck Abbey, funded the new town hall at Chesterfield (just across the border in Derbyshire) and presumably involved him in repairs to his parish church at Babworth. His brother, Lord Edward Bentinck, headed the move to build new Assembly Rooms and grandstand at Nottingham. Carr's other Nottinghamshire com-

missions included Colwick Hall for John Musters, one of the chief subscribers to the Nottingham grandstand; Newark Town Hall; Thoresby Lodge for the Duke of Kingston; Langford Hall for Henry Duncombe; as well as alterations to Staunton Hall, Clifton Hall and Grove Hall and a design for a house in Southwell. Had Carr just worked in Nottinghamshire he would have been considered an active local architect.

Perhaps Carr's most unexpected group of commissions is in Ireland, although in each case the contact lies back in the North of England, Coolattin House and the Flannel Hall at Rathdrum, both in Co. Wicklow, for Earl Fitzwilliam; the Sessions House at Lismore for the Duke of Devonshire; an obelisk and mausoleum in Armagh for the Yorkshire-bred Archbishop of Armagh, Richard Robinson. But it is still hard to explain why Carr received his largest and most unexpected commission, for the vast hospital of San Antonio in Oporto. It is true that Portugal, and particu-

larly Oporto, were strongly influenced by England at that time, but it might have been expected that an architect would have been sought in London, or in Bristol, where the trading links were strong, not in York. The answer may lie with Carr's close friend William Mellish whose family traded with Oporto or with the Yorkshire-born chaplain to the English Factory there, Dr Wood, whose family subsequently employed Carr at Bolling Hall, but the exact route, which must have lain through the influential British consul John Whitehead, remains undiscovered.

Not that Carr was without his setbacks. Building was looked upon by the gentry as a fashionable and enjoyable pastime and they frequently indulged themselves by asking several architects for schemes. At Harewood, Lascelles consulted at least four architects and Carlisle employed two for the design of the stables at Castle Howard where Carr supplanted Chambers. At Burton Constable, a range of architects — Adam, Lancelot Brown, Carr, Thomas Atkinson

and Thomas Lightoler — offered designs for alterations. It was the last named whose proposals were accepted, as they were at Platt Hall, near Manchester, where Carr and William Jupp had also submitted designs. Ten years later, about 1770, Charles Hotham asked Carr, William Middleton and Thomas Atkinson to design a new Dalton Hall. It was Atkinson, Carr's principal competitor in York — whom he had once used for the bricklaying at Fairfax House — who was successful. At Parlington designs were sought from Thomas Atkinson and Thomas Leverton. Neither was used. Thomas Yarborough, sought designs for Campsmount from Henry Flitcroft, Carr and James Paine.[44] At Busby Hall in the North Riding (Fig. 40), Carr who had carried out several works for the Turners of Kirkleatham, was called in by Jane Turner to draw up a scheme of reconstruction. But the job went to a local builder Robert Corney, whose drawings were clearly based on those of Carr. Beilby Thompson, having acquired a plan for alterations to old, four-gabled

Wetherby Grange from the London-based 'great Mr Wyatt' — to use his own description — decided on further amendments and brought in Carr to carry them out.[45]

But what is all too clear from Carr's list of works is how he dominated Yorkshire. In York his main rival was Thomas Atkinson, who has fewer than twenty commissions to his name, many of them for the Yorkshire Catholic gentry, a market he dominated thanks to his own conversion to Roman Catholicism. William Belwood, who supervised Adam's interiors at Harewood, set up in York in 1774 but is credited with only six commissions. Carr's other local rivals were more builders than architects with only a handful of buildings to their credit: William Middleton in Beverley, Robert Corney from Cleveland, John Foss of Richmond in the 1790s, John Platt of Rotherham whose surviving journal sheds more light on his practice than most. Their principal interest is in showing how far Carr had climbed.

If Carr had a metropolitan rival it was not Robert Adam, Sir William Chambers or James Wyatt, whom he saw off effectively, but James Paine. Like Carr, Paine (six years older than Carr) had begun as clerk of work on a great Yorkshire house, Nostell Priory. His early years were focused on Doncaster where his success in winning the commission for the Mansion House in 1745 ensured him a mass of local work between then and the early 1750s. But Paine lost out to Carr over the design for Campsmount in 1751 and, more importantly, the York grandstand in 1754. He was also increasingly drawn to London. Despite a number of fine houses designed there in the 1750s Yorkshire played an increasingly limited part in Paine's practice. Whether out of discretion or because the work was no longer available for him he bowed out for Carr in the early 1760s. But there seems to have been no animosity. Paine was happy to give credit to Carr for his work at Raby Castle, a commission where Carr replaced him.

LONDON AND ABROAD

Although Carr was, in the best sense of the word, a provincial architect, he knew London well. He visited the capital as early as 1751 when William Gossip commented to Edmund Garforth that he was thinking of visiting Bath as well.[46] He was there again in March 1758 when Popplewell explained to Edwin Lascelles that 'Mr Carr's sons left for London last Monday'.[47] More mysteriously, a letter in the Leeds Infirmary book dated 7 June 1768 mentions that 'My sudden call to London and long stay there has unavoidably delay'd a great deal of my Business and thrown me into a great hurry at present'.[48] Quite what called Carr to London so suddenly and for so long is unknown.

It was in the late 1770s, the 1780s and 1790s that Carr visited the capital virtually every year, sometimes for only a few days, sometimes for nearly two months, as in 1785 when he arrived on 8 May and left on 26 June, but usually for about a month around May.[49] While in London Carr carried out major alterations to Burlington House, which the Duke of Portland leased from the Duke of Devonshire, between 1771 and 1776 and supervised alterations and improvements to Earl Fitzwilliam's house in Grosvenor Square between 1781 and 1783. A design, which must date from after 1774, also survives for the dining room of Cleveland House in St James's Square for the 2nd Earl of Darlington. It is not known if it was executed. However, in Carr's terms such works were minor and it was not architecture that drew him repeatedly to London.

Carr certainly used London as a base for excursions, and perhaps jobs, outside the city. In 1784 he commented that he had been '5 days out of Town of the seven I have been here'.[50] Basildon Park near Reading, built between 1776 and 1783, must have been supervised in this way. In 1777 it was suggested that he might visit Earl Harcourt at Nuneham Courtenay when he was in London and in 1782 he visited Latimers about twenty-three miles north-west of London to draw up a report on its condition for Lord George Cavendish. He is also known to have visited the Dowager Marchioness of Rockingham at Hillingdon House near Uxbridge, Middlesex, although apparently only on a social visit.[51]

It has been suggested that, following in the steps of Adam, Chambers and Paine, Carr indulged in the occasional building venture in London, perhaps on the estates of the Dukes of Portland or Devonshire. York, where the population remained fairly static throughout the century, offered few such possibilities. London, growing at a prodigious rate, was the real centre for speculation. But no evidence to support this has been found. There is no reference in any of his letters nor in his will. Moreover, had Carr wanted to involve himself in speculative building fast-expanding cities such as Wakefield or Leeds were closer to hand. An annual visit sounds an unlikely approach for the practical Carr to take to anything as risky as property development.

More probably Carr's trips were essentially social, evidence of the growing social circles of the well-established architect. Samuel, Carr's erudite brother, was a prebendary of St Paul's Cathedral. Although he is never mentioned in correspondence their relationship must have been satisfactory as Carr provided generously for his family in his will. The sculptor Joseph Nollekens, described as 'my friend'[52] and who sculpted Carr in the 1790s, would have been well placed to introduce him to artistic and architectural circles, where his membership of the Architects' Club shows him to have been comfortable.

39 Courteenhall, Northamptonshire; the stables built for Sir William Wake after 1766

In 1790 he recommended Mr Harvey and Mr Scofield of Golden Square, London, who had been staying with Carr at York in 1790, to the steward at Wentworth Woodhouse, introducing them as 'my particular friends'.[53] He was also very friendly with his patron William Mellish, in whose house in Albermarle Street off Piccadilly he regularly stayed.

A mysterious, and irritatingly unsupported, reference in 1771 suggests that Carr may have visited France. John Grimston's agent reported in a letter of 30 May 1771 that 'Mr Carr is gone (I believe) to France'.[54] Perhaps Carr was celebrating his freedom from the troublesome office of Lord Mayor which ended on 4 February that year. He certainly had time to make a French excursion. It would appear that there are no letters fixing his location between 4 February, when he wrote to Samuel Shore from York, and 8 October, when he wrote again from York to John Grimston.[55] However, this period lies between the regular years of correspondence with Popplewell at Harewood, which end in 1762, and with Benjamin Hall at Wentworth Woodhouse, which begin in 1772, so the evidence remains thin. Certainly it would have made sense for Carr, who never had the chance to travel abroad as a young man, to visit France. By 1771 he was prosperous enough to afford the excursion, we know from his later records that long distances did not trouble him and the long years of peace between the end of the Seven Years War in 1763 and the outbreak of war with France again in 1778 provided the opportunity.

SOCIAL LIFE

Carr appears to have been an acceptable, honest companion though, in his early life, more concerned with business affairs than with conviviality. The record of attendances at the York Assembly Rooms during Race Week, published in the local press, seems to prove the point. Carr was not consistent in his attendance. In 1753, society flocked into York and 'There was the greatest Appearance at the Assembly-Rooms in Blake Street ever known since that Building was erected'. Perhaps the consideration then being given to a new race stand intrigued young Carr, for he entered his subscription for the first time. 1755 was another boom year and again we note Carr, in fact, two Mr Carrs, presumably John and his father, subscribing to the proceedings which marked the opening of the Standhouse on the Knavesmire. In subsequent years, Carr's presence was variable. Once he was accompanied by a Miss Carr but there is no specific mention of Mrs Carr.

40 Busby Hall, Yorkshire, unexecuted design made for Jane Turner in about 1757

The Minute Books of the Assembly Rooms provide another slant on Carr's interests.[56] Carr indulged himself in the purchase of a £25 share (No. 143) in the Rooms from William Staniforth and Jerome Dring, Rockingham's political agent. In 1779 he was elected by ballot to one of the twelve directorships, along with the Duke of Devonshire and the Marquis of Rockingham. In 1782 Carr signed the minutes as chairman, noting that attendances had dropped. Carr transferred his share to his nephew William in 1792, about the time when he was apparently withdrawing from most of his business activities. On taking over Carr's directorship William Carr was appointed treasurer, a post which he held until 1805 when his place was taken over by another director, friend of the family, Thomas Swann.

The friends of Adam and Chambers provide valuable pointers to their intellectual interests. Carr's friends are not so easy to identify. His early life was limited and circumscribed by his family. His closest associate was his father and it is likely that his other friends were drawn from the building trade. For example, Carr was a witness at the wedding of Daniel Shillito, carver of Wakefield, who worked with Carr's father at Heath Hall. James Henderson of York, who plastered at so many of Carr's buildings, must have had a close relationship. There are several other master craftsmen in the same category.

By joining the Rockingham Club in 1754 Carr widened his circle to include not only York tradesmen but minor gentry. It also indicated social aspirations. However, the most illuminating personal record of social status occurs in the Harewood correspondence of the 1750s where Carr emerges as an equal to the steward, Samuel Popplewell, with whom he stayed on occasions and who in turn accepted hospitality of the Carrs in Horbury. Carr's wife was friendly with the Popplewells. In the 1770s, Carr's relationship with Benjamin Hall, the steward at Wentworth Woodhouse was on a similarly friendly basis but Mrs Carr was no longer mentioned in the correspondence. Carr had by now moved up in the world — he could place 'Esquire' after his name — and though he still stayed with the steward, being on excellent terms with the chaplain and housekeeper, he was sufficiently important to ask in polite though offhand manner for the extension of hospitality to acquaintances. Thus, in 1775 he introduced 'my friend Mr Nollikins the Eminent Sculptor' (1775); then in 1781 'A Gentleman of consequence whose name is Mr King is on Tour (with his Lady), a great and curious Antiquarian … I take the liberty to desire you will show him all the Civilitys in your power'. Particularly interesting is his introduction of Sir William Robinson and his brother, Richard Robinson, Lord Rokeby, Archbishop of Armagh and Primate of All Ireland. The former had succeeded to the baronetcy on the death of his brother, Sir Thomas, the amateur Palladian architect. The Primate, according to Carr, 'is a curious man and will ask many questions'. Like his elder brother, the archbishop was building mad and after seeing Wentworth Woodhouse, its stables and Keppel's Column, proposed to visit Raby Castle then being altered by Carr. The latter added 'I have been with them at Castle Howard', where Carr had designed the stables. The Primate commissioned an obelisk and a mausoleum from Carr. Mr Harvey and Mr Scofield of Golden Square, London, who had been staying with Carr at York in 1790, were introduced as 'my particular friends'; and, in the following year, the architect warned the Steward that he would be arriving for dinner at three o'clock with 'Alderman Myers and another good friend of our party Joseph Atkinson' ('our party' presumably meaning the Whig persuasion).

Myers (or Mires) was a York tradesman. A miller, he attended the same church as Carr and shared with him an interest in the Yorkshire Tontine. Another aldermanic friend of earlier and closer acquaintanceship was William Siddall, successful woollen draper and tailor — also a director of the Tontine — about whom Carr was once rather patronizing, referring to him as 'poor Sydall' when the latter's turn came round for the chairmanship of the Rockingham Club as he felt that the unpopularity of his friend would be unlikely to bring out much support at his investiture. Even so, 'poor' Siddall sat with Carr on the Bench, and accompanied Carr on trips. In 1783 we find him with the architect at Wentworth and in 1785 Carr wrote that he had arrived in London 'with my friend Sydall'.[57] Siddall was sufficiently distinguished to be elected Lord Mayor of York and to become 'Grand Master of the most Ancient Grand Lodge of All England'.

The diaries of Carr's various travelling companions also provide an insight into Carr's circle of friends. Some, like William Rigge who provided slates for many of Carr's buildings and with whom he stayed in the Lake District, were business acquaintances.[58] His link with others, such as Mr Cox and Mr Lethulier whom he met near Andover, is less clear.[59] Perhaps the closest of Carr's gentry friends was William Mellish of Blyth Hall. Carr worked for him at Blyth and stayed at his town house in Albermarle Street in London.

Universal social acceptance belonged to Carr, culminating in his joining the exclusive York Club, membership of which was confined to the nobility and gentry.

Carr's relationship with the most eminent of clients was almost invariably cordial. Rockingham was kindness itself and even the sharp Fitzwilliam grew to rely on Carr and treat him as friend. Carr took a modest pride in knowing so many of the nobility and, while he certainly kept his place, his letters to them all have a quiet assurance. The correspondence between Carr and the Duke of Portland illustrates his attitude for while the bulk of it is straightforward and business-like, the two men became sufficiently intimate to discuss their sicknesses. When the duke asked Carr to stay at Welbeck in October 1781, Carr replied with alacrity:

My Lord Duke, I assure your Grace a very little invitation will at any time bring me to Welbeck, the regard and pleasure which I have so long enjoyed there, will be remembered by me with gratitude so long as I exist. I had resolv'd before I received Your Graces obliging letter, to take the first opportunity of visiting Welbeck, in consequence of the message which I received from Wentworth house, and therefore can only add that I hope to enjoy that pleasure the latter end of next week.[60]

Carr also played a central part in the most important social occasion that took place in eighteenth-century York, the visit of the Prince of Wales and his brother, the Duke of York in 1789. In preparation renovations were carried out to the Assembly Rooms 'according to Mr Carr's approbation', although the decision over the colours of the decorations was left to Mrs Fawkes. A full day of amusements at the Mansion House, accompanied by dinner with the choicest wines and fruits, was attended by three dukes, eleven lords, eleven knights, Yorkshire gentry and eight aldermen, including John Carr. On the Monday, amid scenes of wildest enthusiasm, the Prince of Wales and Duke of York arrived on the raceground. During an interval in the running Carr, at the command of the royal brothers, stood between them and with admirable spirit and sweetness sang the patriotic ballad, 'Heart of Oak', to the great delight of the company.[61]

The princes left for Wentworth Woodhouse where 20,000 people assembled in front of the mansion, bonfires were lit and fifty hogsheads of ale were distributed to the populace 'which did amazing execution'. Three hundred carriages brought guests to a ball of unparalleled brilliance. In the great saloon, which had been completed by Carr, 'fireplaces were hidden by a profusion of flowering shrubs and aromatics in pyramidal forms, which had a cool pleasing effect'. Two hundred tapers blazed from the central chandelier and 850 lamps were used, including three rows of multi-coloured lamps lining the balcony and others hanging festooned from the columns. Supper was eaten off solid gold plates. The guests included Carr and his two nephews, William and John.

CHAPTER THREE

THE PRACTICE

THE OFFICE

DESPITE THE SCALE OF HIS PRACTICE Carr
ran a small office. There was nothing, for instance,
to compare with Adam's extensive drawing office.
Staff were few, one or two at a time, and in 1762 there must
have been no one in the office as Sarah Carr twice had to
answer Carr's mail for him. During the election of 1770
Carr had to apologize for not being able to give more assistance in collecting votes as he had then only one clerk at
home.

The limitation of staff is intimated in a letter of 1758 in
which Robert Carr, reported that Carr was returning to
York to set 'the lad' on to a revised scheme for Harewood
House. The boy could have been William Lindley or possibly Thomas Orvin who wrote to the steward at Harewood
in 1758 explaining Carr's absence on tour. Another whose
name emerges briefly from the Harewood correspondence,
this time in 1763, is James Hartley. There is also the Charles
Mason who made a laborious copy of Batty Langley's
Ancient Architecture Restored in 1768. The document in ink,
now in Sir John Soane's Museum, is signed by Carr and was
possibly set by him as a student exercise.[1]

Joseph Halfpenny (1748–1811), limner of Bootham, is
said by George Benson, the York historian, to have been an
assistant but there is no evidence of a professional connection. Born the son of the archbishop's gardener, he became
first a house painter, later developing into a well-known
local artist. His principal claim to fame is that as Clerk
of Works to the Minster during Carr's survey of 1794 he
took advantage of the scaffolding to measure and draw
details which were published in twenty numbers between
1795 and 1800 as *The Gothic Ornaments of the Cathedral Church
of York*.

Two clerks less shadowy and of considerably greater
stature than these are William Lindley (*c.* 1739–1818) and
Peter Atkinson (1735–1805). Both subscribed in 1774 to
Thomas Skaife's *The Universal British Builder*, the former
calling himself Architect of York and the latter Surveyor of
York.

Lindley was probably Carr's first assistant and must have
joined him in the mid-1750s as the practice was rapidly
expanding — in 1773 he stated that he had been employed
by Carr for nearly twenty years. His well-developed aes-
thetic capabilities are shown by the drawings he produced
while still a youth of Kirby Hall, the York Grandstand and
the York Assembly Rooms, which were used for prints.[2]
Like the other assistants, he was probably given little independence of action. Thus, when John Grimston wrote
about the alterations to Kilnwick Hall in June 1769, Lindley
replied 'Mr Carr has been from home about a week, but as
soon as he returns I will show him your letter when you
may expect his answer.'[3]

In 1773 Lindley left Carr to set up his own practice,
placing advertisements in the *York Chronicle* of 18 October
and in the *York Courant* of 19 October. Had their names
been swapped, the *York Chronicle* advertisement could easily
have described Carr's practice:

Architecture

WILLIAM LINDLEY, Architect, and Director of
Buildings, who has been an assistant to Mr. Carr of York,
in that Business, near 20 years, Draws and Designs all
Kinds of Edifices, from the plain Farm House to the most
stately Mansion; Also Designs for Churches, Chapels,
Monuments, Temples, Pavilions, Green-houses, Baths,
Bridges, Gateways, Stables, etc. — He likewise makes
Alterations, Additions, and Improvements in old or
inconvenient Houses, and designs all Manner of Inside
Finishings, as Door-cases, Chimney-pieces, Cornices,
Ceilings, etc., etc., in the genteelest Taste, with proper
Directions for execution of each Design. He hopes the
long study of his Profession, and the great Practice he has
had (while with Mr. Carr) will enable him to give entire
Satisfaction to those that please to favour him with their
Commands, who may depend on having them executed
with the greatest Expedition and on moderate Terms. Mr.
Lindley may be heard of at his Lodgings, at Mr. Milner's,
Coach-Painter, in Blake Street, York.

Lindley soon moved to Doncaster after being invited by the corporation in October 1774 to design the playhouse. He developed a substantial career in south Yorkshire, often working on former commissions of Carr's including Kirklees Hall, Ossington Hall, Bretton Hall and Campsmount.[4]

The other assistant was Peter Atkinson, whose strength lay in the measuring and costing of buildings. Initially a carpenter and then a surveyor, he aspired to higher things, describing himself as architect on the occasion of his second marriage at St Mary Bishophill Senior in 1775. He first appears in 1769 when he measured and certified some carving at Harewood on Carr's behalf. In February 1779 Carr wrote introducing him to the steward at Wentworth Woodhouse: 'Mr Atkinson is one of my Clerks who has never before been at Wentworth House, he is on his way to Buxton and I have ordered him to measure up all the work.'[5] In 1781, Carr again refers to Atkinson as 'My Clerk', which was his description in Carr's 1789 draft will, where he was left £20.[6]

Although Atkinson seems to have succeeded to Carr's practice — the biography written by a successor to the practice for Wyatt Papworth's *Dictionary of Architecture* (1852–92) states that Atkinson succeeded to a portion of Carr's engagements — their relationship is anything but clear. It scarcely supports the suggestion that they went into partnership in 1785. Although Atkinson was responsible for writing the occasional letter, as were Lindley and the other clerks, Carr always remained very much in control, clearly not sharing the responsibility with anyone. Indeed, there is a case for assuming that Atkinson was something of a freelance. In 1780, for example, he applied unsuccessfully for the post of Receiver of the Rents of York, sometimes known as City Steward. He attained the post and its salary of £40 a year in 1786. In 1782, he is listed amongst the members of the Rockingham Club as 'Mr Peter Atkinson, Architect' (note the status symbol of 'Mr') and in the *York Guide* of 1787 as 'Architect' with an address in North Street. This is a little confusing for about the same time information was being sent from Wentworth 'to Mr Atkinson in Mr Carr's office at York'. How far this independence went it is difficult to say as Carr was still relying on him in 1787 for the settlement of accounts, and in 1790 the two were still in association, although Carr rather tersely commented to the Steward at Wentworth Woodhouse 'Mr Atkinson show'd me this morning what he had ordered for the chimney tops, which I do not approve of …'.[7] The date, 1790, has some significance for it probably marked Atkinson's acquisition of the commission to design Hackness Hall, finished about 1795. It would be reasonable to assume that it was about this time that he distanced himself from Carr who was then approaching seventy and slowing down in his career. This inference is reinforced by the fact that the reference to Atkinson in Carr's draft will of 1789 was not repeated in the draft will of 1792, suggesting that Atkinson was no longer in Carr's employment.[8]

The two men seem to have remained in some form of association as we find them together over buildings at Wortley Hall in 1797. Eventually Atkinson was joined by his son, Peter (1776–1846) and together they continued the Carr tradition of keeping abreast of the times with sound, sensible work. The Hackness estate has outbuildings, particularly the stables, in the Carr manner, and the mansion itself, on occasion understandably attributed to Carr, has a plan based on that of Wiganthorpe Hall. Its elevations, though essentially Carr, have a touch of the increasingly fashionable Greek detail. So, in Lindley and the Atkinsons Carr lived on.

Equally important were members of Carr's family. In the 1750s Carr had a close connection with his father Robert, based on Horbury, in works at Thorp Arch, Campsmount, Harewood, Heath Hall and in bridge surveys for the West Riding magistrates. The association extended to his brothers, James and, in particular, Robert. Robert's son William was born in Askham Richard in 1749, suggesting that Robert was involved with Carr on work to Askham Hall, living near the site and perhaps acting as clerk of works. Robert supervised the construction of Kirklees Hall, visiting eleven times between July 1759 and February 1760, and the relationship became especially close after their father's death in 1760. It was presumably Robert who was the brother sent to Towneley Hall in Lancashire to give assistance to the workmen in 1766 'as he was more conveniently situated for waiting upon you than me'.[9] In the same year Carr noted in a letter to John Spencer that 'My Brother has taken the dimensions of all Marsden's work which I shall examine and make out the Bill of when I go next to Cannon Hall'. It must have been a busy year for in August Robert Carr, together with Luke Holt a carpenter from Horbury, contracted to built the new county house of correction at Wakefield to John Carr's designs for £2,650. Five years later the infirmary there was built to his own designs. It was again to his brother that Carr turned when work on the Leeds Infirmary ran into difficulties in 1769 because Wilkinson the original supervisor was too ill to carry out his job leading to the construction of defective foundations. Robert Carr was brought in on 10s 6d a day to supervise building work, visiting one day a week.[10] Carr had considerable faith in Robert's ability, and worked hard, and successfully, to gain him the Surveyorship of the West Riding Bridges when he relinquished the post.

Carr later employed Robert's son, William Carr (1749–1820). William was clearly not a dominant figure. Although he was held in affectionate regard by his uncle he had little more status than the other assistants. He sent the occasional adequately written letter to clients on behalf of Carr and references to him in the Wentworth Woodhouse papers give a general idea of his duties. For example, in 1779 he was busily arranging the dispatch by water of a model of Keppel's Column, interesting himself in designing the plaster flowers to be fixed to the Riding House ceiling, making the model for the stable gates and, in 1784, was again dispatching goods — this time a marble table and three chimneypieces. In 1787, Carr mentioned that 'my nephew and Mr Atkinson remember the drawing' suggesting they worked together,[11] and it was William who signed the receipts for the fees concerning Lincoln Gaol and Grimston Garth.

Carr trusted William Carr enough to leave some of the financial management of the practice in his hands, as can be seen from evidence of his paying bills into Carr's account at Goslings Bank.[12] He was also a valued draughtsman. In 1778 Carr described a large drawing and small drawing of chimneypiece in the tower room 'neatly drawn by my nephew',[13] and in 1787 Carr explained to Lord George Cavendish that he had given his nephew directions to make a fair drawing of the temple at Holker.[14] Carr certainly missed him when he fell ill in the winter of 1783, explaining to the steward at Wentworth that he had ordered Waterworth to make a drawing of the tables as he had no one else who could do that business except his nephew 'and he is so much worse than he was that I am at present much distressed in my business for want of his aid'.[15] It is not surprising that he wrote a fortnight later with concern that 'my nephew grows weaker every week, and we are in doubt whether he can hold out until warm weather returns'.[16] His interest extended beyond ordinary drawing for there is an entry in the York Chamberlain's accounts showing a payment to him for engraving.

William followed in his uncle's steps by joining the Rockingham Club and took his turn in the vice-presidency in 1783. He also followed in a directorship of the Assembly Rooms, having been given a share by his uncle. His immediate appointment as treasurer implies some knowledge of accountancy. But in 1782 his aspirations to becoming a civic dignitary received a set back when he failed to be elected a commoner for Monk Ward. By the time he married Henrietta Fermoy in 1785 at the church of St Mary Bishophill Senior he had achieved some status for the clerk described him as 'William Carr of this Parish Esquire'.

Like Carr, he died childless at Carr's country mansion, Askham Hall, which he had inherited after his uncle's death. He had been appointed a Deputy Lieutenant of the West Riding, an honour which but for Carr's earlier acquisition of the estate would never have come to him.

Why William failed to take over the lucrative practice which Carr had built up is a mystery. Maybe sickness prevented it. He spent two months in 1795 taking the waters at Buxton in an effort to cure his rheumatism. Maybe Carr's

bounty was sufficient for him, or maybe he was simply not up to the responsibility.

SUPPLIER OF CHIMNEYPIECES

Estate accounts show that Carr was occasionally paid for the supply of various materials, for example, slates and even reeds for the plasterers at Harewood. His most consistent supply was of marble slabs, plain marble chimneypieces and a certain amount of cut stone. Carr was involved in this trade from the very start of his career when he provided hearths and mantelpieces for William Gossip at Thorp Arch in the early 1750s and again for Gossip's house in York in 1757. This presumably explains his entry in the York's Freeman Rolls as a stone cutter. One workman, at least, is known, Robert Rhodes who was apprenticed to him for seven years in 1757 and obtained his Freedom in 1770 as a mason.[17] Rhodes may have continued a business partnership with Carr. In about 1778 he was paid £20 10s 9d for marble chimneypieces for Denton Park, which Carr designed.[18]

Numerous references can be found to Carr being paid for chimneypieces in the 1760s, at Tabley Hall, at Everingham Hall in 1762, Swinton Park in 1764 and 1767, Aske Hall in 1765 and Allerton Park in 1768. At Harewood, where Robert Adam designed the chimneypieces in the state rooms, Carr provided twelve marble chimneypieces for the bedchambers. The trade was clearly profitable. He was paid £146 18s for marble chimneypieces, including a black and gold marble slab, for Ravenfield in 1771 and £170 6s 8d for marble, fireplaces and grates at Thirsk Hall in 1775. However, he did not insist on his designs being used. He advised George Donston at Worksop in 1769 that though willing to design chimneypieces Donston should buy a marble chimneypiece for the best room from Walsh's in South Street, Berkeley Square, when he was in London 'as they are sometimes to be met with cheaper than having one made on purpose'.[19] Nor did he insist on executing his own designs. At Burlington House in 1771 he was quite happy for Devall to make the dining room chimneypiece to Carr's design and indeed for him to design the drawing room chimneypiece, taking note of the dining room chimneypiece design.[20]

TRAVEL

With such a small office and so many commissions Carr was endlessly travelling, surveying sites, visiting clients, making sure the workmen were doing what they should be. It was a hectic life which made co-ordinating different jobs difficult. 'I have been in Lincolnshire this fortnight & just

41 St Peter's church, Sheffield, restored in 1772–74, view from the south-east in an eighteenth-century drawing

got home & am obliged to set out in the morning to the Marquis of Rockinghams', he wrote to Popplewell at Harewood on 22 September 1754. 'I know not how to get your things drawn pray can you excuse me a week longer as I am afraid it will be seven or eight days before I return to York.'[21]

The twenty-six visits Carr made to Thorp Arch Hall between 8 August 1749 and 14 September 1750 were exceptional. This was, after all, Carr's first major commission. But he was scarcely less assiduous at Harewood and Plompton. The first payment made to him for work on the Harewood Estate notes: 'By 10 times coming to Gawthorpe on sundry occasions from July 9th to Oct. 23, 1754. £10.10.0.' Similarly his invoice of 1 November 1756 to Daniel Lascelles at Plompton, records:

Sepr. 22, Octr. 1, 8, 29, Nov. 8, 1756, Feb. 22, Mar. 29, 30, Ap. 12, 13 — Eight times at Plumpton to direct the work going on and considering how to alter the old house and taking a plan of the old house: £8 8s od … May 22, July 20, 28, 28, 30, Augt 31, Sep 14 — Seven days at Plumpton to direct the work and meet Mr Lascelles to determine the plan and operation for altering the House and

taking an account how everything shou'd be done in order to calculate the Expense. Riding about to seek a situation etc: £7 7s od.

His invoice for repairs to St Peter's church at Sheffield (Fig. 41) reveals the sequence of visits on a single commission:

To four journeys to Sheffield at the request of the burgesses on account of the repairs proposed, & executed in order to support the old church viz: The first to take their direction concerning the repairs, and to make a plan of the old part of the south and east sides of the church in order to make a proper design for the repairs thereof agreeable to the other parts of the church. The second journey to lie before the burgesses the new designs made for the south and east sides of the church and to make a report of the expence thereof and of the manner the work should be executed in order that workmen might bring in proposals for undertaking the work. The third, to meet the gentlemen in order to contract with the workmen for the execution of the work. And the fourth to examine the execution of the work, and to direct the proper manner of raising and finishing of the parapet the lead work gutters etc … And calling at Sheffield church three times

THE PRACTICE

56

during the time the work was doing in order to examine the execution thereof and lastly to measuring of all the masonry, windows etc and making out the charge thereof according to the contract.[22]

Five letters from the winter and spring of 1762/63 give a flavour of Carr's frenetic activity. On 27 September 1762 he wrote to Bacon Frank: 'I have been abroad in the North for some time and am but just returned, or would have been sooner with you and given an answer.'[23] On 13 November he wrote again: 'I am truly sorry to inform you that I am unavoidably engaged for this next fortnight or rather longer I am afraid … am obliged to be at Aske [near Richmond] on Friday and Sir Peter Leicesters [Tabley Hall in Cheshire] on Wednesday next.'[24] He was still at Tabley when Sarah Carr wrote to Popplewell on 5 December: 'Mr Carr is in Cheshire and I this day Received a Letter from him wich tells me he intends being at Stapleton [near Doncaster] ye next week.'[25] On 26 February his clerk James Hartley wrote again to Popplewell: 'Mr Carr unfortunately left for the North two days before your letter arrived and wont be back until about 8th March. He'll see you as soon as he returns.'[26] He was soon on the road again, On 6 April Hartley wrote again to Popplewell: 'Mr Carr is in Nottinghamshire and he'll probably return on the eighth and proposes to be in Pontefract on the thirteenth. When he returns you'll receive an answer from him.'[27] Cheshire, disparate parts of Yorkshire, the North (presumably County Durham or Northumberland), Nottinghamshire … the round never stopped. Sometimes it was all nearly too much. On 26 March 1764 Carr wrote despairingly to Bacon Frank:

It is with the utmost difficulty I can perform my business so to oblige the Gentlemen I am concern'd for, the Spirit of Building rages so much at present, and am truly sorry I shoud incur your displeasure by not calling when I was so near, my calling at Stapleton was very late in the Evening in order to be nearer York where I was obliged to be Early the next day and really had not time to call any where. I am setting out for Leeds this morning and will if possible contrive to be with you on Wednesday next.[28]

In 1769 he was forced to explain to George Donston that he would send drawings as soon as he could, but that he had 'been abroad 23 days and have another journey of 5 days to make before I can sit down and draw'.[29]

To the demands of his private practice must be added those of his two successive bridge surveyorships, for the West Riding from 1761 to 1772 and from then till his death for the North Riding. These took time. On 24 March 1779, for instance, he reported that he was setting out for a fortnight on the bridge survey.[30] So did his activity as a magistrate. Several letters refer to the Sessions at Northallerton requiring his presence. In March 1802, for instance he wrote to the steward at Wentworth Woodhouse that 'I cannot come before the second Sunday after Easter as I must be at Northallerton the first whole week after easter'.[31]

Thus it comes as no surprise to find William Mason writing to Earl Harcourt in 1778 that he had difficulty tying Carr down as he 'has so much employment that he is seldom at York'.[32] Nor had things improved by 1787 when Carr wrote to Thomas Grimston on 10 December: 'I left home before your Letter of the 25th Octor came to hand, & I did not return from Buxton before the 8th of this month.'[33]

The extent of travelling was hard enough without the inevitable knocks on the road. Thus on 27 July 1777 he wrote from Brancepeth Castle that he would wait on Lord Rockingham as soon as he had completed business on this 'circuit'. 'I have been so way laid this journey I have not got on as intended and I am in great pain with a broken shin that I find will never be better until I get some rest, and when that will be I cannot tell.'[34] Nor should the hazards of horse travel — his common practice — be forgotten. In 1784 he feared that he would be confined to his room for some time because 'in mounting a young horse I was thrown by him upon the pommel of the saddle with my stock under me which has bruised the testicle in such a manner that I can with great difficulty write and will be confined to my room for some time'.[35] Carr was at least sometimes accompanied by a manservant, Thomas, who forgot the slippers which his master had lent to a fellow guest, a clergyman, at Wentworth in 1776.[36]

DRAWINGS

As well as visiting in person Carr controlled his practice through endless detailed letters and a myriad of drawings (Fig. 42). Although no family archive survives and his own drawings have been lost, the extent and length of his practice mean that several hundred letters and probably as many drawings survive. Particularly valuable are the two major caches of letters at Harewood, where there are more than twenty letters from 1754 to 1762, and above all Wentworth Woodhouse, where there are 181 letters from 1772 until shortly before his death in 1807. With a few side references to his latest illness and his travels these generally stick closely to the matter in hand, often including very detailed and lengthy instructions for the work in hand.

Drawings were equally important, and indeed his letters often include sketch drawings to make his message clear. It was through drawing that Carr worked out his ideas, explained them to the client and then communicated them to the craftsmen. The process started with sketches and the extensive sequence of drawings for Everingham Hall (though mainly for unexecuted work) show with rare clarity the precise sequence followed by Carr when designing a country house. One catches a glimpse of the process at work when Carr wrote to Popplewell 'I have sent you a

THE PRACTICE

57

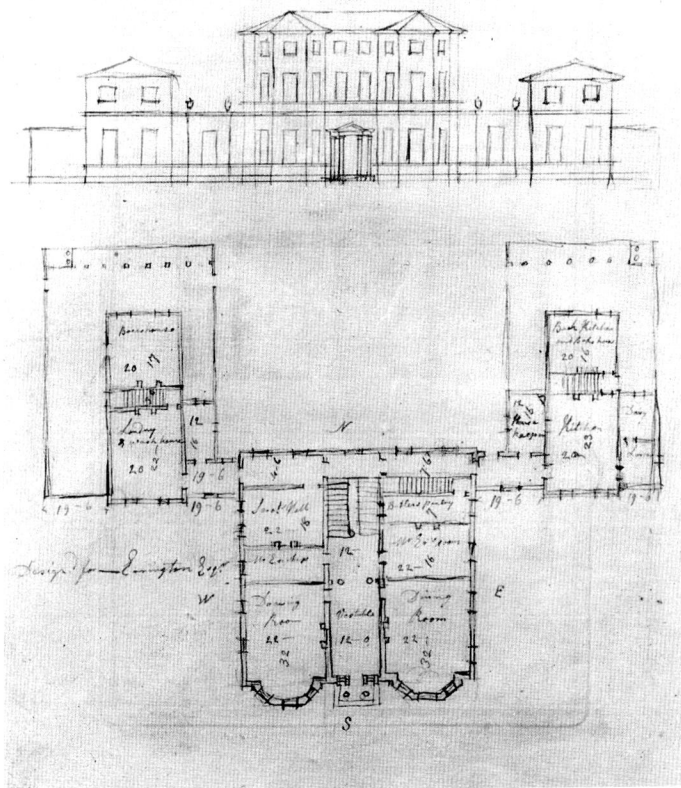

42 Drawing by Carr of the plan and elevation of Chesters, Northumberland, built for John Errington in 1771

sketch of the intended Portico ... If Mr Lascelles approves of what I have Drawn, please to acquant me & I will send you the directions at Large for the Execution of the Desin'.[37]

Presentation drawings such as that for rebuilding Wiganthorpe Hall (Fig. 43) or for extending Nuneham Park (Fig. 44), were invariably well-drawn, usually on Whatman paper, with edges bordered, having been fixed on the drawing board not with pins but with black or red sealing wax. One idiosyncracy of Carr's drawings is that he often marked the line for five on his scale with three dashes. Pencil was rarely used, the finish being in ink line, often brown, with areas in plan and elevations tinted with light washes of colour. The lines outlining walls in plan were usually thickened on one side to simulate shadowing and to give greater definition, a method adopted by many contemporary draughtsmen.

A good example of Carr's technique is given in the design in the Harewood papers which he drew for the Temple of Venus, a surprisingly large eye-catcher, erected on the hillside facing across the valley towards Harewood House (Fig. 45). There are four sheets of standard size, all bordered and inscribed 'J. Carr, Architect 1780'. The scale

is not written but, in Carr's usual fashion, there is a diagrammatic horizontal scale divided, in this instance, on the basis of one inch representing four feet. The walls in the plans are drawn in black ink line, thickened on one side with an infilling of yellow ochre wash. The description, in flowing script, not block lettering, is in brown ink. Black ink line is used for the elevation, washed in with grey Chinese ink, but without colour. Shadows are cast and darkened by one who obviously had an adequate knowledge of sciagraphy — even reflected light is shown in the shadows of the podium and dome. In the section, a wider range of colour washes is employed — grey, yellow ochre, raw sienna and gentle green for the glass of the windows.

Drawings were executed in a wide variety of scales. Random samples give: $1\frac{1}{8}$ in = 10 ft; 1 in = 8 ft; $9\frac{1}{16}$ in = 10 ft; $1\frac{1}{8}$ in = 10 ft; $1\frac{1}{2}$ in = 10 ft; 1 in = 10 ft; $\frac{1}{4}$ in = 10 ft; 1 in = 4 ft; 1 in = 5 ft; $\frac{3}{16}$ in = 1 ft; $\frac{1}{5}$ in = 5 ft; $9\frac{1}{4}$ in = 40 ft and so on. Although there seems to have been little consistency, multiples of sixteenths or eighths of an inch predominate.

Undoubtedly, the factor that gives most character and unity to a Carr drawing is the flowing writing, which makes the efforts even of Adam appear pedestrian. Not all of Carr's drawings are signed: some are plain, some simply initialled 'J.C.' in the bottom left-hand corner and some, including the early ones, are inscribed with 'J. Carr', for example, the sketch schemes for Harewood House. In correspondence, however, the architect signed himself John up to about 1762 when he then turned over to the signature Jno Carr.[38]

Drawings emanating from Carr's office, apparently all in the same hand, were never signed other than with the architect's name or initials. Carr could not have done them all so that we must assume that his clerks assimilated Carr's style of drawing and lettering — as they did, for instance, in Chambers's office — resulting in work indistinguishable from that of the architect.

Where Carr gained was in his willingness to produce alternative schemes. There are many designs for a bridge over the lake at Wentworth Woodhouse and no fewer than seven for the Lion Gateway at Brampton. The Rockingham Mausoleum had at least two carefully drawn proposals, each topped by a lofty obelisk. And for Parlington, he offered three schemes for a mansion, the permutations of which could be extended by raising flaps of alternative designs hinged over the wings, and a Gothic design for a chapel and chaplain's house (Figs 46 and 47).

43 *opposite above* Wiganthorpe Hall. Yorkshire, drawing of an unexecuted design made for William Garforth in about 1778

44 *opposite below* Nuneham Park, Oxfordshire, drawing of an unexecuted design made for the 2nd Earl Harcourt in 1778

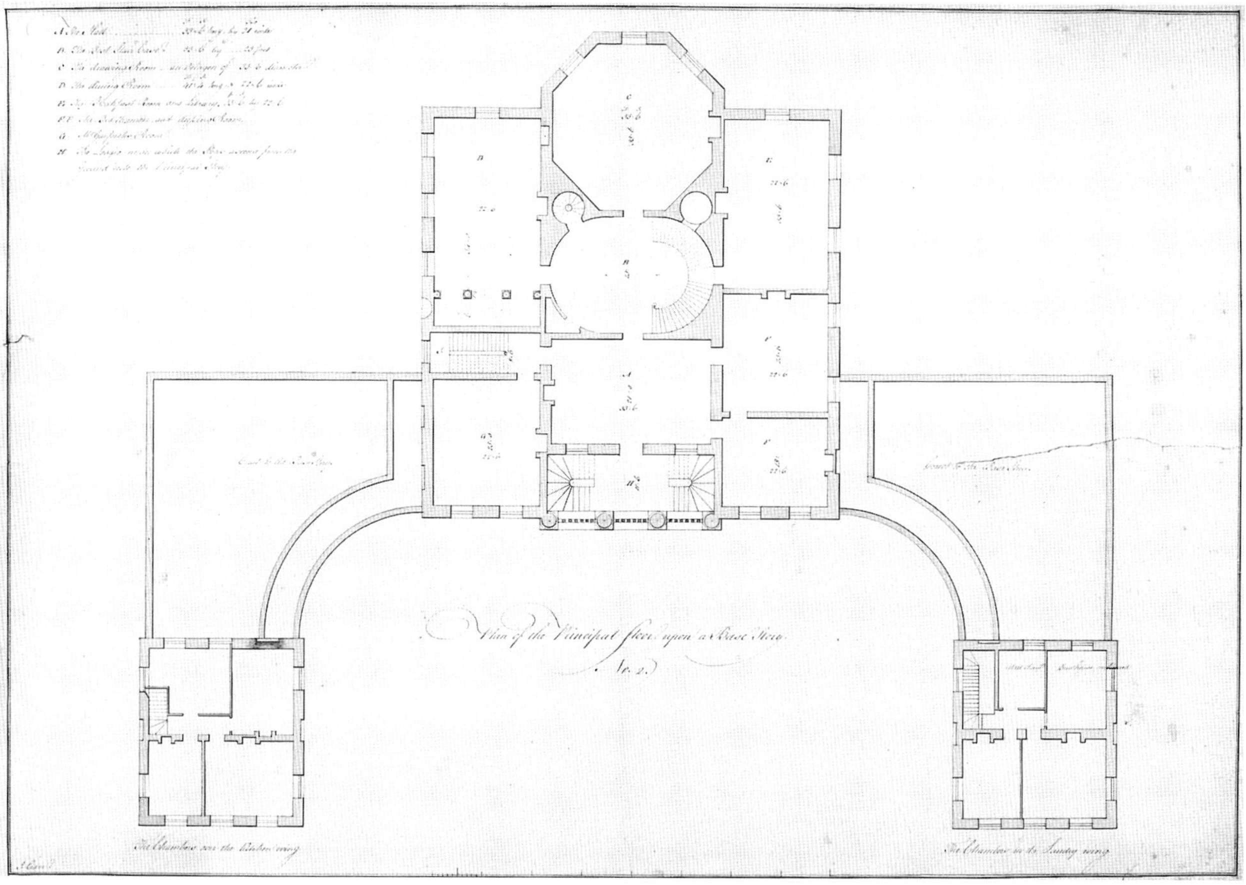

Plan of the Principal floor upon a Base Story
No. 2

The Chambers over the Eating wing

The Chamber in the Sowing wing

The Principal Elevation

THE PRACTICE

59

45 *above* Harewood House, Yorkshire, the Belvedere or the Temple of Venus, built in 1780; drawings by Carr
46 *opposite above* Parlington Hall, Yorkshire, unexecuted design for a chapel made for Sir Thomas Gasgoigne in 1772, ground plan
47 *opposite below* Parlington Hall, Yorkshire, unexecuted design for a chapel made for Sir Thomas Gasgoigne in 1772, elevation

Even in the presentation drawings, Carr frequently added overall room sizes to simplify understanding by the client and, on acceptance of a scheme, completed the measurements so that the drawings became working drawings. His designs for the parsonage at Alderton of 1772, for instance, were 'so particularly figured & delineated that I think the workmen cannot err in the execution of it', a phrase that he frequently repeated and would have applied to the drawings for Ossington Church (Figs 48 and 49).[39] This explains why the design of the building as erected is nearly always missing. There seems to have been no regular practice of making record drawings as there was in Adam's office, later taken to a highly organized state by Soane. When Carr had to discuss designs by post he made care to keep a copy of the original, as in 1771 when he wrote to Samuel Shore about his proposals for the Hollis Hospital: 'I have kept a Copy of the Design & can now Correspond with you or Mr Hollis upon the Subject.'[40] However, earlier he had been forced to confess in 1764 to Bacon Frank that 'I have not a copy of the dining room [drawing] therefore cannot send the moulding at large for the panels'.[41] Carr had either to make do with the original or laboriously to

prick through — he was a great hand with the dividers — in order to produce a copy. Lack of time frequently caused him to make do with the original. This could, and did, lead to difficulties. In March 1769 Carr wrote to John Craven, the mason on the Leeds Infirmary, answering his questions by explaining that if he wanted answers he would have to send Carr the working drawings where most of the details he wanted to be informed about could be found. 'I cannot learn where the working Plans & Elevations are which I draw'd for the proper Execution of the work, I imagine Mr Wilkinson has them, they shoud be fix'd upon Boards & always remain upon the place.'[42] An item in the Buxton A/cs for 1781 reads, 'Making Boards for Pasting Drawings on'.

Supplementing the small-scale working drawings were the larger scales used for doors, windows and chimney-pieces approximating to quarter, half and one inch scales. There are several illustrations ranging from those for Everingham Hall, to drawings for ceilings for Wiganthorpe Hall in the Victoria and Albert Museum.

Finally, there were full-size details called 'directions at large' or 'in great'. These, too, were usually drawn in ink,

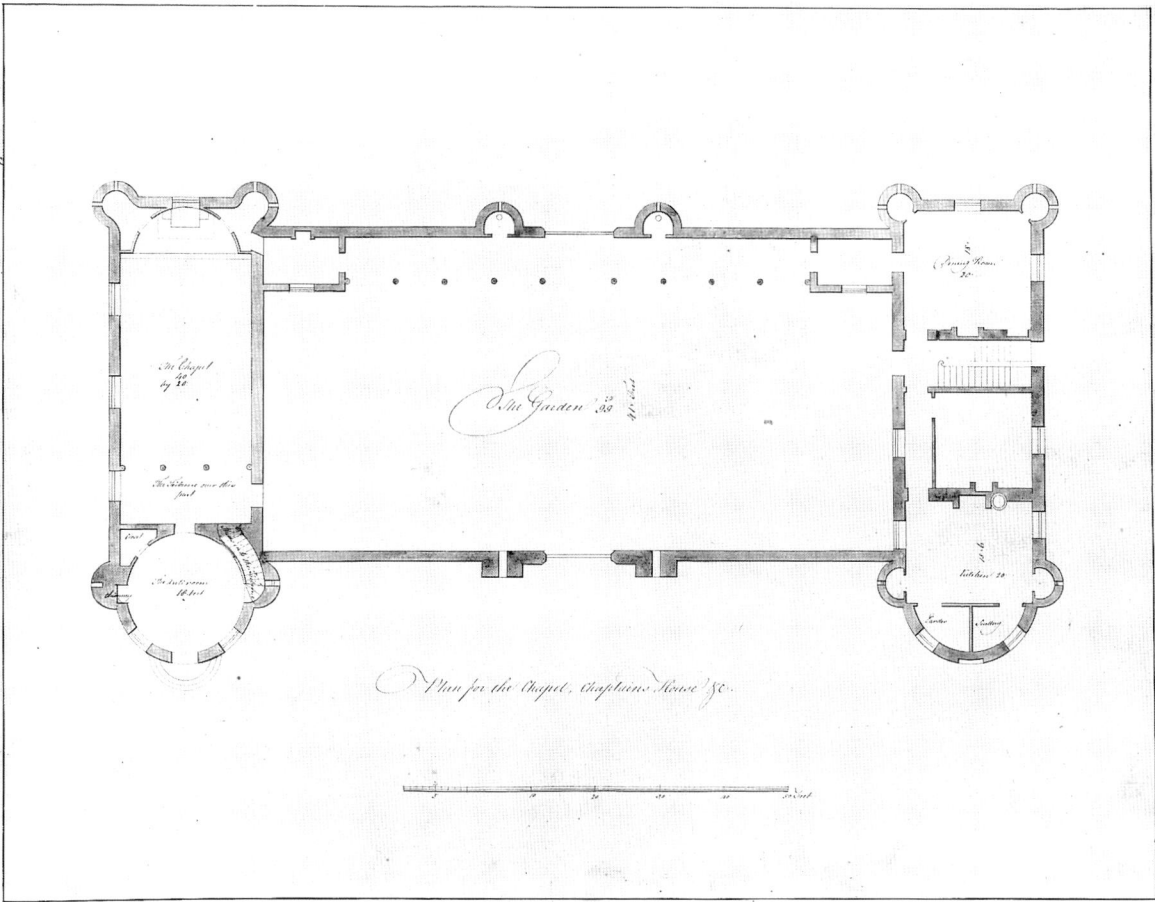

Plan for the Chapel, Chaplains House &c.

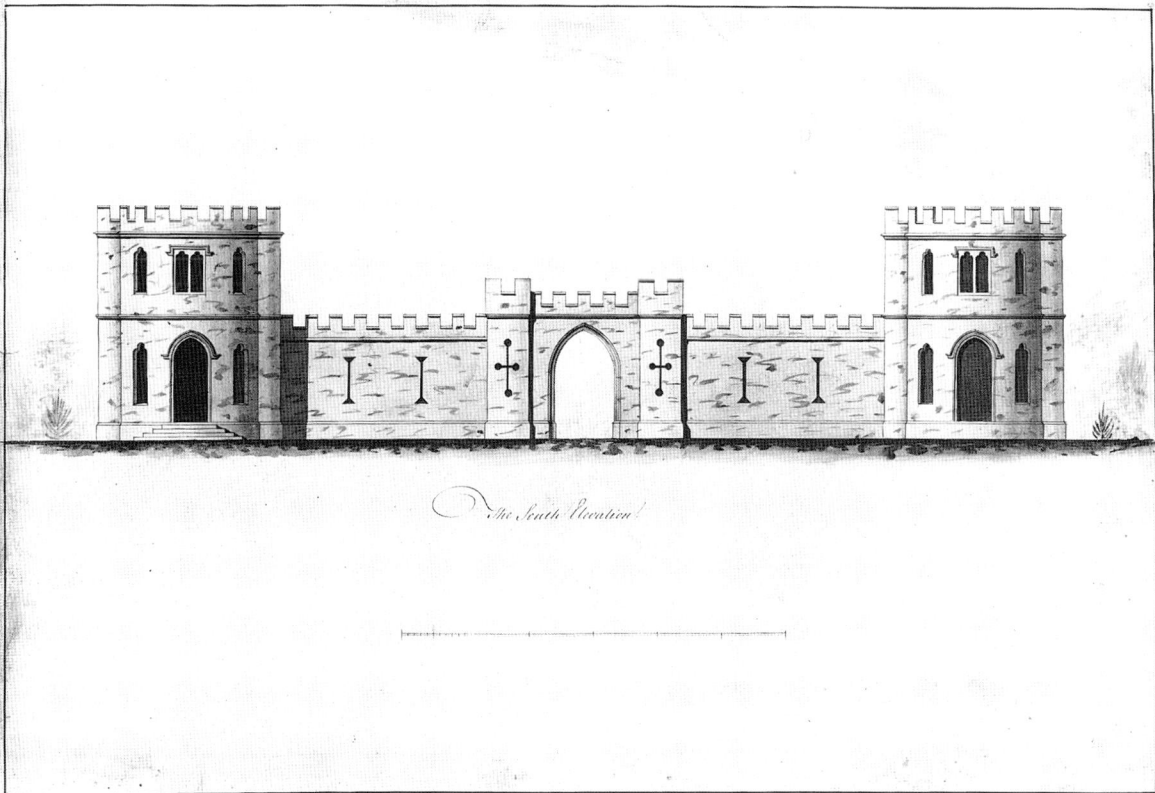

The South Elevation

THE PRACTICE

61

Section of the Steeple end of Church
All the Windows in the tower are Blank
except the West side is open

Plan of the Belfrey Floor
& Groining above

Plan of the Collumns above the Belfrey
The Bells must hang in the 3 Recesses
that is raised for hinging the Arches off

NB The inside Arch must Spring
at 24. 3/2 above floor

10   20   30   40   50 feet

Islington Church & Mausoleum by Carr

48 *opposite above* Ossington Church, Nottinghamshire, built for Robert Denison in 1782–84; drawing by Carr
49 *oppoasite below* Ossington Church, Nottinghamshire, built for Robert Denison in 1782–84; drawing by Carr
50 *above* Denton Park, Yorkshire, built for Sir James Ibbetson in about 1772–78; entrance front

though, on site, Carr was known to draw in chalk on the nearest convenient object, in one instance, a piece of furniture. In 1781 he wrote to Wentworth Woodhouse asking that 'Tommy Hobson send the profile as he has it drawn of the great troughs as I first intended them, figured particularly, as he has it on a paper, which he took from my chalk drawing against the press in Mr Fenton's office, I think one may draw it full size from Tommy's sketch'.[43] Carr was not always best pleased when the workmen expected such detailed designs, as he wrote to Bacon Frank in 1764: 'I had better keep a man to do the ornament as be obliged to draw them their ornament at large. I could not do a tenth part of my business. Tis sufficient to show where I woud have the pannels broke with ornament and where to introduce it.'[44]

Carr seems to have varied the number of drawings which he prepared for a job. At Denton Park (Fig. 50), even the detailing of the curved cupboards in the bedroom, quite apart from the more obvious features such as chimney-pieces, cornices and architraves, was given the most careful consideration. Everingham Hall is also fully covered with small-scale drawings of both constructional and design details. There are designs for interiors — walls, ceilings, chimneypieces — leaving little to the imagination of crafts-men. One drawing of ornament was executed 'at large' in red chalk on brown paper. The bridge at Ferrybridge received extremely close attention, as the drawings prove, and similar care must have been taken over the detailing of the Buxton Crescent and of Newark Town Hall.

Unlike Adam or Chambers, Carr seems to have designed little furniture, although he did on occasion. In 1783 he wrote to the steward at Harewood 'I have ordered Water-worth to make a drawing of the tables as I have no person that can do that business but my nephew.'[45] This was followed by references in 1784 to Elwick making a table 'a dr of which have given my lord'[46] and to Lord Fitzwilliam wanting Carr to design a frame for the glass in the drawing room between the window frame.[47] Carr also designed pier tables and mirrors at Chatsworth at about the same time and perhaps a set of pier tables at Ribston. He was probably

THE PRACTICE

51 *above* Denton Park, Yorkshire. Niches and tables in the breakfast room
52 *left* Burton Constable, Yorkshire. Design by Carr for a candlestick for William Constable

also responsible for the tables placed in niches at Denton Park (Fig. 51) and Norton Place[48] and for the bookcases at Colwick Hall (Fig. 123) and Grove Hall, both of which were clearly designed to fit in with the decoration of the room. More unusual were the two candlesticks he designed for Burton Constable, somewhat uncomfortable pieces based on Ionic columns (Fig. 52).

Not that Carr was uninterested in the furniture in his interiors. Walter Spencer Stanhope's diary for 29 April 1768 notes: 'Mr Carr went with me to Mr Tyler the Notary and paid his bill, from there he went with me to Cobbs, Chippendales and several other of the most eminent Cabinet makers for the order of proper furniture for my Drawing Room.' On 18 May, 'Mr Carr called upon me, discoursed him about furniture of my drawing room, said he would speak to Ellick [Edward Elwick of Wakefield] & write to me.'[49] Elwick won some of the contract, though furniture did come from London.

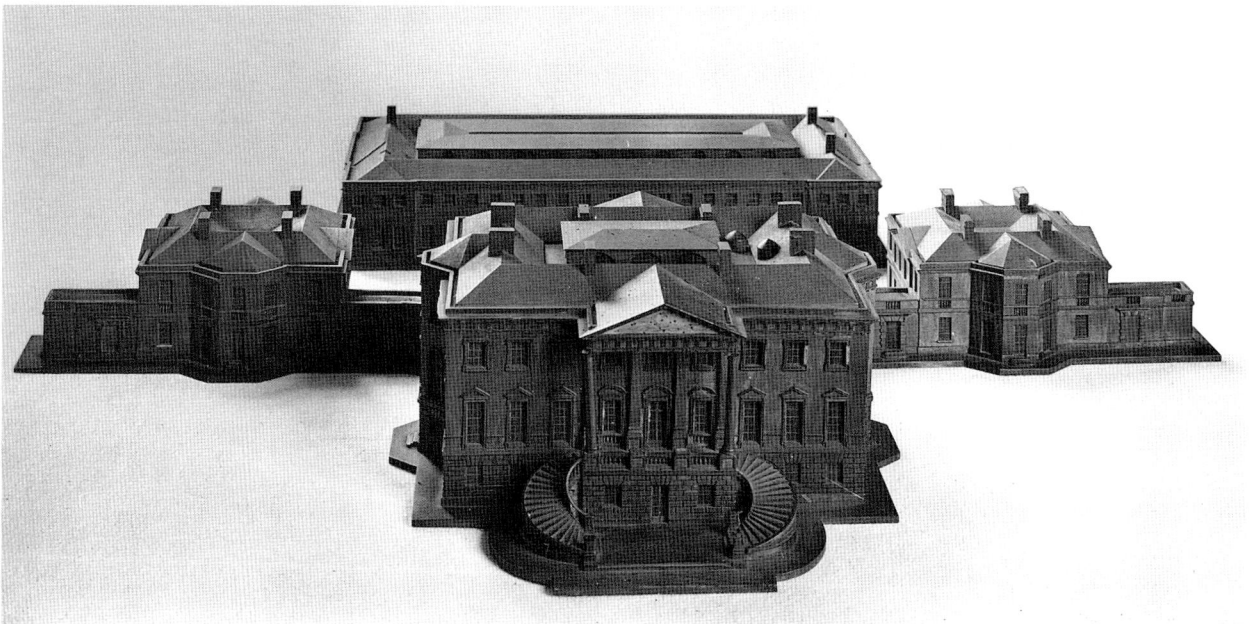

53 Tabley Hall, Cheshire, built for Sir Peter Leicester in 1760–67; contemporary model

MODELS

Carr communicated by drawings, by frequent correspondence and, particularly, by his visits, but also by models, such as that for the great mansion of Tabley Hall, Cheshire, where the wooden model of house and stables, not quite the same in all detail as the finished building, is still kept (Fig. 53). A model was also made for Thoresby Lodge, for the Duke of Kingston. Payment was made in 1767 to the joiner 'Robert Barge for making a model of the new buildings £1.14.3.'

Carr's appreciation of models is also illustrated in a letter which he sent to the Marquis of Rockingham in 1774, suggesting an improved design for the cupola over the enormous stables then building at Wentworth Woodhouse. 'I wish if your Lordship would be pleased to let me give directions to Smith to make a little model of it about 2 ft 6 in high.' On a less elevated plane, we find that in the following year Carr was dispatching to the Wentworth Steward '... the Model for the necessary house Water closet ... it is but a very small thing 8 or 9 inches square'.[50] Carr had arranged the installation of water closets at Thoresby Lodge and was probably trying to gain a convert in Lord Rockingham. The mansion was certainly fitted out with water closets for, a few years later, Fitzwilliam, Rockingham's successor, waxed exceeding wrath over the provision of a new seat to his W.C. in marble instead of the warmer, more comfortable, mahogany. In 1779, the marquis was considering various possibilities for an eye catcher in Wentworth Park, for which Carr submitted several proposals. A model of the

base was made by William Carr and despatched by the Rotherham boat.[51] In 1781 Carr sent a model of the roof of St Ann's Well to Buxton, presumably as a constructional guide.[52]

ESTIMATES

Presentation drawings, or schemes, were either accompanied, or were eventually followed, by estimates, as we see in a letter of February 1769 from Carr to Samuel Shore concerning the Hollis Hospital:

I have sent you by the Sheffield Carrier to be left at Mr Watsons in Sheffield the Plans, Elevations and Estimate of the 16 Alms Houses, the School and the Masters house; The whole of which design is particularly delineated, and the dimensions of every part figured, and in the Estimate of the expence I have put down the prices of almost every article, from which directions the undertakers will be enabled to ascertain the quantity of materials wanted, and the Trustees inform'd how to make Contracts with them without being imposed upon.[53]

A full estimate is contained in a report accompanied by plans which he made in 1782, concerning radical alterations to Latimers, Buckinghamshire, for Lord Chesham.[54] The recommendations were complete with a summary, broken down into three sections, the first part of which reads:

Expence of uncovering the House, and laying on the Tyles again, repairing the Roof, recasting the Lead Gutters, and Building a new parapet wall on the South &-East parts of the House, Taking

54 Newark Town Hall, Nottinghamshire, built in 1773–76; entrance front

down the Gable ends & repairing the Garretts and making the proposed alterations in the Chamber story the four Bed chambers & five dressing rooms according to the plan marked No. 2 will cost as near as can be computed ....£1840.

A similar but lengthier report and estimate was prepared by Carr in 1770 on the state of York Minster.[55] Extracts and comments from the survey give the gist:

The High Roof over the middle Aisle from the Center Tower to the West end ... This is an exceeding bad Roof, and has been very injudiciously repaired ... The Belfry Window in this Tower is made so ugly by filling up the intermediate parts thereof with Brick and Plaister, that one cannot help lamenting the disagreeable appearance it now makes ... Great East Window ... many decayed parts thereof in the inside, which may be preserved from further decay by a good Coat of Plaister being put upon the decayed places ... The Vestry Roof ... N.B. There is an ugly Brick Chimney upon this part, and another upon the Library which ought to be taken down.

Carr expressed concern about the roof over the south end of the 'Great Cross Aisle' recommending repairs to the rafters and ceiling, and noted that the side walls of the south transept were bulging. He continued: 'N.B. A Great many

of the Grotesque Ornaments which project from the walls ... decayed ... [should be] taken down ... to prevent their doing mischief by falling.' He concluded: 'Since this report, of the state of this noble Cathedral was made, I have carefully Estimated the Expence of the several necessary Repairs herein mentioned, which upon a moderate valuation amount to the Sum of Four Thousand two hundred Pounds and upwards. Dated February 22nd 1773.' Carr was paid 21 guineas for the survey.

Estimates for completely new buildings are rare: £11,000 for Thoresby Lodge and the estimate of 'a little more than £2,500 if properly managed' for Leeds Infirmary. Writing to the Trustees of the Infirmary in 1768 Carr explained 'I have ... finished the Estimate of the expence of building the whole and finishing such a part of the Infirmary as was proposed when I was last with you, according to the Plans and manner specified in the inclos'd instructions which with working Plans (in my opinion) should be open for Workmen to Inspect and make their calculation from in order to undertake the execution'.

A frequent method of the time was to base the estimate not on the cubic capacity of the building but on the number

55 Bootham Park Hospital, York, built in 1774–77; entrance front

of squares comprising its plan. A square was a hundred square feet and was priced according to the quality and height of the proposed structure. Outbuildings — also special features, chimneypieces, door furniture and so on — were regarded as extras and treated separately. Thus in Carr's 1769 letter to Shore concerning the Hollis Hospital he noted.

As you will not build the whole of this design at once, I have calculated from my Estimate the expence of Building one Square of it, or 100 feet Superficial, and find that every 100 feet will cost about £22.3.0, So that if you multiply the Length by the breadth (of any part you think proper to build at one Time) & divide the product by a 100 you will readily know the Expence of Erecting a part of the building.[56]

Carr, trained as a building surveyor, was quite capable of measuring off and pricing trades in detail. On the contract of 30 November 1756 with James Sanderson, Benjamin Child and John Newland for two farm houses which he designed at Plompton, every element was minutely priced, either by individual item, the yard or the square. Thus chimneypipes were 12s each, slating 'laid on dry & pointed' was 2s the yard and the house roof 'finding

all materials and Workmanship' was £18s the square. The contractors pledged to have the buildings covered by 29 September and completed by 25 December 1757 on penalty of £100.

But, as ever, pricing new buildings remained an uncertain science. William Mason, who had a high regard for Carr, passed on his own cynical view to Lord Harcourt when he suggested that Carr should be asked 'what he thinks it [alterations to Nuneham Park] may be executed for, and if he says for £2000 or £2050 call it in your own idea £5000 & you will not be disappointed. I say this not to depreciate my friend Carr, but to shew you that this is the case in all Architectural or even common building estimates'.[57] This certainly seems to have been the case in a number of Carr buildings. At Thoresby the steward waspishly noted on the account that Carr's original estimate had been for £11,000 and that the house had actually cost £17,000. Similarly the Bootham Park Hospital in York (Fig. 55) went so far over the estimate that a further appeal for money had to be launched. But Carr would not have attained the reputation he did had he come in habitually over budget, and it is fair to guess that at Thoresby, at least,

THE PRACTICE

67

the extra cost came from changes of mind and extravagance on the part of the client.

After designs and estimate had been accepted, and drawings completed, the next step was its execution. Public bodies, such as town councils or hospital committees, were more or less standardized in constitution and methods. A policy was agreed and recorded in minutes. Monies authorized for projects were made available and accounted for by the treasurer or chamberlain. Usually public bodies advertised for tenders or proposals from workmen. A good example is the advertisement appearing in the *York Courant*, (and *Nottingham and Newark Advertiser*) in December 1773, for the building of Newark Town Hall (Fig. 54) where, it was stated, drawings could be seen at 'Mr Carr's, York'. Another example, printed in the *York Courant* on 14 September 1779, concerned the new Female Prison in York Castle (Fig. 56): 'All workmen willing to undertake the Additions proposed to be made to the said Castle, are desired to deliver in Estimates, with the lowest Terms for which they will undertake the same, at the Castle, on Friday the 24th inst. by Ten o'clock in the Morning according to Plans, Elevations and Method of Doing the Work which may be seen in the mean-time at Mr Carr's Office in York.' Corresponding procedures were adopted for the hospitals at Lincoln, Leeds and Bootham, all by Carr. The erection and repair of bridges in the Ridings for which Carr was responsible, were also advertised in the papers.

A closing date was given for the proposals which might be required in writing and sealed, as they were for Newark Town Hall and for Bootham Park Hospital. A relevant advertisement for the latter in the *York Courant* of 1 December 1773, reads: 'Those workmen who are inclined to undertake the bricklayer's work of the intended Lunatic Asylum by measure, finding bricks, and all other materials in that branch, are desired to send their proposals, as soon as possible, sealed up, to Mr. Samuel Waud, to be laid before the Committee.' There were similar advertisements for joiners, carpenters and masons.

Sometimes, workmen were asked to turn up at the appointed time to give their propositions verbally. As the committee was unversed in the technicalities of building, the presence of the architect or surveyor was essential to 'assist the Justices in making Contracts with Workmen' — the expression used in the Surveyor's contract with the West Riding Authority. This was a very necessary requirement for, as the archives of the Riding prove, many estimable tradesmen were often illiterate and incapable of adequately putting forward their proposals in writing or, indeed, even verbally, to amateurs. In many cases, to complicate matters, labour and the supply of materials were separately agreed upon.[58]

It would appear that on occasion the magistrates did not always relish the task and, where the surveyors were trustworthy, would delegate the work to them. An example occurred at the Barnsley Sessions in 1779 when, for the Female Prison at York Castle, John Gott and John Carr were empowered to 'proceed to contract with Workmen for completing the said works according to the Plan and Estimate'.

In 1766, John Carr and his fellow surveyor to the West Riding, John Watson, produced a design and estimate for a new House of Correction at Wakefield. Advertisements asking for proposals appeared in the York, Leeds and Sheffield papers. At the Rotherham Sessions in August, 1766, the Court, after deliberating on the proposals, did not contract with individual tradespeople nor with a single entrepreneur; instead they compromised, contracting with Robert Carr of Horbury, mason, and Luke Holt, of the same place, carpenter, to erect the building for the sum of £2,650 within two years from Michaelmas, 1766. Thus, quite apart from the unusual situation of John Carr presumably recommending his own brother for the job, we see that the contract provided for a date for completion. The provision was not a wholly exceptional one since it was also incorporated in the agreement with the Peacocks, the mason family who built Carr's graceful bridge over the Greta in the North Riding in 1773. Here the builders were required to furnish security for satisfactory completion, which they did with the backing of Thomas Swann, the York banker, whose son married Carr's niece. Payments were to be made on an interim basis subject to the work being approved by Carr or his representative. Finally, the Peacocks were expected to maintain the bridge for seven years.

CONSTRUCTION

On works where several trades had been 'contracted for', a co-ordinator was needed. Carr with his extensive commitments could hardly be expected to do this, even in York, and a superintendent of works was a necessity. The latter, a superior tradesman or even architect, was something more than a clerk of works. He was also the builder and even draughtsman, producing drawings of details when the occasion arose. Good men were in the minority. Carr could recommend only Wilkinson for the Infirmary at Leeds, and when the latter found the job too much for him the architect's brother Robert had to take on the work. The erection of the House of Correction, Northallerton, was superintended by John Whitehead, who was also responsible for the masonry. At Newark Town Hall, and at Buxton Crescent, it was William Matthews, and for the Standhouse on the Knavesmire, Thomas Terry of York.

For private commissions the procedure, though similar, was more variable. A major difference implicit in most

56 The Female Prison, York, built in 1779–83; entrance front

private work was the great difficulty in getting materials, labour and artists to a building, often of great sophistication, sited in the country miles from a centre of population. The accounts and correspondence relating to the alterations to Cannon Hall, near Barnsley, indicate how Carr negotiated with and brought in tradesmen, arranging for his brother, Robert, to supervise the work. The whole project was done on a very personal basis, relations with the client being extremely cordial. Many years later, in 1790, Stanhope noted in his diary that Carr had stayed at the Hall for a couple of days preparing an estimate and scheme for raising the wings and 'refused to take a farthing'.

Labourers, and sometimes tradesmen if the jobs were difficult to estimate, were engaged at so much the day or week. For instance, Clerici, the craftsman in scagliola at Wentworth Woodhouse, was paid at the rate of a guinea a week including his board. Again, at Cannon Hall, where Carr was unable to find tradesmen who could provide both labour and materials, the architect settled for labour only on a daywork basis. Writing to the client, Spencer Stanhope, in June 1778, he said, 'I have agreed with the Mason for 2/2 per day and Tweedale has promised to send some diligent workmen as it is impossible to do the work in any other manner than by days work, but at a much greater expense, I am certain, for I do assure you they have not the least idea of judging of the value of doing the work by the yard'. Even so, circumstances obliged him to accept a similar arrangement for the joiners in later work at Cannon Hall in 1786, payment being at the high rate of two shillings a day.

In other cases, Carr treated with tradesmen for payment on the basis of measured work where rates were agreed for various different types of labours. Carr had his own very definite ideas as to what the charges should be. A blue notebook in the Galway Manuscripts includes prices

'allow'd by J. Carr Esq. for Whiteaker's Building at Haworth'. Plastering is given at so much a yard, blue slating at 8d per yard and 7s 6d per square, figures were given for a square of flooring and, surprisingly, for a square of roof trussing.[59] Sometimes we find that agreement was reached before work started; sometimes, perhaps where the tradesman was illiterate or inexperienced, it was simply left to Carr to measure and evaluate the work fairly during and after completion. This was the case at Wentworth Woodhouse in 1786. The Steward, having obtained prices for brickwork, submitted them to Carr who replied firmly, 'I am so much amazed at the prices you have sent me for building the garden walls, that I cannot consent to give the prices proposed by either of the different workmen'. Also, 'the proposals which you have received are very incorrect'. The architect dilated at length on his objections and finished 'but if they will leave the prices to me, they shall have what the work deserves in a fair honest way'.[60]

In these instances, materials specified and approved by Carr were supplied by the client or through his steward. If the latter saw fit, a simple contract was drawn up. Very often, Carr went beyond advising and specifying. For instance, during the building of Harewood House he accompanied the Steward to Hull where he chose materials including the timber; and for work on the Wentworth Woodhouse estate he called for and examined samples of stone, one of which from the Steetley quarry was left for his collection at the Red Lion, Rotherham.

Ideally, of course, the most professional system of contracting was where labour and materials were combined as single items in a schedule of prices, conforming generally to one of the present-day procedures. It could only be achieved if the tradesman had the organization and capital to provide the materials, unusual in the case of the small, local man. However, most large buildings needed work of elaboration and often of considerable extent. The plastering, for example, necessitated the importation of specialist tradesmen who, employing several hands, customarily worked to the inclusive system.

Once initial agreement had been made with the workmen, Carr, if he had not already done so, rode about the site determining the position of the building, as the Plompton correspondence later shows, and when satisfied, pegged out the ground plan as he did at Harewood. His subsequent supervisory visits depended on the requirements of the particular job. Lascelles, checking on the architect's supervision, was assured by the steward Popplewell that Carr had never been found 'awanting'. Visits also depended on requests from clients — there are several illustrations of Rockingham, Fitzwilliam and Lascelles ordering their stewards to arrange a visit from the architect. His willingness to travel and accommodate the client was one of his principal attributes. However, the day-to-day supervision on site varied according to circumstances: the client and, perhaps, a master tradesman on small projects; on large mansions, the steward and the superintendent of buildings were usually the responsible people. During the building of Harewood House both a superintendent and an assistant superintendent were employed; similarly, there were two professionals at Buxton Crescent.

ACCOUNTS

Accurate accounts were essential to all payments. Carr in his capacity as architect or surveyor had this final responsibility. Thus in October 1787 William Carr wrote to Thomas Grimston enclosing 'the remainder of the Workmen's Bills carefully examined by my Uncle, but by being suddenly called from home he has omitted signing two of them'. He added 'I am sorry you have had so much Trouble with Brown. He was here yesterday. If any the best way to settle his Bill, will be to let him bring it over himself to my Uncle, & I have not a doubt about its being settled to your satisfaction.'[61] Usually Carr did the work himself, at other times he used his clerks, as at Staunton Hall, where Peter Atkinson did the measuring.[62] At Thoresby Lodge the job was so large that Carr and Atkinson did the job together.[63] At Cannon Hall the work was carried out by his brother Robert.

In exceptional circumstances Carr allowed the superintendent of works or even a tradesman to take measurements and submit accounts for his approval. In 1795, bedridden and without staff, he found a solution to the surveying of the Lion Gateway at Brampton, Wentworth, by using the steward's nephew and Samuel Sykes, the estate mason. He wrote to the steward, Benjamin Hall, 'I should

imagine by this time, the Masons must have almost built the Gateway and Lodges, which when done Mr Byrom and Sikes can measure off, keeping each sort of work separate, and for which separate works, you have prices by you that will suit most of them: therefore Mr Byram will be able to make out the Bill for my inspection.'[64]

Some of the better-off workmen were content to wait for completion but usually interim payments were made according to Carr's certification which must have involved the architect and his clerks in considerable work in measuring up and pricing. A check through the accounts of Thoresby Lodge shows that there were over thirty payments to the carvers and well over forty to the masons. During relatively minor alterations to St Peter's Church, Sheffield, between 1772 and 1775 John Bishop, the mason, received twelve payments from the Duke of Norfolk. Most of them were standardized at the round figure of £30, eliminating the need to establish accurately the interim value of work completed.

The final accounts themselves were neatly drawn up, one document or one set of documents for each contractor. Work was separately itemized, measurement given, and costed according to the figures agreed in the schedule of prices. Approved and signed by Carr, they were presented to the client or steward for payment. There are several excellent illustrations, perhaps the most impressive being the folio of twenty-seven pages concerning work on the Rockingham Mausoleum in Wentworth Park. The Harewood Archives offer many competent accounts. At a rather more domestic level are those for Thirsk Hall: there are the bills of James Henderson, the plasterer, John Peacock, the mason, Robert Blakesley, the carver — and Carr himself as supplier of chimneypieces. All were passed by the architect 'Examined and allow'd Jno Carr'. Elsewhere, in other projects, the format was the same. The bill started off with 'A Note of the Carpenters work' (or the Bricklayers work, etc.) finishing with the architect's certification varying in style from the above to 'This Bill examined &-prices prefixed per Jno Carr' or, perhaps, 'The whole measurement examined and setled by Jno Carr'.[65]

But occasionally even Carr could slip up, as an embarrassed letter to Ralph Bell of Thirsk Hall in 1775 makes clear:

Worthy Sir, I have not words to express the sense of Gratitude which I feel at your sending back my Bill, as I could not from my own find out where the Error was. I herewith return the Bill just as it was, from which you will in amount see where the mistake was. You will observe that the Total of the Bill is £289.7.8. And I had received of you sometime since £57.0.0. Subtract £57 from £289.7.8. and you will find the Balance is £232 7s 8d. And in my Bill it is only put down £132.7.8. So that I fell short of the right sum Just £100. You will please to observe I have not altered a figure in the Bill, but at the bottom thereof have shown that the

Error was in Substracting the fifty seven pounds from the whole Sum — and that Error is 100 pounds in my favour, which I am very sorry should have hapned in my account to you, but I am very happy that it has hapned in the hands of a Gentleman who I am confident will take no advantage of it, but will I hope excuse it, and remit the balance when it is convenient.

The letter is endorsed: 'July 12th, 1775. Recevd of Ralph Bell Esqr One hundred pounds being the Sum due as is herein specified — which is in full of all demands. Recd by me Jno Carr.'

Finally, a word on the spirit in which Carr carried out his duties. In 1787, he wrote a letter to Benjamin Hall concerning the erection of a small building on the Wentworth Estate. Feeling that circumstances did not warrant the taking of careful measurements for an interim payment, he suggested the payment of a lump sum of £25 or £30 and the balance when the job had been completed and measured. The architect continued, 'surely we may all be trusted till then. I want to do nothing but justice to them and the same too is proper to be done for my Lord.'[66]

FEES

The Architects' Club, of which Carr was an honorary member, from time to time concerned itself with professional matters. In 1795, for example, a heated controversy arose over professional charges with Soane holding that a 5 per cent charge for fees should cover all duties, whereas Holland and others wanted an additional 2 per cent for measuring. Carr could have contributed very little to the debate as percentage payments were very much the exception in his case. The only indication of a definite percentage fee occurs in the documents relating to Thoresby Lodge. The ledger accounts do not give payments to Carr — except for the supply of chimneypieces — but an abstract prepared by Samuel Shering, the steward, showing Carr's fee, presumably paid direct to the architect by the duke notes: 'Mr Carr had paid him for his Drawings Attendances his Clerk coming over twice to assist in Measuring as it is always proper to have two Persons in great Measurements & Settlings which was 5 per Cent for the House: £850'. The cost of the house had been £17,000. The account also notes that 'N.B. The Offices Alterations & Repairs coming under my Inspection, Mr Carr made no charge.' Here the relevant section states: 'The offices altering repairing Patter Walling, Bason, Engine House, Engine Works and Stable Building under the care of T. Simpson. £9267' The fee charged, 5 per cent, did not include extra for measuring. Visits, for which some architects made additional charges, were included.[67]

At Lincoln the committee for the new gaol preferred to work on a percentage basis but was thwarted by delays to the start of the building. When Carr put in a bill for £97 5s in March 1779 for the plan and estimate he had submitted more than four years earlier, the committee 'resolved to make an order to pay Mr Carr £50 on account', but since the gaol was still needed 'this Plan may in a short time be adopted when the Mode of Paying the whole will then be discharged in the usual manner of so much per cent upon the Building'.[68]

Attempts can be made to establish a percentage by extracting costs for building works and relating them to the fees charged. Unfortunately, the accounts, not always complete, are frequently vague in description. Sometimes materials for more than one building are lumped together under one heading or, if they have been obtained from the estate itself, may be omitted altogether. Thus, often we can only obtain an approximate idea of the true cost of the building. Similarly, the fees are difficult to assess. They may not even be recorded, being a private transaction between client and artist.

The earliest extant account, and one of the neatest, is provided in the notebook for the Grandstand on the Knavesmire, compiled by George Thompson, in the Wentworth Woodhouse papers. The total cost of the building in 1755 came to £1,896 0s 7½d. Carr was paid £160 10s, approximating to the unusually high fee of 8½ per cent. But there is no indication as to whether the sum was simply for designing and superintending or whether it also included sums for extra work in measuring or in negotiating for materials. Further examination shows that the accounts are not complete. They do not, for example, include stone donated by the Marquis of Rockingham.

Another simple illustration concerns the refacing of St Peter's Church, Sheffield. Items can be fairly easily extracted from 'The Book of the Twelve Capital Burgesses of ye Town and Parish of Sheffield in the County of York'. John Bishop, the mason, was paid no more than £361 5s 2d. Yet in 1775 on completion of the work there is the entry: 'Pd Mr Carr in full of Bill for Church Designs £54 12s 0d', a fee of apparently 15 per cent, which must have included designs that were not executed. To confuse the issue further the accounts of the Duke of Norfolk, who had similar responsibility for maintenance of part of the fabric of the church, show payments of £366 8s 10d for building and £26 5s 0d to Carr: a percentage of only 7 per cent. However, the duke's payment of £26 5s 0d — a round 25 guineas — suggests a fee rather than a percentage.

A further instance emerges from the North Riding Archives in the shape of 'Christopher Goultons Account of Cash Received and paid respecting Building the new Court House and House of Correction at Northallerton'. So far as can be ascertained, the total cost of the premises was £5,217 9s 2d. Omitting the cost of purchasing the land, legal expenses and stamp duty the costs were about £5,000, with

57 *above* Basildon Park, Berkshire, built for Sir Francis Sykes in 1776–83; the garden front
58 *opposite* Basildon Park, Berkshire; the hall

Carr being paid £200 for 'planning and for superintending the Building thereof', the balance of £20 2s 6d being a sum to cover 'the last works'.[69] This gives a fee percentage of approximately 4 per cent.

Much of Carr's work in his early days was paid for on a daily rate. This was the case with first payment made to him for work on the Harewood Estate was on a day rate: 'By 10 times coming to Gawthorpe on sundry occasions from July 9th to Oct. 23, 1754. £10.10.0.' A guinea a day gives a useful indication of Carr's status. His well-established surveyor father was paid only 7s 6d a day, while the ordinary tradesman often had to be content with one shilling or even less. Carr charged similarly to Daniel Lascelles at Plompton, as his invoice of 1 November 1756 reveals: 'Eight times at Plumpton to direct the work going on and considering how to alter the old house and taking a plan of the old house: £8 8s od ... Seven days at Plumpton to direct the work and meet Mr Lascelles to determine the plan and operation for altering the House and taking an account how everything shoud be done in order to calculate the Expense. Riding about to seek a situation etc: £7 7s od'. Drawings were charged separately: 'To making Designs for the Pond heads, one of them executed and two more made in London: £3 11s 6d ... April 20 — To making two different designs for

altering the old House which were sent to London: £5 15s od ... Octo. 16 — To making Designs for Farmhouses and Estimate of their expense and coming over with them and seeking their situation: £6 6s od, £1 1s od'. A separate invoice records 'By making drawings at York for the portico and moulding at large for it and Ballustrade and three Different Designs for Gateways and Gates. £4.4.0.'

Little had changed by 1772 when Carr made out a new invoice to Lascelles 'for designs, surveying works, measuring of the several works etc. for the year 1772. To myself seven times at Harewood to set out the buildings at Stank, and direct the proper execution of them, and the Dove house, the Gallery in the Church, and fitting up the Brewhouse, making the Design for the Inn at Harewood, the several Plans and Elevations thereof particularly delineated. Measuring of the Joyners and Carvers work of the Gallery at Harewood House, and making out their Bills Measuring of the Masonry of the Pigeon Court, and making out the Bills thereof and also an account of the Stone Getting, etc. for the whole. £37.16.0.'

On frequent occasions Carr charged an annual salary or flat fee for a year's work instead of charging a percentage or for time expended. Some of these were official salaries, as were the £50 and £100 a year, respectively, paid to Carr in

THE PRACTICE

59 Blyth bridge, Yorkshire, probably built for William Mellish

his capacity as surveyor, first to the West Riding and later to the North Riding Authorities. Similarly when 'he directed the repairs to the Minster' in York from 1794 to 1797 he was paid 'after the rate of one hundred pounds a year'. But Carr regularly followed the same system with his private clients, both on longstanding commissions and on relatively short ones.

At Harewood Carr's payments fluctuated but from 1765, when decoration of the State Rooms began to Adam's design, Carr received regular annual payments first of £50 and then from the following year of £60. Payments were made either at the end of December or the beginning of January and continued until the house was virtually complete in 1772. A receipt from Carr acknowledges £60 as his salary, not his fee.

At Wentworth Woodhouse Carr received a first payment of £80 in 1763 'for sundry Journies and plans'. The plans may have been the initial proposals for the Great Stables started in 1766. Turning to the accounts of the Agent, William Martin, we find under 'New Stables': 'John Carr 1 years salary £84', a sum which was paid annually until his death in 1807. It became an inclusive salary embracing the architectural work on all the estates of the Marquis of Rockingham and his successor, Earl Fitzwilliam.

Another case is provided by the Kirkleatham Estate Book.[70] About 1765, after Charles Turner had succeeded, though descriptions are vague, alteration work was undoubtedly progressing on the old mansion house. On 9 February, 1766, an entry appears: 'By remitted Mr Carr architect Draft on Rondean £65'. Presumably, this was a late payment covering the previous year for, on 22 November 1766, we see 'By remitted Mr Carr for a yrs stipend due August £65'. Clearly, some annual arrangement had been agreed and although the word stipend was not again used Carr received subsequent payments totalling £159 13s 10d in December 1767 and in January 1768.[71] The same arrangement can be seen at Basildon Park (Figs 57 and 58) where Carr was paid £100 every summer from 1777 to 1781.[72]

The sum paid varied again at Aske Hall, but the notion of an annual stipend remained, with Carr being paid variously 50 guineas in October 1764 and October 1765, 200 guineas in 1766, £100 in November 1767 'for a year's attendance', £80 in September 1768 and £100 in September 1769. The same system can be found at Escrick where on 26 December Carr wrote to Beilby Thompson alerting him to an intended visit, when he hoped to collect 'my interest and annual stipend'.[73] Regular payments, though the amounts vary, from John Mellish, suggest that Carr was working at Blyth (Fig. 59) on a fixed-fee basis, with the fee perhaps varying on the amount of work undertaken each year. Thus Carr was paid £42 (40 guineas) in January 1770 and another £42 on 29 December (presumably the fee for 1771), and £21 (20 guineas) in February 1774 and May 1777.[74]

Our final illustration concerns Thirsk Hall, owned by Ralph Bell, who employed Carr to raise this relatively small house by one storey and to add simple wings.[75] The work

60 York Assize Courts, York, built in 1772–76; entrance front

of alteration continued for about four years from about 1770 to 1774 and the salary basis appears again. His invoice of 8 June 1771 reads:

Made the plans of the Old house, and the new Wings and all the parts thereof at large for the workmen, and making all the drawings for the chimney pieces, bases, surbases Architraves and all the other drawings for the Joyners, plasterers etc. and measuring of their several works, and giving all the necessary directing for the proper execution of the work for 32 years from June 8 1771 the whole designs drawings and directions included at 30 Guins a year: £110 5s.

The vital point is that '30 Guins a year'.

In large projects, such as those at Harewood and Wentworth, the accounts are sufficiently detailed to show that Carr rarely concerned himself with the minutiae of supplying goods so that it is unlikely that he made much on the side. The possibilities are more obvious in small or individual projects where there was no established estate organization controlled by a steward through whom or by whom materials were ordered and paid for. For instance, at Fairfax House, in York, the bills were often disbursed through Carr for slate, gravel, timber, painting and even for two 'bustos' from the sculptor, Cheere. It would seem strange for Carr to have done this work gratuitously, and a fee may be tucked away somewhere. Possibly, he included for it in his overall fees, 25 guineas in December, 1764, and 50 guineas in March, 1765 'on account of attending and designing his [Lord Fairfax's] building'.

Carr's role, assuming that it extended beyond that of simply preparing drawings, was generally supervisory, for which, as we have seen, he was paid a fee. At two of his largest commissions, however, the York Assize Courts (1772–76) (Figs 60 and 61) and the Bootham Park Hospital in York (1774–77), nearly all the payments were made through Carr, which suggests he accepted a much more direct role. At the Assize Courts he was paid nearly £8,500, at Bootham Park Hospital almost £4,000. Carr must have felt that taking on this greater responsibility was practicable as the buildings were within walking distance of his office. The attraction was presumably the potential of much greater financial rewards.

CRAFTSMEN

Carr did not employ fashionable London talent. The Ciprianis, the Zucchis, the Kauffmanns were never available to him and, as a result, he did not develop the painted panel in the full Adam manner. The one exception came when he engaged Theodore de Bruyn — who specialized in painting imitations of sculpture in low relief — to decorate panels at Basildon Park in 1776 and Farnley Hall in 1790. Instead Carr's closest relationships were with craftsmen in his own county.

Joseph Cortese did the rather chaste decoration at Kilnwick Hall, in the East Riding and plasterwork at Lytham Hall in Lancashire in 1764 — assisted by John Rains and

61 *opposite* York Assize Courts, York, the civil court
62 *above* Ormesby Hall, Yorkshire, the lodges built for Sir James Pennyman in about 1772

William Stephenson. The plasterwork at Arncliffe Hall of 1753 may also be by Cortese. From the *York Courant* we learn that Cortese died in 1778 and that his executors were Mr Edward Elwick, upholsterer of Wakefield, and James Henderson, plasterer of York.

Elwick, either the upholsterer made a Freeman of York in 1758 and a Chamberlain in 1759, or his son, whom he took into partnership, had an extensive business supplying furnishings, cabinets and carvings to mansions all over the north of England, including several designed by Carr: Campsmount, Kilnwick Hall, Grimston Garth, Wentworth Woodhouse, Ravenfield Hall, Cannon Hall, Harewood House, Wynyard Hall and even Tabley Hall, in Cheshire. Carr had a good opinion of him.

The other executor, Henderson, was even closer to Carr. Like Elwick and Carr, Henderson was a new figure in York. He avoided taking up the Freedom of York until 1764 when he was obliged to put down the fee of £25, and was duly entered in the Rolls on 17 February. All businessmen in the city were required to take up their Freedom: if they could claim patrimony it cost nothing; otherwise there was the levy of £25. That Henderson came from a York family is, therefore, unlikely.

When, in 1755, Henderson advertised in the *York Courant* for an apprentice, it is clear that he was already well-established near Bootham Bar, and could very well have been responsible for the distinctive plasterwork in Carr's three houses in Micklegate. We lose track of him until the early 1760s when he was then busily working for Carr on the alterations to Lord Fairfax's house in Castlegate. One of the few remaining vouchers records a payment to him in 1762 of 30 Guineas for 'ye Drawing Room ceiling'. It is likely therefore that he executed the other fine, Rococo ceilings in the mansion.

It would seem that Henderson held the dominant position of plasterer in the York area. Having designed additions to Cannon Hall, near Barnsley, Carr confessed to his client Spencer Stanhope: 'I am at a loss how to advise you as to the Execution of it [the dining room ceiling] as I assure you we have no person in the County that can execute it but Henderson, and if you do not chuse to have him Imploy'd, some person must be sent from London.' Henderson was engaged: in 1766, he did the ceiling to the library, with a centre piece of 'musical Trophies in the Antique manner' and, in the following year, the ceiling to the drawing room, with an interesting overall pattern of

THE PRACTICE

entwining vines. At Kirkleatham Hall, Henderson was again called in. His most elaborate work was the coved ceiling of the saloon, with its central feature comprising an assortment of spears, arrows, birds, a horn, a hare and foliage, indicating a move away from classical subject matter to one more akin to everyday life and incorporating naturalistic objects. A lightening of detail was also apparent. When the works were finished in 1767, Carr, Henderson and Corney (the builder) were lavishly wined and dined by Charles Turner, the client, at a cost of £10. Not that all Henderson's work was so elaborate. At Whitkirk Church in 1772 he was paid for plastering the wall and repairing the figures of the Irwin Monument.

Critical to Henderson's stylistic development was his involvement from 1765 at Harewood House with his partner, James Rothwell. Henderson and Rothwell were responsible for all the plastering at Harewood House, except the State Rooms, which were being done by the Rose family. It was here that Henderson, and also Carr received an early and intimate view of the new Adam style of decoration. The experience resulted in a breakaway from their varied and inconsistent, although often interesting, designs based vaguely on Rococo, Palladian and York motifs. Henceforth the Adam/Rose influence is clearly apparent on the Carr/Henderson partnership. At Thirsk Hall, where the architect added wings and an additional storey between 1770 and 1774, Henderson's new saloon exhibits all the delicate two-dimensional Adam characteristics. The Saloon ceiling corresponds closely with one at Lairgate Hall, Beverley, a building owned by Sir James Pennyman who almost certainly used Carr at Ormesby Hall (Fig. 62). Thus, it is likely that Carr and Henderson co-operated at Lairgate Hall. The two also came together at Swinton Park (c. 1766) near Masham, at Thoresby Lodge (c. 1768) at Ravenfield Hall (c. 1770) near Rotherham, and again, in 1771, on some small alterations to Temple Newsam and on a 'Gothic Temple' at Gilling Castle, and finally at Denton Park in the 1770s.

James Henderson died in 1778 and his son, Thomas, took over the business in Blake Street. Thomas continued the relationship with Carr on the extensive works at Buxton, 1787, Horbury church (1791–94), the Minster (c. 1794) and Wentworth Woodhouse, particularly on the Mausoleum (c. 1790) in company with Ely Crabtree. The latter, a good plasterer, lived for a time in Lendal. His acquaintanceship with Carr went back to the 1760s as at Thoresby Lodge, where he was an assistant to Carlo Clerici. In 1803 he worked on almost the last of the architect's designs: the apsidal staircase at Wentworth Woodhouse.

Carr used other plasterers, for example, Thomas Oliver at Tabley (c. 1768) and John Wood at Northallerton Court House (c. 1788). There was also James Rothwell, one-time partner of Henderson at Harewood where he too assimilated the style of Rose, producing similar Adamesque details at Denton Park (c. 1778) and Bolling Hall, Bradford (c. 1780).

Scagliola was used occasionally by the Italian stuccatori in the first part of the century, for example, at Castle Howard, although not accepted generally until 1770 or later. Consequently, its employment by Carr in the lofty circular hall of Thoresby Lodge in the early 1760s is unusual. Even more interesting is the fact that it was carried out by Carlo Clerici and Vassalli, the latter, presumably being the famous Italian stuccoist. Clerici is little known. After Thoresby, where he had been assisted by the young York plasterer, Ely Crabtree, he worked at Lord Rockingham's town house in Grosvenor Square and transferred in 1774 to Wentworth Woodhouse, where his principal work was in the Grand Saloon. The niches, the eighteen Ionic fluted columns beneath the gallery, the eighteen Corinthian pilasters above the gallery and the fine 'marble' floor which he executed are superb.[76]

The successful use of scagliola at Wentworth Woodhouse encouraged Carr to employ the material in the great entrance hall of Raby Castle (Fig. 63). The columns that support the high, vaulted ceiling are covered in a composition of dull brown. The effect is not unpleasant but if Carr had stuck to masonry, a more convincing atmosphere of the Middle Ages would have been achieved. J. Brown, the craftsman, was brought in from London.

Carr made frequent demands on Doncaster carvers. Christopher Richardson (1709–81), master carver, had sufficient interest in architecture, and the necessary money, to subscribe to James Paine's expensive *Noblemens and Gentlemens' Houses* of 1767. He carved at Welbeck Abbey during Carr's alterations for the Duke of Portland, at Ravenfield Hall (c. 1770) where his assistants were Charles Jones and Jonathon Morris, at Wentworth Woodhouse and, partnered by Burnet Butler, at Harewood. Christopher Theakston, his son-in-law, carved the statue of Justice over Carr's Town Hall, at Newark although Gunnis in the *Dictionary of Sculptors* credits the figure to his one-time associate, Waterworth. Theakston too, operated at Harewood, Ravenfield Hall, and even acted as builder for Carr's grandstand at Doncaster. When he died, his wife Harriet continued the business and was paid for some of the carving on St Ann's Well at Buxton designed by Carr.

Then there was Thomas Waterworth (1753–1829) of similarly high reputation. He also worked at Harewood, on the mausoleum at Wentworth Woodhouse and on Buxton Crescent where his bill amounting to £318 included £65 for carving 'His Grace's Coat of Arms in front of the building'. Finally, a small commission, he carved Carr's name on the bridge at Ferrybridge.

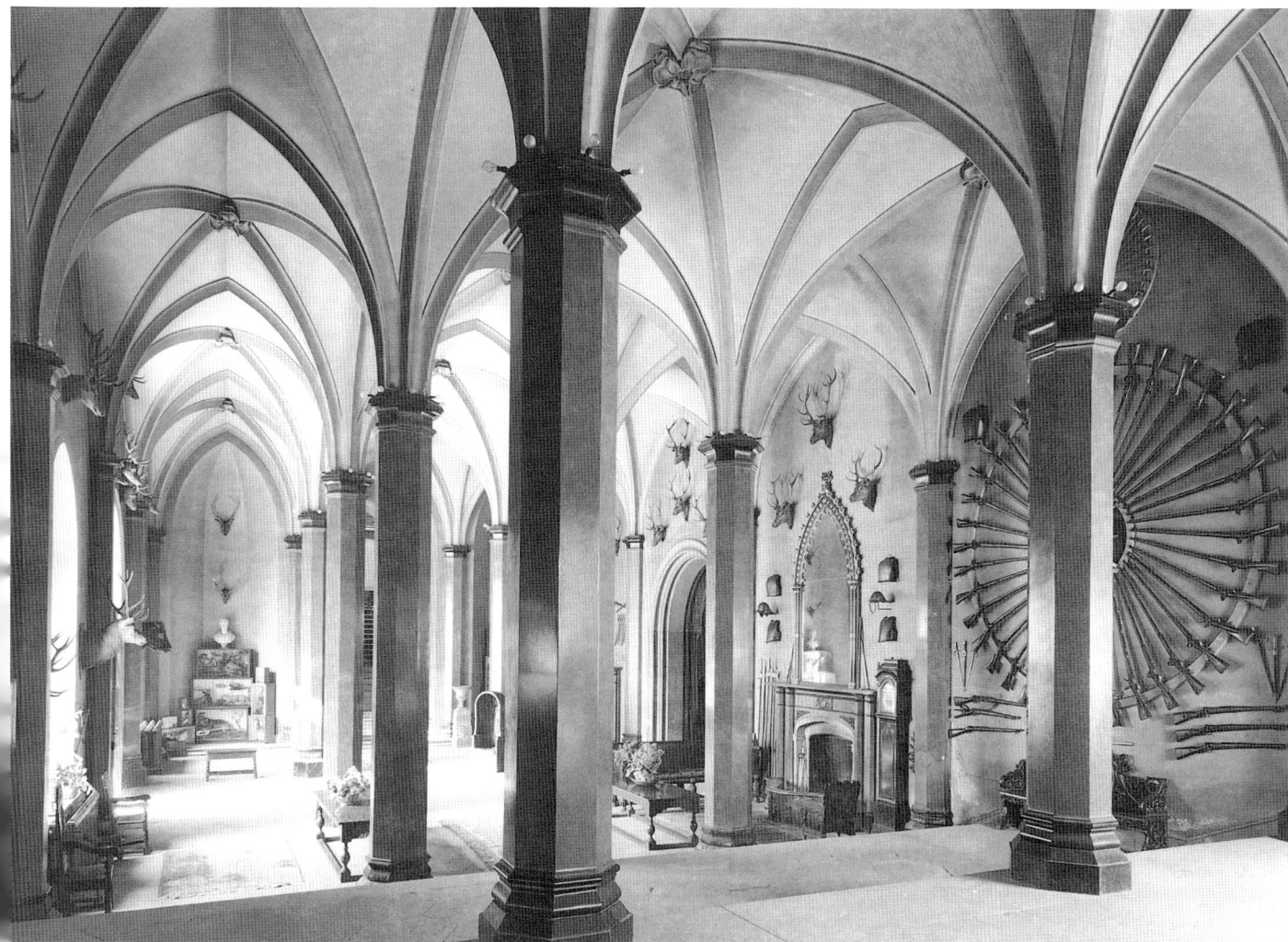

63 Raby Castle, Co. Durham, the Great Hall of 1780–85 built for the 2nd Earl of Darlington

Of carvers based farther north, Daniel Shillito is perhaps the earliest of merit to have associated with Carr. He was certainly operating at Heath Hall, near Wakefield, in the 1750s, at Everingham Hall (*c.* 1764) in the East Riding, also at Lytham Hall (*c.* 1764) in Lancashire, at Stapleton Park (1762–64) and at Tabley Hall (*c.* 1767) in Cheshire. Shillito worked at Harewood where, like the other associates of Carr, he noted the Adam detail carrying the characteristics into the carving at Thoresby Lodge, Nottinghamshire, which he did in company with another carver, Matthew Bertram.

Shillito, a resident of Wakefield, could have been a childhood friend of the architect, for Horbury, Carr's birthplace, was only a mile distant. When he married Jane Hinchliffe at St Mary, Bishophill Senior, York, in 1762, John Carr was a witness.

Robert Blakesley of York was a similarly accomplished carver. Like Carr, he was a Whig and member of Rockingham Club. When a number of York tradesmen were threatened in 1776 with prosecution for not taking up their

Freedom, 'Robert Blakesley, Carver, Micklegate', was quickly added to the Roll. In 1772, the year he dissolved his partnership with a James Officer, he was working on the carving at Thirsk Hall where James Henderson and Dodsworth, another York carver, were also engaged. He appears momentarily in the York Sessions Book for 1779 where, as a constable of the Parish of St Martin, he is recorded as witnessing an assault by Samuel Sleightolinino (*sic.*), carver, on Thomas Woolstonholme (*sic.*) When the 'new Drawing Room' at Wentworth Woodhouse was to be gilded in 1784 Carr suggested that Blakesley would execute the gilding 'as well as any man in this County and he certainly will do it as well as anybody out of London'.[77]

Of all the provincial carvers, who associated with Carr, Shillito did the most work, but it was the Fishers of York who were the most widely known. The senior Fisher, Richard, said to be the illegitimate son of the first Lord Rockingham, moved to York in about 1750, the same time as Carr, and occupied a house at the corner of St Saviour's Gate and Spen Lane, to which was attached a garden, yard

THE PRACTICE

79

and workshop. He was probably the 'Mr Fisher' who exhibited at the newly formed Society of Artists in London in 1761. Eventually he was joined in partnership by his son, John, with whom Carr was principally concerned, and by Samuel, probably another son. After the father's death, about 1773, the two sons continued the business. Like Henderson and Blakesley, they were loath to take up their Freedom, but after the threatened prosecution in 1776, 'John Fisher and Samuel Fisher carvers and statuaries in North Street ... exercising that business in a Yard there' duly paid up and had their names entered on the Roll. In 1780, John announced, in the *York Courant*, the dissolution of the partnership, and in 1783, describing himself as a 'Sculptor in St Helen's Square' advertised, most politely, for an apprentice: 'A youth who has a taste for drawing will be most agreeable'. In 1794 he was not in a position to advertise for anyone: he was bankrupt.

A member of the Rockingham Club, John Fisher, had a wide practice, one might even describe it as monumental. Among other things, he was responsible for the statue, with the 1780 petition for Parliamentary reform in hand, of Sir George Savile, erected in the Minster in 1789. He also provided 'Enriched and Plain Marble Chimney-pieces, finished in the highest taste'. It was principally these which he supplied to the buildings designed by Carr. Fisher's largest commitment where Carr was the architect was at Wentworth Woodhouse. He provided several carved marble chimneypieces, and there is among the Wentworth Muniments, an excellent drawing, presumably by Fisher, accompanying his detailed specification and estimate of cost, of a proposed chimneypiece for the Grand Drawing Room. But the statuary was very dilatory: he took six years to complete one chimneypiece and ten years for another. Carr complained 'there's no trusting what he says' and, indeed, on measuring up two chimneypieces, found that the client had been overcharged by nearly £40.[78]

Fisher also supplied carved pieces to Milton, near Peterborough, and to Farnley Hall. The steward at Farnley was slow in paying, and Fisher sent a very pathetic appeal asking for an early settlement so that he could buy marble advantageously from a consignment at Hull. But he was not paid for two years. Fisher also provided the statue of Justice — remarkable for its not being blindfolded — over the Law Courts at York Castle and pedestals for the busts by Nollekens, a medallion and lettering ('281 Dozen Capital Letters in the Inscription at 2s per dozen') in the Mausoleum, Wentworth Woodhouse.

Fisher, an excellent craftsman but a poor business man, was eventually imprisoned for debt. Carr wrote, in 1792, 'Mr Fisher is still in Jail, and nothing has been done for the new room at Milton, but I hear (that he) is upon a plan to cheat his Creditors of 13 Shills in the pound, which will enable him to go on again.' Fisher was soon released but, apparently did not apply himself urgently to work: Carr, in 1795, informed the steward at Wentworth Woodhouse 'I am afraid Fisher will never get your little monument done I most sincerely wish you had applied to Nollikens just to have done the head, the rest might have been done here, all Fisher's best men have left him, they cannot get their wages of him, and they have set up here in York two of them very good workmen ...'.[79]

One final craftsman with whom Carr was regularly involved was the ironsmith Maurice Tobin, who provided locks, hinges, balustrade for the stairs and gates of the Leeds Infirmary in 1770. He had earlier worked with Carr on Kirklees Hall, Fairfax House, St John's Church in Leeds and Cannon Hall.

Practical, hardworking, obliging, Carr was held in high esteem by all who had dealings with him. Samuel Shore described him in 1768 as 'a very ingenious man, [he] has a good taste and I have always found him consult convenience and economy ... Mr Carr will draw as plain and simple a design as is wished for but in a better form and proportion and with more taste than any other person we have about Sheffield'.[80] Ten years later William Mason, though affronted by his accent, explained to Lord Harcourt that 'you will find him wonderfully adroit in expediency'.[81] Thomas Whitaker, writing after Carr's death, recorded that 'In his designs of houses Mr Carr was eminently happy: no one had more studied or more thoroughly understood the arrangement and proportions of private apartments'.[82] Even his rival James Paine, who might have been expected to have reservations about the man who displaced him as dominant architect in the North, observed that 'I am bound to say I have never met with [clumsiness] in any of Mr Carr's designs.'

CHAPTER FOUR

OLD AGE

—————

As CARR ENTERED HIS SEVENTIES a portrait of a contented and fulfilled man emerges from a note made by Bishop Porteus, whom Carr visited at Lambeth Palace on 27 June 1794:

Had a Visit this day from Mr Carr of York the Architect of the North, with whose conversation I was highly pleased. He gave me a short account of himself wch was very amusing. He had been in business as an architect above half a century. At the outset his pay for many years was but very slender, being allowed for his Journeys only 5 shillings a Day … But his increased by Degrees, & by great Oeconomy he raised a considerable Fortune. He said he had been always contented & happy, never formed any great expectations & was therefore never disappointed. Scarce any thing had ever happened throught. his whole life to give him any disturbance, nor did any of those whom he befriended & assisted ever behave ill or give him any uneasiness. He had no children of his own, but He had a large number of nephews & nieces, all of whom he Educated well, given the Girls three thousand pounds each to their Fortune, married several of them very advantageously & placed the young men in good Employments. He now allowed to various Relations & dependents 800£ a year. He this year finished a Church which he began in the year 1790 at his native Village in Yorkshire. He built it of the finest stone in the Kingdom, at his own Expence, & it cost him upwards of 10,000£. On the day he opened it 33 of his Relations dined with him in the village, a thousand of the inhabitants met him & conducted him into the Church, & a great niece of his, 17 years of age played the Organ. He said all his relations prospered & did Well. He himself enjoyed constant health & a perfectly tranquil mind, & believed he was the happiest & most contented man in the world, & truly thankful to Providence for all his Blessings …[1]

It is a charming picture of a man at peace with himself and the world.

FAMILY AND FRIENDS

As Porteus makes clear, family was always important to Carr. His wife Sarah had died on 19 January 1787. Following her death his nieces came to play an important part in his later life. He certainly enjoyed their company, as his comments at Christmas 1793 reveal: 'I have got my sister — 2 clever nieces and two Miss Heatons with me from Chevet so that I may say I have excellent company in so many young folks only they kick about and break my chairs.'[2] A succession of nieces served as his housekeepers. The first was probably Ursula, his brother Robert's daughter. She was certainly living in the parish when she married in 1792, the Register of Bishophill Senior recording 'Ursula Carr of this Parish spinster m. Robert Swann 1792.' The ceremony was witnessed by Carr and by two other nieces, Maria Elizabeth Carr and Harriet Ann Clark.

Ursula's place was taken by another niece, probably Harriet Ann. In a letter of 1795 Carr requested the help of Mrs Croft, housekeeper at Wentworth, in finding a steady maidservant to assist 'my old good servant they do their work in common as cooking and cleaning alike. The present (maid) is the most saucy ill tongued girl … and abuses my niece if she goes into the kitchen — I give 17 guins they have a deal of work to do but we keep good house and they live very comfortably and quiet.'[3] Mrs Croft, apparently, was able to assist, for Carr sent his love, thanked her for the present of 'roll'd Beef which was vastly good' and engaged a man and woman servant, Robert and Mary Hinchcliffe.[4]

Carr's love for his family was also shown by the rebuilding of his native church, which his father had altered forty years earlier (Figs 65 and 66). The new church was opened on 17 May 1794, to great celebrations and, as Bishop Porteus recorded, dinner for thirty-three relations. For Carr this was to be a family church. An effulgent monument to his father was set up. The proof for the inscription survives at Browsholme with detailed comments by Carr on the size and the spacing of the letters, addressed to Mr Waterworth, Carver in Doncaster, that is Thomas Waterworth the elder who was responsible for the decorative stone carving of the mausoleum at Wentworth Woodhouse, erected in 1788. The church included a private vault for the Carr family, 35 ft long by 10 ft wide.

By now Carr was busy assuring his posterity. A portrait bust was ordered from his friend the sculptor Joseph Nollekens in 1800 (Fig. 64) and two portraits commissioned from Sir William Beechey, one, dated 1791, remained with the family, the other was presented to the Corporation of York in 1803 to hang in the Mansion House.[5] The first portrait was engraved C. H. Hodges and prints distributed to friends in 1793.[6] An engraving survives at Browsholme Hall. Carr also had his church at Horbury engraved by Thomas Malton so that he could again send out prints. Mrs Croft, the housekeeper at Wentworth Woodhouse was sent two in June 1796.[7]

Carr also sought the final proof of gentleman status, a coat of arms. This was not without some family infighting. In 1805 his nephew John Carr, who was arranging for a coat of arms for Carr, took exception to William Radcliffe, Rouge Croix, asking another nephew, the Reverend Robert Lascelles Carr, for information. The Reverend tartly informed Radcliffe 'The fact is, that the late Mr Carr … gave his children that sort of education, which is too apt to make its possessors the object of hatred with such persons as are inflated with the pride of wealth — a pride which is invariably and inseparately united with most abject meaness … I am greatly surprised that my Uncle should commit the direction of his pedigree to a man so illiterate as my cousin J Carr.' The Reverend Carr lived in somewhat straitened circumstances as chaplain to Earl Clanwilliam and Lord Mendip. The coat of arms — per pales gules and azure; on a chevron embattled argent, three estoiles argents — was duly delivered to Askham in the autumn of 1805 while Carr was on tour in Scotland. The cost was £57 16s.

FINANCES

'A considerable fortune' was how Carr described his wealth to Bishop Porteus, and *The Gentlemen's Magazine* reported him to have been worth £150,000 at his death. For someone who had started as a simple mason and who shared the limited inheritance he gained from his father among numerous brothers and sisters, this was a remarkable achievement.

Tracing the origins of Carr's wealth is not easy as no account books survive and the records of his bank in York, Messrs Raper Clough and Swanns,[8] have been destroyed. However, it is possible to gain some idea of the true extent of his fortune and how he gained it, principally from two draft wills of 1789 and 1782, and from his final will of 1807 and the probate record of his estate.[9] The draft will of 1792 is particularly useful as its cover carries a series of rough calculations in which Carr worked out his wealth.

Carr's wife Sarah, a domestic servant, presumably brought him no dowry when they married and he did not receive much when his father died in 1760.[10] Robert Carr's will shows that he left his eldest son the house in which he lived in Horbury, the surrounding buildings and adjoining

64 *above* Bust by Joseph Nollekens of Carr, dated 1800
65 *opposite above* St Peter's church, Horbury, Yorkshire, built by Carr for himself in 1791–94. Engraving by Thomas Malton
66 *opposite below* St Peter's church, Horbury, Yorkshire; the interior

one and a half acres, together with one acre in Mill Field and half an acre in West Field, both of which had quarries, and two pews in Horbury church. Carr's brother Robert was given permission to use the quarries without recompensing Carr.

Nevertheless, Carr was soon accumulating property, first in York as we have already seen, and then nearer Horbury. In 1769 Carr bought the estate of New Laithes, about two miles north of Barnsley and four miles south of Horbury.[11] Two undated valuations on his draft will survive for this. One states that it brought in a rent of £210, but should bring in £250, and was worth £7,500. The other valued it at £15,000.

OLD AGE

83

67 New Lodge, Barnsley, Yorkshire, built by John Carr for himself in 1795

68 New Lodge, Barnsley, Yorkshire; one of the lodges

By 1792 he had also bought a valuable estate at Ellenthorpe near Boroughbridge, about sixteen miles north of York and conveniently situated close to the Great North Road. The property, which is described as 'newly purchased', was a valuable one. In the calculations of his wealth Carr puts it as worth variously £17,000 and £20,000 and notes that it brought in rents of £400–£450, which he described as 'very low'. When the estate came to be sold in 1842 it encompassed 550 acres, together with tithes, and was formed of two substantial farms, Ellenthorpe Hall of 274 acres and Ellenthorpe Lodge of 275 acres. Ellenthorpe Hall was described as a 'capital mansion house which is a modern, well-built brick edifice, covered with blue slate — breakfast room, dining room, drawing room, seven bedrooms, two commodious kitchens with chambers over for servants, spacious arched cellars, dairy, larder …'.[12] Carr was probably responsible for building the house, which is a very plain three-bay, two-storey brick house. Its only architectural embellishment is a handsome pedimented Doric porch over the front door which is characteristic of Carr.

Carr may have been drawn to Ellenthorpe by family connections. Norton-le-Clay, where his mother came from, is only a couple of miles to the north. In 1789 one of the farms was occupied, on a rent of £270, by Thomas Clark, who was married to Carr's niece Ann (his brother Robert's elder daughter). Carr spent a week with them in mid-December 1796.[13] It seems likely that the Clarks had lived there for some time as an abstract of title for 1755 refers to 'John Clarke the younger of Allenthorpe, York, woolstapler'.[14] Edwin and Heaton Clarke were the tenants in 1842.

In about 1795 Carr rebuilt the old house at New Laithes, which was renamed New Lodge (Fig. 67).[15] He also designed impressive octagonal gate lodges (Fig. 68) apparently inspired by the then-fashionable Temple of the Winds in Athens.[16] He seems to have used the house himself but in 1803 Elizabeth Chivers noted that it was lived in by his nephew John Clark, Ann Clark's son.

In 1784 Carr had made over the family land he had inherited from his father to his nephew John Carr.[17] A successful attorney who married in 1785, the younger John Carr was made a commissioner for Land Tax in the West Riding in 1798 and by 1805 was an acting commissioner for Affairs of Taxes in the West Riding.[18] By 1790 the younger John Carr was living at Horbury in Carr Lodge, which was described as 'a charming house belonging to Mr John Carr of Wakefield' by Amelia Clark, who visited in 1796.[19] In 1803 writing to the steward at Wentworth Woodhouse to clear up a confusion over gifts of venison he explained that he had 'long since' purchased the house and estate of Mrs Cookson.[20] It is likely that the money was provided by his uncle.

Carr carried on acquiring land in the area, buying about a rood of land in Denton Lane Shut from Joseph Raynor, clothier of Horbury, in about 1793 and Dewsbury Rectory Manor in 1802. (Dewsbury is about three miles from Horbury.) By 1805 this had conveyed to his nephew John.[21]

By 1801 Carr had also bought Askham Hall in Askham Richard, leaving New Lodge to the sole occupation of his nephew. This was about five miles from York and conveniently close to the main road from York to Leeds. The house had been one of Carr's first commissions and was not intended as an investment but as a country house to which he could retire. It had been described in the York Courant when advertised for rent in 1787 as a 'mansion house pleasantly situated near the City of York … with the

OLD AGE

gardens, coach house, stables, dovecote, brewhouse and other convenient outbuildings, &c for the reception of a genteel family; together with 30 acres of land adjoining the premises'.²² It is unclear how much land Carr brought but it must have been smaller than at his other two estates. In 1806 it brought in a rent of £250, the same as the rent for New Laithes, but it was valued, together with the remaining property in York, at £11,000 where New Laithes was worth £15,000.

Carr also invested heavily in stocks and shares and was a director of the Yorkshire Tontine. The calculations on his 1789 draft will refer to his investments in the Calder and Hebble Canal, which in one calculation were valued at £20,000. The same calculation also refers to £1,000 invested in the Market Weighton navigation. This seems to have been a later acquisition as it is not referred to in 1789 or 1792.

Carr also held varying sums in Bank of England stock. The 1789 draft will refers to £10,000 held in 4 per cent stocks (subsequently crossed out) and to an unstated figure in the 3 per cents. The 1792 draft will refers to £10,000 in 4 per cents. A later calculation refers to £6,000 in the 5 per cents and £2,000 in the 3 per cents.²³ At the time of his death Carr owned sixty-one shares in the Calder Navigation and a hundred shares in the Market Weighton Navigation, together with £6,000 in Navy 5 per cent stock.

Carr also had substantial sums lent out on mortgages. From very early on Carr seems to have worked the money markets. In 1755 he wrote to Popplewell: 'I begin to be in Tribulation about the £100 Bill coming, as I must deliver my money in on Fryday at furthest.'²⁴ In 1761 he revealed that he had bought a six-year bond 'of her ladyship and sons ... which I think was a good thing'.²⁵ Walter Spencer Stanhope recorded in his diary for 29 April 1768 'Mr Carr went with me to Mr Tyler the Notary and paid him his bill'.²⁶ In 1774 he was asking for payment of his salary from the steward at Wentworth Woodhouse as 'want of cash and difficulty of getting it makes me apply everywhere to raise some money for ensuing payments made about xmas'.²⁷ But perhaps the most intriguing reference comes in 1794 when we learn that the Hon. Henry Willoughby had mortgaged Birdsall to John Carr for £10,000, with interest set at 5 per cent.²⁸ This is confirmed in one of the set of rough calculations which lists mortgages worth £17,500, £10,000 to Willoughby, £7,500 to Marton and £1,000 to 'Lawyer'. Interestingly, we know that one of Carr's contemporary provincial architects, Thomas Pritchard of Shrewsbury, also lent money to cash-strapped gentry, in his case £1,000 to Noel Hill of Tern Hill in Shropshire between 1771 and 1776.²⁹

Despite this information it is not easy to pin down Carr's exact worth at any one moment, but though only one is dated, the rough calculations on the back of the 1792 draft will allow us to gain some idea of his wealth in the last decade and a half of his life. One — before the purchase of Askham Hall — calculated his income as £1,765, that is £730 as rent and £1,035 as interest from his stocks. Against this was the £405 cost of legacies and annuities he was committed to, leaving a surplus of £1,360. According to this calculation Carr was worth £44,500, that is £29,500 in land and £15,000 in stocks.

However, another calculation, dated 1806 puts his income as £2,000. That is £1,250 for land (including Askham) and £750 which was the income from £15,000 at 5 per cent. Another calculation values his land at £46,000, his mortgages at £17,500, his canal shares at £21,000 and his stocks at £8,000.

These figures can be compared with Carr's probate. The two principal beneficiaries were William and John Carr. William Carr received all the property in York and Askham Richard, all Carr's mortgages and the money due to him on bond, all his stock in the funds and all his ready money. This was valued at £22,336 5s 5d. John Carr received the sixty-one Calder and Hebble Navigation shares and one hundred Market Weighton Navigation shares together with the stock invested in the Navy 5 per cents (valued at £6,000). In the will he was also to have received cancellation of £1,500 debt and conveyance to him of the Manor and Estates at Dewsbury. Presumably that happened in the interim. The total estate was valued at £35,000, a very substantial sum. It does not include any reference to Ellenthorpe or New Laithes. Presumably these had been handed over in the interim. Nor in calculating Carr's total fortune should we forget that he spent a reported £10,000 building Horbury church and substantial sums educating and setting up his nephews and nieces, the last receiving handsome dowries of £3,000.

So how did Carr make this fortune? Diligent though he was the income from his fees on their own could not have been enough. There was then his business supplying marble, chimneypieces and hearths but that, though no doubt profitable, cannot have brought in great riches. There is no evidence that Carr made money from property development nor of Carr's involvement in the family quarrying business, a potential source of wealth. The key appears to lie in Porteus's remark that: 'At the outset his pay for many years was but very slender, being allowed for his Journeys only 5 shillings a Day ... But his increased by Degrees, & by great Oeconomy he raised a considerable Fortune.' We know that Carr was involved in the money market and in land purchase from relatively early in his career. It would appear that careful investment of his fees in land, mortgages, stocks and shares coupled with an essential frugality and long life allowed him to accumulate his remarkable fortune.

Carr's comment to Bishop Porteus that he enjoyed perfect
health says much for his generally positive frame of mind,
for what strikes anyone reading his letters are the repeated
comments on his poor health. In business letters Carr was
direct and to the point. He rarely mentioned other jobs but
he did allow himself the luxury of a 'postscript' on the
current malady. Rheumatism was one of his principal weak-
nesses. The first recorded attack confined him to his room
on the last day of 1774 and appears to have accompanied
another complaint. As Carr explained in January to the
Duke of Portland in excusing his absence from Welbeck:
'When I had the honour of being at Welbeck the last time,
I proposed to myself the pleasure of waiting of your Grace
in Christmas to have spent a few days free from business,
but alas how Vain is human schemes, the day before New
years day I was Violently attacked with the Gravel it almost
tore me to pieces and brought on an obstinate fever, that I
have not since been able to quit my Bed before yesterday
which reduced me to so weak a state that I am not able to
walk.' The handwriting of the letter is very weak and Carr
concludes with an evidently heart-felt note: 'May your
Grace long enjoy uninterrupted health is the sincere wish of
Your Graces Most obedient and most humble servant'.[30]

For Carr it was a bad winter. Early in April he wrote
from Buxton apologizing for letting the duke down again:

I am now so disabled by the Rheumatism (from which I have not
had a moments ease since Christmas) that it is with the greatest
pain & difficulty I can crawl over the floor in the day time, and in
the night as soon as I grow warm, I am tortured with the most
excruciating pain in my Back & Thighs, which has reduced me
into so weak a state, that I fear it will be a long time before I can
be recovered. I have been here one week, in three weeks more the
Physicians tell me they will be able to judge of the Effect of this
water in which I Bathe once a day.[31]

Fortunately, the waters proved efficacious and ten days
later Carr was able to write again to the duke:

I have not words to express the gratitude I feel on account of your
Grace's kind concern for my health, which I now begin to hope I
shall restore by persevering in Bathing here, as my pains for two
days past have begun to abate, and I can now Crawl about with the
help of a stick; but I have been so much cautioned against getting
cold, that I hope your Grace will excuse my waiting of you at this
critical turn of my Disorder, which I was flattered woud be the
case after I had Bathed Eighteen or twenty times.[32]

In April 1780, tortured by pain in back and shoulders, he
was unable to rise without help but wrote to the Duke of

69 The Crescent, Buxton, Derbyshire, with the
stables beyond, built for the 5th Duke of
Devonshire in 1780–90

OLD AGE

OLD AGE

87

70 The Assembly Rooms in the Crescent, Buxton, built for the 5th Duke of Devonshire in 1780–90

Devonshire that he hoped 'in a fortnight or 3 weeks to see you for I am very anxious to see the work which I have directed to be begun at Buxton' (Figs 69 and 70). In January 1781 he was 'almost demolished with pain this weather'.[33]

It was not just ill health that laid him low. Accidents were also a nuisance. A broken shin troubled him during a circuit in 1777: 'gt pain broken shin will never mend till I get some rest and when that will be I cannot tell'.[34] In 1784, at the age of 61, he hurt himself mounting a young horse, being 'thrown on pommel of saddle wh has bruised my testicle in such a manner I can with gt diff write will be confined to my room for some time.'[35] It was the start of another bad winter. In February he was 'so demolished with the Gravel I am unable to stir this severe weather, & am at present confined here with my friends at Carlton'.[36] And in April, was 'still so weak I can hardly crawl across the floor'.[37]

A lame leg was the principal complaint in 1785. In January 1787 he was 'confined to room by severe hurt on top of right foot three weeks and by drenching me with physick they brought the gout into my left foot therefore am obliged to lie like a log and write upon a board on my knees'.[38] In August 1789 'since I left you I have been exceeding ill with a severe cold and cough'.[39]

September 1790 saw the return of an old problem: 'I have an old wound broke out on my ankle that has been healed and well upwards of 50 years to which an humour has lately fallen and it is become so sore that it will I fear be the work of a tedious time to heal it'.[40] It was slow to heal and at the beginning of October: 'I was told this morning by the surgeon that my wound is now got into a way of healing, but he said I must be confined for two months'.[41]

A cold laid him low in January of 1792[42] and in September he was confined to his room by a 'bilious disorder which has almost demolished and cannot yet get quit of it and am so harassed with it and the pain in my bowels I dare not stir out and I want something to do'.[43] The winter and spring of 1793 was little better. A dreadful cough and a pain in his bowels laid him up at the house of his friend William Mellish in Albermarle Street for over a week: 'I am somehow or other very unwell of myself besides the violent cough and rheumatism in my head and teeth.'[44] In April, back again in London, he was complaining: 'I don't like the Gout at all, I never had it before I cannot go out of my room and I have a little wound in my other ankle which I made with my shoe heel in scrambling down stairs which with some drying liquid would soon be healed but the rascals here made a job of it.'[45] Three weeks later: 'I can now just hobble about again but the east wind plagues me very much.'[46]

1794 was no better.

It is a melancholy truth [he reported] that I have never been able to get out of my room but twice on horseback for an hour since I last saw you at Wentworth house, the complaint in my bowells brought me to deaths door and reduced me so weak incessant evacuations that the Rhumatism seized from head to foot, and I am still unable to crawl over the floor without crutches. The pain on my back and shoulders is somewhat-abated, but the constant sluggish pain in my feet never varys, they swell a little, but are never red or inflamed and they are better a little and worse as the weather varys. My lord has wished me to come last week to Milton to plan him some alterations which he wants made there in his absence, Sorry I was to tell him I was unable to come to him, and I feel no hope of getting better until warm weather puts in.[47]

In February 1795 the severity of the weather had made a cripple of Carr with rheumatism from head to foot and his signature quite lacked its usual flourish.[48]

It is almost an age since I last heard from you, during which time I have never been able to get out of my room; and for some time past: I have not been out of bed: owing to a dropsical complaint which attacked my legs and thighs, the swelling of which could not be reduced without my being confined to bed: fluids as well as solids pass thro my weak bowells that we never could procure, an increase of water: tho I have every Dieruetic that ever was administered; we have however diminished the swelling so much: that if the weather was but favourably mild and warm that I coud out to enjoy the benefit of it either on horse back or in my Phaeton I might recover my strength and throw off the disorder.[49]

But, as Porteus's comment makes clear, for all this it would be wrong to think that ill health dominated Carr's life. His afflictions were insufficient to stop Carr from busying himself with work, and, as with many of his contemporaries, it was the long cold winters that really caused the problems. When the seasons warmed up, health tended to improve. It may be no coincidence that he gave Porteus such a positive account of his health at the end of June. But he was also active in the search for ways to improve his health. He took patent medicines, once leaving 'my round wood bottle with my Bark in it in the office window', at Wentworth Woodhouse, causing him to bemoan the fact that 'I have no memory my dear friend, I

fail alike in every part except my respect & affection to my friends' and asking that a boy be sent over with it.[50] In May 1795 he reported that his doctor had advised him to bathe in a shower bath and asked that a sketch be made of one which he had provided for Lady Rockingham at Wentworth Woodhouse so that he could have it copied.[51] But it was not shower baths or patent medicines that were to transform Carr but the open carriage. The following January he told Lord Fitzwilliam that 'I drive out every morning before breakfast for an hour and a half which keeps me vastly well'.[52] What really put him in good health was travel.

Carr had always been an active traveller. He was reported in 1771 to have visited France.[53] However, just at the age when his practice was slowing down and he might have considered spending more time abroad the outbreak of the French Revolution and the subsequent revolutionary wars which lasted for most of the rest of his life closed the Continent to travellers. Instead, like many of his compatriots Carr took to travelling in Britain, particularly to the more picturesque areas. But even given the growing fashion for British tourism Carr is surely exceptional for the length and extent of his travels, particularly given his advanced age.

The first recorded pleasure trip was from June to December 1795, passing through Derbyshire, the Lake District into Scotland and back to York through Northumberland and Durham. Carr had been sick for some months previously so that the tour was also in the nature of a convalescence. He was accompanied by two young ladies, one of whom, Harriet Clark, his niece, kept a journal in which she referred to buildings by 'my Uncle Carr'.[54] The itinerary was not entirely architectural. Growing demands of industry were changing the face of the country which Carr had earlier known. A visit to the Carron Ironworks was recorded by Miss Clark: 'the great casting-rooms are very astonishing, from the roaring of the bellows and the dreadful fires, out of which the liquid metal runs into the moulds and is cast into cannons, pots, grates, and various other things, by such figures of naked men as we had never before seen'.

The tour was accomplished in some style. Carr's own carriage with a pair of horses was driven by himself and following behind on horseback were two servants. The old man was rather proud of the extent of his peregrinations, boasting to Lord Fitzwilliam in January 1796, shortly after the tour ended, that 'the Open Carriage agrees best with me in which I travelled upwards of two thousand miles since the first of June'.[55]

Later that year Carr was in London, this time with Harriet, showing her the sights. For her, it was in the nature of a last fling before returning to York for her marriage. John Carr witnessed the girl's nuptials to Thomas Swann of the banking family in St Mary Bishophill Senior but, even before the ceremony, had fixed on another tour with

71 Mausoleum of the 2nd Marquis of Rockingham at Wentworth Woodhouse, Yorkshire, built for the 4th Earl Fitzwilliam in 1785–91

Amelia, Harriet's sister and 'another pretty young woman who are to be her (Harriet's) Bridesmaids'. Writing to the steward at Wentworth Woodhouse he declared: 'I shall have the pleasure to shake you by the hand along with two nice young damsels. You see I travel like the Grand Turk with my Ladies along with me — we are going to make the Grand Tour, but I know not where we shall go.'[56] The tour was a great success, as Carr recounted to the steward at Wentworth Woodhouse:

After we had been three weeks at the Lakes we visited Ld Frederick and Ld John Cavendish at Holker, crossed the 10 mile sands to Lancaster, Garstang, Duston, Chorley, Manchester, Stockport, Buxton, Chatsworth, Matlock, Derby, Burton on Trent, Birmingham, Litchfield, Worcester, Glouster and then cross'd the Severn into Wales, Monmouth Ross, Chepstow down the Wye then Cross'd the channel to Bristol, from thence to Bath where we spent a week, then to Frome, Stourhead & Alfreds Tower near the Mendip hills from thence to Longleate the Marquis of Baths in Wiltshire. Beckfords at Font hill near Maiden

Bradleys & over the downs to see Stone henge that famous druid temple, from thence to Salisbury over the plains by the famous Roman Camp. thence to Ld Pembrokes at Wilton, from thence to Newbery, Reading, & Basildon where we spent 10 days delightfully with Sir Francis & Lady Sykes & their lovely daughter, from thence to Henley on Thames to Mr Freemans who married Lady Stricklands charming daughter with whom we spend 8 days charmingly from thence we set sail for Oxford where after visiting Blenheim we spent another week, from thence we came to Hillenden & spent three days very pleasantly with Lady Rockingham and Lady Charlotte Wentworth, & from thence to London & spent 3 weeks in seeing all the London sights to the great delight of my Companions and as I before said we arrived safe at York Man & horse on the 26 Novemr after a journey of upwards of two

72 *opposite above* Farnley Hall, Yorkshire, built for Walter Hawksworth Fawkes in 1786–92; the south front

73 *opposite below* Farnley Hall, Yorkshire, built for Walter Hawksworth Fawkes in 1786–92; the library

OLD AGE

92

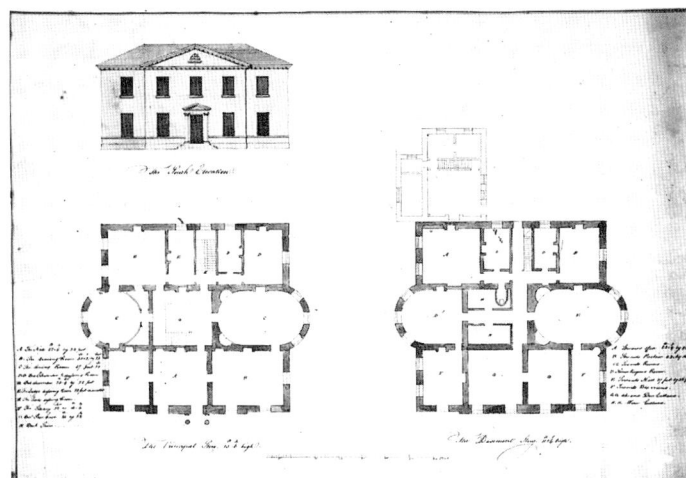

74 *opposite above* Eastwood House, Yorkshire, built for Joseph Walker in 1786–87; front elevation

75 *opposite below* Milton House, Soke of Peterborough, the former library made for the 4th Earl Fitzwilliam in 1792

76 *above left* Coolattin House, Co. Wicklow, built for the 4th Earl Fitzwilliam in 1799–1807

77 *above right* Coolattin House, Co. Wicklow, built for the 4th Earl Fitzwilliam in 1799–1807; plans by Carr of the principal and basement floors

thousand miles during which journey we had never less than 2 breakfasts, one dinner and tea and supper when we coud eat it — never had a stop or accident 5 minutes on the Road nor any rain except about 2 showers from Lancaster to Preston.[57]

Harriet Clark's account of the trip survives in the form of another diary.[58]

He was keen to be on the road again, as he explained in January 1796 to Strickland Freeman: 'Yesterday I bought another horse to match those I have in order to enable me to make another tour as soon as the season of the year will permit my setting out again for I never have been for many years in so good repair as I am at present and have been ever since I reach'd York, therefore I think I cannot do better than take another journey.'[59] Such was the importance of his open carriage that if he was unable to exercise he soon felt the result 'the severity of the long winter and the severe season', he told Strickland Freeman in April 1799, 'we have had here for two months past has almost demolished me as I could never get out'. Not surprisingly, the tours continued. One from August to November 1798 with Amelia Clark saw Carr visiting Snowdonia,[60] another, in 1799, embraced Norfolk where he intended to visit the 'my dear friends' the Mellishes 'who have most of them houses there'.[61]

A distinctive feature of Carr's travels was the regularity and length of his stays with former clients, in some of the

grandest houses in the land. Thus in the 1795 trip he and his companions spent a fortnight at Wentworth Woodhouse and three weeks at Chatsworth. In 1796 they had ten days with Sir Francis and Lady Sykes at Basildon, eight days with the Freemans at Fawley Court and three days with Lady Rockingham at Hillingdon, as well as visiting Lord George Cavendish at Holker. It says much for the social distance Carr had travelled since he was the young son of a local mason and speaks highly of Carr's practical ability as an architect that many of his patrons were not only prepared to commission him again and again but to invite him to stay. Clearly Carr was good company, as is evident from one of his letters to Mrs Chivers, 'Lord Fitzwilliam has been in a very weak state of health and has often begged I woud stay with him for a little company until he goes to Scarborough'.[62]

However, even Carr occasionally overstepped the mark. In September 1783 the Duchess of Devonshire wrote to her mother from Chatsworth:

When we arrived here, we found Mr Carr, I found to my great displeasure that he had been entertaining Ld and Lady George with entering upon every particular about Gaubert & the expense & so the Duke had wished the contrary — this exposed me all day long to the Georges finding fault with everything & I had not been suckling wd have made me much mauvais sang. The Duke stop'd Carr's mouth the next day but I am afraid to late as all the country seems to know that things are sending back & so ... the Drawing is the prettyist & most comfortable room I ever saw, but when we came here at first Mr Carr has set George into such a finding fault way that at first both he and Ld George w'd provoke me exceptionaly tho' I never said a word, for it was always this would have been better so & he carry'd it so far once as to say the room was very well but he would have put all the furniture of the Drawing Room into the Music Room & so vice versa — however everyone who comes admires the drawing room so much that the Georges now are among its puffers.[63]

Despite his travels and the long absences they caused, it would be a mistake to think that Carr had retired from practice. He was to continue working until his death.

Nevertheless, there is a distinct sense by 1790 that he was easing off. Whereas 1785 had seen the new bridge at Boroughbridge and the Rockingham Mausoleum at Wentworth Woodhouse (Fig. 71), three new houses were begun in 1786, Farnley Hall (Figs 72 and 73), Sand Hutton Hall and Eastwood House (Fig. 74), followed by Chesterfield Town Hall in 1787, he took on very few new buildings thereafter. What work he did was nearly all for his old clients. There was substantial work to be done for Earl Fitzwilliam in the house and on the estate at Wentworth Woodhouse and at Milton House (Fig. 75). He returned to Ravenfield Hall, Thoresby Lodge, Cannon Hall and Bretton Hall to make alterations and visited his old clients the Curwens to make improvements to Belle Isle on Lake Windermere. Plans to add wings to Harewood House were considered and he probably designed the new gates there. And, unexpectedly, there was a completely new house, Coolatin Park in Ireland, designed in 1799 for Earl Fitzwilliam after the old house was burnt down in 1798 (Figs 76 and 77). It was a major project and not completed until the year of Carr's death.

THE LAST YEARS

The new century saw old age creeping up on Carr who was now in his late seventies. An inflammation of the eyes kept him indoors and prevented him reading or writing, forcing his niece Amelia Clark to act as his amanuensis.[64] In February 1801 he left York (although he retained the house in Skeldergate) and moved with a niece into Askham Hall. As he explained to his friends at Wentworth Woodhouse: 'I am now removed to this place to end my days, a good house 15 rooms on a floor with the offices.'[65] The best description of his new home comes in a letter he wrote to Miss Heaton on 25 January 1805:

You will find my habitation and its environs very antique, but comfortable. In front is a grass plot with a dial in the centre thereof, and on each side were a couple of haymakers, but as they are not wanted at this season of the year, they now guard the fish pond in the garden, as my old gardiner, as antique as everything about him, is become incapable of cultivating more than half the garden, and my Scrubbery and Turpentine walk are quite neglected, but if you don't come to see me before May, I will during that month get them into a little better order; in June the shrubs are beautiful; my dear friends, I do not mention this by way of saying when I should wish to see you (for I shall be very happy to see you, come when you please), but at that time Nature begins to dress herself in her best attire to receive her summer visitants.

From my gravel walk you ascend three steps into my hall, at the ends of which stands two objects of very different sizes, the one an organ, the other a clock upon a table, and a weather glass above it, so that I daily see how time flies and the weather changes; at one end of the hall is a very small, but a warm little parlour, the sides

thereof wainscotted with little pannels one foot square, at the other end an oak wainscotted library with some books in it, beyond that is a strong room with an iron door and shutters of the same metal, answering to which at the other end is the butler's pantry, so that you find out I have five rooms in front, and over them three bed chambers and three dressing rooms. On the back part behind the hall is a pretty good dining room and a drawing room, which fifty-five years ago I added to the front part of the house for the owner thereof, beyond which is a train of offices as long as any lady's gown in the Kingdom, which, and also the stables, coach-houses, &c., were also added by me for the owner, Mr Garforth. Now this description, my dear friends, will save me the trouble of showing you my premises, and you will know your way about the house without a conductor; therefore you will be able to chuse your own apartment. You travel four miles beyond Tadcaster, York road, a hundred yards more will bring you to a little ale house, by the end of which you turn to your Left hand to a gate which leads into a field, keep the hedge side, and in four hundred yards more you will see the grand village of Askam, and my house at the end thereof, and two lofty gates, which for want of a porter cannot be opened; proceed, however, towards that on your right hand, and go close by the door and palassades of a neat small house on your right hand, and by the side of my garden wall on your left, and you will see a white garden door, there get out and come in.[66]

Even now Carr did not abandon his practice, with the North Riding's bridges coming to play an increasingly predominant role from about 1789. At least half a dozen of his designs were completed in the North Riding between 1797 and 1806 and three or four more built soon after his death in accordance with his proposals. But his greatest bridge was in the West, not the North, Riding on the Great North Road at Ferrybridge (Fig. 78). It still stands, high and robust, an impressive feature in the countryside carrying an important highway over the navigable River Aire and intended to be seen and admired. The commission for Ferrybridge was secured in open competition. A notice announcing the competition, dated 14 January 1797, first appeared in the *Leeds Mercury* on 21 January 1797, soliciting proposals which were to be delivered on 26 January. The shortness of time prompted one writer to suggest that the conditions had been fixed to give the former Surveyor of Bridges, by then a magistrate of the West Riding, the most favourable opportunity of using his superior knowledge of the site.[67] However, the requirements did not deter at least six other competitors from entering the lists, four of them — John Rawsthorne (the designer of Sheffield Infirmary); Charles Watson, of Wakefield; Joseph Lockwood and J. Beal; and Richard Thorpe — winning 'proper gratuities'.

The Ferrybridge archives give the impression that the magistrates felt entirely responsible for getting the bridge built, and that it was extremely good of Carr to take an interest. Thus in 1798, the architect, 'having expressed his readiness to give every Advice and Assistance in the

78 Bridge over the River Aire at Ferrybridge, Yorkshire, built for the West Riding Magistrates in 1797–1804

Prosecution of the Work', was requested to view the structure; this he did, awarding Mr Hartley full marks as a practical man but 'instructing him how to keep the accounts more distinct and intelligible'. However, if Carr did not provide constant supervision, he prepared virtually all the working drawings — one large-scale detail turned up on the back of a piece of wallpaper. He also issued copious written instructions to Hartley on matters of construction and design, worried about the correct placing of the voussoirs, and became anguished over the position of the towpath arch — 'for God's sake my friend set the arch as far off as possible, or the appearance of the whole bridge will be spoiled'. Tragedy was averted, and the bridge was at length finished in 1803, at the massive cost of £24,864.

With the completion of Ferrybridge Carr appears to have decided he had had enough of bridges and on 19 April 1803 the following entry appeared in the North Riding Quarter Sessions Order Book:

John Carr Esquire having on account of his advanced age resigned his appointment of Surveyor of Bridges of this Riding and this Court having taken into consideration the integrity assiduity and skill exerted in the discharge of his office and the great Services he has thereby rendered the Riding during the period of upwards of thirty years do hereby vote him their unanimous thanks and direct that the same shall be inserted in all the York papers as a Public testimony of the high Esteem in which he is holden by the several Magistrates of this Riding.

After this handsome tribute, Carr underlined his devotion to the bridges of the North Riding by compiling a volume, parallel in achievement to that prepared nearly half a century earlier for the neighbouring riding. This *The North Riding Bridges*, he presented to the magistrates, who ordered that their acknowledgements

be returned to John Carr Esquire for the very handsome and useful present which he has made the North Riding of Yorkshire containing Plans of the Bridges now belonging to the North Riding and Suggestions for the reconstruction and improvement of these which may in future want repair which they consider as an additional mark of his Esteem for them at a Time when they can no longer derive Benefit from the more active Services which they have experienced for more than thirty years. And that this Resolution be communicated by the Chairman to Mr Carr and be entered among the records of the Session.[68]

The book is preserved in the North Yorkshire County Record Office: a large, leather-bound volume measuring 2 ft 6 in by 1 ft 9 in. It contains eighty-five pages of plans and elevations of bridges drawn in ink and lettered in Carr's distinctive style. Each bridge has its construction and history noted, sometimes accompanied by a pertinent comment. For instance there is the 'well built handsome little bridge by Shout' and also 'the former bad bridge by John Peacock'; there is the bridge 'built upon a shivery kind of rock' and the one whose 'contractor is a bad workman'.

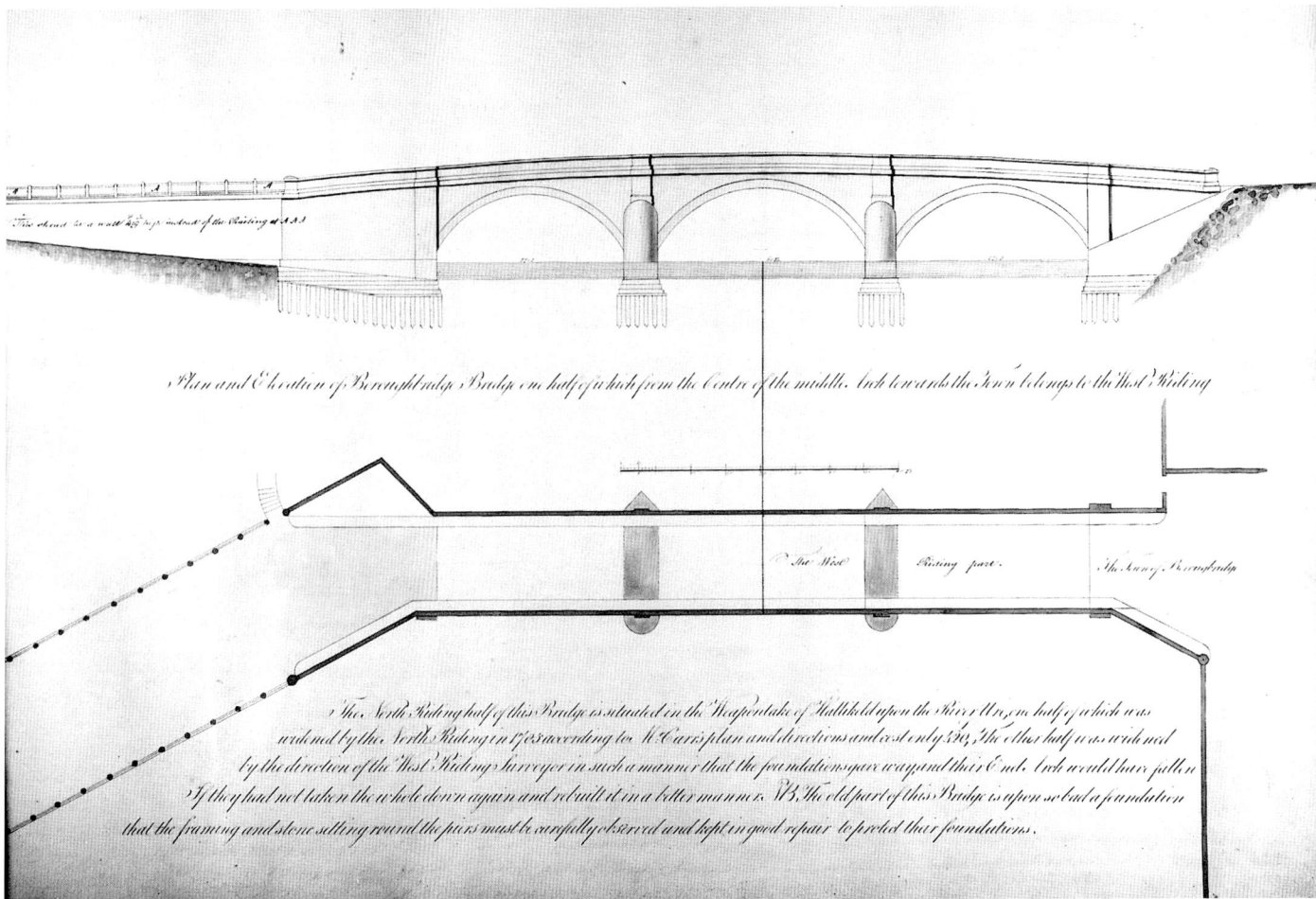

The North Riding half of this Bridge is situated in the Weapentake of Hallikeld upon the River Ure, one half of which was widened by the North Riding in 1785 according to Mr Carr's plan and directions and cost only £420. The other half was widened by the direction of the West Riding Surveyor in such a manner that the foundations gave way and their end arch would have fallen if they had not taken the whole down again and rebuilt it in a better manner. NB The old part of this Bridge is upon so bad a foundation that the framing and stone setting round the piers must be carefully observed and kept in good repair to protect their foundations.

79 Bridge over the River Ure at Boroughbridge, Yorkshire, widened for the North Riding Magistrates in 1785; drawing by Carr

Modesty departs at Boroughbridge 'one half of which was widened by the North Riding in 1785 according to Mr Carr's plan and directions and cost only £420. The other half was widened by the direction of the West Riding Surveyor in 1785 in such a manner that the foundations gave way and their end arch would have fallen if they had not taken the whole down again and rebuilt it in a better manner' (Fig. 79).

Though Carr had retired as surveyor, he could not resist one final return. The bridge at Yarm, near Middlesbrough, was built originally in 1400 by Walter Skirlaw, Bishop of Durham. For three centuries the only crossing over the Tees joining Cleveland and Durham and as such was the joint responsibility of Durham County and the North Riding. During the Civil Wars, its strategic importance led to the most northerly arch being used as a drawbridge, and this same arch, pointed like the other four, was rebuilt, in 1799 to Carr's instructions in the form of a semicircle of wider span. At the same time he also suggested widening the bridge but, in 1803, his proposal was rejected and a recommendation to rebuild anew in iron, at half the cost, was accepted. The work was finished in 1806, but before it could be opened, the abutments failed and the new part of

the bridge collapsed into the river. A court of inquiry was held, with Bernard Hartley as one of the expert members, and the surveyors — the Peacocks of the same family who had built Greta Bridge — were severely censured. It was decided, in future, to adhere to time-honoured methods and to avoid newfangled ideas of construction.

With the surveyors in disgrace Carr, then aged eighty-three, busied himself, despite advancing infirmities, in putting his original scheme into effect (Fig. 80). The three pointed Gothic arches in the centre of the bridge were widened on the east side — although the detailing was classical, the medieval shape was retained — and a new semi-circular south arch erected to match Carr's earlier alteration on the north. The bridge was completed in 1810, three years after the architect's death.[69]

Even after moving to Askham Carr's private practice continued much as before, a steady trickle of work for long-established clients. Major alterations were in hand at Wentworth Woodhouse, particularly the creation of a semi-circular grand staircase (Fig. 81) and there was more work at Milton.

For Carr the key to good health remained activity and so in June 1802 we find him writing from Askham to

Wentworth Woodhouse: 'I should move more from home, I feel I lose my strength by sitting still so much. I will come over and see how the staircase goes.'[70] The winters remained bad. In March 1803 Carr concluded a letter 'I am in such terrible pain that I cannot add more'.[71] But he was resilient, writing later in the month that: 'my Spirits are yet good but the pain wears me out before night. They wanted me much at Milton but I cannot move from my sofa without the greatest pain'.[72] Harriet Carr writing from Askham to Elizabeth Chivers at Bath, gives a picture of the bleakness of the Yorkshire winter:

My dear Miss Chivers. Colds have been bad and very durable. I have had one. Mr Carr begun with a very bad wch brought on the gout wch obliged him to keep up stairs near a fortnight he now much better not yet abel to ride to York he saunters about his little farm he hobbles in walking as well as myself my feet and uncles swell and are very painfull we have cruell cold North and East winds and rain the country is quite a swamp it blackens our little improvements as we can't paint our new pails till that is done we cant plant our greens.[73]

July 1804 saw a crisis. Ed Crabtree waited on Carr and found him poorly indeed, having had a low fever for three days. Not that that kept Carr from his work. Crabtree came away with Carr's opinion on the balustrade of the bridge at Ferrybridge. Carr was not optimistic, writing a few days later that: 'I have had a long struggle betwixt life and death, which is not yet decided, though my weakness is now so great that I am not able without assistance to walk over the floor, I have been devoured for a month with a slow fever which has intirely destroy'd any appetite and taste for anything which is set before me, & in the night I have a very troublesome cough. Indeed I feel to myself that I am so weak that it will be impossible for me to be recovered.'[74] On the 20th of the month he wrote that he 'been in the hot bath today and am not much affected by it physicians great hopes is from the baths'.[75] From the handwriting it is obvious Carr was weak and could hardly write. But by November his health had clearly improved and his neat script had been restored.[76]

That winter he was disconsolate over the news of the death of his much-loved Marchioness of Rockingham, in January 1805, pouring out his sadness to the steward at Wentworth Woodhouse.

Alas my dear friend 'tis a melancholy reflection to see so many (as you and me have seen) of our dear friends drop on every side of us, they remind us of our own dissolution, which must soon happen; but I trust in God we shall met again in a better world with all our friends, never more to be separated … from sudden death good Lord deliver us … I thank god am vastly well but the cold affects me very much. I drink never less than six or seven glasses of wine at my dinner and a Glass of goodneques at night after swallowing the yolk of an poach'd egg, I think that at our age one shoud live well and keep up a good circulation.[77]

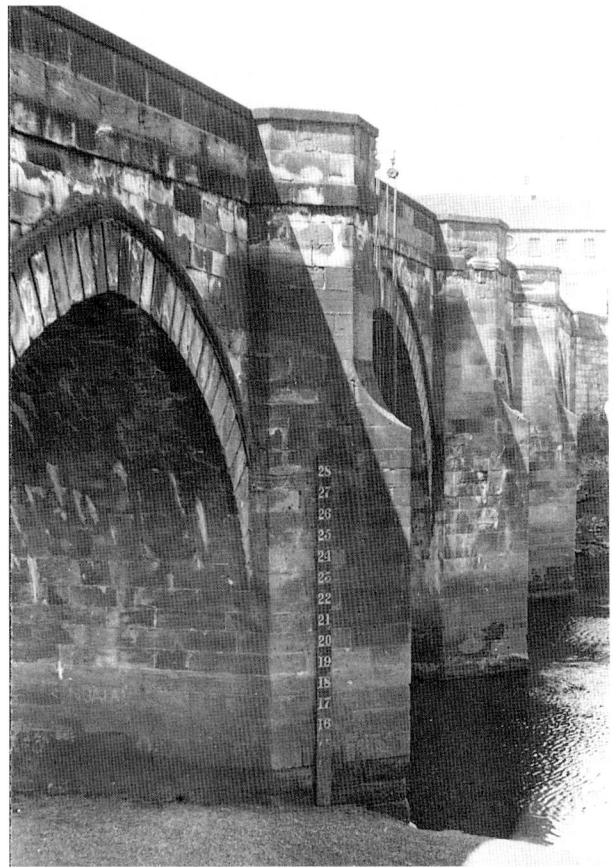

80 Bridge over the River Tees at Yarm, Yorkshire, widened for the North Riding Magistrates in 1806–10

But there was nothing like the thought of a tour with some pretty accomplices to cheer him up. On 1 January 1805 he wrote to Miss Heaton:

I generally make a Tour during the summer to some place or other, and when you come here we may perhaps fix upon a Tour to the Lakes, Scotland, or some place or other, but I don't like to set out before about the middle or latter end of June, the weather then becomes settled. I think you mentioned that you wished to make a Tour when I had the pleasure of seeing you at Wakefield, and I shall be very happy in your company to any part of the world, and I have good neighbour, whose daughter, your age, would perhaps go with us two in your chaise, and two in my phaeton. Perhaps you will come here in March, April or May.

Thus in July 1805 he was travelling again like the Grand Turk accompanied by two Misses Heaton and Elizabeth Chivers (with whom he had already made tours in 1803 and 1804) who kept a diary of her travels.[78] A lively record, it is of particular value in that it mentions works claimed by Carr as his own design for which there is no previous record. The party made its way up Wharfedale where there seemed scarcely a house that Carr had not built or altered and over Rumbels Moor to Gordale Scar, where Elizabeth

Chivers responded with all the emotion of a young lady at the height of romanticism: 'Rocks piled on Rocks and lacerated by torrents ... stupendous masses of stone overhanging at least 30 feet from a tremendous canopy which seems to threaten with destruction the dairing mortal ... the scene is grand and the astonished spectator is struck with the majesty of the surrounding objects.'

This time the weather was not kind. Their first view of Lake Windermere was swathed in mist, although it cleared the next day, allowing a visit to Belle Isle where Carr had recently worked. The view of Keswick which had been keenly anticipated was again hidden by cloud, but worse was to come on ascending Dunmallet: 'sad to relate just as we began to descend an ungracious cloud poured its contents on our suffering heads, every step we took from the excessive heavy rain was as slippery as ice and we one or other of us kept perpetually tumbling, it is impossible to conceive our miserable forlorn condition, happy for us there were no spectators of the scene, for we fell, laughed, and I may add cried, all in the same moment.'

Their first sight of the Scots did not impress them, but the mills at New Lanark did, and even more so Glasgow, after which they did a tour round Loch Lomond and on to Edinburgh. They made their way home via Alnwick Castle, where they saw a grand parade of the local volunteers, Warkworth Castle, which had particular poetical connotations and crossed the Wear at Sunderland over the great iron bridge which spanned the gorge in a single span of 236 feet. Elizabeth Chivers described the bridge, which had been built between 1793 and 1796, as the 'wonder of the present age'. Carr, the great bridgemaster, was sceptical, as Elizabeth Chivers reported: 'This bridge is indeed a wonderful piece of ingenuity but Mr Carr doubts its stability.' (Clearly he was not surprised when he was called in to replace the failed ironwork on Yarm bridge the following year.) Carr's comments were prescient. In 1805 the bridge over the Wear began to show signs of weakness and had to be considerably modified.[79]

They took their time making their way across Yorkshire, visiting old haunts such as Aske Hall and Hornby Castle, where the Duke of Leeds invited them to breakfast — which they declined as they had already eaten. They visited the gardens at Fountains Abbey, Hackfall and Plompton (one of Carr's earliest commissions exactly half a century earlier). Here Carr revealed an interest in natural history, commenting that he was certain the Devil's Arrows at Boroughbridge (famous standing stones) had come from Plompton. Eventually,

we arrived safe at Askham about seven o'clock after having had a most delightful ramble of near nine hundred miles, been always favoured with the blessings of health and without any accident whatever, with either the carriages or the horses. We shall ever feel a most agreeable sense of the kindness of our good friend Mr Carr

for having took up and protected us in the long and charming tour. He drove a pair of spirity little horses in his phaeton the whole of this long journey, although in his eighty third year of his age; we shall consider ourselves greatly obliged to him for this very wonderful performance by which he conferred a pleasure and favour on us that will never be erased from our memory.

Carr's good spirits and his affection for his young companions emerges from a letter to her mother, Mrs Chivers.

The next pleasure to seeing those friends we expect is the hearing from them, therefore I am determined to give you the trouble my dear Mrs Chivers to acquaint you that I am pretty well and have been so ever since I left Askham where I hear from your obliging letter by my fellow traveller there has been some revolutions and additions to that celebrated place. I hope I have heard of a maid that will supply my maids place but I am not yet certain, what cocking of Caps we shall have this winter from the couple of smarts which has arrived from Pontefract lately I heard of the gay figure they made there. You will disappoint my dear Mrs Chivers very much Miss Heatons if you do not call of them for a day or two on your return home they will will be very happy to see you and it is but 15 miles from Doncaster to Barnsley and 1 more to Painthorp and from thence you go by the noble seminary at Ackworth and may call of our friends at Carlton in your way to [Ackworth], Pontefract I shoud have said, the weather is fine and you will not have a better opportunity, take time by the fore lock. Lord Fitzwilliam has been in a very weak state of health and has often begged I woud stay with him for a little company until he goes to Scarborough, which will be sometime next week. I shall then return by Carlton to see Miss Hinchcliffe and some other friends before I return home which I fear will not be before you, you are also in the center of your old friends and therefore why shoud you not injoy them, we shall have a winter long enough.[80]

He was still working hard, as Harriet Carr explained writing from Askham to Elizabeth Chivers at Bath: 'Mr Carr begs his kind rememberance to your father and thanks for delivering his letter to Mr George we have got the order from him if you should go that way you will tell him and that Mr Carr will write to him as soon as he has time he's just now very much engaged about Mr Wentworth's affairs he get up at six or before'.[81] Long detailed letters had to be written to control the work at Wentworth Woodhouse. But the effort was becoming too much. In March Carr reported (in a letter that was feebly written and in places illegible) 'I am pretty well, but cannot write have no use in my right hand - only sometimes'.[82] In May he was concerned that the workmen 'have I fear too little for the job indeed, but I cannot remember what they was have, I told you but I have no memory left'.[83] It was a complaint he repeated sadly in June 'let S. Sykes show by a drawing the impossibility of seperating the plinths to Lord Milton for I cannot draw ... I am much distressed about it and I wish I was able to think better about it but I cannot think as once coud'.[84]

Clearly there were rumours about Carr's health as in June his nephew William stated that the reports on Carr

81 Wentworth Woodhouse, Yorkshire, the staircase built for the 4th Earl Fitzwilliam in 1800–06

OLD AGE

were entirely unfounded, that he had dined in York the previous day and that he had not seen him so well for many months. It is perhaps some such confusion which explains the strange story of Miss Heaton of Painthorpe House related in 1806 to Elizabeth Chivers,

John Carr who has done some business for us lately but nothing for which we thought he could possible charge us more than 6 or 8 pounds and today he sent us a bill of £20 and some shillings. We were astonished, I assure you, and very much provoked at the enormity of the name it what you like ... I believe he has charged for every technical word he in his wisdom has uttered.[85]

In July Carr was so weak that he could not walk 100 yards, 'I eat well enough but am burnt in bed all night without clothes on'.[86] A week later he was unable to write and was relying on his niece.[87] He recovered his strength but was increasingly despondent. On 30 October he wrote to the builder of Ferrybridge, Bernard Hartley, to arrange for the engraving of his name on the Ferrybridge parapet, began 'Dear Barney, I hope this will meet you in good health to go through the toils of this life which you have hitherto done with great Credit to yourself and friends. I am quite worn out and my facultys also, I pray God yours may long be preserved to you.'

His last letter was dated Sunday, 7 December 1806. It contained matter of fact instructions about the dimensions of the hall and concluded 'I am much better than I have been, but my facultyes are much impaired in writing; mark the height of the pedestal under Busts of marble. God Bless you my dear friend'.[88]

Shortly afterwards, on 23 February, 1807, a despatch was sent by William Carr to the steward at Wentworth Woodhouse announcing Carr's death:

I am sorry to be the messenger of bad news, my dear Uncle died yesterday morning. I am happy to say that he had a very easy death and was perfectly sensible to the last moment. I have lately had the Gout in my right hand and write with difficulty but it was a great satisfaction to me to be able to attend my Uncle in his last moments, pray tell Mrs Croft that he desired the medecin Chest might be sent to her after his death which I will do by the fish Cart very soon.

Carr had died the previous day at Askham Richard. His death received a lengthy notice in the *Gentleman's Magazine*:

22 February 1807. At Askham Hall, near York, aet 84. Jn Carr Esq, an eminent architect, one of the aldermen of that city, of which he served in the office of mayor in 1770 and 1785 and uncle to Rev Robert Lascelles Carr, of Stamford, Co. Lincs. He built the Crescent at Bath, the mausoleum of the Marquess of Rockingham, the much admired town hall at Newark and the bridge over the Ure at Boroughbridge and founded and built the church at Horbury near Wakefield. He also designed several noble residences, particularly the seat of Lord Harewood. He is said to have left property to the amount of £150,000 to be divided among collateral relations.[89]

Carr was brought to rest in the vault of Horbury Church on 28 February 1807. The first sermon in the church had anticipated the event, the text preached from having been: 'This shall be my rest for ever; here will I dwell, for I have a delight therein'. Carr had presumably chosen the verse.[90]

In due course a monument was put up to him:

To the memory of John Carr, gentleman of Askham Parva in the County of York who gave distinguished service to his country by reason of his outstanding industry, congenial chracter, exceptional benevolence and upright life. So diligently did he serve Architecture that he is rightly counted among the most famous masters of this art, bringing honour and distinction to his country. Within the narrow bounds of this tablet it is impossible to express in words how many splendid and noble buildings, both public and private, arose happily under his direction. He was honoured by election to the London Society of Architects. He fulfilled the duties of Justice of the Peace with the utmost loyalty and sense of justice. He was twice Lord Mayor of the City of York. Reader, if you wish to know how outstanding he was in generosity and piety, in ability and knowledge, look upon this hallowed Church, erected thanks to his most praiseworthy munificence.

The echoes of Wren's monument in St Paul's were presumably deliberate. They were not inappropriate, for Carr's architectural impact on his native county was as profound as that of Wren on the City of London.

POSTSCRIPT: CARR'S LEGACY

Carr's will was proved on 25 May 1807. His nephew William was the sole executor and received all the household furniture, plate, linen, books, pictures, china etc., articles contained in his houses in York and Askham Richard together with the cattle, stocks, crops and implements of husbandry at Askham. He was also left all Carr's mortgages and the money due to him on bond, all his stock in the funds and all his ready money, goods, chattels, personal estate and effects not otherwise disposed of. This was valued at £22,336 5s 5d. The other major beneficiary was William's brother John, who received the shares in the Calder and Hebble and Market Weighton Navigations and government stocks.

Carr's brother James was forgiven all the debts and fees owed him and Elizabeth Carr (wife of the Revd Samuel Carr, Carr's brother) and Mary Hinchliffe (his maidservant) received annuities of £100 and £40 respectively. For the other nieces and nephews there were substantial capital sums, £1,000 each for Robert Lascelles Carr, his nephew, and Maria Elizabeth Carr, his niece, £1000; £500 for Ann, wife of Thomas Clark (his niece), Mrs Harriet Ann Swan (daughter of Ann Clark), John Swan and Amelia Clark, daughter of Ann Clark (who had married since the will was written and was now Amelia Rainier). There were smaller sums of £100 for James Carr, Thomas Wilson and Robert Swann and £50 for John Hoyland jnr, Enoch Morgan (his servant) and Thomas Hinchcliffe (another servant). Swann, who married his niece Ursula, was to have been given Ellenthorpe Hall in the will, presumably again the gift had already been made. Finally he directed the mayor and communality of the City of York in whom he had entrusted £666 13s 4d in 3 per cent reduced annuities to apply the dividends to the person who for the time being shall be the organist of the church at Horbury by half-yearly payments. The Lord Mayor and Aldermen of York, Thomas Swann, Robert Swann and Mr Clarke were given mourning rings. Alderman Thomas Wilson and Robert Swann were appointed trustees. Henry Bland and William Champney of York were to be the bankers.[91] The total estate was valued at £35,000, a very substantial sum.

Carr had hoped to establish a Carr dynasty, or rather two, his nephew William Carr at Askham and his other nephew John, William's brother, at Carr Lodge. But William had only a single daughter, Henrietta, who died an infant. On his death in 1820 Askham Hall passed under the provisions of Carr's will to Robert Swann, William Carr's brother-in-law. Even before that the Skeldergate house in York was offered for sale in 1813 and when that proved unsuccessful was advertised for demolition, which again cannot have been successful as the house survived until 1945 when it was finally demolished. Albion Street was built on the house's gardens in 1815.[92]

Shortly after William Carr's death, on 13 February 1822, Sir John Soane bought two books with inscriptions by Carr from the bookseller William Boone, John Wood's *The Description of the Hot-Bath at Bath* of 1777 and Roger Morris's *Select Architecture* of 1755. He also acquired a manuscript copy of Batty Langley's *Ancient Architecture Restored* which had been made by one of Carr's clerks, perhaps Charles Mason.[93] The books were clearly bought at a sale as Soane's records refer to their lot numbers, but no supporting catalogue survives.

It would appear that following William Carr's death Carr's library, which would either have been in the York house in Skeldergate or at Askham Hall, was dispersed. Sadly, no list of books survives, although it is possible to identify some of its contents from his recorded subscriptions, including those to George Richardson's, *Iconology, or a Collection of Emblematical Figures* of 1779 (an English edition of Cesare Ripa's *Iconologia* of 1593); Richardson's *A Book of Ceilings, composed in the Stile of the Antique Grotesque* of 1776; James Paine's *Plans, Elevations and Sections of Noblemen and Gentlemen's Houses*; and Joseph Halfpenny's *Gothic Ornaments in the Cathedral Church of York* of 1795–1800. Carr's copy of the first three volumes of *Vitruvius Britannicus* was recently acquired by the York Civic Trust. Carr must also have owned a copy of Volfmann's new and enlarged edition of

Joachim von Sandart's *Deutsche Academie*, a popular source book published in 1768, as some of the orders he regularly used are derived from it.[94]

The suggestion that Carr's library was broken up after William Carr's death is supported by the appearance of several lots of Carr drawings in *Bibliotheca Architectonica*, the catalogue of the Bloomsbury bookdealer Priestley and Weale, Bloomsbury, in 1825.[95] These include 'Drawings, a Collection of Designs for Ceilings, Pannelling, &c. 56 in numbers, 6s'; 'Drawings, 2 folio volumes of original Designs, consisting of Plans, Elevations, Details, Ceilings, &c., £1 11s 6d'; 'Drawings, a 4to volume of Designs of Chimney-pieces, Ornaments, Mouldings, &c, 7s'; 'Drawings, a large and thick folio volume of various Designs of Carvings, Elevations, Plans, &c, &c, £1 11s 6d'; and 'Elevations of Buildings; a folio Volume of Drawings of the Elevations of Buildings, public and private, erected in the County of York by the late Mr Carr, £2 2s.'

The subsequent history of these drawings is unknown, although it is possible that the 'Collection of Designs for Ceilings, Pannelling, &c' could refer to the collection of drawings of ceilings by Carr in the Victoria and Albert Museum if the panelling was removed. It can only be hoped that they survive somewhere and will one day emerge. If they do, and in particular if the 'Drawings of the Elevations of Buildings, public and private, erected in the County of York' were to be discovered, they would undoubtedly transform our knowledge of Carr's work.

However, it is unlikely that these represented all Carr's surviving drawings as a group of drawings seem to have survived in his office and were inherited by Peter Atkinson, who succeeded to much of his practice. The survival of such drawings would explain the form of the list of works in the *Architectural Publications Society Dictionary*, where Carr's entry was based on information from J. B. Atkinson, Peter Atkinson's grandson. Certainly Harry Speight claimed to have seen the original plans and working drawings for Harewood in Atkinson's office early in the twentieth century.[96]

The firm, latterly Brierley, Leckenby, Keighley and Groom, survives in York and maintained a large archive of architectural drawings, most of which are now in the Borthwick Institute in York. However, very few drawings of Carr's date survive. One report suggests that these were removed by a former partner in the firm with the intention of writing a study of Carr, but were accidently destroyed after his death.

Ellenthorpe, which had been left to William Carr and then passed to his brother John Carr, was advertised for sale in 1842. The vendor was John Francis Carr, John Carr's son. J. F. Carr had married Mary, only daughter and heiress of William Robinson of Hemingbrough near Selby. His monument in Hemingbrough church refers to him as being 'of Carr Lodge and Hemingbrough Villa, Esq., A Magistrate and Deputy Lieutenant for the County of York'. On his death, aged 81, in 1862 the Carr line died out. His property passed to his daughter Mary, who had married Colonel Robert Parker of Browsholme Hall. Carr had not been happy with the proposed marriage, and sadly he was proved right, the couple became estranged in the 1860s.[97] Carr Lodge was retained but let until 1936 when most of the estate was sold. The Beechey portrait of John Carr passed to Browsholme but is now in the National Portrait Gallery. The surviving family papers have all been deposited in the Lancashire Record Office.

CATALOGUE

82 Alderton rectory

Alderton Rectory, Alderton, Suffolk (Fig. 82)
Revd Richard Frank
New house, 1772

In October 1772 Carr wrote to Bacon Frank, his patron at Campsall, enclosing a design for his brother's parsonage 'so particularly figured & delineated that I think the workmen cannot err in the execution of it'. From White's directory it is clear that this must refer to Alderton in Suffolk, where Richard Frank was rector for forty years until his death in 1813 and where he is reported as having built a large, handsome rectory house. This was of brick with a hipped roof, three-bay entrance front and a canted bay on the garden front. The design is convincingly Carr, although the doorcase (which has typical Carr side windows) is unusual in its use of the Greek Doric order.

Sheffield Archives, BFM 1326/44
William White, *History, Gazeteer and Directory of Suffolk* (Sheffield, 1844), 259

Allerton Park, Allerton Mauleverer, Yorkshire (WR/NY)
Lady Arundell
Marble hearth for the drawing room, 1768

In 1770 Carr was paid £3 19s 6d by Lady Arundell's heir, 2nd Viscount Galway, for a marble hearth for the drawing room at Allerton supplied in May 1768 to Lady Arundell. Allerton was rebuilt in the 1840s.

Nottingham University Library, Galway MSS 12,379
Clive Aslet, 'Early History of Allerton Park', *Country Life*, 26 January 1989

83 Appersett bridge

Appersett Bridge, Hawes, Yorkshire (NR/NY) (Fig. 83)
North Riding magistrates
Bridge widened, 1795

The bridge over the River Ure on the Hawes-Sedbergh road became the responsibility of the North Riding Magistrates in 1791. It was widened and improved in 1795 under Carr's direction. The cost, including piling the foundations and making the roads was £580. Its span was 45 ft.

North Yorkshire County Record Office, Book of Bridges, 1772–1803, 2

Armagh, County Armagh (Fig. 84)
Richard Robinson, Archbishop of Armagh
Obelisk, 1782, and design for a mausoleum

In his copy of Roger Morris' *Select Architecture* in Sir John Soane's Museum, Carr wrote against a sketch of an obelisk

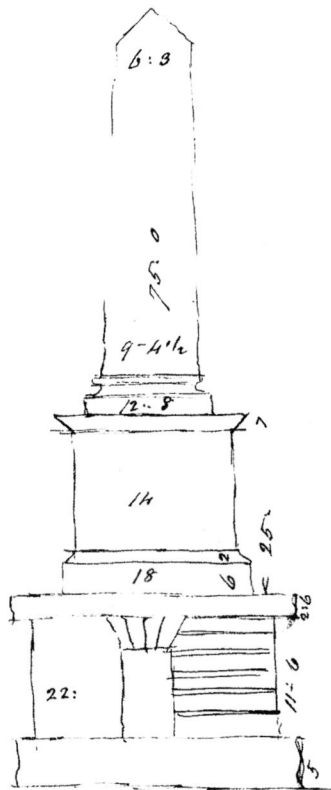

84 Design for Armagh obelisk

'designed pr J. C. and built by the ld primate of all Ireland 1782'. The obelisk was erected on Knox's Hill as a memorial to the Duke of Northumberland by Robinson, who is known to have visited houses in Yorkshire with Carr. Although the dimensions of the executed column are close to those of the drawing, the details vary. The original had a short obelisk on a plinth raised above a rusticated base, a design of considerable power. The executed design is a more conventional, tall obelisk. Francis Johnston, an Irish architect, also claimed responsibility for the obelisk and it would appear that while Carr provided the design it was executed by Johnston, perhaps adapting Carr's design. Carr also produced a design for a substantial, circular, mausoleum similar to that by Nicholas Hawksmoor at Castle Howard, Yorkshire, or to the Doric Rotunda at the Rievaulx Terraces, Yorkshire, but with eleven attached baseless Roman Doric columns. The ultimate source is the Temple of Vesta at Rome and the design, particularly the use of baseless Roman Doric columns, is unusually literal in its neo-Classicism for Carr. A possible inspiration may have been the baseless Doric columns of the Thompson Mausoleum at Little Ouseburn, Yorkshire, of 1742–43, which Carr would have known from his work at Kirby Hall.

Armagh Public Library, Dwgs. Cat X.1.g
Sir John Soane's Museum, Roger Morris, *Select Architecture* (London, 1755), drawing on rear flyleaf
C. E. B. Brett, *Buildings of County Armagh* (Belfast, 1999), 267–68

Arncliffe Hall, Ingleby Arncliffe, Yorkshire (NR/NY)
(Figs 6–8, 85)
Thomas Mauleverer
New house and stables, 1753

Thomas Mauleverer rebuilt the late sixteenth-century house at Arncliffe after marrying an heiress, Miss Wilberfosse. Carr is listed as the architect by the A.P.S.D., which dates the house to 1753, a date confirmed in the pediment. The new house is two and a half storeys high over a rustic, with a tall ground floor and emphatic quoins. The garden front has a central three-bay pediment and an elegant Palladian perron; the entrance front is unrelieved. The house is one of Carr's earliest and the plan (similar to that at Huthwaite Hall) is surprisingly crude, owing more to the smaller manor houses common in Yorkshire since the 1680s than to Palladian models. However, the drawing room and stairwell have elegant Rococo plasterwork and chimneypieces. The east wing additions were made in 1841-43 and the house was much damaged by fire in 1912 when the original pyramidal roof was replaced by one with a flat top. The stable block (Fig. 8) is a typical Carr composition with round-headed windows set in relieving arches and there are a pair of pedimented pavilions flanking the entrance gateway.

Wyatt Papworth (ed.), *The Dictionary of Architecture issued by the Architectural Publications Society* (London, 1877), II, 36
J. Whellan, *History and Topography of the City of York and the North Riding of Yorkshire* (Beverley, 1859), II, 73

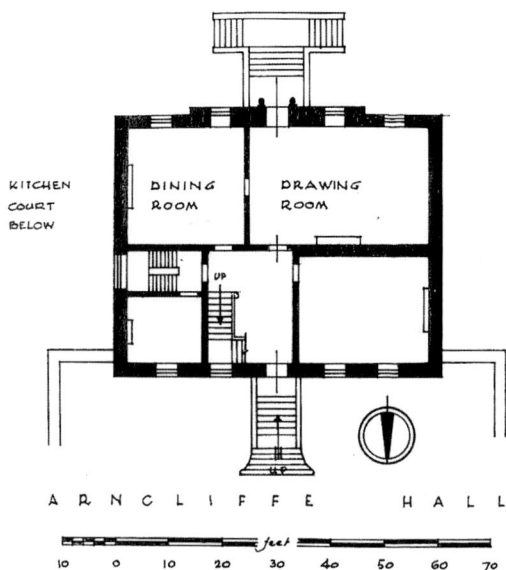

85 Arncliffe Hall, plan of ground floor

Sidney Kitson, 'Carr of York', *RIBA Journal*, 3rd ser., 17 (1910), 242, 246-47, plan

Victoria County History, *Yorkshire, North Riding* (London, 1923), ii, 240

Christopher Hussey, 'Arncliffe Hall, Northallerton', *Country Life*, 25 December 1920

BE/NR/200-01

Arthington Hall, Arthington, Yorkshire (WR/WY)

(Fig. 86)

Thomas Arthington

Remodelled house, *c.* 1760–70

Harriet Clark in 1795, Amelia Clark in 1796 and Elizabeth Chivers in 1805 all record Carr's involvement at Arthington. This must have been for Thomas Arthington, born Thomas Hardcastle, who inherited the Arthington estate (and changed his name) in 1750 at the age of twenty-four following the death of his second cousin Cyril Arthington. He died in 1801. The history of the house remains obscure. Its plain exterior and proportions do not suggest Carr but the interior makes it clear that at least part of the present house is his work. Arthington's brother-in-law Sir Cecil Wray is traditionally believed to have used Carr at Fillingham Castle, Lincolnshire, in about 1770.

Arthington Hall is remarkable for its flying timber staircase, set in an oval stairwell with a central, unsupported flight. This can be compared with that at Kirklees Hall of 1759–60, although this lacks the fluidity and gravity-defying leap of that at Arthington Hall. The date of the staircase is unknown. Family tradition records

86 Arthington Hall staircase

CATALOGUE

a fire in 1790 but the detail of the lower part of the staircase and entrance hall suggest the 1760s or early 1770s. The decoration of the first-floor landing and dome may have been carried out in 1875 by Alfred Waterhouse, whose drawing room was in the 'Adam' style.

Cragg Cottages, a symmetrical row of six two-storey cottages on the road leading west from Arthington Hall could be by Carr. The round-headed windows in giant relieving arches are typical of his style. The cottages have been extended and much altered. An extra bay has been added on the right and the tops of the arches cut off by a new, lower roofline.

York Minster MSS Add. 328/1, fol. 9, 328/2
Giles Worsley, 'Crediting Carr', *Country Life*, 5 May 1988
Peter Thornborrow, 'John Carr's West Yorkshire Buildings', *York Georgian Society* (1992), 29

Aske Hall, Richmond, Yorkshire (NR/NY)
(Figs. 35)
Sir Lawrence Dundas, Bt, MP
Alterations and extensions, 1763–69

Member of an impoverished younger branch of an old Scottish family, Dundas made an immense fortune estimated at £600,000–700,000 supplying the army during the Seven Years War. He bought Aske for £45,000 from Lord Holderness in 1763, shortly after he had acquired a baronetcy.

Dundas was anxious to carry out extensive alterations as soon as possible and Carr was at Aske in November 1762, before the purchase was complete and plans were well advanced by March the following year. Work was concentrated on creating a suite of family rooms, together with offices, leaving thoughts of improving the state rooms for later. By July 1765 the family rooms were complete, together with a new kitchen, brewhouse, bakehouse, laundry, wash house and stables. £1,550 had been spent on the stables and cellars, £2,409 on the rest of the work. The design of the Morning Room ceiling was a paraphrase of Robert Adam's contemporary Great Dining Room at Syon House, Middlesex. The chimneypiece was provided from Florence by the expatriate English sculptor Francis Harnwood, at a cost of £100.

In 1767 Carr produced plans for a massive extension on the front of the house which would have turned Aske into a great Classical mansion. The intended new work would have included a hexastyle portico, an apsed hall 60 ft wide by 27 ft wide, dining room, drawing room and a gallery 80 ft by 27 ft. Nothing came of the grand scheme. Carr was paid 50 guineas in October 1764 and 1765 on account of supervising works at Aske, 200 guineas in 1766, £100 in November 1767 for a year's attendance, £80 in September 1768 and £100 in September 1769. He was also paid £49 3s 7d for six marble chimneypieces in 1765.

Carr's handsome stables were converted into a chapel in 1887. Virtually all Carr's offices were demolished in the 1960s, as were the end two bays of the four-bay family wing.

North Yorkshire County Record Office, Zetland Archives, ZNK; M9/1/1-2; X1/2/17, 18, 28, 29, 81; X 1/7/57-66
Sheffield Central Library, BFM 1314/67
Giles Worsley, 'Aske Hall, Yorkshire', *Country Life*, 1-8 March 1990
BE/NR/65

Askham Hall, Askham Richard, Yorkshire (WR/NY)
Revd Edmund Garforth
Alterations, 1750–51
Rebuilt, 1889

The Revd Edmund Dring inherited a reputed £100,000 from his uncle in 1746 on the condition that he changed his name to Garforth. This allowed him to rebuild Askham Hall and his house in York. The work on Askham Hall was among Carr's earliest commissions, as he explained many years later in a letter to Miss Heaton, after he had bought the house himself. According to the letter Carr added 'a pretty good dining room and a drawing room' and 'a train of offices as long as any lady's gown in the Kingdom', as well as stables and coach-houses. The alterations can be more precisely dated in letters from Garforth's friend William Gossip, who lived nearby at Thorp Arch Hall and involved himself closely in the designs. In a letter of 5 March 1750 Gossip discussed Carr's proposal to pull down the whole house, which Garforth did not relish, preferring to retain the front rooms, and a letter from Gossip to Garforth in May 1751 referred to problems getting into the chamber over the best dining room. The house was of brick, of two storeys with projecting wings. A plan of the ground and chamber floors made by J. B. Atkinson in July 1848 in York Central Library is believed to show Carr's house but is currently missing.

West Yorkshire Archives Service, Leeds, Thorp Arch papers, TA 19/4
National Westminster Bank, Coney Street, deeds
Thomas Allen, *A New and Complete History of the County of York* (London, 1828), i, 473
R. Davies, 'A Memoir of John Carr', *Yorkshire Archaeological Journal*, 4 (1877), 212–13
North Yorkshire County Library Service, *Askham Bryan, Askham Richard: Village Outline* (1988), 31
Brett Harrison, 'Thorp Arch Hall, 1749–1756: "dabbling a little in Mortar"', *Thoresby Society*, 2nd ser., 4 (1994 for 1993), 27

Aston Hall, Aston-cum-Aughton, Yorkshire (WR/SY)
(Figs 87, 88)
4th Earl of Holderness
New house, stables and cottages, 1767–72

Aston Hall, the ancient seat of the d'Arcys, was rebuilt after a fire in 1767. Carr, whom Holderness had earlier

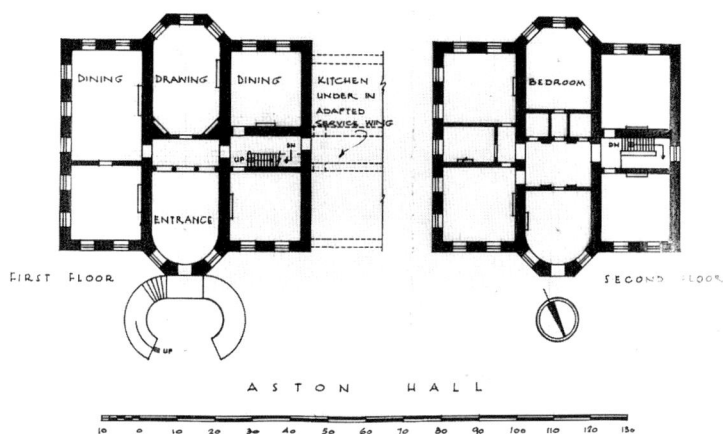

87 *above* Aston Hall, north front

88 *left* Aston Hall, plan of principal and bedroom floors

used at Hornby Castle, Yorkshire, probably viewed the site that year as he wrote from Aston to the promoters of the Leeds Infirmary in 1767. The new house was a substantial, compact, square, stone building with rustic, *piano nobile* and attic, and canted bays on the entrance and garden fronts. It was carefully placed for the views at the end of a ridge. There were originally curving external stairs to the first-floor entrance. Offices were probably in an attached wing.

In 1772 Holderness decided to live solely at Hornby, according to the rector William Mason 'because it is too near the ducal seat at Kiveton', that is to Kiveton Park, seat of the Duke of Leeds. Perhaps because of this the interior of Aston Hall is fitted up much more plainly that the exterior would suggest. In 1774–75 the house was bought by Harry Verelst, former Governor of Bengal. Verelst added a new staircase to the designs of John Platt in 1776–77 and may have removed Carr's external staircase. The office wing was probably rebuilt in about 1825.

The house subsequently became a hospital and the interior has been much altered. It is now a hotel and Carr's stables have been converted to housing.

An undated and unsigned plan and elevation of six cottages to be erected at Aston, by Carr, survives in the Egerton papers in the British Library. These can be identified as a terrace of six (much altered) cottages on the south side of Aston's main street.

British Museum, Egerton MS 3436, fol. 401
Thomas Allen, *A New and Complete History of the County of York* (London, 1831), II, 233
Sir John Soane's Museum, Roger Morris, *Select Architecture* (London, 1955), drawing opposite pl. 4
The Correspondence of Horace Walpole, ed. W. S. Lewis (London, 1955), XXVIII, 91, 172, 231
Mary and Robert Brian Wragg, 'Two Houses by Carr of York', *Country Life*, 12 April 1956
BE/WR/86

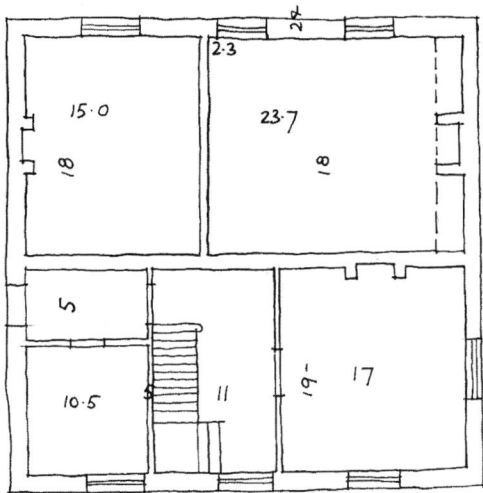

89 *above* Aston rectory

90 *left* Aston rectory, plan of ground floor

"REVD MR MASONS HOUSE AT ASTON"

Aston Rectory, Aston-cum-Aughton, Yorkshire
(WR/SY) (Figs 89, 90)
Revd William Mason
New house, 1770–71

William Mason, the poet, inherited the Hutton estate at Marske in 1768, prompting him to rebuild his rectory at Aston. He retained part of the old house as offices and built a plain, brick, three-bay, two-storey, hipped-roof house commanding a fine view towards Derbyshire. The interiors were simple except for the Adamesque detail of the drawing room. Carr at the time was rebuilding Aston

Hall. Mason recommended Carr to the 2nd Earl Harcourt as a possible architect for alterations to Nuneham Park, Oxford, in 1778.

Sir John Soane's Museum, Roger Morris, *Select Architecture* (London, 1955), drawing opposite pl. 3
Mary and Robert Brian Wragg, 'Two Houses by Carr of York', *Country Life*, 12 April 1956
BE/WR/87

Auckland Castle, Bishop Auckland, County Durham
(Figs 91, 92)
Richard Trevor, Bishop of Durham
Alterations, *c.* 1771
John Egerton, Bishop of Durham
Alterations, *c.* 1771

Richard Trevor, appointed in 1752 and a rich man in his own right, was the first Bishop of Durham for a century to be an energetic builder. The gatehouse at Auckland Castle was built in 1760 to the designs of Sir Thomas Robinson and a rainwater head dated 1764 survives on the main building. There are drawings by Carr at Auckland Castle, one inscribed 'Plan of a new Drawing-room given to Bishop Trevor by Mr Carr of York', another, initialled JC, relates to the picture gallery.

John Egerton completed the south wing after Trevor's death in 1771. Like the rest of the castle the new work was

CATALOGUE

91 *above* Auckland Castle, south wing

92 *left* Auckland Castle, bedroom ceiling in south wing

93 Aysgarth bridge

Gothic in style, although the interiors are classical. Egerton also fitted up the Great Room as a chapel, built Coundon Gate and Stewards House and enlarged the offices and stables before his death in 1787. The extent of Carr's involvement at Auckland Castle both for Trevor and for Egerton is unclear and the proposed new drawing room, which would have been north of the Great Room, was never built. However, the very fine plasterwork, chimneypieces and doorcases in the south wing are characteristic of his work and he is known to have worked for Egerton's brother at Monkwearmouth. The castle was extensively altered by James Wyatt for Bishop Barrington in 1794–96.

William Hutchinson, *The History and Antiquities of the County Palatine of Durham* (Carlisle, 1795), III, viii
James Macaulay, *The Gothic Revival 1745–1845* (Glasgow and London, 1975), 139–40, 145
John Cornforth, 'Auckland Castle, County Durham', *Country Life*, 3 February 1972
BE/Durham/106

Aysgarth Bridge, Yorkshire (NR/NY) (Fig. 93)
North Riding magistrates
Bridge widened, 1788

The bridge over the River Ure, with its 73 ft span and described as 'a very old and substantial bridge', was widened by 10 ft to Carr's design and under Peacock's direction at a cost of £420.

North Yorkshire County Record Office, Book of Bridges, 1772–1803, 1
BE/NR/67

Ayton Bridge, Ayton, Yorkshire (NR/NY) (Fig. 94)
North Riding magistrates
New bridge, 1775

A new bridge was built over the River Derwent on the Scarborough–Thirsk road with two spans of 28ft and two spans of 35ft. Work was carried out to Carr's design and directions. The cost, including making the roads and a temporary bridge, was £1,421. Robert Shout, the builder, failed to perform his contract properly, leaving part of the work to be finished by the Riding.

North Yorkshire County Record Office, Book of Bridges, 1772–1803, 4
BE/NR/68

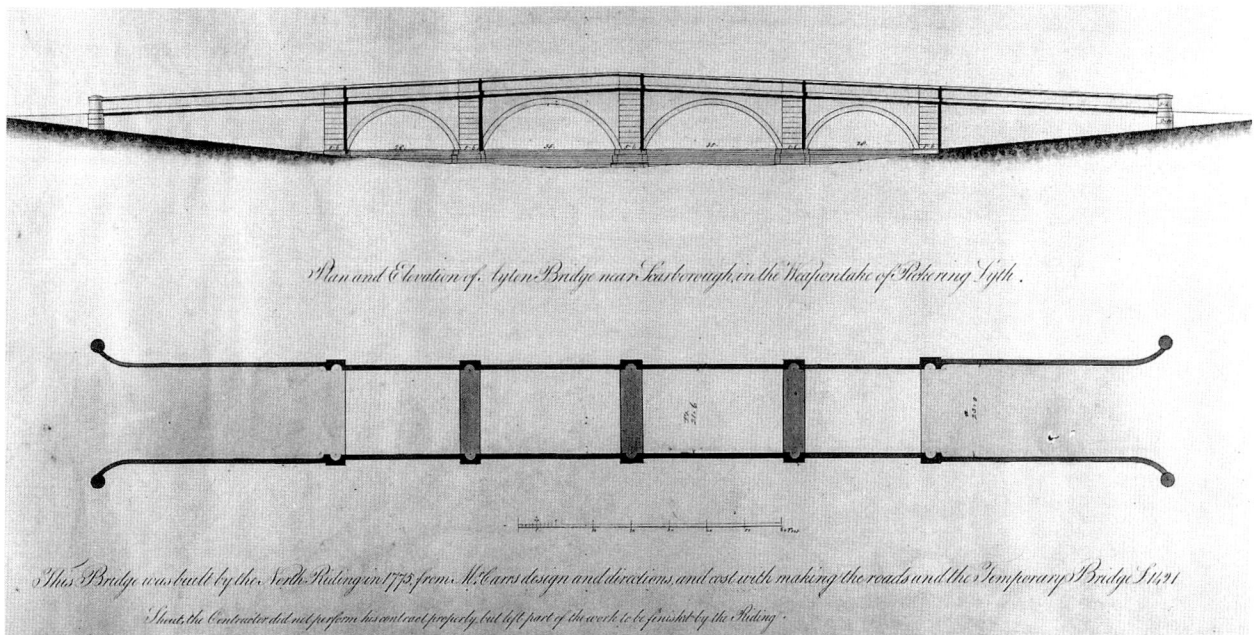

94 Drawing of Ayton bridge

CATALOGUE

All Saints' Church, Babworth, Nottinghamshire

Alterations to the interior, before 1784

Carr was paid for alterations to the interior of All Saints', Babworth, a church used by his patron the Duke of Newcastle and his servants and by Sir George Savile. The total cost of the work was £158 13s 2d, out of which 'John Carr Esqr. Survy'or' received £8 8s. Edward Beardsall was paid 7s 6d, for 'Drawing a Plan of the Old Pews to send to Mr: Carr'. The account is undated but, the vicar, John Simpson, died in 1784. The church was restored in 1859–62.

Nottinghamshire Archives, PR21, 302; information from Dr
    Terry Friedman
BE/Notts/63

Badsworth Hall, Yorkshire (WR/WY)

2nd Marquis of Rockingham
Alterations, n.d.
Ruinous by 1965 and subsequently demolished

Mary Bright, sole daughter and heiress of Thomas Bright of Badsworth, who died in 1739, married the 2nd Marquis of Rockingham in 1752. Thereafter the late seventeenth- or early eighteenth-century house was usually tenanted, although Hunter notes that the house was well maintained. This fits with an undated memo in the Wentworth Woodhouse muniments referring to work done by Carr at Badsworth.

Sheffield Archives, Wentworth Woodhouse Muniments,
    Stewards' Papers, Memo, Work to be done at Badsworth by
    Mr Hartley, Pontefract, (undated)
Joseph Hunter, *South Yorkshire* (London, 1831), II, 438
Edward Waterston and Peter Meadows, *Lost Houses of the West
    Riding* (Welburn, 1998), 63, fig
BE/WR/88

Bainbridge, Yorkshire (NR/NY)

North Riding magistrates
Bridge widened, 1785

The old rough stone bridge over the Bain on the Aysgarth–Hawes road, with its 28ft span, was widened and improved and founded on rock, under Carr's direction.

North Yorkshire County Record Office, Book of Bridges,
    1772–1803, 6
Quarter Sessions order book, Easter and Midsummer 1785
BE/NR/69

Basildon Park, Berkshire (Figs 57, 58, 95–97)

Sir Francis Sykes, Bt, MP
New house, lodges, 1776–83

Born of yeoman stock at Thornhill in Yorkshire in 1732, Sykes made a vast fortune in India. On his return in 1761 he bought Ackworth Park, Yorkshire, a house now demolished and apparently undocumented. In 1774 he married his second wife, the sister of the 3rd Viscount

95 Basildon Park, corridor on bedroom floor

Galway who employed Carr on his Serlby estate. After another brief period in India, Sykes bought the Basildon estate and employed Carr to build a new house there, which is dated 1776 in *New Vitruvius Britannicus*. However, the first payment to Carr in Sykes's account at Goslings Bank, for £100, occurs on 21 May 1777. Carr was paid £100 a year until 1781 with a final payment of £85 in June 1783, making a total of £585. Sykes may have considered employing James Wyatt. His account lists a payment of £84 to James Wyatt on 19 July 1775. Decoration continued until 1784, with Theodore de Bruyn paid £200 in 1783 and 1784. Carr spent a week at Basildon with his nieces in 1796.

Although the house has a *piano nobile*, entrance is through the rustic, up stairs to the portico-in-antis. The main entertaining rooms on the *piano nobile*, hall, staircase hall and octagon and dining room interlock with the family rooms with their own secondary stairs. Thus Carr was able to integrate the entertaining rooms with

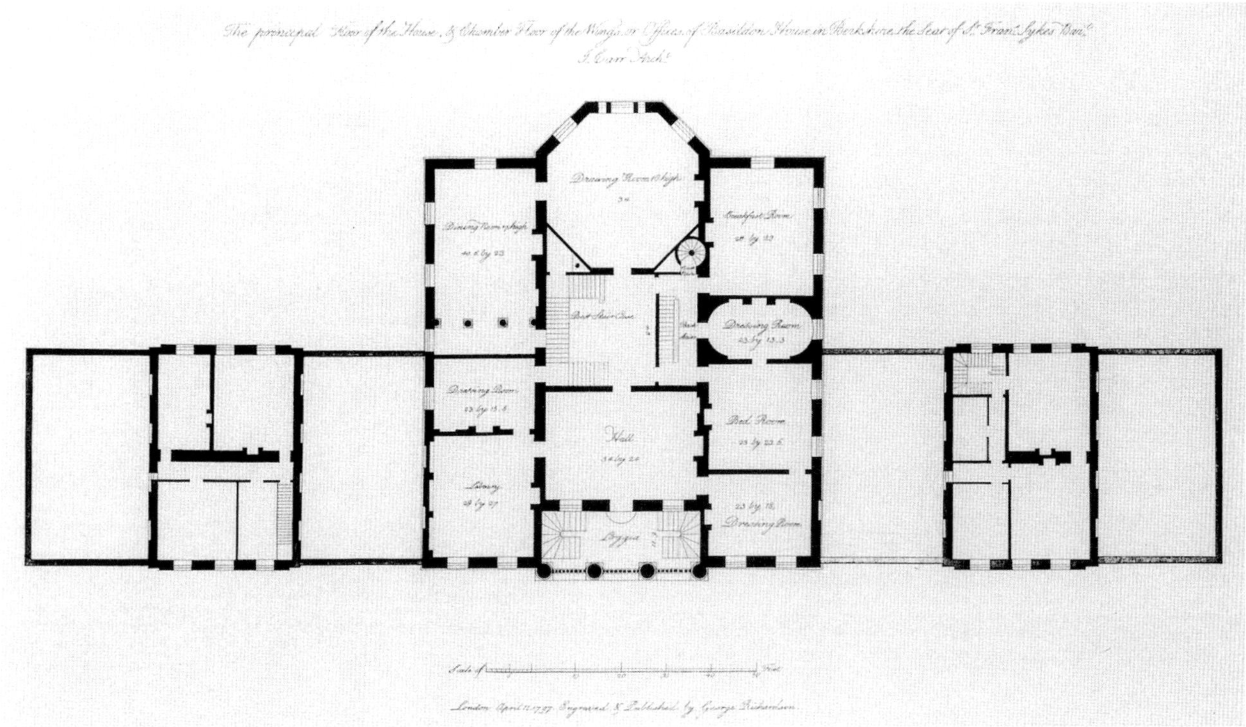

96 Basildon Park, plan of ground floor

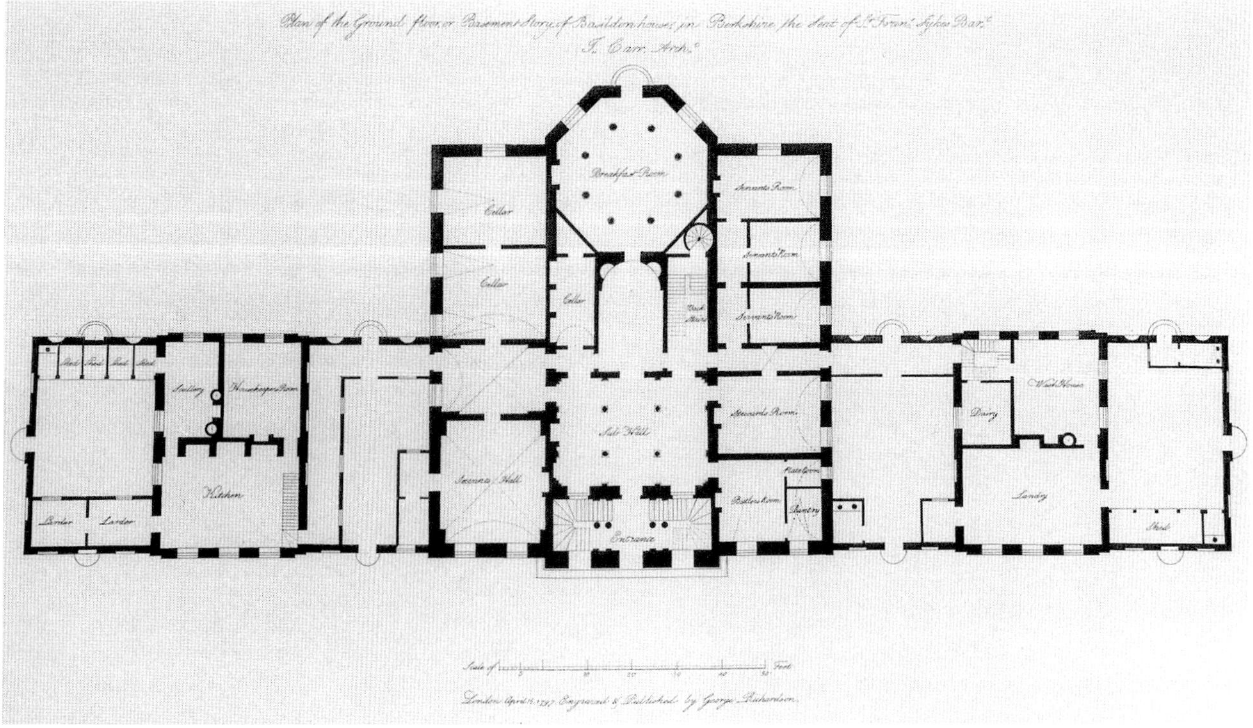

97 Basildon Park, plan of basement

CATALOGUE

112

comfortable provision for the family. The breakfast room, in the octagon on the ground floor, is the only family room on that floor. Sykes never finished the main floor.

J. B. Papworth altered the house and lodges between 1839 and 1844. Basildon was restored in the 1950s by Lord and Lady Iliffe using fittings from Carr's Panton Hall, Lincolnshire.

Sir John Soane's Museum, drawings, dated 1794, signed by Carr
British Architectural Library, drawings by J. B. Papworth showing Carr's work, garden buildings and lodges, etc.
Barclays Bank Archives, Goslings Bank, 56/99,102, 60/112, 60/114, 64/107, 64/273, 68/525, 72/124, 72/125, 72/126, 72/127
George Richardson, *New Vitruvius Britannicus* (London, 1802), I, pls. 12–14
John Cornforth, 'Basildon House, Berkshire', *Country Life*, 5, 12, 19 May 1977
BE/Berks/76

Belle Isle, Windermere, Westmorland (Cumbria)
John Christian Curwen
Alterations, *c*.1795

According to Elizabeth Chivers in 1805 'Mr Carr made some alterations in it [Belle Isle], and designed the elegant door way to it about nine or ten years ago'. Belle Isle was begun by John Plaw for Thomas English in 1774–75 but bought in 1781 as a shell by Isabella Curwen. It was fitted up after her marriage to John Christian Curwen in 1782, perhaps by William Heaton who is known to have worked at Ewanrigg for Curwen. It is not known how extensive Carr's work was at Belle Isle but it may have included the addition of the single-storey offices. He also worked for the Curwens at Workington Hall between 1783 and 1791.

John F. Curwen, *A History of the Ancient House of Curwen* (Kendal, 1928), 180
John Martin Robinson, 'Belle Isle', *Connoisseur*, March 1981
Giles Worsley, 'Crediting Carr', *Country Life*, 5 May 1988

Belle Vue, Nr Hawkshead, Lancashire (Cumbria)
Revd William Braithwaite
Belvedere, *c*.1794

Braithwaite, the rector of Hawkshead from 1762, was a friend of Carr's, who visited him on his tours of the Lakes. He lived at Belmount, a substantial Classical house built in 1774. Carr designed a two-storey summerhouse for Braithwaite on Claife Heights overlooking Lake Windermere with dining room on the ground floor and drawing room on the first floor and a canted bay to take advantage of the view. Another canted bay at the rear housed the semi-circular staircase. Known originally as Belle Vue and now as Claife Station, the building was described in a sale advertisement in the Carlisle Pacquet in September 1800 as 'from a design of Alderman Carr's of York'. The building is not mentioned in West's third guide

of 1789 but is in the eighth edition of 1802. It was probably built around 1794 when Claife Heights was enclosed and the site bought by Braithwaite. The building was subsequently enlarged with two rectangular wings and is now ruinous.

It is tempting to suggest that Hawkshead Market Hall, which was built in 1790 and has characteristic rounded-headed first-floor windows in recessed arches, was designed by Carr on Braithwaite's prompting. Braithwaite certainly contributed to its cost.

York Minster Library, MSS Add. 328/1, fol. 13, 328/2, fol. 18
Thomas West, *Guide to the Lakes*, 3rd edn, 1789; 8th edn, 1802
John Martin Robinson, *A Guide to the Country Houses of the North-West* (London, 1991), 159
Howard Colvin, *Biographical Dictionary of British Architects* (New Haven and London), 1995, 225

The Assembly Rooms, Norwood, Beverley, Yorkshire
(ER/Humberside) (Fig. 98)
New Assembly Rooms, 1761–63
Demolished, *c*.1938

The original Beverley Assembly Rooms in North Bar Street were replaced with a 'commodious edifice' built by subscription in Norwood, a broad suburban street. Building work began in May 1761 and was completed in March 1763. The ground cost £210, the building £790 6s 10d, the lustres or chandeliers (bought from Mr Broadley) £144 15s 6d and furniture £120. Carr was paid 10 guineas for his plans and the builder was William Middleton.

The new assembly room was a relatively simple building in brick with a central, two-storey, three-bay block with a broken-based pediment, flanked by single-bay wings with round-headed windows in relieving arches. The ballroom was 50 ft by 27 ft with six Ionic pillars on each of the side walls and an orchestra gallery over the entrance. The card room to the left was 20 ft by 30 ft and the tea room on

98 Beverley Assembly Rooms

the right 25 ft by 18 ft. Beverley Public Library holds two views taken before demolition.

East Riding of Yorkshire Record Office, DDBC/21/95, 99
George Poulson, *Beverlac* (London, 1829), 447

Lairgate Hall, Beverley, Yorkshire (ER/Humberside) (Fig. 99)
Sir James Pennyman, Bt, MP
Attributed
Alterations, *c.* 1773

99 *above* Lairgate Hall, dining room

Thomas Pennyman bought Lairgate Hall in 1753 and had remodelled it by 1765 when it was acquired by Sir James Pennyman. In about 1773 the house was enlarged to the west by a dining and drawing room, both with canted bays. At the same time the staircase hall was redecorated. Dining and drawing rooms both have finely carved marble chimneypieces and doorways with framed, carved and cross-banded mahogany doors. The ceiling of the dining room duplicates one by Carr for the great dining room at Thirsk Hall of 1771 and its doors have Greek fret borders, a motif Carr repeated at Wiganthorpe and elsewhere. This, and the fact that Pennyman almost certainly employed Carr at Ormesby Hall in 1772, suggests the alterations were by Carr.

John Carr of York, Architect 1723-1807, Catalogue of the Ferens Art Gallery (Hull, 1973), 8
Victoria County History, *York: East Riding* (Oxford, 1989), VI, 187
BE/ER/303

St John the Evangelist's Church, Bierley North, Yorkshire (WR/WY) (Fig. 100)
Dr Richard Richardson
New church, 1766
Altered, 1828

100 *below* St John the Evangelist's Church, Bierley

101 *above* Billing Hal, entrance front

102 *below* Billing Hall, staircase

A compact, aisleless church, three bays deep, with round-headed windows in shallow relieving arches, emphatic pediment over the entrance façade and a small cupola. The interior, which includes a handsome Doric entrance screen, is largely intact and was almost identical to that of Carr's Farnley Chapel. The church was enlarged in 1828 when the Tuscan porch was added.

W. Hiles, *History of the Parish of St John, Bierley* (1925), 19, from information supplied by a former vicar, Revd C. W. N. Hyne
W. Cudworth, *History of Bolton and Bowling* (1891), 266
Derek Linstrum, *West Yorkshire Architects and Architecture* (London, 1978), 189, pl. 144
BE/WR/136

Billing Hall, Great Billing, Northamptonshire
(Figs 101, 102)
Lord John Cavendish MP
House remodelled, *c.* 1776
Demolished, *c.* 1935/1956

Cavendish, uncle of the 5th Duke of Devonshire, was Chancellor of the Exchequer during the short-lived Rockingham and Coalition administrations. He bought Billing in 1776 from the O'Brien family and shortly afterwards 'completely transformed it from the Jacobean mansion that it was into the solid block it now is'. On first appearance the house, nine bays wide with a central three-bay pediment and two and a half storeys high, with a

CATALOGUE

115

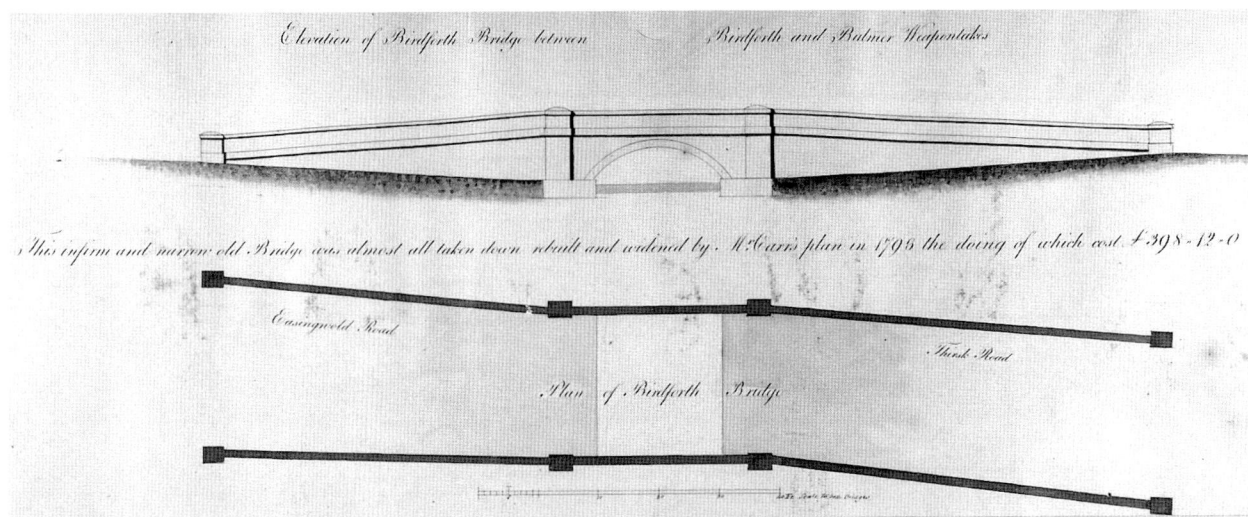

103 Drawing of Birdforth bridge

double plat band below the first-floor windows and single plat band above, seemed a new Georgian construction. Baker, who ascribes the design to Carr, describes it as a new building on a site close to the old house. However, the slightly uncomfortable proportions, irregularities in the plan and the survival of a Jacobean window on the first floor landing shows that Carr thoroughly remodelled an existing house. The building was Georgianized inside and out and given an elegant imperial staircase approached through a Doric colonnade.

After Cavendish's death in 1796 the house was sold to Robert Cary Elwes who made alterations to Hakewill's designs in 1819–20. Further changes were made in 1909 when evidence of the original Jacobean house was uncovered. Part of the house was demolished about 1935, the rest in 1956. The spire of the church fell down in 1759, after which much of the body of the church had to be rebuilt, as well as the upper part of the tower. As the church parapets include sixteenth-century balustrading from the pre-1776 mansion this work may have been carried out by Carr.

G. Baker, *History of Northamptonshire* (London, 1822–30), I, 22
Victoria County History, *Northamptonshire* (1937), IV, 69
BE/Nhants/349–50

Birdforth Bridge, Yorkshire (NR/NY) (Fig. 103)
North Riding magistrates
New bridge, 1795
Demolished 1971

The infirm and narrow old bridge over Birdforth Beck on the York-Stockton road was almost all taken down, rebuilt and widened to Carr's plan at a cost of £398 12s. The span was 20 ft.

North Yorkshire County Record Office, Book of Bridges, 1772–1803, 13

Blyth Hall, Blyth, Nottinghamshire (Fig. 59)
William Mellish
Alterations, possibly including gate piers, stables, bridge, and village housing, 1773–76
House demolished 1972

Mellish, Receiver General of Customs, was a close friend of Carr who frequently stayed in his house in Albermarle Street, London. Carr extended the original 1680s house, *The Beauties of England* reporting that 'the additions and alterations have been so considerable, that we may say it has been rebuilt on the site of the ancient hall, and is now of considerable magnitude'. The description includes 'a most elegant' drawing room with a circular bow and a chimneypiece 'of extreme elegance' with Ionic pillars of Egyptian granite fluted with stripes of white marble and supporting a frieze with a tablet bearing an ancient sacrifice in bas-relief.

Carr and Mellish's accounts in Gosling's Bank record regular payments throughout the 1770s. In February 1769 Carr was paid £60; in January 1770, £42; in December 1770, £42; in June 1773, £82 2s; in February 1774, £21; in January 1775, £42; in April 1777, £21; in August 1779, £112 8s; in August 1780, £20; in November 1782, £10 10s; and in May 1784, £69. This suggests Carr's work extended beyond the house. It probably included the 'extensive pile of stabling' Mellish built, although this is unusual among his stable designs in its use of Diocletian windows. The entrance gate, with elegant urns on the piers and handsome iron gates, was characteristically Carr and particularly fine. A keen improver, Mellish greatly increased the size of the estate. He built the elegant bridge over the River Ryton in 1770. This is probably by Carr and resembles his bridge in the park at Norton Place. Mellish also built several farm houses, the Gothic rectory, almshouses and over thirty cottages with Gothic window casements.

Barclays Bank Archives, Goslings Bank, ledger 42/89, 44/272, 44/274, 49/192, 51/147, 53/210, 55/179, 63/172, 63/174, 67/154, 71/149
J. Hodgson and F. C. Laird, *Beauties of England and Wales* (London, 1813), XII, i, 319
F. C. Laird, *A Topographical and Historical Description of the County of Nottingham* (London, 1820), 319–20
John Raine, *The History and Antiquities of the Parish of Blyth* (London, 1860), 80, 84
BE/Notts/479

Bolling Hall, Bradford, Yorkshire (WR/WY) (Fig. 104)
Capt. Charles Wood, RN
Alterations, 1777–79

Wood, a younger son who married Caroline, daughter and co-heiress of Thomas Barker of Otley, inherited the Bolling estate on the death of his 78-year-old second cousin Thomas Pigot in 1770. He soon set about improving the medieval and seventeenth-century house, remodelling the interior and adding the east wing with a canted bay. This makes no attempt to fit stylistically with the earlier structures. One of the ceilings is modelled on plate six of Richardson's *Book of Ceilings* of 1776.

Work was clearly well in hand by October 1777 when the beams for the first floor and roof were being prepared. It was supervised by Mr Rodwell, apparently the estate steward, and the chief contractor was Mr Harrison. By March 1779 the ironwork on the staircase had been completed and in London Francis Wood was looking out for grates and for carpets from Mr Dyson for the drawing room, the room above it, the fore-bedroom and the dining room. Building work was not without its difficulties and in the same month Carr promised to send a 'clever man' to sort out problems caused by the 'idleness and stupidity of those employed at present'. By September the alterations were largely complete and Carr had sent 'his man' over to measure up. By then Wood was again at sea. He never saw the completed building as he died of wounds sustained off Madras in October 1780. He was succeeded by his 7-year-old son. The house has been a museum since 1915.

Borthwick Institute, York, Wood Papers, A.2.2.3, A.2.4.1, A2.6
BE/WR/132, 620

Bridge over the Ure, Boroughbridge, Yorkshire (WR/NY) (Fig. 79)
North and West Riding magistrates
Widened, 1785
Reconstructed 1969

104 Bolling Hall, ceiling

Responsibility for maintaining the bridge over the River Ure, with spans of 50 ft and 60 ft, was shared between the North and West Ridings. In 1785 the bridge was widened, half of it to Carr's plan and directions, at a cost of £420. On the other half, widened under the direction of the West Riding surveyor, the foundations gave way.

North Yorkshire County Record Office, Book of Bridges, 1772–1803, 12
BE/WR/118

Bow Bridge, Rievaulx, Yorkshire (NR/NY) (Fig. 105)
North Riding Magistrates
New bridge, 1789

A new bridge with a 45 ft span was built across the River Rye at a cost of £218 14s 8d. The builder was T. Peacock.

North Yorkshire County Record Office, Book of Bridges, 1772–1803, 18

105 Drawing of Bow bridge

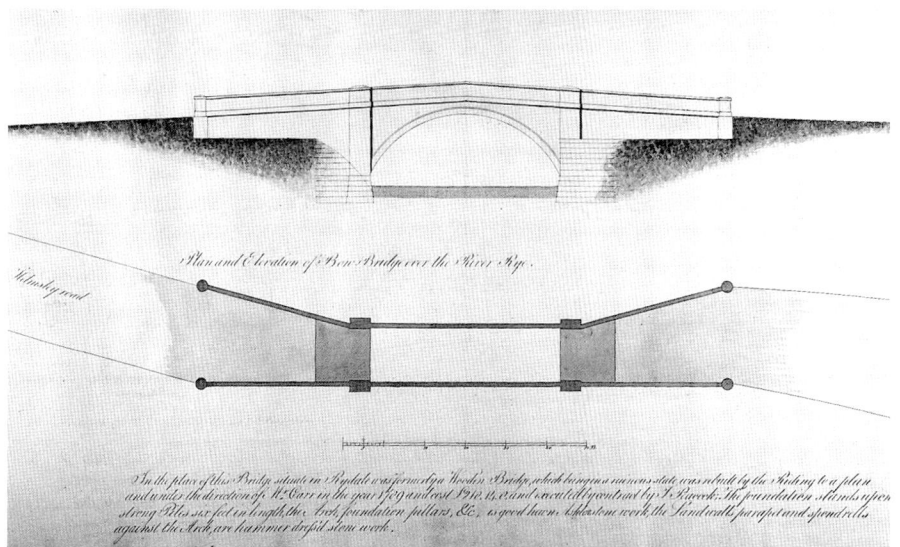

106 St Andrew's Church, Boynton

St Andrew's Church, Boynton, Yorkshire
(ER/Humberside) (Fig. 106)
Sir George Strickland
Attributed
Rebuilding except for tower, 1767–76

A faculty for rebuilding the old, dilapidated parish church was granted in 1767. Churchwardens' accounts record payments to workmen between 18 May 1768 and 21 November 1776. Although there is no reference to Carr in these or in craftsmen's accounts belonging to members of the family, Carr was probably responsible for the design, which would have been commissioned, and presumably paid for, by Strickland, for whom he also worked on Boynton Hall. The general builder was Joseph Armitage; the mason William Ellis; the joiner and carpenter William Scott; and the plasterer William Greenhough. The National Monuments Record holds copies of a contemporary coloured plan, section and south elevation preserved by the church.

The medieval tower was retained and the body of the church rebuilt on the old foundations with a very simple brick exterior with arched windows and a charming Gothic interior. The full length of the chancel was retained but the altar was brought forward to its west end where it was set between columns and pilasters, with the east end occupied by the family pew. The inspiration for this arrangement may have been the similar plan of Andrea Palladio's San Giorgio Maggiore in Venice. The interior was altered in 1910.

Borthwick Institute, York, R.IV.F. 1767/2b; information from Dr Terry Friedman

East Riding of Yorkshire County Record Office, PE143/11; information from Dr Terry Friedman

A. R. Duffy, 'Boynton Church', *Archaeological Journal*, 105 (1948), 85

Arthur Oswald, 'Boynton Hall, Yorkshire', *Country Life*, 22 July 1954

Francis Johnson, 'Boynton Hall and Church', *Transactions of the Georgian Society for East Yorkshire*, 4.i (1955), 27–30

R. B. Wragg, 'John Carr: Gothic Revivalist', in *Studies in Architectural History*, ed. by W. A. Singleton (London and York, 1956), II, 18

BE/ER/333

107 Boynton Hall, north front

Boynton Hall, Boynton, Yorkshire (ER/Humberside)
(Fig. 107)
Sir George Strickland, Bt
Alterations, 1765–80

Drawings for a grand Palladian mansion, almost certainly by Carr, show that as a young man Strickland had ideas of building a new house on a new site at Boynton. Instead he modernized the Tudor house, which Lord Burlington had improved. The recessed centre of the north front was filled in with a canted bay and screens of Doric columns were introduced in the hall. He also added the service wing. There are unsigned drawings for most of this work carried out between 1765 and 1780, probably by Carr, who was paid 17 guineas on 21 September 1767. Carr may have been responsible for the Carnaby Temple and the bridge over Gypsey Race. Strickland also built a large woollen manufacry employing 250 people in the 1760s.

Arthur Oswald, 'Boynton Hall, Yorkshire', *Country Life*, 22, 29 July 1954
Francis Johnson, 'Boynton Hall and Church', *Transactions of the Georgian*
Society for East Yorkshire, 4.i (1955), 27–30
Drawing by John Carr for the service wing, formerly owned by Francis Johnson
BE/ER/334–36

Bramham Park, Bramham-cum-Oglethorpe,
Yorkshire (WR/WY) (Fig. 108)
2nd Lord Bingley
Obelisk, *c.* 1763–73

The obelisk, which is topped by an urn, is mentioned as being by Carr in the travel diary of Elizabeth Chivers. It was built to commemorate Lord Bingley's son who died in 1763 and so was presumably built before Bingley's own death in 1773.

Chivers, cited by H. M. Colvin, *Biographical Dictionary of British Architects* (New Haven and London, 1995), 226
BE/WR/142

Bretton Hall, West Bretton, Yorkshire (WR/WY)
(Fig. 109)
Col. T. R. Beaumont
Alterations, 1793, and designs for garden temples

Bretton passed on the death of Sir Thomas Wentworth in 1792 to his illegitimate daughter Diana and her husband Colonel Beaumont. According to Derek Linstrum, improvements began almost immediately. Designs by Carr for pilasters in the dining room are dated October 1793. Both the dining room and the library, which he also suggests was designed by Carr, have elaborate plasterwork. The dining room walls were decorated with grisaille medallions and the capitals were to be cast by Mr Waterworth of Doncaster. Carr may also have been responsible for the chimneypieces in some of the bedrooms, which are characteristic of his designs. That in the portico bedroom has a carved relief of the fable of the bear and the bees also found at Wiganthorpe Hall. However, Dr Wright argues that Carr had no involvement in the interiors of Bretton Hall. Designs by Carr also

108 Bramham obelisk

109 Bretton Hall

survive for a large Gothic 'Bella Vista' and a composite 'Temple of Virtue and Honour'.

Bretton Hall, Allendale Papers, BEA/C2/MPD 17/15 and 17A
Derek Linstrum, *West Yorkshire Architects and Architecture* (London, 1978), 79
S. J. Wright, 'A History of the Architecture of Bretton Hall, near Wakefield', *Yorkshire Archaeological Journal*, 72 (2000), 156–57
BE/WR/146

Burton Constable Hall, Burton Constable, Yorkshire (ER/Humberside)
William Constable
Unexecuted design for alterations, 1760

Carr was one of several architects who submitted schemes for remodelling the great hall. Carr's was the boldest, suggesting a giant Corinthian order under a high coved ceiling, but it was rejected as too costly. Lightoler's cheaper version was preferred. Carr may also have surveyed the house as a twentieth-century letter refers to a drawing by Carr of the first floor. This is now lost. Carr also produced two drawings for candlesticks (Fig. 52). These are not known to have been executed.

Burton Constable, drawing dated 1760
Christopher Hussey, *English Country Houses, Early Georgian 1715–60* (London, 1955), 225, fig. 405

Busby Hall, Little Busby, Yorkshire (NR/NY) (Fig. 40)
Jane Turner
Unexecuted design for alterations, c. 1757

Carr proposed a major remodelling of Busby Hall for Jane Turner, widow of Cholmley Turner of Kirkleatham who died in 1757. She was the daughter of George Marwood of Little Busby and when her nephew Charles Turner inherited the Kirkleatham estate she moved back to Busby Hall, which she commissioned Carr to improve. Six drawings survive, one signed by Carr, two of them surveys of the old house. The existing structure was to be retained with one corner filled in to create a more impressive elevation and two staircases replaced with a single imperial staircase. An elegant new façade of seven bays and two storeys would have been created, with a three-bay pediment with a Rococo cartouche and a parapet with balusters over the windows. The proposed office wing was surprisingly architectural with a central hen house with a broken-based pediment flanked by laundry and brewhouse behind blind arches.

Carr's design was not accepted. It was presumably felt to be too extravagant. Instead two further drawings, clearly part of a contract, show that Turner used Robert Corney, a carpenter and joiner, who was employed at Kirkleatham Hospital from 1741 and built Kirkleatham church to Carr's designs, both for the Turner family. Corney's designs, only 57 ft wide as opposed to 73 ft, were less ambitious than those by Carr, but retained the idea of an imperial staircase. Jane Turner died in 1764.

North Yorkshire County Record Office, Marwood of Busby
    Papers, ZDU Roll 4
BE/NR/104

Buttercrambe, Yorkshire (NR/NY)
North Riding magistrates
Unexecuted designs for a new bridge, n.d.

Carr's design was not executed. The present bridge of 1840 is to another design.

North Yorkshire County Record Office, Book of Bridges,
    1772–1803

Buxton, Derbyshire (Figs 69, 70)
5th Duke of Devonshire

The Crescent, alterations to the Hall and Baths, 1780–90; two small bridges over River Wye, 1780; New St Ann's Well (dem.), 1780–82; Great Stables and Coach Houses, 1786–90; alterations to the Eagle Inn, 1787; small house, two lodgings, four small stables, 1788–90; small house, Smith's shop and Tap House, 1789

In 1778 a correspondent of Thomas Grimston of Kilnwick reported 'Great alterations at Buxton under the direction of your countryman Carr — The whole Plan is upon a very large scale … said to be in the Estimate of £120,000 and upwards'. The Duke of Devonshire had decided to turn the remote Peakland village into a centre of civility worthy of the metropolis and was to invest over £60,000 in improvements from about 1777 to 1790. Carr's initial scheme for new baths adjacent to the Old Hall at Buxton survives at the Sir John Soane Museum in a copy of John Wood's designs for the Hot Bath at Bath, published in 1777. This would have had a central circular bath with three baths opening off it behind a pair of Ionic colonnades but was rejected in favour of a Crescent and Great Stables.

Building began in earnest in 1780. The new St Ann's Well was completed in 1783. Two years later the semi-circular form of the Crescent, over 300 ft in outer diameter, was described as emerging from the 'Fog, Noise and Confusion' by Lady Newdigate. The carcase was completed by March 1785 when Thomas Waterworth was paid the balance of his bill for carving the ducal arms in the façade. Some of the lodging houses were ready for occupation in 1786 and the Assembly Rooms fitted out in 1787.

The Crescent (Fig. 69), a semi-circular structure with a ground-floor colonnade and Doric pilasters, encompassed a variety of different uses, despite its uniform appearance. These included lodging houses, a house for the duke and two hotels, one with an elegant 76 ft-long assembly room with columned, apsed ends and elaborate plasterwork (Fig. 70). The complex range of uses led to an equally complex plan and the Crescent has three storeys to the front and four to the rear. The plasterwork was by James Henderson of York, carving by Thomas Waterworth, and the two fine marble chimneypieces in the assembly room were supplied by Mails of London at a cost of £163 12s 10d.

The building came in for much contemporary comment. One writer described it as 'a pile that will ever claim the admiration of all amateurs of Grecian architecture'. In 1784, Faujas de Saint Foud, the inveterate traveller, noting that Carr had planned and superintended the construction of the 'superb edifice', reported delightedly that the 'able artist' himself had personally conducted him round the works and noted accommodation for two hundred guests with their servants. Carr's pride in the design is clear from Beechey's portrait, in which his hand rests on a plan of the Crescent.

According to Jewett the 'New Stables … are considered as so completely suited to the purpose for which they are intended, as not to be exceeded by any in Europe, and will remain a lasting monument of the munificence of the founder and the ingenuity of the architect.' They provided accommodation for 300 horses, with 'a range of commodious apartments' above and an adjacent coach house for seventy carriages. The octagonal plan enclosed a circular courtyard, whose perimeter was colonnaded to provide a covered ride. Stables and coach house were finished early in 1790 at a cost of £16,290 19s 7½d. Some of the tradesmen and suppliers — Sykes and Marriott the joiners, Rigge the slater, Moxon the timber merchant — were old associates of Carr. The brickmaker, Onesiphorus Beet, had not previously worked for the architect.

The stables subsequently became a hospital and were roofed with a great dome in 1878.

Chatsworth House, Devonshire Archives, Buxton Building
    Accounts, C38
East Riding of Yorkshire Record Office, Grimston Papers,
    DDGR/42/28

Sir John Soane's Museum, John Wood, *The Description of the Hot-Bath at Bath* (London, 1777), additional interleaved drawing

Alexander Hunter, *The Buxton Manual* (York, 1797)

Richard Warner, *A Tour through Northern Counties of England* (Bath, 1802), 157–58

R. B. Wragg, 'A Bath on the Peak', *Country Life*, 6 July 1978

Ivan Hall, *Georgian Buxton* (Chapel-en-le-Frith, 1984)

Ivan Hall, 'Buxton, The Crescent', *Georgian Group Journal*, 2 (1992), 40–55

BE/Derbs/113–14

Byram Hall, Knottingley, Yorkshire (WR/WY) (Fig. 110)

Sir John Ramsden, Bt

Extensive alterations and stables, *c.* 1762, and possibly *c.* 1770

Demolished 1930s and 1955

As Huddersfield boomed in the second half of the eighteenth century, thanks to the growth of the wool textile industry, the Ramsdens' rental soared and they decided to remodel Byram Hall, a sprawling sixteenth-century house extensively altered in the seventeenth century. The A.P.S.D. and Davies record Carr working at Byram for Sir John Ramsden, Bt and the eighteenth-century elevations fit his style but it is not certain what he did when. Building was in hand in 1762 when John Coe informed Bacon Frank that he had sought an estimate for work at Campsall from 'the man who is building for Sir John Ramsden', implying that he was working for Carr. It has also been suggested, without firm evidence, that Carr worked for Ramsden's son, also Sir John, 4th baronet, who succeeded in 1769. It is possible that, as frequently happened elsewhere, he was employed by father and son. The 4th baronet's sister married another patron of Carr, William Weddell of Newby.

Carr unified the disparate styles of the house under an austere classical dress but the result was ungainly and comparison of photographs with Samuel Buck's sketch of about 1720 shows that the original fabric was simply reclad. The entrance front was of three storeys with curiously paired windows and two-storey projecting wings. The fifteen-bay west wing was of two storeys with a pair of canted bays in the centre. Adam was employed to make internal alterations in about 1780, his finest room being the library. Carr also designed the surviving stables, which were similar to those at Castle Howard and was probably responsible for the handsome Home Farm. The Orangery and lodges have also been attributed to him but this is unlikely and the surviving lodge would be more plausibly attributed to Adam. The stables and farm survive.

Sheffield Archives, B.F.M. 1314/74

Wyatt Papworth (ed.), *The Dictionary of Architecture issued by the Architectural Publications Society* (London, 1877), II, 36

R. Davies, 'A Memoir of John Carr', *Yorkshire Archaeological Journal*, 4 (1877), 205

John Martin Robinson, *Georgian Model Farms* (Oxford, 1983), 120

David Pickersgill, *A History of Byram Hall and its Park* (1996)

Edward Waterson and Peter Meadows, *Lost Houses of the West Riding* (Welburn, 1998), 22, figs

BE/WR/153, 621

110 Byram Hall stables

CATALOGUE

111 *left* Campsall
Hall, east elevation
112 *below* Campsall
Hall, drawing room
doorcase

Calder Abbey, St Bridget Beckermet, Cumberland
(Cumbria)

Joseph Tiffin Senhouse

Unexecuted design for a new house, 1785

A ground plan for Calder Abbey dated July 1785 and
signed by Carr survives in the Jackson Library. This
proposed a substantial house, with a central hall, flanking
drawing and dining rooms with canted bays, imperial
staircase and an office range behind, which was never
executed. A truncated front was added with two reception
rooms at first-floor level. It is not certain whether this
work was carried out by Carr.

Jackson Library, Carlisle, drawing; information from John
    Borron and Sir Howard Colvin

Campsall Hall, Norton, Yorkshire (WR/SY)
(Figs 111–13)

Bacon Frank

House remodelled, entrance gates, designs for garden
buildings, 1762–70

House, demolished 1983

Campsall had been the seat of the Frank family from the
early seventeenth century. In 1752 Richard Frank
(1698–1762) obtained designs from John Watson and
James Paine for Campsall which were never executed. His
nephew Bacon Frank employed Carr to remodel Campsall
in 1762-64, with extensive demolition and new build,
doubling the length of the east elevation and adding

113 Campsall Hall lodge

canted bays to the projecting wings on south elevation. The result was an austere house of three storeys. Letters refer to designs for the drawing room, dining room, study, staircase and servants' hall. The staircase was similar to that at Stapleton Hall, which Frank admired, and Marmaduke Wyvill called to examine the dining room as a model for his own at Constable Burton. A letter from Carr of 1770 referring to joiners' work shows that work continued after 1764. The doorcases of the south-east room, probably the drawing room, were particularly elegant.

Barnsdale Lodge of 1784 is a large Gothic summerhouse, for which there is a plan initialled JC and an elevation signed William Lindley, delineavit. The attractive gate lodge with its central urn, characteristic of Carr, survives on the edge of a housing estate. A portfolio of drawings with a Campsall provenance in the RIBA includes designs for additions and alterations to Campsall Hall, together with a design for a garden temple and a design for 'The rough Arch at the Head of the River', both signed JC. Other drawings in the collection attributed to Carr include a design for a three-storey tower, designs for gates and a design for five cottages at Knottingley New Hall. These last may be identified with a much battered barn at New Hall on the Pontefract–Knottingley road.

Sheffield Archives, BFM 1314/60,67,74; 1315/2; 1316/1,6,22,26; 1317/11; 1319/2; 1325/61,73; 1326/44
British Architectural Library, AF 10/1–12
Four drawings in the possession of Mr John Goodchild
Buckinghamshire Record Office, Drake Papers, D/DR/4/15 and 19
Edward Waterson and Peter Meadows, *Lost Houses of the West Riding* (Welburn, 1998), 64, figs
BE/WR/156

Campsmount Hall, Norton, Yorkshire (WR/SY)
(Fig. 5)
Thomas Yarborough
New house, 1751–56, and farm buildings, n.d.
House demolished except for a few outbuildings in 1959; farm buildings partly demolished 1962 and 1973

Yarborough considered building a new house from 1728, acquiring designs from John Howgill of York that year and from Henry Flitcroft in about 1742. On 8 January 1751 John Carr was paid £5 5s for 'making a Design of Plans and Elevations of a house proposed to be built at Campsall by Thomas Yarborough', together with £3 3s for four journeys. In December James Paine was paid for making a sketch of a plan for a house and offices and two journeys but his proposal was not accepted.

Robert Carr provided an estimate to 'Erect and finish a house and Offices' for £4,707 9s 4d, and in January 1752 signed a 'Memorandum of an agreement' with Yarborough. The house, on a new site, was occupied in February 1756. It was a plain design of five bays and two and a half storeys with three-bay, two-storey wings. Many of the interior furnishings were provided by Edward Elwick of Wakefield.

John Carr also appears to have been responsible for the substantial farm buildings built to an essentially Classical design though with Gothic details. Undated designs by Carr for the farm buildings and for a bridge survive in the Yarborough papers.

T. Connor, 'The Building of Campsmount', *Yorkshire Archaeological Journal*, 47 (1975), 121–32
Edward Waterson and Peter Meadows, *Lost Houses of the West Riding* (Welburn, 1998), 65, figs.

Cannon Hall, Cawthorne, Yorkshire (WR/SY)
(Fig. 114)
John Spencer
Alterations, 1764–67
Walter Spencer-Stanhope
Alterations, and possibly also a windmill, kennels and the stables, *c.* 1778–86; possibly a porter's lodge, north lodge and a Gothic folly, 1789; extra storey added to wings 1790–94; new wing, 1804

Cannon Hall was a late seventeenth-century house owned by the Spencers, prosperous ironmasters. John Spencer employed Richard Woods to landscape the park and Carr to add simple three-bay, two-storey wings to the house. The first reference to Carr in Spencer's diary is for 5 May 1764: 'at home all day, busy with Mr Carr the architect in setting a plan for wings for my house'. He received plans and elevations on 17 July and on 2 January Carr visited to agree prices with the mason, John Marsden. Carr attended the site six more times in 1765 and on 2 and 3 January 1766 presented his bill for superintending and planning the building. Work had clearly not been progressing smoothly as Carr blamed Marsden for not pushing things forward and it was agreed that the library, bedchamber and dressing room should be finished by 1 June.

The library floor was being laid in October 1766. In May 1767 Spencer was writing to Carr about the chimneypiece in the drawing room and in September was discussing the frieze and finishing of the dining room. Edward Elwick of Wakefield was closely involved in fitting up the interior, although some of the furniture came from London where Carr escorted Spencer round leading furniture makers, including Cobb and Chippendale, to discuss furniture for the drawing room. Joinery work was by Mr Tweedale, the fine stucco ceiling of the dining room was by James Henderson who first visited in September 1766 and Maurice Tobin was also involved.

114 Cannon Hall

After John Spencer's death in 1775 Carr was brought back by his nephew, Walter Spencer-Stanhope. The work included major alterations in the old part of the house, including the creation of a pillared entrance hall, and the addition a new kitchen, whose foundations were laid in 1778. Carr often dined at Cannon Hall. He provided a plan for raising the wings one story in 1790. The work was completed in 1794. A further wing was added by Carr in 1804.

Sheffield Archives, Spencer-Stanhope Archives, 60633, 60584 and papers cited by Geoffrey Beard, *Craftsmen and Interior Decoration in England 1660–1820* (London, 1986), 219–20
A. M. W. Stirling, *Annals of a Yorkshire House* (London, 1911), I, 146–48; II, 116–18, 314–15
Ruth Simpson, 'Walter Spencer-Stanhope, Landlord, Business Entrepreneur and Member of Parliament of the 18th century' (BA thesis, University of Nottingham, 1959); cited by Geoffrey Beard in *Georgian Craftsman* (London, 1966), 94–95
BE/WR/156

Carlton Ferry Bridge, Carlton, Yorkshire (WR/NY)
New bridge, 1774

Although Carr had ceased to be the West Riding's Surveyor of Bridges in 1773 he designed a stone bridge at Carlton Ferry near Snaith in 1774. The designs could be seen at his office in York, where tenders could also be left.

York Courant, 8 November 1774

Castle Howard, Henderskelfe, Yorkshire (NR/NY)
(Fig. 115)
5th Earl of Carlisle
Stables, designed 1771, executed *c.* 1774–81

Vanbrugh's stable wing was never built, nor was Sir Thomas Robinson's proposed quadrangle with corner towers of 1755. The 5th Earl of Carlisle commissioned a design by Sir William Chambers in 1770 and orders were

115 Castle Howard stables

given to lay the foundations in 1771, but the project was suddenly abandoned for reasons of economy. Instead Carlisle informed George Selwyn that he had 'made Mr Car of York give him a plan for stables of a very different kind of expense from that of Mr Chambers'. Carr's stables were 'going on as fast as any Building in that place can do' in October 1778, but were not completed until October 1781. In 1784 Robert and Ralph Campleman presented their account for 'all the masonry of the New Stables, sheds against the garden walls, getting all the stone at the quarrys and other masonry executed at Castle Howard'. This totalled over £3,000. Though not the largest of Carr's stables they are perhaps the most elegant.

Castle Howard Muniments, Masonry A/C 1774–82, stewards correspondence J 14/18/12 and 16
British Museum, Add. MSS 41133, fol. 38
J. H. Jesse (ed.), *George Selwyn and his Contemporaries* (London, 1843–44), III, 7
H. Avray Tipping, 'Castle Howard, Yorkshire', *Country Life*, 25 June 1927
R. B. Wragg, 'Stables Worthy of Stately Homes', *Country Life*, 1 November 1962
John Harris, *Sir William Chambers* (London, 1970), 200
BE/NR/114

Catterick Bridge, Catterick, Yorkshire (NR/NY)
North Riding magistrates
Bridge widened, 1792

The bridge over the River Swale on the Great North Road was widened by 16 ft at a cost of £2,980. The bridge has two spans of 35 ft and two of 60 ft.

North Yorkshire County Record Office, Book of Bridges, 1772–1803, 22
BE/NR/120

Chapelthorpe, Sandal Magna, Yorkshire (WR/SY)
(Fig. 116)
New chapel, 1771
Attributed
Demolished, 1951

A petition was submitted to rebuild the ruinous chapel on 18 June 1771. The estimate for rebuilding was £1,194 and the trustees were Sir Lionel Pilkington and Thomas Beaumont. The building was destroyed by fire in 1951 but is recorded by a drawing in Leeds University Library. The design follows a typical Carr pattern, close to that by Carr for Farnley Chapel, classically disciplined but with pointed arch windows, as at St Helen's, Denton.

116 Chapelthorpe

Borthwick Institute, York, R. IV. F1771/2a; information from
Dr Terry Friedman
Leeds University Library, Special Collection, 'Churches of the
Diocese of Ripon', III, fol. 37
Yorkshire Archaeological Journal, 17 (1903), 61
Terry Friedman, *Church Architecture in Leeds 1700–1799*, Thoresby
Society, 2nd ser., 7 (1997), 123

Chatsworth House, Derbyshire

5th Duke of Devonshire
Repair and redecoration, *c.* 1774–84

The 5th duke inherited as a minor in 1764 and married in
1774. That year he appointed James Wyatt as his surveyor,
although in practice it was Carr who received most of the
major commissions. Carr had worked with the duke's
grandfather, the Earl of Burlington, in the late 1740s and
had been regularly employed at Welbeck Abbey, seat of
his brother-in-law, the Duke of Portland. He was
concurrently employed by the Duke at Buxton and
Hardwick and by the Duke's uncles at Holker Hall,
Lancashire, and Billing Hall, Northamptonshire.

Work had begun by the mid-1770s and eventually more
than £10,000 was spent on repairs and redecoration. Carr
was involved in repairs, including those to the chapel
paintings, but his most extensive work was to the private
apartments where work was shared with the Frenchmen
Guillaume Gaubert and Francois Hervé. Carr was
responsible for the structural alterations and some, but not
all, of the decoration of the chimneypieces, doorcases and
window openings. The Frenchmen were responsible for
most of the furniture but Carr designed pier tables and
mirrors. Confusion over the split responsibility led to
arbitration in 1783.

Carr retained a watching brief at Chatsworth. In 1799,
for instance, he examined the decayed state of the
chimneys and suggested how they should be repaired, and
also looked at the state of the deer fence near the kitchen
garden.

Carr's carved overdoors were dismantled during the 6th
duke's remodelling of the private apartments in the 1830s
and put in store, where they remain. Carr's marble and
granite chimneypiece, executed by Richard Maile, was also
removed.

Chatsworth House, Devonshire Archives, Furniture and
Furnishings: A Book of Accounts copied from vouchers
found at Devonshire House; letter dated 20 August 1799 from
John Carr to John Heaton
Ivan Hall, 'A Neoclassical Episode at Chatsworth', *Burlington
Magazine*, June 1980, 400–14

Town Hall, Chesterfield, Derbyshire (Fig. 117)

3rd Duke of Portland
New building, 1787–88
Demolished, *c.* 1860

117 Chesterfield Town Hall

The new town hall, described as a 'neat town house', was
paid for by the Duke of Portland, Carr's client at Welbeck,
who owned considerable property in Chesterfield. It was
built in the north-west corner of the Market Place at the
junction of High Street and Gluman Gate, a position
comparable in importance to that of Newark Town Hall,
but no attempt was made at similar architectural effect.
The town hall was a plain, rectangular stone building, hip-
roofed, with entrance on the short side and, in most
respects, a copy of the Northallerton Courthouse. Hall
notes that the town hall was built 'under the direction of
Mr Carr' and this is confirmed by the A.P.S.D. and
Davies.

The plan, though possibly on a more limited scale,
follows the pattern of Northallerton with accommodation
on the ground floor 'for the reception of debtors' and
gaolers' apartments. The upper floor had a small room for
the magistrates and a large room for the sessions.

Gentleman's Magazine (1819), pt ii, 498
George Hall, *History of Chesterfield* (Chesterfield, 1823) (extended
by Ford Thomas (London, 1839)) 185, 289
Wyatt Papworth (ed.), *The Dictionary of Architecture issued by the
Architectural Publications Society* (London, 1877), II, 36
R. Davies, 'A Memoir of John Carr', *Yorkshire Archaeological
Journal*, 4 (1877), 205

118 *above* Chesters, entrance front | 119 *below* Clifton Hall, south elevation

Chesters, Nr Humshaugh, Northumberland (Figs 42, 118)

John Errington
New house, 1771

Among the sketches in Carr's copy of Morris's *Select Architecture* in the Sir John Soane Museum is one inscribed 'Designed for — Errington, Esqr'. This was John Errington (d. 1783), who presumably wanted a more modern house to replace his nearby family seat Walwick Grange, an extended peel tower. Tomlinson states that the new house was built in 1771. It was greatly extended and almost entirely remodelled internally by Norman Shaw in about 1894, but a survey drawing and the largely unaltered façade shows that the house must have been designed by Carr.

Finely set on rising ground with an extensive view, Carr's house was two and a half storeys high and built of stone. The entrance flanked by a pair of canted bays led to a narrow hall passage with stairs at the far end and a dining room and drawing room on either side. At the rear of the house were a pair of office pavilions set in yards, one for the kitchen, the other the laundry.

Sir John Soane's Museum, Roger Morris, *Select Architecture* (London, 1955), drawing opposite pl. 5
J. Hodgson and F. C. Laird, *The Beauties of England and Wales* (London, 1813), I, 135
William Tomlinson, *Comprehensive Guide to the County of Northumberland* (London, 1889), 185
R. B. Wragg, 'Chesters', *Archaeologia Aeliana*, 4th ser., 36 (1958), 221–26
BE/Northd/224

120 *above* Clifton House | 121 *below* Clifton House, plan of ground floor

Clifton Hall, North Clifton, Nottinghamshire

(Fig. 119)
Sir Gervase Clifton, Bt
Alterations and additions, *c.* 1778–90

Clifton began to modernize the large Tudor house at
Clifton but broke off when his wife died suddenly in 1779.
As a result Throsby, writing in 1790, commented that
rebuilding had been going on for more than twelve years
and was not yet finished. Carr regularized the old house,
levelling the gables and adding a square block of offices to
the north. He also rebuilt the square block to the south,
with its deep bow window, and fronted the link block
which connected the two with a Doric colonnade. The
lofty octagonal entrance was built *c.* 1750 and is not by
Carr. Bray particularly noted that Lady Clifton's dressing
room opened into a greenhouse (similar in design to the
arcade on the Knavesmire grandstand at York). An
impressive cubic gazebo, now ruinous, with Venetian
windows set in relieving arches and framed by niches may
have been by Carr.

William Bray, *A Tour into Derbyshire and Yorkshire*, 2nd edn
   (London, 1783), 358
Robert Thoroton, *History of Nottinghamshire*, ed. John Throsby
   (Nottingham, 1790), I, 113
Christopher Hussey, *Country Life*, 25 August 1923, citing
   accounts
BE/Notts/270–72

Clifton House, Rotherham, Yorkshire (WR/SY)

(Figs 120, 121)
Joshua Walker
New house, 1783–4
Attributed

Walker was the second son of the great ironmaster Samuel
Walker, who died in 1782. Clifton House must have been
built almost immediately after his death as the company
minute book noted in 1783 that 'Mr Joshua Walker nearly
completed his new house, stables, etc at Clifton'. The
house has a datestone of 1783 over the back door and
John Platt began laying the staircase and hall floors in June
1784.

   Like Eastwood House, designed for Walker's brother
Joseph, Clifton House fits firmly within Carr's manner and
can be compared most directly with Middleton Lodge. Its
attribution to Carr is reinforced by the statement by
Guest, who seems to have had access to the now-lost
Walker papers, that two out of the three new Walker

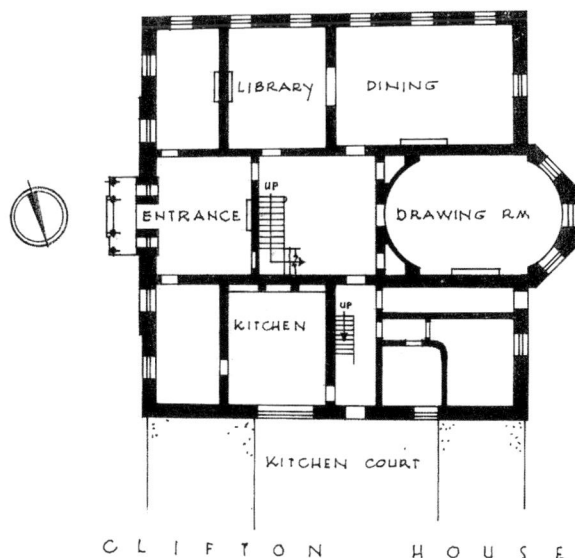

houses, Clifton, Eastwood and Ferham, were designed by Carr. Ferham is known to have been built by John Platt.

Clifton House was a villa, not a country house, although its grounds extended to nearly 70 acres. Sited about half a mile outside Rotherham in an elevated position overlooking the Doncaster road, the house was planned primarily for the prospect. The main rooms face north and east to take advantage of the excellent views while the entrance hall and service wing are orientated west and south. The two-storey stone house is elegant, five bays by six bays with an attached office wing. The entrance front has a three-bay pediment, a central Venetian window and a Doric porch. The interiors are richly decorated with plain ceilings apart from central paterae and handsome doorcases and chimneypieces. Clifton House has been a museum since 1893.

John Guest, *Historic Notices of Rotherham* (1879), 485–502, 681
A. H. John (ed.), *The Walker Family. Minutes Relating to Messrs Samuel Walker & Co., Rotherham, Iron Founders and Steel Refiners 1741–1829*, The Council for the Preservation of Business Archives (1951), 21
R. B. Wragg, 'The Houses of Clifton and Eastwood, Rotherham', *York Georgian Society Report*, 1978, 57–65, plan
BE/WR/421

Clints Hall, Clints, Yorkshire (NR/NY)
Charles Turner MP
Alterations, 1762–63
Demolished, *c.* 1845

Clints Hall, a compact late sixteenth- or early seventeenth-century battlemented house, was left by Charles Bathurst to his three sisters on his death in 1740. One of these was Jane, wife of William Turner, and in 1761 their son Charles, who had already been living at Clints for some time, purchased the estate outright. He employed Carr to make alterations but sold the house to Viscount Downe in 1767, concentrating his attention instead on Kirkleatham. It is not clear how extensive Carr's alterations were but he could have added the three-bay wing to the south shown by Angus.

North Yorkshire County Record Office, Kirkleatham account book beginning 1761, ZK 6565
James Raine, *Marske* (Newcastle, 1860), 75–78
William Angus, *Seats of the Nobility and Gentry* (London, 1787), pl. XXIV
Edward Waterson and Peter Meadows, *Lost Houses of York and the North Riding* (Welburn, 1998), 10–11, figs.

Colwick Hall, Nottingham, Nottinghamshire
(Figs 122, 123)
John Musters
Remodelled house, new stables and kennels, 1774–76

John Musters, who succeeded his father in 1770 and came of age in 1774, married an heiress in 1776 and served as High Sheriff of Nottinghamshire in 1777. He must have set about remodelling Colwick Hall, on the outskirts of Nottingham, almost immediately as the rainwater heads are dated 1776. Musters was one of the chief subscribers to Carr's grandstand of 1777.

The original early-eighteenth-century two-storey house was roughly square with projecting wings on the north, entrance front. Carr left this front unaltered, adding only a balustrade, a screen of Corinthian columns linking the wings and a covered colonnade to the front door. The south front was transformed by the addition of an elegant attached Ionic portico and lower wings housing the ballroom and dining room. The interior is very fine. The library, with a columned screen at each end and fine plasterwork and panelling, takes up most of the old south front. The ballroom in the west wing leads off it and has apsed ends with screens of Corinthian columns, good plasterwork and a plain ceiling. The main stairs form an imperial staircase and open off the entrance hall, which has more handsome plasterwork and panelling.

Musters, who kept a famous pack of hounds, also built new stables, a long, low, single-storey building with a central, two-storey, three-bay pavilion, together with kennels, which were about a quarter of a mile from the house. These were described in 1814 as 'a well designed and indeed elegant, dog kennel'. House, stables and kennels were all built by Samuel Stretton. In 1777 Musters had himself and his wife painted by Stubbs in front of house and stables in a pair of portraits. The house is now a restaurant for the adjacent racecourse.

Robert Thoroton, *History of Nottinghamshire*, ed. by John Throsby (Nottingham, 1790), III, 8
E. W. Brayley and John Britton, *The Beauties of England and Wales* (London, 1813), 12.i, 210
James Dugdale, *The New British Traveller* (London, 1819), IV, 18
The Stretton Manuscripts, ed. by G. C. Robertson (Nottingham, 1910), ii
George Stubbs 1724–1806, Catalogue of the Tate Gallery Exhibition (London, 1984), 157–59, figs 116–17
BE/Notts/251–52

Compton Place, Eastbourne, Sussex
Lord George Cavendish, MP
Unexecuted plans for alterations, *c.* 1781

Lord George Cavendish married Elizabeth, only daughter and heiress of the 7th Earl of Northampton, in February 1782, and through her acquired Compton Place, which had been remodelled by Colen Campbell in 1726–27. Cavendish employed first Wyatt and then Carr to propose extensive alterations to Compton Place, for which four drawings by Carr survive at Chatsworth. One drawing is endorsed 'Carrs Plan from Wyatts' and shows that Carr was following a scheme by Wyatt, which is dated 1781. The other is inscribed 'Mr. Carrs second Plan with our

122 *above* Colwick Hall, south elevation | 123 *below* Colwick Hall, library

alterations inclosed'. Wyatt and Carr's plans were referred to in Repton's Red Book of 1802 but not carried out and instead Compton Place was extensively altered by Jacob Harvey in 1806–08.

Both schemes are principally concerned with the offices and stables, although they include minor alterations to the house. Large office ranges would have been added at one end of the house and equal to it in scale. These would have included new kitchen, steward's and housekeeper's rooms and servants' hall, as well as other outbuildings such as brewhouse and laundry. New stables, similar to those at Raby Castle, were proposed.

Chatsworth House, Devonshire Archives, unreferenced drawings in box marked 'Compton Place Maps and Plans'; information from Richard Hewlings

Cold Coniston Bridge, Yorkshire (WR/NY)
West Riding magistrates
Bridge rebuilt, 1763

The three span bridge over the River Aire on the Skipton–Kendal road was rebuilt in 1763.

West Yorkshire Archive Service, Wakefield, Book of Bridges 1752–1770

Constable Burton Hall, Constable Burton, Yorkshire (NR/NY) (Fig. 23)
Sir Marmaduke Wyvill, Bt
New house, 1762–68

Wyvill succeeded his uncle in 1754 and died in 1774. He replaced the earlier Elizabethan house with a compact villa with a portico-in-antis and a central staircase lit by lunettes. Although the external staircase is inspired by Lord Burlington's Chiswick House the entablature of the portico was at the cutting edge of neo-Classicism in its bold elimination of the architrave, as at Robert Adam's Compton Verney, Warwickshire, of 1761. Wyvill visited Bacon Frank's dining room at Campsall Hall so that 'he might form some notion how to finish his own'. Kitchens and offices were in the rustic, with the family rooms on the first floor, the main rooms facing south and the entrance on the west front. Stables and kitchen court were tucked informally and asymmetrically into the hillside on the north, leaving the house isolated, like Palladio's Villa Capra at Vicenza.

In 1809 Joseph Farington was told by Lord Muncaster — who had the story from Sir Marmaduke's successor Revd Christopher Wyvill — that Wyvill commissioned Carr to modernize the house and then left for extensive travels in Scotland. On his return five months later he discovered that instead of part of the house being pulled down to enable alterations the entire house had been demolished. According to Farington it cost Wyvill £10,000 to build a new house. The story is uncorroborated and no records of the building survive beyond the references in *Vitruvius Britannicus*.

Foal Park Farm, a Gothic design quarter of a mile north-east of the hall, may have been designed by Carr.

Sheffield Archives, BFM 1317/11
James Woolfe and John Gandon, *Vitruvius Britannicus* (London, 1771), v, pls. 36–37
The Farington Diary, ed. James Greig (London 1809), v, 168, 21 May
Marcus Binney, 'Constable Burton, Yorkshire', *Country Life*, 28 November 1968
Curius Crow [Christopher Hussey], 'John Carr's Plan of Constable Burton', *Country Life*, 19 December 1968
John Martin Robinson, *Georgian Model Farms* (Oxford, 1983), 122
BE/NR/124

Coolattin House (later Malton House), Nr Shillelagh, Co. Wicklow, Republic of Ireland (Figs 76, 77)
2nd Marquis of Rockingham
Advice and drawings for alterations to the old house, 1776
4th Earl Fitzwilliam
Advice and drawings for alterations to the old house, 1789–96; new house, 1799–1807

Coolattin was the Rockingham/Fitzwilliam estate house in Ireland, not far from Dublin. It was described in 1775 by John Scott as ill-constructed and built. A drawing of the house by Scott dated August 1776 includes a stable sketched in pencil with notes apparently by Carr. It is not clear if his suggestions were executed.

In 1796 Carr wrote to Fitzwilliam severely criticizing plans for a new house by John Lascelles and suggesting alterations to the structure and elevations. The same month he commented to Benjamin Hall, steward at Wentworth Woodhouse, that 'I have made two setts of plans for the house at Malton in Ireland'. Carr had not visited the site. £613 was spent in the year 1796/7 and £1,336 the following year, but the house was destroyed by fire during the 1798 rebellion leaving only the kitchen.

Carr provided plans for the replacement, which retained the old kitchen. Accounts and correspondence show the ageing Carr held a firm grip on building operations. He produced all the detail drawings and instructions until his death in 1807, using first John Lascelles and then Thomas Hobson (sent from Wentworth Woodhouse) as superintendent. He was paid £400 for his work on 12 January 1807. There is no evidence that he ever visited Ireland.

The house is a simple, square, two-storey, five-bay structure with a central pediment and projecting bays in the centre of the side elevations. The interiors are satisfyingly simple, following the contemporary trend towards an increasing plainness of detail. His instructions and drawings, for example, specified black slab marble for many of the chimneypieces and the omission of bed

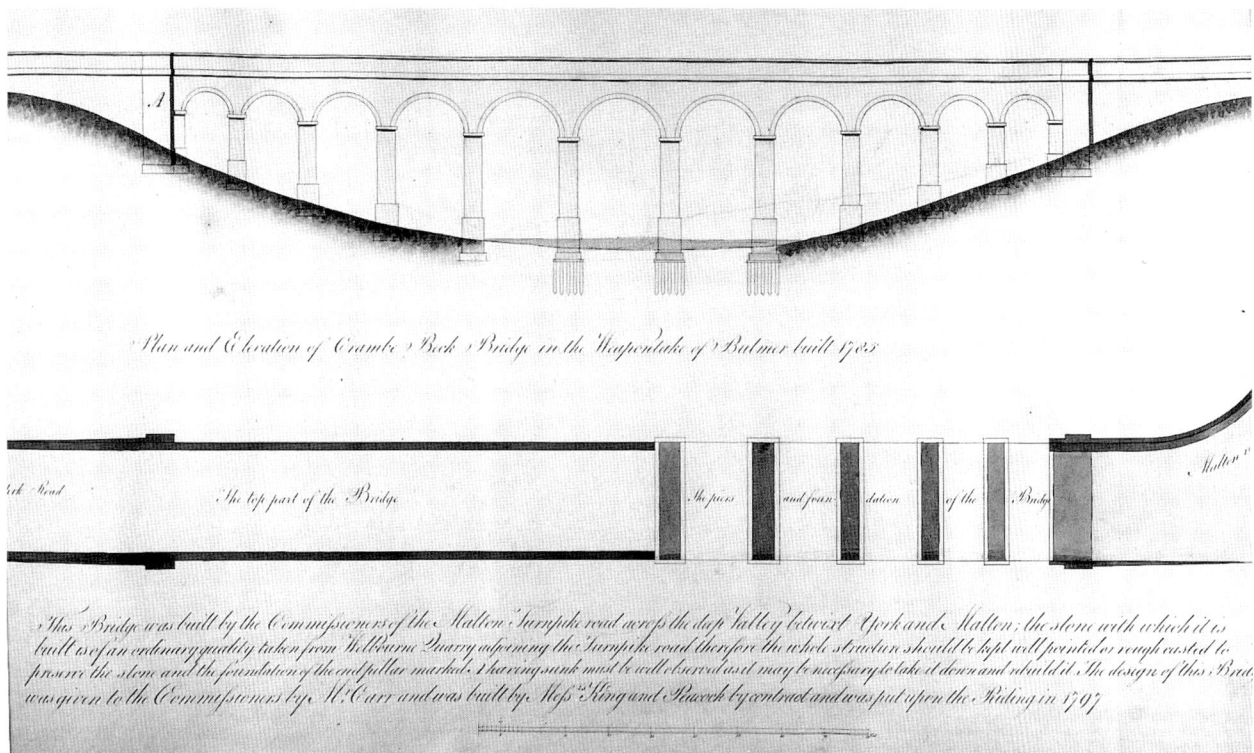

The drawing contains handwritten script:

Plan and Elevation of Crambe Beck Bridge in the Wapentake of Bulmer built 1785

York Road   *The top part of the Bridge*   *The piers and foundation of the Bridge*   *Malton*

This Bridge was built by the Commissioners of the Malton Turnpike road across the deep Valley betwixt York and Malton; the stone with which it is built is of an ordinary quality taken from Welburne Quarry adjoining the Turnpike road therefore the whole structure should be kept well pointed or rough casted to preserve the stone and the foundation of the end pillar marked A having sunk must be well observed as it may be necessary to take it down and rebuild it. The design of this Bridge was given to the Commissioners by M.r Carr and was built by Mess.rs King and Peacock by contract and was put upon the Riding in 1797

124 Drawing of Crambeck bridge

moulds and cornices, which in earlier days would have been unthinkable.

National Library, Dublin, MSS 6012–25, Coolattin Account
    Books,
Coollattin Estate Office, papers, including rough drawings
Sheffield City Library, Wentworth Woodhouse Papers, WWM,
    MP 30 (d), 32, 33; account book of the 4th Earl Fitzwilliam
Northampton County Record Office, (Milton) MSS, miscell.
    vols, No. 778
Irish Architectural Archive Accession 89/28
Information from Dr Edward McParland

Courteenhall, Northamptonshire (Fig. 39)
Sir William Wake, Bt, MP
Stables, after 1766
Attributed

Courteenhall was a small country house used principally as a hunting box when the impressive stable block was built. Sir William Wake's main seat was Waltham Abbey in Essex. It was not until 1791 that Samuel Saxon built the large present house. Although no contemporary records survive the stables fit closely with Carr's distinctive manner, particularly in the use of the pavilion turrets and round-headed windows.

    As the stables are not shown on a survey of 1766 they must have been built after Sir William inherited in that year. Wake had strong Yorkshire connections, his mother was Sarah Walker of Weston and his wife Mary, whom he married in 1765, was the daughter and heiress of Richard Fenton of Bank Top.

    The stables have been converted to a house.

Giles Worsley, 'Carr at Courteenhall', *Country Life*, 30 October
    1986

Crambeck Bridge, Welburn, Yorkshire (NR/NY)
(Fig. 124)
North Riding magistrates
New bridge, 1785
Subsequently widened on the north

The eleven-arch bridge over the Crambeck on the York-Malton road, the Malton turnpike, was rebuilt by King and Peacock.

North Yorkshire County Record Office, Book of Bridges, 1772–
    1803, 27
Drawing by Carr of Crambeck Bridge, formerly at Boynton Hall,
    in the possession of Malcolm McKie

Croft Bridge, Yorkshire (NR/NY) (Fig. 125)
North Riding magistrates
Bridge widened, 1795

The seven-arch bridge over the River Tees was widened by 15 ft at a cost of £3,577.

North Yorkshire County Record Office, Book of Bridges,
    1772–1803, 28

CATALOGUE

133

Dalton Hall, Yorkshire (ER/Humberside)
Sir Beaumont Hotham, Bt
Unexecuted design for a new house, 1769

Carr, Thomas Atkinson and William Middleton were all
asked to prepare schemes for a new house. Atkinson's
design was accepted. Charles Hotham's younger brother
Beaumont, intimate friend and legal adviser to the 3rd
Duke of Portland, would have had knowledge of Carr
through his work at Welbeck Abbey, Nottinghamshire.

East Riding of Yorkshire Record Office, Hotham Papers,
    DDHO/4/27, DDHO/13/5
A. M. W. Stirling, *The Hothams* (London, 1918), I, 309–10

Danby Wiske Bridge, Yorkshire (NR/NY) (Fig. 126)
North Riding magistrates
New bridge, 1782

Responsibility for 'the former and bad built bridge' was
taken on by the North Riding in 1780 and it was rebuilt
to Carr's plan and directions in 1782.

North Yorkshire County Record Office, Book of Bridges,
    1772–1803, 7

125 *left* Croft bridge
126 *below* Drawing of Danby Wiske bridge

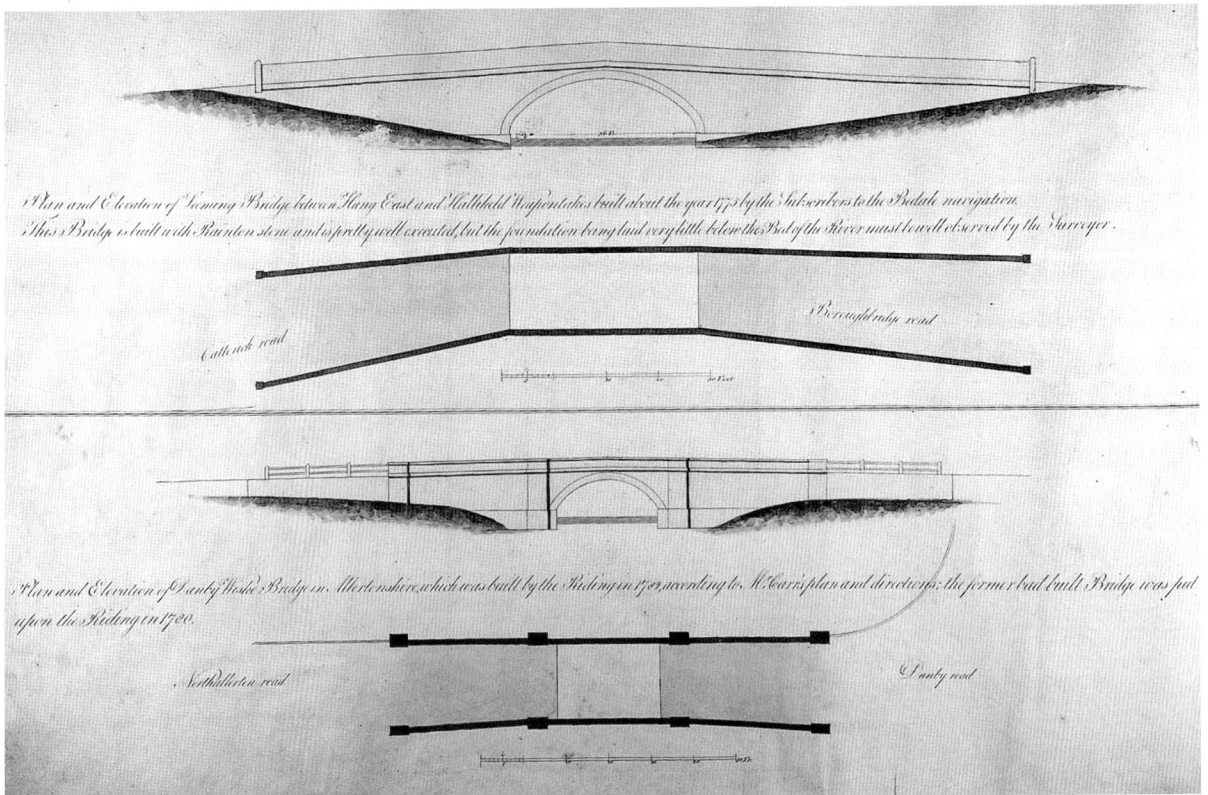

Deepdale Bridge, Startforth, Yorkshire (NR/County Durham)
North Riding magistrates
Bridge widened, 1781

The 40 ft span bridge over Deepdale Beck, otherwise known as Balder bridge, on the Barnard Castle-Alston Road was widened by T. Parkin.

North Yorkshire County Record Office, Book of Bridges, 1772–1803, 31

St Helen's Church, Denton, Yorkshire (WR/NY)
(Fig. 127)
Sir James Ibbetson, Bt
New church, 1776
Attributed

The old Fairfax chapel at Denton was demolished at the same time as the house in 1772 and a new chapel built, at a convenient distance, which opened on 14 July 1776. No documentation survives but the three-bay Gothic building with pointed windows and a tower fits stylistically with Carr's work and it is assumed that he was commissioned by Sir James Ibbetson for whom he was currently rebuilding Denton Park. The west porch is a later addition.

West Yorkshire Archives Service, Leeds, Parish Records 11, curate's notes; information from Dr Terry Friedman
Leeds University Library, Special Collections, *Churches of the Diocese of Ripon*, III, fol. 4; information from Dr Terry Friedman
Thomas Whitaker, *Loidis and Elmete* (Leeds, 1816), 196
BE/WR/178

Denton Park, Denton, Yorkshire (WR/NY) (Figs 50, 51, 128–31)
Sir James Ibbetson, Bt
New house, stables, lodges and possibly church,
c. 1772–78

Denton, the ancient home of the Fairfax family, was bought by James Ibbetson, a wealthy Leeds clothier, in 1735, who rebuilt the house on a modest scale. On his death in 1739 the estate passed to his eldest son Samuel, at whose death in 1768 it passed to his nephew Sir James Ibbetson. In the same year Ibbetson married Jenny Caygill, the sole heiress of John Caygill, a Halifax merchant of 'immense fortune'.

Ibbetson's trustees had sold off the family business, which he had inherited at the age of fifteen on his father's death. One of his first acts on coming of age was to rebuild the 1730s house at Denton, claiming that it was in a 'ruinous condition', on a handsome scale and on a site with extensive views across Wharfedale. According to Richardson the house was erected in 1778. However, this was probably the date of completion as Mr John

127 St Helen's Church, Denton

Goodchild has several pages of accounts with tradesmens' details totalling £9,459 11*s* 7*d*, unsigned and undated but from 1772. A further £10,541 18*s* 7*d* was spent on furniture.

'Mr Carr Architect' was paid £630, but the most expensive bill was that of the (unnamed) mason, £2,105 18*s* 2¼*d*, with Robinson, 'stonegetter', receiving £728 2*s* 9*d*. The joiner, Newland, was paid £1,407; the plasterer, Rothwell, £837 15*s*; the carpenter, Bradley, £338 17*s* 8*d*; the painters, Boynton and Kemp, £235 16*s* 10*d* (Yeoman, also a painter, received £38 18*s*); the bricklayer, Dodgson, £229 1*s* 8*d* (with Sutcliffe, also a bricklayer, paid £76 3*s* 5*d*); the carver, Mr Wade, £112 16*s* 10*d*; the slater, Cowell, £29 11*s* 2*d* (and Cowell junior, also a slater, £45 0*s* 2¼*d*). Camm was paid £33 for the best staircase rails. Wilfred Skirrow was paid £350 for lime; William Rigg £187 3*s* for slate; Jonathan Cawood £276 for nails; Maude £410 14*s* for timber; Summers £246 2*s* for lead; Dixon and Moxon £237 10*s* for timber; Thomas Dodgson £173 14*s* 3*d* for iron; Clay £64 for lead; Robert Rhodes £20 10*s* 9*d* for marble chimneypieces; Fenton £19 8*s* 3*d* for skylights. The unidentified brickmakers were paid £658 4*s* 9*d*.

According to Richardson, Denton Park was one of Carr's favourite works. The nine-bay house, which has no rustic, is unusually long and low for Carr and can be compared with Colwick Hall, Nottinghamshire. The

128 *above* Denton Hall, north elevation | 129 *below* Denton Hall, plan of ground floor

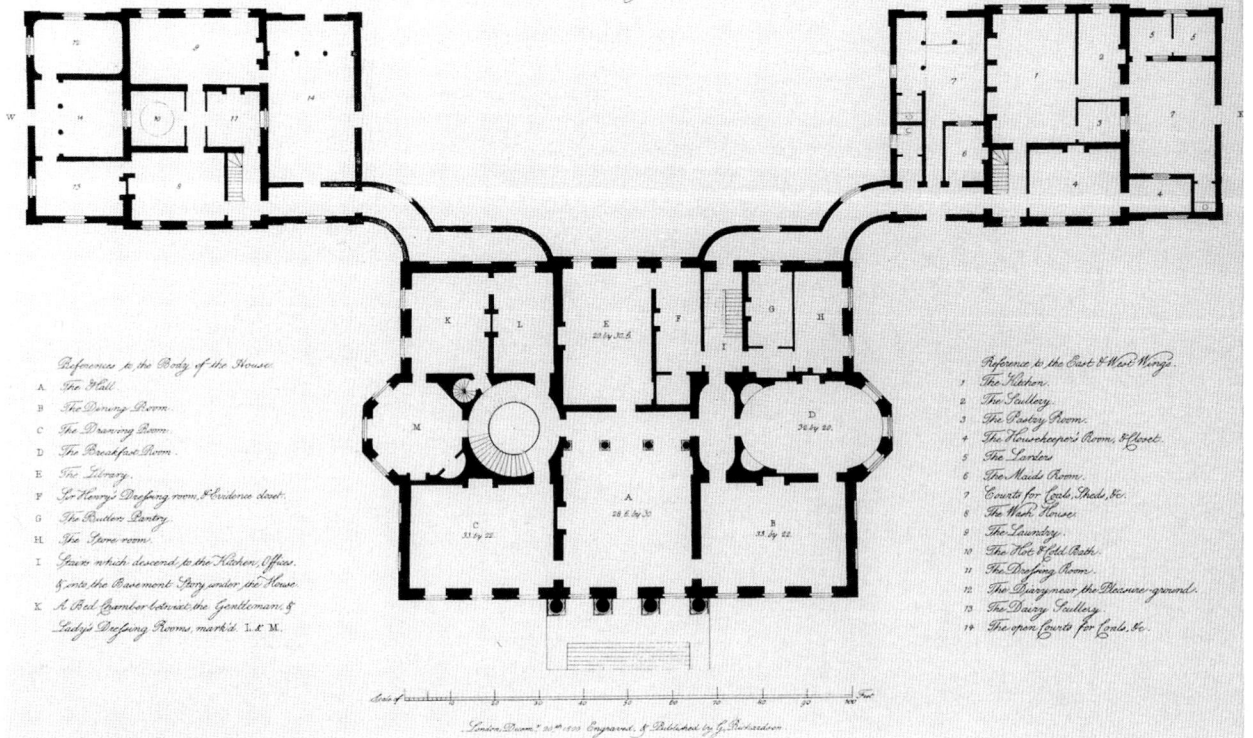

Principal Story of Denton Hall, in Yorkshire, the Seat of Sir Henry Ibbetson Bart.

John Carr, of York, Architect.

References to the Body of the House

A. The Hall
B. The Dining Room
C. The Drawing Room
D. The Breakfast Room
E. The Library
F. Sir Henry's Dressing room, & Evidence closet.
G. The Butlers Pantry
H. The Store-room
I. Stairs which descend to the Kitchen, Offices
   & into the Basement Story under the House.
K. A Bed Chamber betwixt the Gentleman's &
   Lady's Dressing Rooms, mark'd L & M.

Reference to the East & West Wings.

1. The Kitchen
2. The Scullery
3. The Pastry Room
4. The Housekeeper's Room, & Closet.
5. The Larders
6. The Maids Room
7. Courts for Coals, Sheds, &c.
8. The Wash House.
9. The Laundry.
10. The Hot & Cold Bath.
11. The Dressing Room.
12. The Dairy near the Pleasure-ground.
13. The Dairy Scullery
14. The open Courts for Coals, &c.

London Decem.r 25.th 1800 Engraved, & Published by G. Richardson

CATALOGUE

entrance front, which differs in minor details from the house as engraved, is richly detailed with an attached Ionic portico, balustrade and window surrounds. The north front is much plainer with round-headed windows on the ground floor. The two side elevations have double-height canted bays and the house is flanked by a pair of service wings linked by an underground passage. One contained the kitchens, the other dairy, laundry, wash house and hot and cold bath.

The planning is particularly sophisticated. The master suite of bedroom and two dressing rooms is on the ground floor with the circular staircase tucked in beside it. Next to it is the library with adjacent Evidence Closet (with its own entrance and strong room), where Sir Henry would have done his business. The plasterwork, particularly in the front hall, drawing room and staircase, is richly elaborate. That in the staircase dome recalls the work at the York Law Courts. White Allom made alterations in the 1930s. The house is now offices.

Original accounts, plan and elevation in the possession of Mr John Goodchild; information from Dr Richard Wilson

George Richardson, *New Vitruvius Britannicus* (London, 1802), I, pls 54–56

John Preston Neale, *Views of the Seats of Noblemen and Gentlemen* (London, 1822), v, pls. 34, 35

T. D. Whitaker, *Loidis and Elmete*, (Leeds, 1816), II, 196

Christopher Hussey, 'Denton Hall, Yorkshire', *Country Life*, 4 November 1939

R. G. Wilson, 'Merchants of Land: The Ibbetsons of Leeds and Denton 1650–1850', *Northern History*, 24 (1988), 85, 87, 92

BE/WR/178

All Saints Church, Dewsbury, Yorkshire (WR/WY)
(Fig. 132)
Rebuilding of tower and aisles, 1764–68

By 1764 the steeple — 'a very antient fabrick' — and the medieval aisle walls of All Saints were so decayed that services were no longer safe. Two shillings was spent 'treating with Mr Carr for plan and overseeing the Tower' on 11 May 1764 and that year the steeple was taken down and work started on a new tower — the clerk was paid 6*d* for 'going for Mr Carr for plan & overseing the tower'. A faculty was granted on 2 December 1765 for the demolition of the old walls. The tower and outer walls of the church were rebuilt in Carr's Gothic manner with light-hearted ogee-shaped doors, one boldly placed so that it cut into one of the new windows. Carr was paid £3 10*s* 9*d* for surveying' on 28 April 1768.

Whitaker observed in 1816 that 'by a judicious forebearance which would not have been exercised now, all the inside of the church which could be preserved was allowed to stand'. Further restoration was carried out in 1823 and the chancel and transepts were added in 1887 when the south windows were altered.

130 *top* Denton Hall lodges | **131** *below* Denton Hall stables

Borthwick Institute, York, FAC 1765/2a; information from Dr Terry Friedman

West Yorkshire Archives Service, Wakefield, D9/299, Dewsbury parish Register Churchwardens Accounts 1745. April 1876; information from Dr Terry Friedman

John Greenwood, *The Early Ecclesiastical History of Dewsbury* (London, 1859), 110–12

S. J. Chadwick, *Handbook of Dewsbury* (1893), 20

R. B. Wragg, 'John Carr: Gothic Revivalist', in *Studies in Architectural History*, ed. by W. A. Singleton (London and York, 1956), II, 18–19, fig. 5

Derek Linstrum, *West Yorkshire Architects and Architecture* (London, 1978), 189, fig. 145

BE/WR/179

132 All Saints Church, Dewsbury

133 Doncaster grandstand

Doncaster Racecourse Grandstand, Doncaster, Yorkshire (WR/SY) (Fig. 133)

New stand, 1776–81
Demolished 1969

Carr received the commission for the Doncaster grandstand from the Marquis of Rockingham, Peregrine Wentworth and Childers Walbanke Childers in 1776. There was no competition from other architects and the design surpassed that at York in size and elegance. John Platt's journal for 6 January 1777 notes 'Gave an Estimate for building a Stand on Doncaster Horse Course, after a Design of Mr Carr, but Theakston ye Carver, & Beardsall of Bawtry, Estimated the lowest & of course they got it.' The cost came to £2,637 and Carr was paid £105 for plans for the Grand Stand on 22 October 1781. It was engraved by W. Sheardon in 1811.

Rotherham Central Library, Archives, Microfilm 101/F, vol. 1, transcription by Mary Didham *c.* 1907–10 of 'John Platt's Journies and his other transactions in Business, f. 59'; information from Dr Terry Friedman
Edward Miller, *The History and Antiquities of Doncaster* (Doncaster, 1804), 158
J. Tomlinson, *Order Books of Doncaster Corporation* (Doncaster, 1887), 207–08, 245
Tessa Gibson, 'The Designs for the Knavesmire Grandstand, York', *Georgian Group Journal*, 8 (1998), 76–87

Durham Castle, Durham (Fig. 134)

Bishop Shute Barrington
Remodelled gateway, 1791

Harriet Clark, Carr's niece, visiting Durham in 1795 with the architect referred to 'the Bishop's palace and new Gothick Gateway into the palace yard, design'd by my Uncle'. This was the Norman gateway which was Gothicized, according to Raine, by Bishop Barrington in 1791. The work is sometimes attributed to Wyatt but is more typical of Carr. Barrington's predecessor, Bishop Egerton, for whom Carr worked at Auckland Castle, had earlier remodelled the drawing room at Durham Castle, for which Carr would be a likely architect.

York Minster Library MS Add. 328/3, fol. 29
William Hutchinson, *The History and Antiquities of the County Palatine of Durham* (Carlisle, 1787), II, 283
James Raine, *A Brief Account of Durham Cathedral* (Newcastle, 1833), 132
James Macaulay, *The Gothic Revival 1745–1845* (Glasgow and London, 1975), 141, pl. 77
BE/Dur/213, 248

Durham Cathedral, Durham

Advice, 1774

Carr's advice was sought on the condition of the cathedral whose 'ragged appearance' was considered 'a scandalous

134 Durham Castle gateway

relexion upon so opulent a body'. However, he made no reponse and instead a survey was obtained from Robert Mylne.

Hertfordshire County Record Office, AH 2263

East Row Bridge, Sandsend, Lythe, Yorkshire (NR)
NY (Fig. 135)
North Riding Magistrates
New bridge, 1777

The four-arch bridge was rebuilt by J. Peacock at a cost of £450.

North Yorkshire County Record Office, Book of Bridges, 1772–1803, 36

Eastwood House, Rotherham, Yorkshire (WR/SY)
(Figs 74, 136)
Joseph Walker
New house, 1786–87
Attributed
House demolished, c. 1920, stables demolished 1949

Walker's Ironworks were one of the great industrial enterprises of Rotherham, founded in 1741 by Samuel Walker and growing rapidly, thanks particularly to the demand for armaments, in the second half of the century. In 1762 the firm was worth £13,500, by 1797, £213,313.

Samuel Walker died in 1782 and three of his sons soon built handsome mansions, surrounded by extensive gardens and plantations, funded by the generous dividends the firm was paying, £38,500 in 1783, £31,500 in 1785.

Joseph was the second son and the firm's minute books record that he built his new house in 1786 and the offices, gardens and stables in 1787. Although the house was demolished in the 1920s measured drawings made by Thomas Salvin in 1905 survive in the Libraries, Museums and Arts Department of Rotherham Borough Council. These show that Eastwood House was a plain house with a five-bay entrance front, three-bay pediment and a canted bay on the garden elevation.

Like Clifton House, built for Walker's brother Joshua, Eastwood House fits closely with Carr's work and though firm documentation is lacking it is confidently attributed to him. Guest, who seems to have had access to the now-vanished Walker papers, mentions that two out of the three Walker houses, Clifton, Eastwood and Ferham, were designed by Carr. As Ferham is known to have been the work of John Platt, and is very unlike Carr's other buildings, this reinforces the attribution of the other two to Carr. Eastwood Farm of 1786, now demolished but formerly part of the estate and one of the largest farms in the county, may also have been designed by Carr.

John Guest, *Historic Notices of Rotherham* (Worksop, 1879), 485–89, 681
A. H. John (ed.), *Minutes Relating to Messrs. Samuel Walker & Co, Rotherham 1741–1829* (1951), 7, 19, 21–22
R. B. Wragg, 'The Houses of Clifton and Eastwood, Rotherham', *York Georgian Society Report*, 1978, 57–65

Dundas House, St Andrew's Square, Edinburgh
Sir Lawrence Dundas, Bt, MP
Unexecuted design for a house, 1768

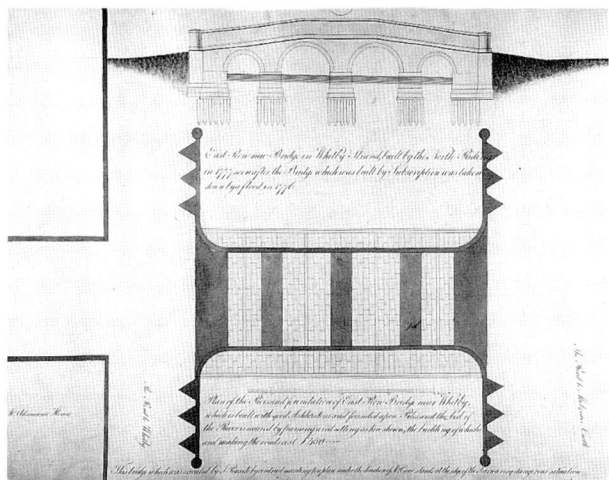

135 Drawing of East Row bridge

Eastwood House, Rotherham.

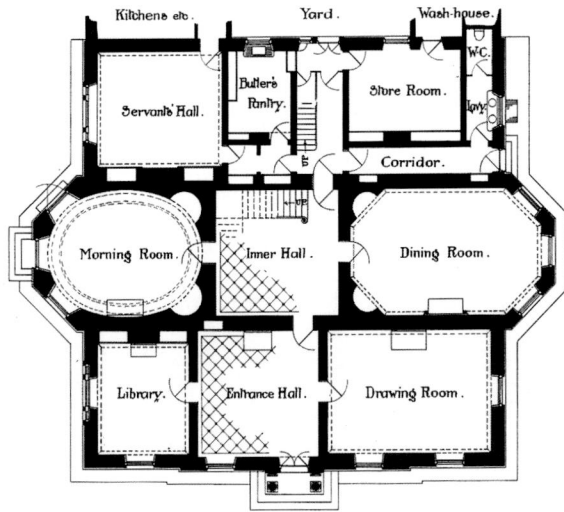

Kitchens etc. — Yard. — Wash-house.

Servants' Hall. / Butler's Pantry. / Store Room. / W.C. / Lav'y

Morning Room. / Inner Hall. / Dining Room. / Corridor.

Library. / Entrance Hall. / Drawing Room.

Ground Floor Plan.

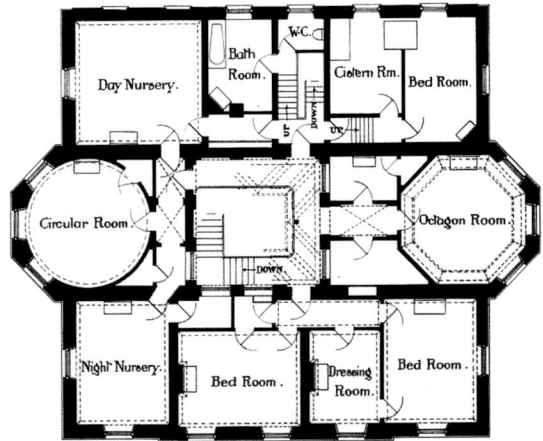

Day Nursery. / Bath Room. / W.C. / Cistern Rm. / Bed Room.

Circular Room / Octagon Room.

Night Nursery. / Bed Room. / Dressing Room. / Bed Room.

First Floor Plan.

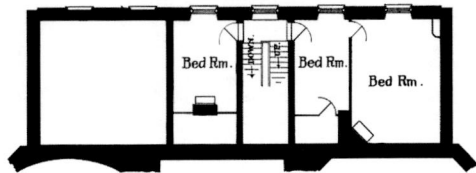

Bed Rm. / Bed Rm. / Bed Rm.

Mezzanine Floor Plan.

Scale _____ of feet.

Thomas Salvin
Mens et Delt Feb 1905.

136 Eastwood House, plan of ground and first floors and mezzanine

Carr was paid £20 for the 'Edinburgh plan' in 1768 and on visits to Edinburgh repeatedly referred to Dundas House as having been designed by him, although it was in fact built to Sir William Chambers's designs in 1771–76. Perhaps Chambers had borrowed extensively from Carr's scheme, which does not survive.

North Yorkshire County Record Office, Zetland Papers, ZNK v/4/1/13; X 1/7/65
York Minster Library, MS Add. 328/1, fol. 15
British Library, Add. MSS 41133, fol. 38
Robert Davies, 'A Memoir of John Carr', *Yorkshire Archaeological Journal*, 4 (1877), 210
John Harris, *Sir William Chambers* (London, 1970), 207–08
Giles Worsley, 'Crediting Carr', *Country Life*, 5 May 1988

Ellenthorpe Hall, Aldborough, Yorkshire (NR/NY)
(Fig. 137)
For himself
New house, n.d.

Carr bought the Ellenthorpe estate, near Boroughbridge, as an investment before 1789. It was occupied that year by Thomas Clark, who was married to Carr's niece, Ann. The house is very plain, of brick with three bays and two storeys, and could be mistaken for an ordinary farmhouse were it not for the handsome Doric porch. This is an unlikely touch for a farmhouse but characteristic of Carr, particularly of New Lodge, which Carr also designed for himself, and with which Ellenthorpe Hall can be most directly compared.

Lancashire Record Office, Parker of Browsholme Papers DDB acc. 6685, box 33, bundle 7

137 Ellenthorpe Hall

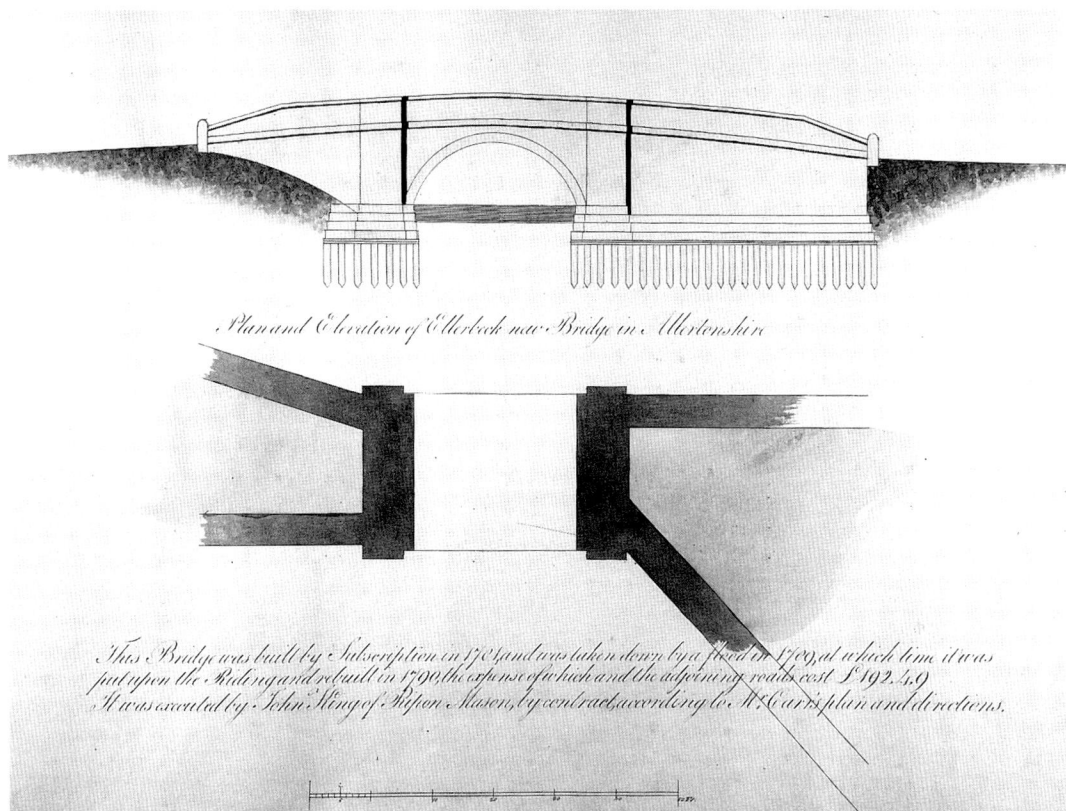

Plan and Elevation of Ellerbeck new Bridge in Allertonshire

This Bridge was built by Subscription in 170[?] and was taken down by a flood in 1780, at which time it was put upon the Riding and rebuilt in 1790, the expense of which and the adjoining roads cost £192.4.9 It was executed by John King of Ripon Mason, by contract, according to Mr Carr's plan and directions.

138 Drawing of Ellerbeck bridge

Ellerbeck, Yorkshire (NR/NY)
(Fig. 138)
North Riding Magistrates
New bridge, 1790
Demolished

The 30 ft span bridge over Cod Beck on the Thirsk–Yarm road was built by John King of Ripon at a cost of £192 4s 9d.
North Yorkshire County Record Office, Book of Bridges, 1772–1803, 41

Eller Beck Bridge, Goathland, Yorkshire (NR/NY)
North Riding Magistrates
Bridge widened, 1803

The narrow existing bad bridge on the Whitby–Pickering road, now known as Kirby Bridge, was improved and widened by 16 ft to Carr's plan and directions at a cost of £221.
North Yorkshire County Record Office, Book of Bridges 1772–1803, 13

St Helen's Church, Escrick, Yorkshire (ER/NY)
Beilby Thompson
New church, 1781–83
Demolished, 1856

The *Gentleman's Magazine* records that Thompson 'pulled down the Old church about the year 1780, and rebuilt it in a different situation, and in a very elegant manner, from a design of John Carr, of York, esq'. A faculty to rebuild Escrick church had been granted to his mother, Lady Dawes, in 1759 but was not acted upon. In 1781 Thompson's private Enclosure Act for Escrick included demolishing and replacing the church, 'an ancient Building, very much in decay and inconvenient for many of the Parishioners', and parsonage. The Act explains that the church was 'so situated as to obstruct many considerable Improvements' intended by Thompson. Thompson agreed to rebuild the church and parsonage at his own expense within three years for no less than £600.

The new church, which was placed to the north of the house, was consecrated in 1783. Allen described it in 1831 as 'a modern edifice of brick with stone quoins and dressings … at the west end is a handsome tower, with a balustrade and small pinnacles at the angles. The south side of the church has four large circular-headed windows. The east front forms a centre and wings; the former has a Venetian window and Tuscan columns and antae and is finished with a pediment. In each of the wings are

139 Escrick Park stables

square-headed doorways with attached Tuscan columns and small pediments.'

In 1856 the church was replaced by the present ambitious building by F. C. Penrose.

Gentleman's Magazine, June 1794, 528–29; information from Dr Terry Friedman

Thomas Allen, *A New and Complete History of the County of York* (1831), II, 349

J. P. G. Taylor, *Escrick: A Village History* (York, 1999), 64–68

BE/ER/409

The Rectory, Escrick, Yorkshire (ER/NY)

Beilby Thompson

New rectory, 1781–83

Attributed

Demolished, 1848

As well as remodelling Escrick Park, rebuilding much of the village of Escrick and erecting a new church, Beilby Thompson 'built a neat parsonage-house adjoining to the church'. This was a substantial building with six bedrooms, barn and stable. As the work on Escrick Park and the design of the church were by Carr it is probable that he also designed the rectory. This was replaced by F. C. Penrose's new rectory in 1848. An undated drawing of the old rectory hangs in the church at Escrick.

Gentleman's Magazine, June 1794, 528–29; information from Dr Terry Friedman

J. P. G. Taylor, *Escrick: A Village History* (York, 1999), 68–69, 102

BE/ER/409

Escrick Park, Escrick, Yorkshire (ER/NY) (Fig. 139)

Beilby Thompson

Alterations, 1763–65, 1776–79; stables, 1774–78; one, possibly more, farmhouse, 1774 and possibly village housing

Escrick Hall, a small, late-seventeenth-century house with a hipped roof, was refronted and raised to three storeys, possibly in 1758, the date of the rainwater heads bearing the initials BT. There is no evidence for the architect and as Beilby Thompson was only sixteen at the time, and his father had died eight years earlier, his mother, generally referred to as Lady Dawes following her first marriage to Sir D'Arcy Dawes, must have been responsible. Thompson came of age in 1763 and that September Carr produced a design for adding wings, for which he charged £14 14s. He returned in October to make a plan of the grounds and set out a way to the menagerie, for which he charged £5 5s. In November he made a general plan of the grounds and the courts round the house, a design for new stables, another elevation of the house and wings and a drawing for finishing the study. Carr's total bill came to £56 14s, which was settled in May 1765.

On the north side of the house a pair of canted bays was added, one containing the kitchen, the other the billiard room, along with a new imperial staircase. This was elegantly plastered and included heads of the Greek philosophers Socrates and Heraclitus, the orator Democritus and the father of medicine Hippocrates. Although two-thirds of the ceiling was destroyed in a twentieth-century flood, enough survives to give a sense of its Rococo exuberance.

The stable design was not carried out at this date and Carr returned in 1774 to fix a site. The work was not without its difficulties. In July 1775 the day book of the agent, John Nevill, records: 'These days Works above of Ellstones [John Elstone, the local bricklayer] was by pulling Down and Building up a Gain by some Mistake and Blunders he made by not Observing the Plan and Mr Carr ordered that he should Do the Alterations at his Own Expense so that will be Just as my Master pleases.' More work, including the creation of a new dining room in 1775–76 and plastering the hall ceilings in 1777–78, was also carried out at this date. The ceiling of the drawing room was probably done then and is a slightly modified version of George Richardson's *Book of Ceilings* of 1776. The house is now a school.

Starting in 1775 Thompson also removed the greater part of the village of Escrick to create a new park, for which he received a private Act of Parliament in 1781. The village was rebuilt to the north of the house and Carr could have provided designs but none of the eighteenth-century houses survive thanks to the extensive rebuilding of the village by Lord Wenlock early in the twentieth century.

Carr also designed at least one new farmhouse in 1774, and possibly others. Whinchat Hall (of 1778), Mount Pleasant and Chequer Hall date from this period.

CATALOGUE

East Riding of Yorkshire Record Office, DDFA/37/28

Diaries of Beilby Thompson for 1763, 1764 and 1774 and estate day book for 1775 in the posession of Nigel Forbes-Adam of Skipwith Hall; information from Mr J. P. G. Taylor

David Neave and Ivan Hall, 'Escrick Hall and Park', *York Georgian Society Report*, 1971, 25–33

J. P. G. Taylor, *Escrick: A Village History* (York, 1999), 50–52, 55, 58–61

BE/ER/406–08

Eskeleth, Yorkshire (NR/NY)

North Riding magistrates
Bridge improved, 1802

The 38 ft bridge over Arkle Beck on the Reeth-Barnard Castle road in Arkengarthdale was improved in 1802.

North Yorkshire County Record Office, Book of Bridges, 1772–1803, 20

St Everilda's Church, Everingham, Yorkshire
(ER/Humberside) (Fig. 140)
New church, 1763–73
Attributed

A petition was granted to replace the decaying village church of St Everilda on 14 July 1763. It was rebuilt in brick, leaving the medieval tower, with a three-bay nave and a lower, canted-bay apse. The 1773 date on the royal arms may mark the building's completion. Originally the windows were wider and set in larger blank arches, but they were replaced in the nineteenth century. The design is similar to the work of Carr, who was just completing the rebuilding of Everingham Hall for William Constable, and is plausibly attributed to him.

Henry Stapleton, *History of St Everilda's Church*
Borthwick Institute, York, FAC 1763/1a; information from Dr Terry Friedman
BE/ER/411

Everingham Hall, Everingham, Yorkshire
(ER/Humberside) (Figs 21, 141)
William Haggerston Constable
New house, 1758–64

William Haggerston was left Everingham and other estates by his great-uncle Sir Marmaduke Constable in 1746, when he took the name Constable. He inherited a Tudor house remodelled in the seventeenth century with an extensive office wing, part of which Carr retained. The new house was of brick with stone dressings, two and a half storeys high and seven bays wide with a central three-bay pediment.

An account book survives for 1757–64. Workmen were paid for pulling down the old house in January 1758 and the carcass of the new house must have been completed by 1759, the date on the one surviving downpipe. The first payment 'to Mr Carr', of £40, was paid on 16 December

140 St Everilda's Church, Everingham

1758. A year later he received £126 on account, in March 1760 a further £74 4s and in January 1762 he was paid £20 'for overlooking' and £23 19s for chimneypieces. Among the memoranda is one dated 3 November 1759 for 'Mason's work done by John Carr', £149 16s 6½d. This included stonework in the window surrounds, the chimneystacks and the Doric porch. Other workmen included Richard Bainton and James Cade, carpenters; William Taylor and Richard Bainton, joiners; Daniel Shillito, carving; Richard Swale, bricklayer; Thomas Beckwith, painter; John Carr, stonework and chimneypieces. Thomas Atkinson also received payment, perhaps for chimneypieces, in 1763. The total cost of the new house was about £3,570.

Surviving drawings show that Carr originally proposed a variation on Kirby Hall with a *piano nobile*, rustic and attic

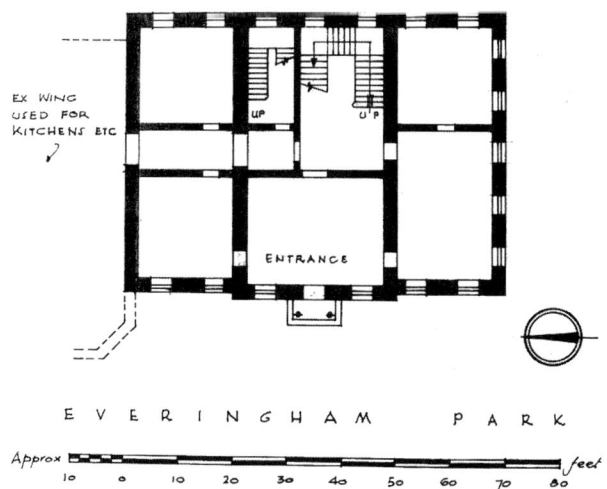

141 Everingham Hall, plan of ground floor

142 Fangfoss Hall, entrance front

and a Venetian window in the centre. As built the main rooms were on the ground floor and the Venetian window was abandoned. There are also drawings for the chimneypieces, one, for the dining room, signed JC. The house was much extended in the nineteenth century and was restored by Francis Johnson in 1962, who returned it to its original appearance and reinstated the staircase. Nearly all the Georgian decoration survives at the upper level and some below.

Hull University Library, Maxwell-Constable papers, DDEV/70/21, DDEV/56/283

R. B. Wragg, 'Everingham Park: Carr's Work Authenticated', *Transactions of the Georgian Society for East Yorkshire*, 4.ii (1957), 57–58

Arthur Oswald, 'Everingham Park, Yorkshire', *Country Life*, 15 February 1968

BE/ER/412–13

Fangfoss Hall, Fangfoss, Yorkshire (ER/Humberside) (Fig. 142)
George Overend
New house, 1766
Attributed

The Overends owned a small estate at Fangfoss, which in 1788 extended to 300 acres, from at least the early eighteenth century. Fangfoss Hall is typical of a number of simple, cubic houses attributed to Carr. Other examples include Knaresborough House and Well Head House, Halifax. It is a modest country house of five bays and two-and-a-half storeys, of brown brick with a pyramidal roof, stone plinth, plat band, running cill and modillion cornice. The east front has a pedimented porch with Ionic columns, the west front a Doric porch. The Doric porch

with its freestanding columns, arched doorcase and chanelled rustication can be compared to the doorway of the Eastwood House, New Lodge and Carr's own house in Skeldergate. The detail of both interior and exterior are characteristic of Carr and David Neave considered the attribution convincing. According to Bulmer Fangfoss Hall was built in 1766.

T. Bulmer, *Topography and Directory of East Yorkshire* (Preston, 1892), 612

Victoria County History, *A History of Yorkshire: East Riding* (Oxford, 1976), III, 166

John Bradshaw and Ivan Hall, *John Carr of York*, duplicated catalogue of an exhibition held at Ferens Art Gallery (Hull, 1973), 44, 45

BE/ER/414

Farnley Chapel, Leeds, Yorkshire (WR/WY) (Fig. 143)
New chapel, 1761
Demolished 1884

In April 1761 the vicar of Leeds, Samuel Kirshaw (for whom Carr also worked that year at St Peter's, Leeds), petitioned the Archbishop of York for a licence to rebuild the ancient chapel of ease at Farnley, which could not hold the congregation. The licence was supplied in May and Carr provided a design for £5 5s. William Danby, for whom Carr worked at Swinton Park in 1764–67, was lord of the manor and instrumental in the rebuilding.

The builders were the mason John Lister from nearby Bramley, the carpenter James Lambeth and the joiner Thomas Teale, both natives of nearby Horsforth. They had earlier built the chapel at Horsforth designed by Carr's co-surveyor of bridges John Watson and had probably been recommended by him. The estimated cost was £494 14s 6d.

The chapel was an austere building under a single gable with a pedimented west front, a pedimented door with Doric half columns and cupola for the bell. It was lit on each side by three round-headed windows under blind arches and at the west end by a Venetian window. Carr repeated the pattern at St John's, North Bierley, in 1766, Chapelthorpe, near Wakefield (1770–71, attributed) and Ossington, Nottinghamshire, 1782-83.

Terry Friedman, 'Church Architecture in Leeds 1700-1799', *Thoresby Society*, 2nd ser., 7 (1997), 34, 120–23, figs 40–41

BE/WR/340

Farnley Hall, Yorkshire (WR/NY) (Figs 72, 73)
Walter Hawksworth Fawkes
Large addition to Jacobean house, and possibly stables, 1786-92

Walter Hawksworth inherited Farnley from his cousin, Francis Fawkes, in 1786, adding Fawkes to his surname and calling in Carr greatly to extend the Jacobean house. Work started swiftly. Foundations were dug in 1786 and

143 Farnley Chapel

by 1790, as the date on the drawing room ceiling reveals, decoration had begun. The house was essentially complete when Fawkes died in 1792, leaving it to his son Walter Ramsden Hawksworth Fawkes to complete the furnishing.

Carr's addition is square, with a canted bay on the south front and a columned imperial staircase. The dining room is among the richest of all Carr's works, with coved ceiling, exuberant plasterwork and painted medallions by the Swiss painter Theodore de Bruyn. By contrast, the music room and library are very restrained. The first, plainly elegant, has a segmental ceiling compartmented by flat bands. In the library the ceiling is circular, translated into a square by shallow pendentives reminiscent of the work of James Wyatt, Thomas Leverton or even Sir John Soane. The family appear to have continued to sleep in the Jacobean wing.

It is possible that Carr had either carried out earlier works for Francis Fawkes or that such work had been considered. A letter from francis Fawkes to Walter Hawksworth of August 1774 requests that Carr let Hawksworth know when he would be at Farnley because Fawkes was worried that he might be away and even if home did not want to agree to a scheme without Hawksworth's presence. This suggests that the new work may have been planned but not executed during Francis Fawkes's lifetime, which would explain the swift start on the project after his death.

John Preston Neale, *Views of Seats of Noblemen and Gentlemen* (London, 1822), v, pl. 37

Gordon Nares, 'Farnley Hall, Yorkshire', *Country Life*, 20-27 May, 3 June 1954

Angela Evans, *The Art and Architectural Patronage of the Hawksworth and Fawkes Families in the Eighteenth Century*, BA Dissertation in Fine Arts, Leeds University, 1983, 18; information from Robert Frost

BE/WR/196

Fawley Court, Henley-on-Thames, Buckinghamshire

Strickland Freeman

Advice on gateway and stucco, 1797–99

Carr was friends with Freeman, with whom he spent eight days in 1796 and again visited in 1803. He assisted Freeman, who acted as his own architect at Fawley, commenting upon and correcting his drawings and giving him practical advice on buying materials. One drawing of the gateway, apparently by Freeman, was returned drawn correctly, with the addition of a Doric frieze. The building was to be of brick covered with Strickland's 'impenetrable stucco', on which Carr gave further advice having had 'a great deal of conversation lately with an eminent Stucco plaisterer'. Carr also enclosed a second, more elegant drawing for the gate and sent designs for a sash rail.

Gloucester County Record Office, Strickland of Apperley Papers, FF38, D 1245/C/4; information from Dr Eileen Harris and Dr Terry Friedman

BE/Bucks/328

144 Fillingham Castle lodges

Ferrybridge, Knottingley, Yorkshire (WR/WY)
(Fig. 78)
West Riding magistrates
Bridge rebuilt, 1765
Demolished 1797–1804
West Riding magistrates
New bridge, 1797–1804

Carr first designed a bridge over the River Aire on the
Great North Road in 1765. The four-arch bridge built by
John Gott of Calverley. This lasted just over thirty years.
On 21 January 1797 notice was given in the *Leeds Mercury*
that a meeting of the Quarter Sessions would be held at
Ferrybridge in five days time 'at which Time and Place
such persons as think proper may deliver in Plans for
building the said Bridge ... a proper Gratuity will be given
to the Person who shall produce the most approved Plan
or Plans for building the said Bridge'. Carr's plan for a
three-arch bridge (one arch of 62 ft 6 in and two of 54 ft
6in) was duly approved. A drawing signed by Carr is
inscribed 'Plan and Elevation for the new Bridge at
Ferrybridge approved of by the Magistrates Jany 26th
1797'. It was varied slightly in execution with a blind
balustrade being substituted for a plain parapet.

The cost of the bridge to 21 April 1803 was £24,864.
Work was carried out by direct labour under the
supervision of Bernard Hartley. The accounts only record
one occasion, in May 1798, on which Carr was asked by
the justices to review the works and report on progress.
Before work was completed the justices passed a

resolution thanking Carr for his plans and authorising his
name be 'engraved' on the parapet. 'John Carr, Esquire, of
York, Architect, 1797' is built into one parapet, 'Bernard
Hartley, of Pontefract, builder, 1804' into the other.

West Yorkshire Archive Service, Wakefield, Book of Bridges
1752-1770; County Clerk Order Book and Accounts
Alfred Booth, 'Notes on "The New Bridge" at Ferrybridge',
RIBA Journal, 21 November 1931, 39, 55–56
BE/WR/200

Fillingham Castle, Lincolnshire (Fig. 144)
Sir Cecil Wray MP
Lodges and gateway, *c.* 1770
Attributed

Wray was brother-in-law to another Carr client, Thomas
Arthington and the lodges and gateway at Fillingham are
virtually identical to a design in a drawing believed to be
by Carr at Raby Castle. They also resemble the gateway at
nearby Redbourne Hall, which is also believed to be by
Carr. The Gothic house which Wray built has also been
attributed to Carr but the attribution seems less plausible.
It was rectangular, raised on a podium with circular towers
at the corners and crenellated parapets. The interior was
Classical.

Alistair Rowan, 'Gothick Restoration at Raby Castle', *Architectural
History*, 15 (1972), fig. 21a
J. S. Miller, 'Fillingham Castle', *York Georgian Society Report*, 1970,
67–69
BE/Lincs/276–77

145 Fixby Hall stables

Fixby Hall, Nr Huddersfield, Yorkshire (WR/WY)
(Fig. 145)
Thomas Thornhill
Stables, *c.* 1780
Attributed

Thomas Thornhill married in 1779 and his arms, impaling Lynnes in the pediment of the greenhouse, suggest a possible date for the alterations to the house, although the greenhouse has no obvious parallels in other Carr buildings. However, the new stables of nine bays with a central pediment, round-headed windows linked by a running cill and blind arches are characteristically Carr. The same pattern can be found on Carr stables at Escrick Park, Ormesby Hall, Ravenfield Hall and Ribston Park and on the side elevation of the stables at Castle Howard. Fixby Hall was also remodelled at about the same time, including the addition of canted bays, work for which Carr could have been responsible.

BE/WR/275

Forcett Park, Yorkshire (NR/NY) (Fig. 146)
Robert Shuttleworth
New stables, n.d.
Attributed

Daniel Garrett rebuilt Forcett Park for Richard Shuttleworth in the 1730s and was probably responsible for the handsome entrance lodges. James Paine added an elaborate banqueting house in about 1762 for his son James Shuttleworth. However, the stables of nine bays with a central arch and pediment, round-headed windows in relieving arches and a running cill are characteristically Carr. They can be compared with similar stables at Ribston Park, Ormesby Hall, Ravenfield Hall, and Byram Park. The stables are undated but could be the work of his son Robert Shuttleworth who succeeded in 1773.

BE/NR/164

146 Forcett Park stables

147 Design for Glamis Castle

Gilling Castle, Gilling, Yorkshire (NR/NY)
9th Viscount Fairfax
Repairs and new Gothic temple (demolished), *c.* 1756–57

The letters of Thomas Weatherill, Lord Fairfax's steward, show that Carr was responsible for reroofing the house. The wing over Fairfax's library and apartments was on the point of completion in July 1756, when work was to begin on the other wing. The laundry was reroofed in 1757. References to the temple in these years suggest that the substantial Gothic temple which once stood at the far end of the park was built at this time. James Henderson, the plasterer, made minor alterations to this in 1771.

North Yorkshire County Record Office, Newburgh Papers, ZDV(F), misc. 1129
R. B. Wragg, 'Some Notes on 18th-century Craftsmen', *York Georgian Society Report*, 1955–56, 60
BE/NR/168

Gilling East, Yorkshire (NR/NY)
North Riding Magistrates
Bridge widened, 1800

Carr widened the 20 ft bridge over the Hole Beck in 1800.

North Yorkshire County Record Office, Book of Bridges, 1772–1803, 47

Glamis Castle, Angus (Fig. 147)
9th Earl of Strathmore
Unexecuted proposals for alterations, 1765

Carr proposed extensive alterations including two balancing service wings in the Gothic style. There are no accounts or correspondence but the cellar book for 1765 records that port 'was brought up for Mr Carr'. As this follows shortly after port for Mr Bell 'architect' it would seem that building schemes were then being considered. In the event Lord Strathmore was content simply to repair the house.

Carr's scheme had more respect for the existing castle than that by Bell. All the earlier work with its heraldry would have been retained and the only noticeable change was to the balustrades and overhanging eaves on the wings, which would have been replaced by castellated parapets. A new entrance would have been created at the first floor with a double-flight stair. Two service courts would have been added, connected to the main castle by short, single-storey links. Slade points out that the scheme anticipates Robert Adam's castle style by several years.

Scottish Buildings Record, copies of signed drawings by Carr of the 'Castle at Glammis' at Glamis
Harry Gordon Slade, *Glamis Castle*, Society of Antiquaries of London, forthcoming

148 Gledhow Hall

149 Gledstone Hall

150 Gledstone Hall stables

151 Goldsborough Hall gates

152 Grimston Garth

Gledhow Hall, Leeds, Yorkshire (WR/WY) (Fig. 148)
Jeremiah Dixon
Rebuilding, 1764–66
Attributed

Jeremiah Dixon, a Leeds merchant, bought the Gledhow estate in 1764 and built or enlarged the house, probably at the same time. It was described as unfinished in 1766, when it was valued at £1,600. The style of the house, which is of stone and has two storeys with a pair of canted bays flanking the entrance hall and a further canted bay on the side elevation, supported by Dixon's employment of Carr to design his town house in Leeds, suggests Carr may have been the architect. The house has been much added to and the stylistic evidence is not conclusive.

Thomas Dunham Whitaker, *Loidis and Elmete* (Leeds, 1816), I, 129–31
Sidney Kitson, 'Carr of York', *RIBA Journal*, 3rd ser., 17 (1910), 253, plan and photograph
Derek Linstrum, *Historic Architecture of Leeds* (Newcastle, 1969), 80
Maurice Beresford, 'East End, West End. The Face of Leeds during Urbanisation 1684–1847', *Thoresby Society*, 60 and 61 (1985/86), 119
BE/WR/332

Gledstone Hall, Martons Both, Yorkshire (WR/NY) (Figs 149, 150)
Richard Roundell, completed by Revd William Roundell
New house and stables, started 1770–72
Attributed
Demolished, except for stables and garden pavilion, 1925–27

Gledstone was designed for Richard Roundell, who inherited from his father in 1770. It was completed after his death at the age of thirty-two in 1772 by his brother William. A compact rectangular house with a *piano nobile* and central canted bay on the entrance front and smaller two-bay pavilions, it can be compared to Aston Hall of *c.* 1767–72, and is safely attributed to Carr.

The house was replaced by a new house designed by Lutyens incorporating some of the doors and chimneypieces. The stables with a domed lantern tower and circular court surrounded by an arcaded ambulatory survives.

Thomas Whitaker, *The History and Antiquities of the Deanery of Craven* (Leeds, 1878), I, 93–95, plate
Edward Waterson and Peter Meadows, *Lost Houses of the West Riding* (Welburn, 1998), 6, figs
Christopher Hussey, 'Gledstone Hall', *Country Life*, 13 April 1935
BE/WR/219

Goldsborough Hall, Goldsborough, Yorkshire (WR/NY) (Fig. 151)
Daniel Lascelles
Alterations, after *c.* 1762

Lascelles bought the Goldsborough estate with its early seventeenth-century house in about 1762 when he abandoned plans to build a new house on his adjoining Plompton estate and decided instead to modernize Goldsborough Hall. The work is documented in the Harewood papers and included rusticated gate piers, replacement of some mullioned windows with sashes, insertion of a classical doorway, and redesigning of some of the interior in the Adam style.

West Yorkshire Archive Service, Leeds, Harewood Estate Papers, Accounts and Correspondence
Mary Mauchline, *Harewood House* (Ashbourne, 1992), 172, fn 51
BE/WR/221

Greta Bridge, Yorkshire (NR/County Durham) (Fig. 28)
North Riding magistrates
New bridge, 1773

The new bridge with its magnificent span of 74 ft 6 in across the Greta on the Scotch Corner–Brough road

153 Grove Hall, south elevation

replaced an earlier bridge swept away in the floods of 1771. The original estimate was for £780, the actual cost £850. The builders, John and William Peacock, agreed to maintain it for seven years. The adjacent George Inn may also be Carr.

North Yorkshire County Record Office, Book of Bridges, 1772–1803, 49; North Riding Sessions bundles, contract, 16 July 1772

R. B. Wragg, 'The Architect of Greta Bridge', *York Georgian Society Report*, 1958–59, 30–33

BE/NR/311

Grimston Garth, East Garton, Yorkshire

(ER/Humberside) (Fig. 152)

Thomas Grimston

New house, stables and possibly temple, *c.* 1781–86

After the old house at Grimston was destroyed by fire in the seventeenth century the family had moved to Kilnwick. On succeeding his father in 1780 Thomas Grimston decided to build a new house at Grimston slightly further inland than the original one. He employed Carr who had earlier worked for his father and was also carrying out improvements at Kilnwick.

Grimston intended a romantic pavilion near the sea, not a regular seat. The Gothic design is triangular with a single central hexagonal room on each floor and a trio of circular turrets. The dining room was decorated with numerous coats of arms and three alternative schemes for treating the windows survive, probably from Carr's office.

East Riding of Yorkshire Record Office, DDGR/43/4/10,12; 43/5/5, 37

M. E. Ingram, 'John Carr's Contribution to the Gothic Revival', *Transactions of the Georgian Society for East Yorkshire*, 2.iii (1949), 43–52

M. E. Ingram, *Leaves from a Family Tree* (Hull, 1951), 114–21

M. E. Ingram and Francis Johnson, *Country Life*, 17 October 1952

R. B. Wragg, 'John Carr: Gothic Revivalist', in *Studies in Architectural History*, ed. by W. A. Singleton (London and York, 1956), II, 27–30

BE/ER/445–47

154 Grove Hall, library

Grimston Park, Yorkshire (WR/NY)

Sir Thomas Gascoigne
New house, n.d.
Attributed

Speight states, with apparent authority, that Grimston
Park was rebuilt in the latter part of the eighteenth century
by Carr. That this is not a wild attribution can be seen in
his footnote where he points out that Grimston is omitted
from the list of Carr's work cited in the *Yorkshire
Archaeological Journal*. It is possible that Speight may have
seen drawings for the house as elsewhere he comments
that the original plans and working drawings for
Harewood House were in the possession of Messrs
Atkinson, architects in York.

   The house was rebuilt by Decimus Burton in 1840 and
there is no documentary evidence to support Speight's
statement, although Carr did provide designs for Sir
Thomas Gascoigne at Parlington in the 1770s.

Harry Speight, *Lower Wharfdale* (London, 1902), 199, 473
BE/WR/227

Grinton, Yorkshire (NR/NY)

North Yorkshire magistrates
Bridge widened, 1797

The bridge over the River Swale on the Richmond-Kirkby
Stephen Road was widened at cost of £1,523 13s. The
span was 42 ft 6 in.

North Yorkshire County Record Office, Book of Bridges,
   1772–1803, 50

Grove Hall, Nr Retford, Nottinghamshire (Figs 153, 154)

Anthony Eyre MP
Alterations, c. 1762
Demolished 1952

Anthony Eyre (1727–88) purchased Grove Hall, which lay
adjacent to other family estates, in 1762. He had married
Judith Letitia Bury, great-niece and heiress of Sir
Hardolph Wastneys, in 1755 and previously lived at
Adwick-le-Street, Yorkshire, which was sold in 1762. As
the adjacent house at Rampton had been demolished by
his father Eyre decided to live at Grove Hall, which had a
fine site with a southern prospect and extensive views.

   Carr was commissioned to add family rooms facing
south in about 1762. Parts of the south-west front were
pulled down or remodelled, though the first-floor Grinling
Gibbons room was retained. A new entrance hall and
staircase was created, together with a suite of dining room,
drawing room with canted-bay window, ante-room with
apsidal end and library. The library had a particularly fine
bookcase clearly designed to follow the detail of the room.
Its detail echoes that of the bookcases in the library at
Colwick Hall. This suggests that it too was designed by
Carr.

   Further alterations were carried out by A. H. Eyre, who
succeeded in 1785. Thomas Waterworth of Doncaster,
who executed the decorative stone carving on Carr's
Fitzwilliam Mausoleum in 1788, provided marble for a
chimneypiece purchased in 1791. Plasterwork was added

by William Holliday of Byland, Yorkshire, formerly an apprentice of James Henderson, Carr's favourite plasterer, in 1792. It is not clear if Carr was involved, but it is more likely to have been the work of William Lindley, who was paid for building two lodges in 1794.

Robert Thoroton, *History of Nottinghamshire*, ed. by J. Throsby (Nottingham, 1790), III, 264

John Piercy, *The History of Retford* (Retford, 1828), 219

H. A. Johnson and Antony Cox, 'The Architecture of Grove Hall, Nottinghamshire', *Transactions of the Thoroton Society*, 89 (1985), 75–85

BE/Notts/136

Grove Hall, Darrington, Yorkshire (WR/WY)
William Sotheron
Alterations, *c.* 1783
Attributed

In 1783 Carr wrote from Darrington to the steward at Wentworth Woodhouse asking him to show the bearer of the letter, one of Mr Sotheron's workmen, how the water closet in the garden worked. Grove Hall near Darrington, just south of Ferrybridge, was the seat of William Sotheron and it is clear from the letter that Carr was carrying out work for him there.

Sotheron had acquired Darrington through his marriage in 1751 to Sarah, only daughter of Samuel Savile of Thrybergh and Darrington and first cousin of Sir John Savile, 1st Earl of Mexborough, of Methley Hall, where Carr is believed to have worked. The gates, now derelict beside the A1, are characteristic of Carr, and the ballroom added to the rear of the house is finely decorated in Carr's manner.

Sheffield Archives, Wentworth Woodhouse Muniments, WWM St P 6 (iii) 10a

Joseph Hunter, *Hallamshire* (London, 1869), 421

Yorkshire Parish Record Society, *The Register of the Parish Church of Darrington* (1913), 98

House in George Street, Halifax, Yorkshire (WR/WY)
Christopher Rawson
New house, n.d.
Demolished

'The mansion in George Street, Halifax, for the Rawson family' is included in the A.P.S.D.'s list of Carr's commissions and Davies lists 'House in George Street, Halifax, for Mr Rawson'. This has been assumed to refer to Somerset House, a combined house, bank and warehouse, built for John Royds and dated on the overmantel in the saloon 1766, which subsequently was occupied by the Rawson family bank. However, this curious composition is quite unlike any other Carr building and would not normally be attributed to him. Moreover, it was occupied by the Royds family until 1805 and was not acquired by the Rawsons until 1807. This

makes its attribution to Carr tenuous. It seems more likely that the A.P.S.D. and Davies references, probably taken from surviving drawings, should be taken literally and that Carr's design was a house for Mr Rawson in George Street.

This is likely to have been Christopher Rawson (1712–80), the third son of John Rawson of Bolton, near Bradford, who settled in Halifax and rose to be a prominent businessman. The Rawson family, involved in the clothing business from the early eighteenth century, were pioneers in manufacturing and trade who developed early and expanding links with the Orient and other overseas countries. Rawson also built a brick house at Stoneyroyd, about a mile outside Halifax, in about 1764.

Wyatt Papworth (ed.), *The Dictionary of Architecture issued by the Architectural Publications Society* (London, 1877), II, 36

R. Davies, 'A Memoir of John Carr', *Yorkshire Archaeological Journal*, 4 (1877), 205

Halifax Public Library, E. J. Walker, 'Our Local Portfolio'

J. Lister, 'Stoney-Royd', *Halifax Antiquarian Society* (1909), 241

T. W. Hanson, 'Royds of George Street, Halifax, and of Bucklersbury, London', *Halifax Antiquarian Society* (1941), 75

Arthur Porritt, 'The Rawson Family', *Halifax Antiquarian Society* (1966), 28–30

Hardwick Hall, Derbyshire
5th Duke of Devonshire
Repairs and alterations, bridge in the park, renovation of the underkeeper's house, 1785–91

Carr's name can be found on numerous vouchers for work at Hardwick totalling £1,226 in the late 1780s. He is known to have visited the house several times. Two visits are recorded in 1788, including one of four days in December, with further three-day visits in 1789 and 1790. The work seems to have concentrated on repairs and domestic improvements. New stonework was carved for the rooftop and chimneys were rebuilt. The roof was strengthened by the carpenter Thomas Sykes using a mixture of new beams and iron cramps, as were ceilings and floors all over the house. Much of the work involved repairs to plasterwork, especially to the ceilings and walls of the Long Gallery, dining room, State Room and Great Hall. The service areas of the house and the attic were plastered. New fireplaces were installed in the attics and service rooms, along with new shelves, cupboards and doors. A new Bramah water closet was installed at the south end of the first floor in 1789. The key craftsmen employed were Thomas Allen, John and Joseph Brocklehurst, plasterers, John Ball, mason, Thomas Sykes, carpenter, and Thomas Mellor, plumber.

It is possible that Carr divided the two-storey chapel into two rooms, with a chapel above and servants' hall below. This was done between 1793 and 1800, although the absence of vouchers after 1793 leaves this to be

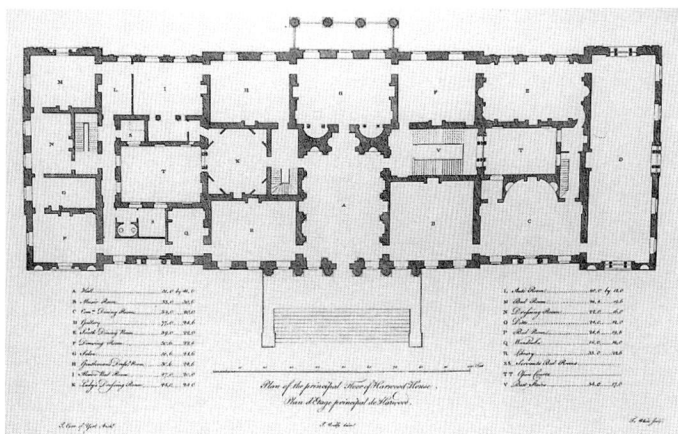

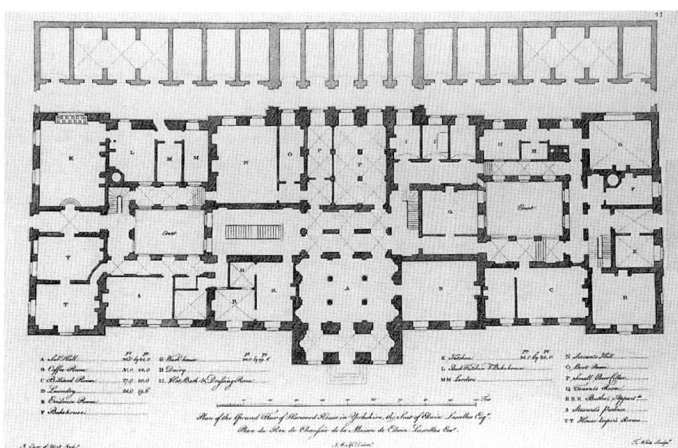

155 Harewood House, plan of the ground floor
156 Harewood House, plan of the basement

proved. In 1790s he completely renovated the house of
John Hall, the underkeeper, providing new doorcases,
stairs, shelves, windows and wainscotting.

Chatsworth House, Devonshire Archives, information from Ben
Cowell/National Trust

Harewood Church, Yorkshire (WR/WY)
Edwin Lascelles
Alterations, 1774; repairs, 1793
Attributed

Proposals by Robert Adam to alter the church in 1759 and
c. 1765–71 came to nothing. In 1774 new pews, gallery
and stairs were added. In 1793 the church was restored,
with a new roof in Westmorland slate, the west gables of
the aisles rebuilt at a lower level than their medieval line,
the tower parapet renewed and the bells rehung. At the
same time the east gable was recast with new battlements,
florid pinnacles and a quatrefoil window. The east drive is
aligned so that the east gable of the church is prominently
in front of the visitor before the drive sweeps southward

to the house. In 1795 the Lascelles vault was constructed
below the chancel.

There is no documentary evidence for the work which
does not seem to be by Adam and is closer to Carr's
Gothic churches at Ravenfield and Denton. The
eighteenth-century fittings have since been removed.

John Jewell, *The History and Antiquities of Harewood* (Leeds, 1819),
39
L. A. S. Butler, 'All Saints Church, Harewood', *Yorkshire
Archaeological Journal*, 58 (1986), 91–92
BE/WR/243

Harewood House, Harewood, Yorkshire (WR/WY)
(Figs 16, 17, 45, 155–57)
Edwin Lascelles
Old Gawthorpe Hall, alterations, 1754-55 (demolished
1771–73); stables, 1755–58; Harewood House (New
Gawthorpe Hall) 1759–71; unexecuted design for wings,
1800; Lofthouse Gate, 1771; 'New Bridge in the Valley',
1771; menagerie 1774; rotunda 1774; Temple of Venus,
1780 (demolished); Main Gateway, 1801; dam head and
undated design for small Chinese bridge

In 1753 Edwin Lascelles inherited Gawthorpe which his
father, a wealthy Barbadian merchant, had bought. It was
part of an inheritance reportedly worth £166,666. A
political ally of the Marquis of Rockingham, Lascelles
soon resolved to build an elegant new house on the estate,
although in the meantime he employed Carr to improve
Gawthorpe Old Hall. Designs were sought from the
young, fashionable William Chambers, recently returned
from Italy, and perhaps from Matthew Brettingham and
Lancelot Brown, but rejected.

Lascelles began by building new stables in 1755. Doubt
has been expressed about Carr's authorship as the design,
with its Kentian centrepiece, differs markedly from his
conventional stable elevations, although there are parallels
with the contemporary stables at Heath Hall. However,
Carr was paid £55 5s in April 1757 'for the drawings and
attendance etc on account of the New Stables' up until
December 1756 and an engraving in the Wakefield Art
Gallery by his assistant William Lindley names Carr as
architect. His family certainly built the stables and letters
refer to his designing the Doric colonnade in the stable
yard after work had begun.

Carr produced designs for the new house, his most
impressive country house, in 1755, but Lascelles also
sought ideas from Robert Adam in 1758 and elements of
Adam were integrated into Carr's scheme. Carr was largely
responsible for the elevation and plan. The main interiors
were wholly by Adam. Foundations were laid in December
1759 and the house was ready for occupation in 1771. In
1762 Carr rebuilt Adam's semi-circular internal court,
which had proved unsatisfactory, with Sir Thomas

157 Harewood House gates

Robinson's advice. While the house was being built Carr was also responsible for designing several farmhouses.

Initially, Carr's father acted as clerk of works. John Muschamp, of Harewood, was mason. Carr was paid £60 a year for his 'drawings and attendance'. After the house was complete he continued to design numerous buildings for the estate and in 1800 prepared a scheme for adding wings, including new kitchens, for the 1st Lord Harewood. These were not executed.

Davies lists the lodge and gateway at Harewood, begun in 1801, as by Carr, noting that it was probably one of his latest works. Carr certainly claimed credit for the design, according to Elizabeth Chivers in 1805, for the triumphal arch at the entrance from Harewood village. Peter Atkinson also made designs for the gate. Harewood House was altered by Sir Charles Barry in 1843–50, when the portico was removed, a balustrade added and the interiors rearranged.

West Yorkshire Archive Service, Leeds, Harewood Papers, accounts, drawings and correspondence

Gott Collection, Wakefield Art Gallery, engraving of the stables by W. Lindley

James Woolfe and John Gandon, *Vitruvius Britannicus* (London, 1771), v, pls 23–28

R. Davies, 'A Memoir of John Carr', *Yorkshire Archaeological Journal*, 4 (1877), 205

A. T. Bolton, *Robert and James Adam* (London, 1922), 157–77

Christopher Hussey, *English Country Houses, 1760–1800* (London, 1956), 61–69

John Martin Robinson, 'In Pursuit of Excellence', *Country Life*, 28 June 1979

R. B. Wragg, 'The Architect of the Harewood Stables', *York Georgian Society Report*, 1979, 66–73, plate

John Martin Robinson, *Georgian Model Farms* (Oxford, 1983), 125–27

Giles Worsley, 'Crediting Carr', *Country Life*, 5 May 1988

Mary Mauchline, *Harewood House* (Ashbourne, 1992)

BE/WR/245–47

CATALOGUE

158 Harewood village

Harewood Estate, Yorkshire (WR/WY) (Fig. 158)
Edwin Lascelles
New village, 1750s–1807; estate buildings including:
Lofthouse Farm, *c.* 1758, farmhouse 1760–61, Stank Farm,
1763, cottages at Stank, 1772–74

As well as designing Harewood House and buildings in
the park, Carr worked extensively for Lascelles on the
surrounding estate. The village of Harewood was moved
from near the church to a new site on the approach to
Harewood Park from Wetherby. The well-proportioned
two-storeyed stone terraces with stone roofs, erected to
Carr's designs, were marked improvements on the houses
they replaced, some of which were described as hovels.
They varied in size, some small enough to be described as
'of a rather meaner kind', the majority relatively generous.
Work began in the 1750s and continued into the early
nineteenth century. According to Caffyn most of the
housing was built between 1796 and 1812. It is not clear
what Carr's involvement was by this stage.

Lascelles also built a ribbon factory to provide
employment, as well as a school, the doctor's and
steward's house and the inn, designed in 1772. The ribbon
factory was architecturally more ambitious than the
houses, with a central tripartite building and flanking
ranges with thermal windows in blank arcading. The
model was Lord Burlington's design for almshouses at
Sevenoaks in Kent.

The hamlet of Stank lay to the west of Harewood. The
steward's annual accounts record work in progress on the
substantial farm buildings and estate workshops in the
1760s, with references to the hog sties, slaughter house,
duck house and tower. The craftsmen, John Muschamp I,
mason, James Norfolk, carpenter, and John Walker, slater,
all worked at Harewood House. The farm buildings
survive with the exception of the middle range, which has
been demolished.

Carr's invoices also record him setting out and directing
the execution of the buildings at Stank in 1772 and their

measurement by his clerk in 1774. These were probably
the symmetrical U-shaped range of cottages to the west of
the farm, which have a five-bay central block with
pediment, lower flanking ranges and projecting pavilion-
like ends.

West Yorkshire Archive Service, Leeds, Harewood Papers,
    accounts, drawings and correspondence
John Martin Robinson, 'In pursuit of excellence', *Country Life*, 28
    June 1979
Lucy Caffyn, *Workers' Housing in West Yorkshire 1750–1920*
    (London, 1986), 25–26

Hawksworth Hall, Aireborough, Yorkshire (WR/WY)
(Figs 159, 160)
Walter Hawksworth
Alterations, *c.* 1774

Hawksworth Hall was a long rambling sixteenth-century
house altered in the seventeenth century and the second
quarter of the eighteenth century. Further work took place
later in the eighteenth century when a canted bay was
added at the western end of the house and the interior
reorganized. A signed drawing in the Fawkes Papers
shows that Carr was responsible for adding the canted bay
and for the design of the dining room within. Though the
room has been much altered sufficient eighteenth-century
decoration remains to show that Carr's plan was executed.
The staircase ceiling was probably carried out at the same
time. Details of the work match Carr's work elsewhere.
The Ionic frieze in the dining room recalls that in the
portico at Colwick Hall and chimneypieces resemble those
at Norton Place, Wiganthorpe and Ormesby Hall. This
would suggest a date in the mid-1770s.

The work must have been carried out by Walter
Hawksworth, who succeeded his father in 1760.
According to Speight, Hawksworth had a high opinion of
his own comfort and 'maintained the character of a
country gentleman with much dignity and circumstance,
and at one time kept above a dozen male servants in about
the house'. He was left Farnley Hall by his relative Francis
Fawkes in 1786 and subsequently employed Carr to add a
substantial new wing to it. In 1774 when Francis Fawkes
was considering employing Carr at Farnley Hall he wrote
to Hawksworth asking him to arrange a visit by Carr. This
suggests Carr may have been working for Hawksworth at
the time.

Yorkshire Archaeological Society, Fawkes Papers, DD
    161/26/c/2
Harry Speight, 'Hawksworth Hall and its Associations', *Bradford
    Antiquary*, new ser., 2 (1905), 293
Angela Evans, *The Art and Architectural Patronage of the Hawksworth
    and Fawkes Families in the Eighteenth Century*, BA Dissertation in
    Fine Arts, Leeds University, 1983, 17–18; information from
    Robert Frost
BE/WR/255

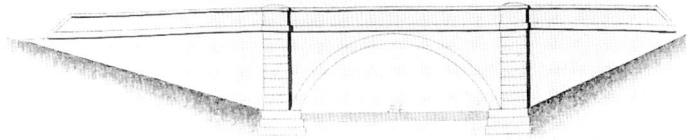

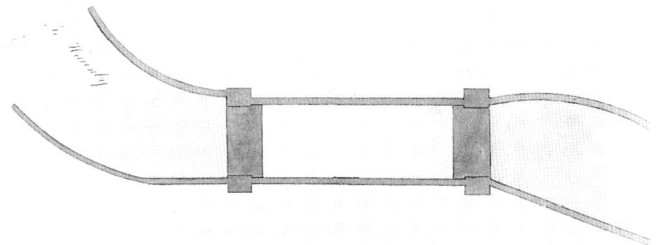

159 *left* Hawksworth Hall, south elevation | 160 *top right* Hawksworth Hall exterior
161 *below right* Drawing of Hawnby bridge

Hawnby, Yorkshire (NR/NY) (Fig. 161)
North Riding magistrates
New bridge, 1800

The new 32 ft 6 in span bridge over the River Rye was
built at a cost of £370 15s.

North Yorkshire County Record Office, Book of Bridges,
1772–1803, 19

Heath Hall, Warmfield-cum-Heath, Yorkshire
(WR/WY) (Figs 162, 163)
John Smyth and his son, John Smyth, MP
Remodelling and enlargement, 1754–*c.* 1780

Heath, a village about two miles from the centre of
Wakefield, had a large number of mansions. Joseph
Hunter, historian of Doncaster and Sheffield, compared it

CATALOGUE

to Hampstead Heath. In 1754 Carr was employed by John Smyth to remodel and enlarge the small house bought, or possibly built, by his grandfather John Smyth, a wool merchant. Carr more than doubled the size of the house, adding an attached Ionic portico and wings with canted bays. One of these held a drawing room, the other a dining room and circular study, with bedrooms above. The drawing room, with rich Rococo plasterwork and arcaded walls, is one of Carr's finest interiors. Some early eighteenth-century interiors survive in the bedrooms but elsewhere the decoration was completely remodelled. Carr also added parallel ranges, one for offices, the other for stables. The Deer House, an anonymous Palladian building in the park, may also be by Carr.

More work was done after Smyth was succeeded by his son John in 1771. The total cost of the house was £8,281 8s 5d and the final payment is said to have been made in 1780. This was to 'Mr Carr's executors', probably referring to Carr's brother Robert, who died in 1777.

An extra floor was subsequently added to the wings, upsetting the subtle movement of the original design. After years of neglect Heath Hall was bought by Mr and Mrs Muir Oddie in 1959 and restored with the assistance of Francis Johnson.

William Watts, *The Seats of the Nobility and Gentry* (London, 1786), pl. 84
Arthur Oswald, 'Heath Hall, Yorkshire', *Country Life*, 19–26 September, 3 October 1968
BE/WR/259

High Bourn, Masham, Yorkshire (NR/NY)
North Riding magistrates
Bridge widened, 1796

The 52 ft 6 in span bridge over the River Burn, also known as Swinton Bridge, on the Swinton–Masham road was widened by William Lister at a cost of £575.

North Yorkshire County Record Office, Book of Bridges, 1772–1803

Holker Hall, Lower Holker, Lancashire (Cumbria)
Lord George Cavendish MP
Temple, c. 1787

The temple had been built by July 1787 when Carr wrote to Lord George Cavendish to check details for a fair drawing to be made by his nephew. Carr may also have been responsible for a Gothic east wing added to Holker Hall in the 1780s and burnt out in 1871.

Lancashire County Record Office, DDCA/22/9/9
Clive Aslet, 'Holker Hall, Lancashire', *Country Life*, 26 June 1980

Holme Hall, Holme-on-Spalding Moor, Yorkshire
(ER/Humberside)
Marmaduke Langdale
Alterations, c. 1756–66

Carr measured and valued work done by the sculptor Jeremiah Hargrave in 1756 and was probably responsible for the elaborate dining room and staircase. He may also have designed the Roman Catholic chapel of 1766.

East Riding of Yorkshire Record Office, Harford (Holme) Papers, DDHA/14/27, 4 May 1756
BE/ER/474–75

Hooton Pagnell, Yorkshire (WR/SY)
William Bawden
Repairs to Hooton Pagnell vicarage, 1797

Bawden, an antiquary, was vicar of Hooton Pagnell. Carr wrote to St Andrew Ward of Hooton Pagnell about repairs for Mr Bawden on 27 May 1797. It is not clear what happened.

Information from Sir Howard Colvin

St Peter's Church, Horbury, Yorkshire (WR/WY)
(Figs 65, 66, 164)
For himself
New church, 1791–94

Carr marked his rise from humble stonemason to architect, gentleman and magistrate with the erection of a handsome new church in his native town. *The Leeds Intelligencer* recorded on 2 June 1794 that 'On Sunday the 18th ult. Divine service was performed for the first time in the new church at Horbury … This beautiful structure … is allowed to be the handsomest building of its size in the country. The spire is truly elegant, and the body of the church is rendered perfectly commodious, by a judicious arrangement of the fittings. The rich elliptical ceiling is stucco executed by Mess. Henderson and Crabtree of York, and an elegant sweet ton'd organ built by Mr Donaldson of the same city, while they form the most pleasing coup d'oeil reflect at the same time the highest honor on the projector of the whole, John Carr … who was born at Horbury, and at whose sole expence the church and organ were built.' Carr had enthusiastically ordered engravings from Thomas Malton and invited all his friends and relations to the opening ceremony.

Carr's petition to rebuild the decayed church is dated 5 December 1789 and was granted early in 1790. The foundation stone, in the south-west corner of the tower is inscribed: 'John Carr/AR/22 Feb A.B.C. 1790/D.D.D./30 Geo III'. The pediment is inscribed: 'Hanc aedem sacram: pietatis in deum et amoris: in solum natale monimentum: propriis sumptibus extruxit Johannes Carr Architectus: anno christi MDCCXCI.'

Construction did not proceed smoothly. In 1792 a storm blew the scaffolding against the side of the tower, threatening to demolish it; but to Carr's great relief — for he had little faith in the ability of his own masons — matters were soon put right. A plan of the 'new Chapel at

162 *above* Engraving of Heath Hall | 163 *below* Heath Hall, drawing room

CATALOGUE

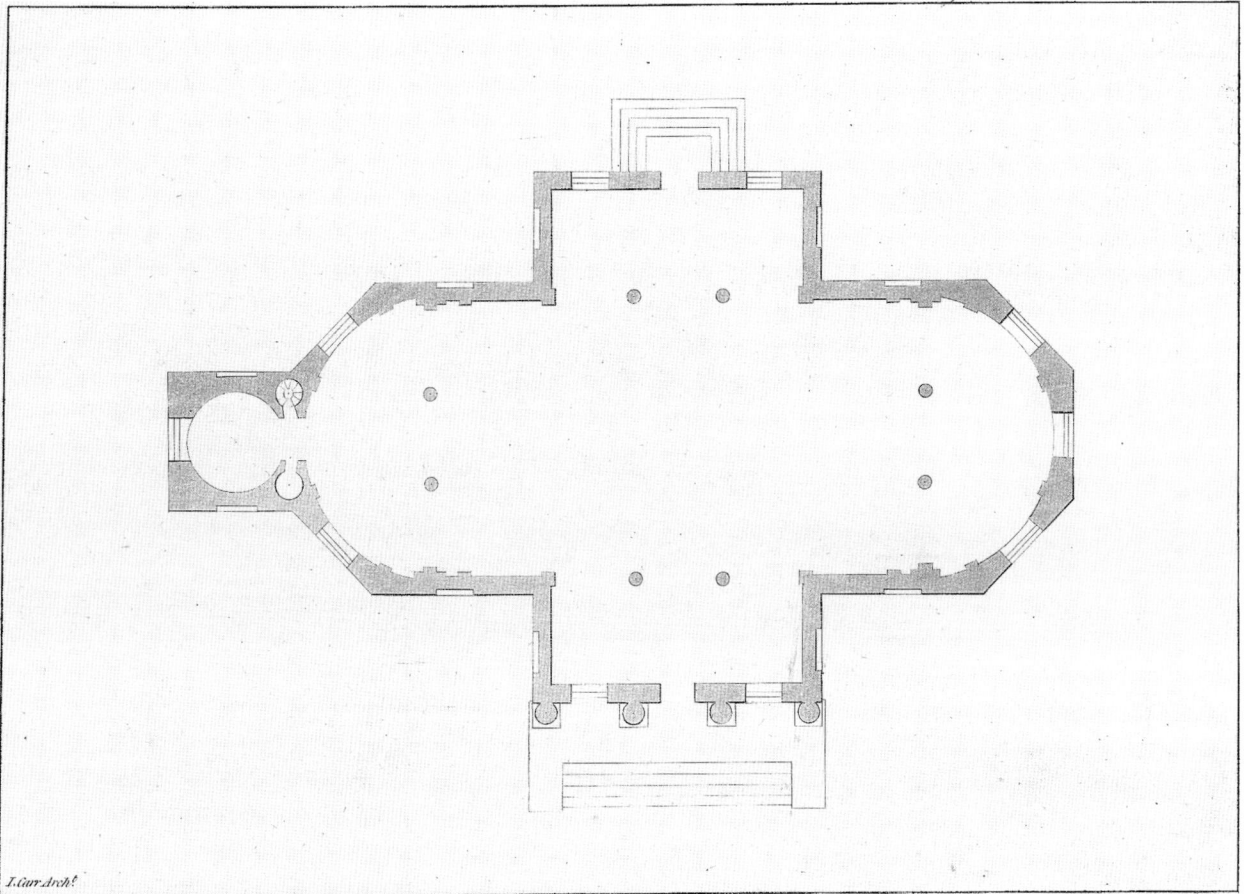

Plan of the Church at Horbury built 1791.

164 St Peter's Church, Horbury plan

Horbury, which shews also the number and disposition of all the Pews', dated 1794, probably records its completion. The cost was £8,000.

This was the most ambitious of Carr's churches. The plan is unusual with the entrances through Ionic porticoes in the sides of the building leading to transepts screened from the body of the church by Corinthian columns. The nave forms a single volume with curved apses at each end set in canted bays and the walls are decorated with Corinthian pilasters. The tower, divided into three sections and topped by a colonnade supporting a spire is particularly elaborate. The spire originally had a gilded urn on top but this fell in the nineteenth century.

Monuments to Carr and his father hang on the wall and Carr lies interred in the vault beneath the church. Horbury vicarage is said to have been built at the same time as the church to Carr's design but has been demolished.

Sheffield Archives, WWM, Stw P6 (iv) 105, 114
Print engraved by Thomas Malton, published 1 November 1791

Borthwick Institute, York, FAC, 1789/4C; information from Dr Terry Friedman
R. Davies, 'A Memoir of John Carr', *Yorkshire Archaeological Journal*, 4 (1877), 206
Sydney Kitson, 'Carr of York', *RIBA Journal*, 3rd ser., 17 (1910), 241–66
BE/WR/268

Hornby Castle, Yorkshire (NR/NY) (Figs 165-67)
4th Earl of Holderness
Alterations, *c*. 1760–70; farmhouses, 1766–67 and bridge, before 1777
House largely demolished 1930s

The Earl of Holderness inherited the great medieval fortified house of the Conyers family as a boy of three in 1722. Lord Lieutenant of the North Riding from 1740 and Secretary of State from 1751, he devoted himself to improving his house and estate after being dismissed from office in 1761. He was helped by the annual profits of

165 *top* Arbour Hill, Hornby Castle | **166** *middle* Castle Farm, Hornby Castle | **167** *bottom* Hornby Castle bridge

CATALOGUE

£4,200 from his wardenship of the Cinque Ports from 1765.

Holderness was a keen architectural patron building or altering two houses in London, his villa at Sion Hill in Middlesex, Aston Hall, near Rotherham (rebuilt after a fire in 1767), as well as Hornby Castle, and employing Giacomo Leoni and James Stuart as well as Carr. Harriet Clark, Carr's niece, visiting with the architect in 1795, referred to 'the great additions and noble offices' added to the castle by Carr for Holderness.

The rebuilding of Hornby Castle may have begun in the 1750s, perhaps using James Stuart, to whom the design of the Grand Hall has been attributed. Carr may have acted as executant architect as a Mr Carr was paid £50 in 1753 and £280 in 1757. Major alterations were carried out in the 1760s. William Mason discussed significant alterations with Lord Holderness in 1760 and John Carr was paid a total of £1,920 17s 10d between 1763 and 1768, when the account ends. Arthur Young describes major improvements underway in 1768 and Lord Holderness and his family moved back into the castle in 1770, where he lived in great style.

Carr rebuilt the south and east ranges of the castle in a simple Gothic manner. He probably designed the rusticated bridge (built before 1777) in the park, which was laid out by Lancelot Brown. Carr was almost certainly responsible for the three model farms built in the late 1760s. The Home Farm may be modelled on Thorpe Farm, designed by Sir Thomas Robinson near Gretabridge. Arbour Hill and Street Farm were extravagantly designed as eyecatchers, with turrets, arcading and canted bays.

Only the south range of the castle survives. Its interior was remodelled in the 1930s when the east wing and much of the medieval fabric was demolished.

British Library, Egerton 3436, fols 368–69, 3497
Yorkshire Archaeological Society Archives, DD 5/32/2
York Minster Library MS 328/3, fol. 32
John Martin Robinson, *Georgian Model Farms* (Oxford, 1983), 127–28
Giles Worsley, 'Hornby Castle, Yorkshire', *Country Life*, 29 June 1989

Horton, Yorkshire (WR/Lancashire)
West Riding magistrates
Bridge enlarged, 1765

The bridge over Horton (alias Stock) Beck was enlarged in 1765.

West Yorkshire Archive Service, Wakefield, Book of Bridges 1752–1770

Howsham, Yorkshire (NR/NY)
North Riding magistrates
Unexecuted design for a bridge, n.d.

Carr produced a design for the bridge which was not used. The present bridge was built in 1812–13.

North Yorkshire County Record Office, Book of Bridges, 1772–1803, 59

Howsham Hall, Yorkshire (ER/NY) (Figs 168, 169)
Nathaniel Cholmley MP
Internal remodelling, c. 1775, Howsham Mill, 1760, and lodges
Attributed

Nathaniel Cholmley handsomely remodelled the principal reception rooms and the main bedrooms of the Elizabethan house in about 1775. The Great Hall with its screen of Doric columns, drawing room with Ionic pilasters and delicate stucco frieze and the gallery with handsome stucco ceiling are all fine rooms. The work has long been associated with Carr but documentary proof is lacking and stylistic comparison is not conclusive. However, Hutchinson refers to a letter seen by Dr Ivan Hall stating that Cholmley was leaving the house while Mr Carr carried out his work. The stables are unlikely to be by Carr.

Cholmley also rebuilt part of the adjacent village after many of the houses were demolished and their sites incorporated in the park in the late 1750s and the 1770s. Elizabeth Montagu commented that 'Mr and Mrs Cholmley … have built a village very near their house, and fitted up and furnished the houses with all the decent comforts humble life requires.'

Howsham Mill (now derelict), a pretty, Gothic structure with ogee door and quatrefoil windows, dated 1760 over the door, is also probably by Carr, as may be the two small hexagonal lodges near Howsham Bridge with round-arched gateways and rounded battlements.

168 Howsham Mill

169 Howsham Hall, Great Hall

Arthur Oswald, 'Howsham Hall, Yorks', *Country Life*, 24, 31
    August 1935
J. P. Neale, *Views of the Seats of Noblemen and Gentlemen* (London,
    1822), v, pl. 41
John Hutchinson, 'Howsham Hall', *York Georgian Society Report*,
    1982
K. J. Allison, *East Riding Water Mills*, East Yorkshire Local
    History Society, 1970, 44
BE/ER/495–96

Huthwaite Hall, Thurgoland, Yorkshire (WR/SY)

(Figs 2, 170)
John Cockshutt
New house and seven-arch stable block, 1748

A house for H. M. Cookschutts Esq at Huckwaite of 1748
is included in the A.P.S.D.'s list of Carr's commissions.
This is Huthwaite Hall, for John Cockshutt, an ironmaster
and owner of the Wortley ironworks. He may have known
the Carr family professionally. Robert Carr later ordered
iron plate from Cockshutt for Harewood House.
Huthwaite Hall is five bays wide and two and a half

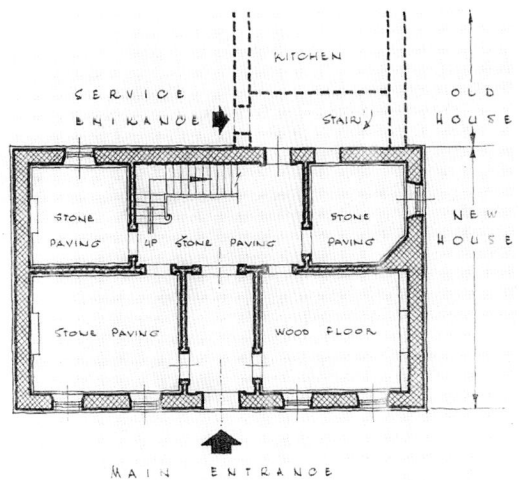

170 Huthwaite Hall, plan of ground floor

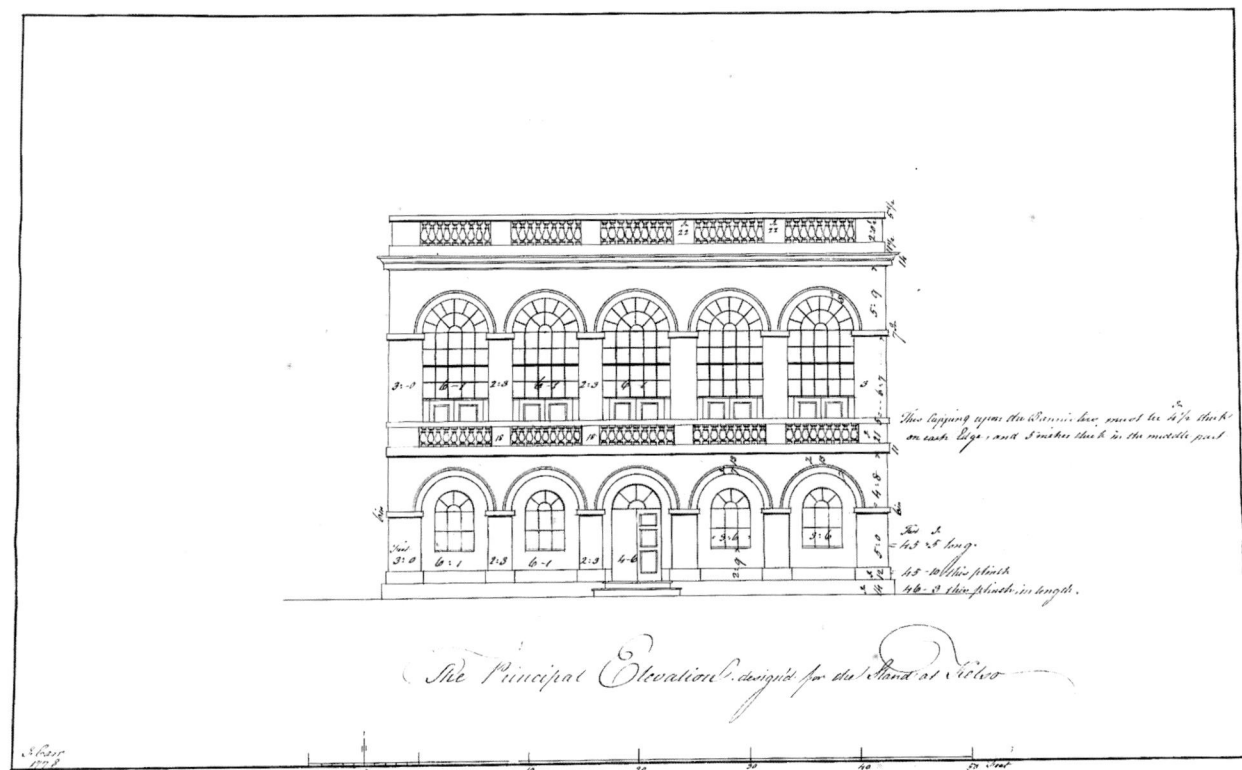

171 Design for Kelso grandstand

storeys high with a pedimented doorway and a projecting rear office wing.

Wyatt Papworth (ed.), *The Dictionary of Architecture issued by the Architectural Publications Society* (London, 1877), II, 36
Mary and Brian Wragg, 'A House for Mr Cockshutt', *Hunterian Society Transactions*, 7.v (1956), 271–75
BE/WR/517
BE/NR/164

Kelso, Berwickshire (Fig. 171)
Sir Gilbert Elliot, Bt, MP, later Lord Minto
Unexecuted designs for a racecourse stand, 1778

Elliot, acting on behalf of 'the gentlemen of the county', commissioned plans for a stand at Kelso. Carr provided two designs, the second simpler and less expensive one incorporated the stairs into the body of the building. Carr suggested an ashlar front with the sides and rear 'a good hammered wall'. He also suggested pitch paper and gravel be used for the roof, adding that if this was unfamiliar to the workmen he would send someone to execute it. The stand would have been of two storeys, with a glazed arcaded first floor and projecting miranda or balcony. The ground floor would have had two rooms, one for tea, the other probably for preparation. A single room, 41 ft 5 in by 18 ft, was planned for the first floor, with stairs leading to the roof, which could also have been used for viewing.

National Library of Scotland, Minto Papers MS 13233, fols 112–131, letters, plans, elevations and sections signed by Carr
Malcolm Airs, 'The Strange History of Paper Roofs', *Transactions of the Ancient Monuments Society*, 42 (1998), 41
Tessa Gibson, 'The Designs for the Knavesmire Grandstand, York', *Georgian Group Journal*, 8 (1998), 76–87

Kilnwick Hall, Beswick, Yorkshire (ER/Humberside)
John Grimston
Alterations, 1769–72
Thomas Grimston
Alterations, 1781
Demolished, 1951

Grimston was a friend of Stephen Thompson of Kirby Hall and frequently discussed building with him. He bought Kilnwick Hall in 1747, which had been substantially reconstructed in the 1720s, and carried out further work before his death in 1751. He was succeeded by his son John who commissioned Carr to carry out further alterations in 1769. Work, which included reroofing, new rainwater goods, and the addition of a bay window added to small drawing room on the east front of the house, began in 1770 and lasted until 1772. Cortese was employed on the plasterwork, as was Addinal, and Edward Elwick was involved with the furniture and internal decorations.

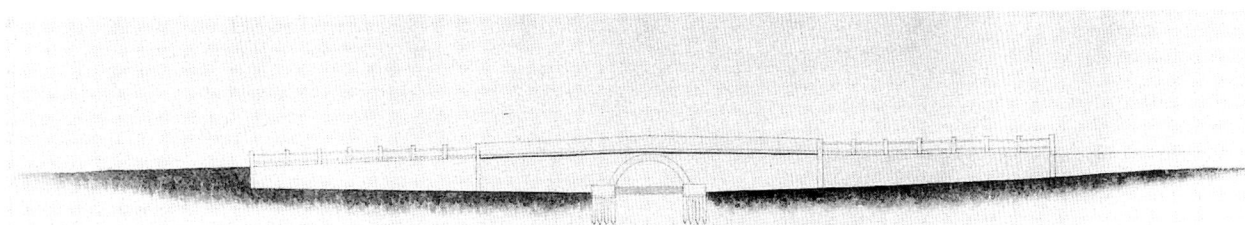

North Kilvington Bridge near Thirsk between Birdforth and Allertonshire Wapentakes.

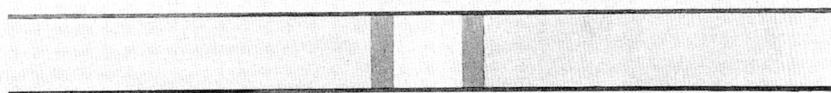

Plan of North Kilvington Bridge which was widened and improved by the Riding in 1775 the doing of which cost £200

172 Drawing of Kilvington bridge

On John Grimston's death in 1780 his son Thomas made further changes. The library was given new woodwork, a fashionable fireplace and delicate low relief stucco ceiling. Carr also proposed a new single-storey drawing room with apsidal ends 22 ft 6 in by 44 ft in 1781 but this was not built.

Two gate lodges and one or two estate buildings, characteristically Carr, remain. Townend Farm at Kilnwick, a three-bay, two-storey farmhouse with the windows set within a recessed arcade similar to Carr's Home Farm at Hornby Castle has been attributed to Carr by Ivan Hall.

Design by Carr inscribed 'Plan of the new drawing Room particularly delineated for the Workmen', dated 1781, and design by Carr for a Greek Doric bath house and entrance gates formerly in the possession of Francis Johnson

East Riding of Yorkshire Record Office, Grimston Papers, DDGR/42/3, 19–22

M. E. Ingram, *Leaves from a Family Tree* (Hull, 1951), 66–70, 113.

Ivan Hall, 'John Carr: A New Approach', *York Georgian Society Report*, 1972, 27, plate

David Neave and Edward Waterson, *The Lost Houses of East Yorkshire* (Bridlington, 1989), 36–39

BE/ER/578

Kilvington Bridge, South Kilvington, Yorkshire (NR/NY) (Fig. 172)
North Riding magistrates
New bridge, 1774–75
Demolished 1970

Tenders were invited in 1774 to build a bridge over Spital Beck on the Thirsk–Yarm road to a plan drawn by Mr Carr.

North Yorkshire County Record Office, Book of Bridges, 1772–1803, 54; North Riding Quarter Sessions April 1775 *York Courant*, 16 August 1774

Kirby Hall, Little Ouseburn, Yorkshire (WR/NR) (Fig. 3)
Stephen Thompson
Supervision and design of interiors, 1748–55
Demolished except the stables, 1920

Stephen Thompson, a wealthy London merchant and money broker, decided to build a new house on the family's Yorkshire estate during the lifetime of his father, who did not die until 1760, aged eighty-three. He consulted Colonel Moyser over the plan and on his advice also approached Roger Morris. He also showed his plan to James Paine. According to a contemporary engraving Thompson provided the plan; the elevations were produced by Morris (who died in 1749) and the Earl of Burlington (who died in 1753) and the building was 'Executed & inside finishings, by J. Carr, Architect'.

The foundation stone was laid on 14 September 1747, but in March the following year Thompson was forced to dismiss the supervisor following a quarrel with one of his father's servants. He was replaced by Carr, who is first mentioned in a letter to his friend Thomas Grimston dated 10 May 1748 in which Thompson commented that he was going 'to Meet my New Overseer to put him in a way of going on with my Workmen'. In 1749 he referred to him as 'a clever Young Fellow of a Mason at the Head of my Works'. Although Thompson hoped to finish the building by 1752 it was not completed until 1755.

British Library, Kings Maps, XLV, 24–1
East Riding Record Office, Grimston Papers, DD GR 41/4/2,3,27,44; 41/5/2,3,5,17,13,17; 41/6/18; 41/7/24
James Woolfe and John Gandon, *Vitruvius Britannicus* (London, 1771), v, pls 70–71
Edward Waterson and Peter Meadows, *The Lost Houses of the West Riding* (Welburn, 1998), 15
Brett Harrison, 'Thorp Arch Hall, 1749–1756: "dabbling a little in Mortar"', *Thoresby Society*, 2nd ser., 4 (1994 for 1993),

Kirkham Bridge, Firby, Yorkshire (NR/NY)
North Riding magistrates
Unexecuted design for a new bridge, 1806

Designs for a new bridge over the River Derwent were presented to North Riding magistrates but probably never used.

North Yorkshire County Record Office, Book of Bridges, 1772–1803, 58

Kirkland Hall, Churchtown, Lancashire (Fig. 173)
Alexander Butler
New house, 1760
Attributed

173 Kirkland Hall, entrance front

Two-and-a-half storeys, handsomely proportioned, the seven-bay brick house with stone details has a central projecting pediment, handsome stone coat of arms in the pediment, plat band and quoins. According to Sir Howard Colvin the houses is dated 1760 over the front door. Colvin also notes that the front elevation is virtually identical to Langford Hall, Nottinghamshire.

The Tuscan porch is unusually light for Carr at this date. The doorway has side windows similar to Clifton Hall, Rotherham, and Lytham Hall. Part of the earlier house was retained as offices.

Peter Fleetwood-Hesketh, *Murray's Lancashire Architectural Guide* (London, 1955), 71, fig. 146
BE/North Lancs/152

St Cuthbert's Church, Kirkleatham, Redcar, Yorkshire (NR/Cleveland) (Figs 174, 175)
William Turner MP
Rebuilt upper part of tower and body of church, 1759–63

A petition was submitted to rebuild the decayed church on 21 June 1756 and Carr was paid £24 3s in 1759 by William Turner for a draught of the church. Turner was the father of Sir Charles Turner who used Carr to remodel Kirkleatham Hall. The builder was Robert Corney, a local master carpenter, who according to Ord was 'both architect and builder' of the church and may have modified Carr's designs.

The church is of stone, of the highest quality of workmanship. The nave, with round-headed windows, is of four bays and the choir has a Venetian east window. The interior has an arcade of Tuscan columns. The lower part of the tower is of 1731 and James Gibbs's mausoleum of 1740 was retained at the north-east end of the church.

Borthwick Institute, York, Reg. 36, fols 167[r–v]
North Yorkshire County Record Office, Kirkleatham account book, 1759
John Ord, *The History and Antiquities of Cleveland* (London, 1846), 374
A. C. Taylor, 'Kirkleatham', *Architectural Review*, 124, 247–50, October 1958
BE/NR/218

Kirkleatham Hall, Redcar, Yorkshire (NR/Cleveland) (Figs 34, 176)
Sir Charles Turner
Alterations and extensions, 1764–67, 1779–80
Demolished, 1954

Turner succeeded his great-uncle Cholmley Turner in 1757 and called in Carr, who also worked for him at Clints Hall. Arthur Young, writing in 1768, was particularly impressed by Carr's alterations: 'Those who would wish to see an excellent living house, in which the agreeable part of convenience is consulted, without destroying the scale of a large family, will be pleased with this seat, which, I must

174 *left* St Cuthbert's Church, Kirkleatham, exterior | **175** *right* St Cuthbert's Church, Kirkleatham, interior

176 Kirkleatham Hall, dining room

be allowed to think, does great honour to the abilities of Mr Carr.'

Carr remodelled the seventeenth-century hall, providing a Gothic elevation with crenellations and hoodmoulds over the windows, and adding tall, two-storey, two-bay wings, one with a broad bow window. The gallery in the east wing was 61 ft long and 21 ft high. Photographs of the dining room show that its coved ceiling had particularly elaborate plasterwork with a central cartouche celebrating hunting, mythological scenes and garlands supported by ox skulls hanging between rosettes. Carr appears regularly in the accounts from 1764, particularly in 1766 and 1767, with Robert Corney as the principal builder. The plasterers James Henderson and William Sutton and Co. are mentioned in the accounts. The stables, built about 1750, are characteristic of Carr but the relevant account book is missing.

There are a number of other Gothic works at Kirkleatham whose date and authorship has never been satisfactorily resolved. These include the entrance gate, a dovecote-eyecatcher, the two angle bastions to the north of the house, and a similar pair of arrow-slitted bastions on Turner's Hospital, which as Pevsner notes, seem unlikely to be part of the original construction of 1742. These may all be Carr's work. According to Young, Turner also erected five farmhouses and associated buildings 'in the strongest manner of brick, tile and proportionable timbers', fourteen cottages round a green together with shops and an inn to form a new village, and in the nearby 'little fishing town' a bathing house, inn and grain warehouse for merchants. He also also built six new farm houses at another estate which he owned, Wombwell in the West Riding, about three miles north of Wentworth Woodhouse.

Carr was still working for Turner at the end of his life. In 1779 accounts show that he was paid £100; in 1780 he was due a further £205 5s 2d and £150 was paid him on account in 1782. In 1783 Carr was receiving interest on debts owed to him and the final balance of Carr's account, £121 10s 6d, was paid in February 1785, two years after Turner's death.

North Yorkshire County Record Office, Kirkleatham papers, ZK 6564, 6565, 9598

Arthur Young, *A Six Months Tour through the North of England* (London, 1770), II, 107

R. B. Wragg, 'John Carr: Gothic Revivalist', in *Studies in Architectural History*, ed. by W. A. Singleton (London and York, 1956), II, 23–25

Edward Waterson and Peter Meadows, *Lost Houses of York and the North Riding* (Welburn, 1998), 22–23, figs

BE/NR/218

Kirklees Hall, Brighouse, Yorkshire (WR/WY)
(Fig. 177)
Sir George Armytage, Bt, MP
Alterations, 1759–60

Sir John Armytage considered remodelling the Jacobean house and had consulted James Paine when he was killed in a raid on the French coast in 1758. He was succeeded by his 24-year-old brother George who converted the house from a Jacobean to a Georgian residence. Carr was brought in to design the main staircase, the back stair, passage, arcade and outside door in 1759. The hanging staircase is particularly impressive. It was made possible by structural ironwork supplied by Maurice Tobin in 1760 at a cost of £249 15s.

Carr invoiced £7 17s 6d in 1761 for five journeys and £6 10s for his designs. His brother Robert, who supervised the work, visited eleven times between July 1759 and February 1760, was paid £20 3s. Work continued until Sir George died in 1783 but it is not known if Carr was involved in the later work. William Lindley was paid for plans in 1777.

177 Kirklees Hall, staircase

'Kirklees Hall, Yorkshire', *Country Life*, 22 August 1908
D. Nortcliffe, 'The Restyling of Kirklees Hall, 1753–90', *Halifax Archaeological Society*, 1982, 28–37
Peter Thornborrow, 'John Carr's West Yorkshire Buildings', *York Georgian Society*, 1992, 29

Knaresborough House, Knaresborough, Yorkshire
(WR/NY) (Figs 178, 179)
James Collins
New house, 1768
Attributed

James Collins was lawyer to the Lascelles family and the new house he built on the High Street in Knaresborough is only two miles from Plompton and Goldsborough. It is dated 1768 by stained glass signed Peckitt 1768.

The house is attributed stylistically to Carr. It is a detached, set-back stone house of two and a half storeys, five bays wide with lower two-bay wings and a porch with Doric columns and pediment. The design, particularly the use of continuous cill and plat bands and pilasters under the first-floor windows and the lower wings, is close to that of Well Head House, Huddersfield. The Chinese fret chimneypiece now in Conyngham Hall, Knaresborough, very similar to those by Carr at Norton Place and Wiganthorpe, may have come from Knaresborough House.

York Georgian Society, *The Works in Architecture of John Carr* (York, 1973), 8, 19
BE/WR/297

Langford Hall, Nottinghamshire (Fig. 180)
Henry Duncombe MP
New house and stables, c. 1774

Langford Hall, originally Langford Place, is a plain, brick house, two and a half storeys high, seven bays wide, with a three-bay central pediment and simple Tuscan porch very similar to Kirkland Hall, Lancashire. It is relieved with characteristic Carr touches, a delicate modillion cornice, a plat band and running cill, balusters under the first-floor windows and a pedimented Doric porch, together with garlands in the pediment. The main rooms were elegantly fitted up.

Elizabeth Chivers ascribes the house to Carr in her travel diary of 1803 where she noted 'a pretty new house which belongs to Charles Duncombe Esq. designed by Mr Carr'. Throsby writing in 1790 described it as 'newly built, at present not inhabited'. However, the house must have been built some time before, probably in the 1770s. The substantial estate had been bought by Thomas Duncombe, of the Yorkshire family of Duncombe Park, in 1722. On his death in 1746 it was left first to his wife Sarah after his death and then to his third son Henry Duncombe, of Copgrove, Yorkshire. Sarah Duncombe died in 1774. A lease made in 1781 by Henry Duncombe

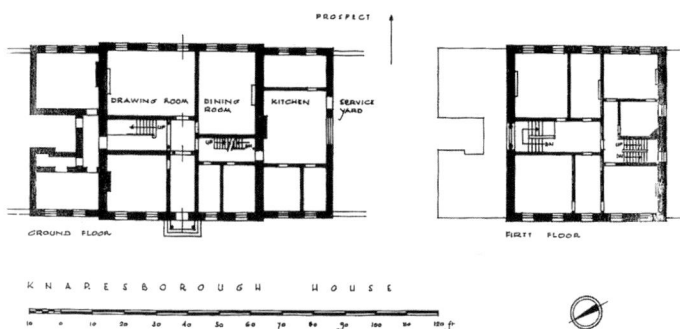

178 *above* Knaresborough House, entrance front
179 *below* Knaresborough House, plan of ground and first floors

shows that he built Langford Hall, referring to it as 'all that capital messuage or mansion house then lately erected and built'. This replaced the old house at Langford, which he would have found small and inconvenient as it had been built as a hunting lodge in the 1630s and had been leased to a farmer for many years. A long, two-storey service wing has been demolished.

Nottingham University Library, Middleton papers, Mi Da 45
Robert Thoroton, *The Antiquities of Nottinghamshire*, ed. by John Throsby (Nottingham, 1790), 1, 369
M. W. Barley, 'Langford Hall: A Probable 17th-century Hunting Lodge', *Transactions of the Thoroton Society*, 92 (1988), 47
BE/Notts/163

Latimers, Latimer, Buckinghamshire
Lord George Cavendish
Proposed alterations, 1782

Lord George Cavendish, uncle of the 5th Duke of Devonshire, inherited Latimers, which had been owned by the Cavendishes since 1615, in 1779. Horace Walpole described the house in 1755 as recently much improved but having 'undergone the Batty Langley discipline'. In 1782 Cavendish married the daughter and co-heiress of the Earl of Northampton. That year Carr, who was also employed by Cavendish at Holker, surveyed the house, providing two plans showing what he thought should be done.

His report stated that the house was in poor structural condition; that the west side was so ruinous that it ought to be taken down and replaced with offices; that the south and east roofs needed retiling; that the wooden parapet on the south and east fronts should be taken down and rebuilt in brick 'in a Gothick form' and the brickwork rendered like the front of the house; and that the gable ends should be taken down to render the roof and gutters less complicated and replaced by proper windows for the garrets. Carr also suggested that the best way to create good new bedrooms was to divide the upstairs dining and drawing rooms into apartments and that tiles from the demolished west wing could be used to roof the new offices and repair the remaining roofs. The cost of the work was estimated at £4,640. It is not known if the proposals were executed and the house was rebuilt in 1832 by Edward Blore.

Carr report in the possession of Mrs R. B. Wragg
Estate Office, Latimers, drawing by Carr of 'Moorish Gothic' building
Victoria County History, *Buckinghamshire* (London, 1925), III, 27
The Correspondence of Horace Walpole, ed. by W. S. Lewis (London, 1973), XXXV, 233–35
BE/Bucks/426

St John's Church, Briggate, Leeds (WR/WY)
Alterations, 1764–65
Overcrowding led to the addition of new galleries on the south and west walls of the church. The scheme was promoted by the vicar, John Murgatroyd, and four prominent parishioners: Francis Blaydes, Thomas Lodge, Richard Wilson and Jeremiah Dixon (for whom Carr had designed a town house in Boar Lane in 1750). The scheme was granted a licence in 1764.

Despite the strong Gothic character of the building Carr designed utilitarian galleries with a plain panelled Classical front. He provided the joiners with full-scale working drawings ('described at large for the Joyners work') for the masons for the new west window. The joiner was William Hargreaves, a leading local master carpenter, whose contract Carr witnessed on 27 March 1764. Cast-iron pillars were provided by Maurice Tobin & Son at a cost of £32 7s 5d, along with other ironwork. Carr sent in his invoice on 10 October 1765, charging £20 for the designs, for arranging the joiner's contract, for measuring the work and for several journeys to direct execution of the work. He was paid on 30 July 1766. The galleries were removed in 1867.

Terry Friedman, 'Church Architecture in Leeds 1700–1799', *Thoresby Society*, 2nd ser., 7 (1997), 52–56, 179–80, fig. 12

St Peter's Church, Kirkgate, Leeds, Yorkshire (WR/WY)
Repairs, 1761, 1766, new vestry room, 1772
Demolished
In September 1761 the churchwardens resolved to apply to 'Mr Jno Carr of York Architect … to view [and] give his opinion as to ye manner & Expence of makg a new Roof'. In December he submitted an 'Estimate of ye Expence of repairing ye Roof … over ye south & north Isles & ye Crossing Roof with his directions as to ye manner of affecting ye sd Repair & deliver'd in his Estimate mark'd … A containing 13 Pages.' It was agreed that the south aisle be repaired to Carr's plan but what work was done is unrecorded. Carr may have been responsible for removing the rails and banisters surrounding the font in 1764.

In 1766 Carr received two guineas for 'a Modell of the West Window'. Again it is unclear if Carr's work was executed. He designed a new vestry room in 1772, which was built by Robert Rhodes whose estimate was £186 1s 6d. Its appearance is unknown.

Terry Friedman, 'Church Architecture in Leeds 1700–1799', *Thoresby Society* 2nd ser., 7 (1997), 34–36, 46

House at Bridge End, Leeds, Yorkshire (WR/WY)
George Green
New house, prior to 1769
George Green was a wealthy Leeds grocer with a family house at Bridge End or Briggate. In February 1769 Carr wrote to Mr Hey discussing work on the Leeds Infirmary and recommending Hawkswell, a Leeds joiner, as a possible surveyor to succeed Wilkinson. Carr described him as a sensible man and commented that he had conducted 'Mr Green's house at the Bridge End under my directions very well'. This may refer to Green's own house, valued in 1768 at £500, or alternatively to the new warehouse by the bridge, valued at £2,100. An earlier house and warehouse on the site had been acquired by the Improvement Commissioners and demolished for street widening under the terms of the Bridge Act of 1760. The warehouse had been described as 'part unfinished' in December 1761.

Leeds Infirmary 31/1, Letter Book 1767–73, letter from Carr, 13 February 1769
Maurice Beresford, 'East End, West End. The Face of Leeds during Urbanisation 1684–1847', *Thoresby Society*, 60 and 61 (1985/86), 117

House in Boar Lane, Leeds, Yorkshire (WR/WY)
Jeremiah Dixon
New house, 1750–53
Demolished
A house for J. Dixon in Leeds in 1753 is included in Carr's list of works in the A.P.S.D. This is presumably Jeremiah

180 Langford Hall, entrance front

Dixon, later of Gledhow Hall. According to Whitaker, Richard Wilson sold Sir William Rooke's estate in Boar Lane to John Dixon, a merchant, whose only son Jeremiah pulled down the house and rebuilt it very handsomely in 1750, the stone for the front being brought from the Huddleston Quarry. Dixon's old premises were advertised for sale in the *York Courant* in 1753. Dixon sold the house to Thomas Lee Jnr for £4,500 in 1763.

Wyatt Papworth (ed.), *The Dictionary of Architecture issued by the Architectural Publications Society* (London, 1877), II, 36
Thomas Whitaker, *Ducatus Leodiensis* (Leeds, 1816), 5
Maurice Beresford, 'East End, West End. The Face of Leeds during Urbanisation 1684–1847', *Thoresby Society*, 60 and 61 (1985/86), 125

House in Kirkgate, Leeds, Yorkshire (WR/WY)
Sir Henry Ibbetson, Bt
Extension, 1752–54
Demolished

Henry Ibbetson succeeded his father James, one of the half dozen leading merchants in the West Riding, in 1739.

He was also left his house in Kirkgate, rebuilt in 1715, and described by Thoresby as 'one of the best houses in town'. Ibbetson further advanced the business and had an annual income of over £1,000 a year. In 1748 he was made a baronet.

Initially Ibbetson preferred his suburban villas at Shadwell and then Great Woodhouse but from 1751 lived principally in the house in Kirkgate. This was substantially extended by a new wing on the site of an adjacent house, which was rebuilt by Carr in 1752 at a cost of £1,800. The rebuilding was controversial as the new front extended into the street on land which did not belong to Ibbetson. Complaints were ignored and the following year Ibbetson was elected to the Leeds Corporation as a common councilman and then mayor.

In January 1754 Ibbetson wrote recommending his carver to William Gossip. Describing him as 'an ingenious and a very good workman' he explained that he had been near a year with him and should be finished by the end of March. Ibbetson explained that it was Carr who had told him that Gossip was looking for a carver and it is clear from the letter that Carr supervised Ibbetson's work. A subsequent letter from Carr in April reveals that the carver was Mr Loan.

The house was valued for sale in 1770 at £2,500 but did not sell until 1781.

West Yorkshire Archives Service, Leeds, Thorp Arch papers, TA23/2

Maurice Beresford, 'East End, West End. The Face of Leeds during Urbanisation 1684–1847', *Thoresby Society*, 60 and 61 (1985/86), 112

R. G. Wilson, 'Merchants of Land: The Ibbetsons of Leeds and Denton 1650–1850', *Northern History*, 24 (1988), 84–89, 92, 94

Leeds General Infirmary, Leeds, Yorkshire (WR/WY)

((Figs 25, 181)

Hospital, 1768–71

Demolished 1893

Although a growing town, Leeds had no hospital so a committee met in May 1767 to 'consider the Expediency of an Infirmary'. Among the members of the committee was Carr's patron Jeremiah Dixon. John Royds, another of Carr's clients, was asked to solicit support for the scheme from the inhabitants of Halifax and Edwin Lascelles of Harewood House, who subscribed £100, laid the foundation stone. The minute and letter books of the building committee contain all the contracts, prices and details of the various problems encountered.

The following April Carr presented plans and elevations to the committee, which accepted them and asked him to produce an estimate. Carr explained that pressure of work meant he could not supervise the building. Instead he recommended Mr Wilkinson of Wakefield, explaining that he would 'wish to give my designs and directions to his care rather than to a set of ignorant workmen'. Drawings and the estimate of 'a little more than £2,500 if properly managed' were produced in June and the foundation stone was laid in October.

Work did not proceed smoothly. Wilkinson was too ill to complete the detailed drawings or superintend construction and resigned his post. Some of the contractors defaulted and the foundations filled with water. Carr visited the site in May 1769 and ordered that the foundation be demolished and rebuilt. After attempts to persuade Mr Gott and John Riley to accept the post of supervisor failed Carr's brother Robert took on the job at 10s 6d per day.

In May 1770 Carr was providing drawings for the vestibule, staircase cornice, chapel cornice and board room. Economy prevailed. The dentil and flute were left out of the staircase cornice, the chapel cornice was left plain and the carved mouldings were left out of the chapel. On 2 January 1771 Carr was asked to send a proper person over to survey and measure the building and it finally opened in February 1771 at a cost £4,599.

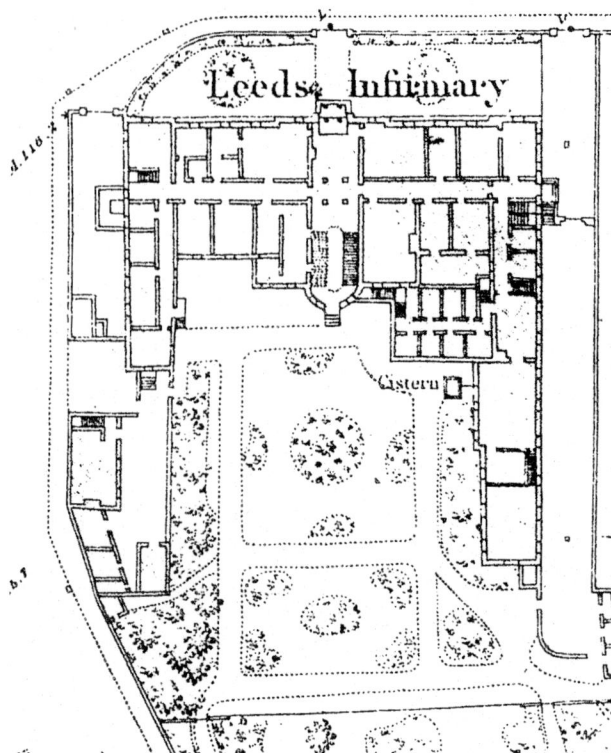

181 Leeds Infirmary, plan of ground floor in 1847

Carr's balance 'for designing and superintending etc the Infirmary at Leeds' of £98 5s was paid in December 1772.

Matthew Reader, Thomas Sutcliffe and William Smith, all of Leeds, were the bricklayers, William Hargreave, John Kendall and Thomas Anderson the carpenters. John Craven and John Lister contracted to do the masons' work, but Lister soon dropped out. Plasterwork was by John Johnson; plumbing by Mary Green; Jos. Boynton was the painter; Maurice Tobin provided locks, hinges, the balustrade for the stairs and the gates; and the carver was Mr Wade.

The building was a handsomely detailed brick structure with stone details. It had two storeys with Venetian windows in the central and end bays and first-floor windows set in relieving arches. John Howard, the lively reformer not given to unnecessary praise, was much impressed by the hospital in 1788, announcing that 'This is one of the best Hospitals in the Kingdom. The building is of brick, and is what such places ought to be — plain, handsome and substantial … The length of the building is 150 ft, width 38 ft. The court is 186 ft by 30. The back court with the offices and gardens 186 ft by 120 … In the wards which are 15 ft 8 in high, there is paid great attention to cleanliness and six circular appertures, or ventilators open into a passage 5¼ ft wide.'

Wings were added in 1782 and 1786 and the attic storey in 1792. The Infirmary was demolished in 1893.

Leeds General Infirmary records 31/1, Building Committee
    Minutes, 1768–74; Book of Letters 1767–73
Engraving after a drawing by Wilkinson owned by Bootham
    Park Hospital
J. Ryley, *Leeds Guide* (Leeds, 1806)
Thomas Dunham Whitaker, *Loidis and Elmete* (Leeds, 1816), 84
Sydney Kitson, 'Carr of York', *RIBA Journal*, 17, 254, 8 January
    1910
S. T. Anning, *General Infirmary at Leeds* (Edinburgh and London,
    1963), i
Kevin Grady, *The Georgian Public Buildings of Leeds and the West
    Riding*, Thoresby Society Publications, 62 (1987), pl. 6 (b), 122,
    139

Leventhorpe Hall, Swillington, Yorkshire (WR/WY)

(Figs 182, 183)
Richard Green
New house, 1774–77

Elizabeth Chivers noted in her travel diary of 1803, 'a
beautiful villa built by Richard Green Esq and designed by
Mr Carr'. This was Richard Green who died in 1790, aged
eighty, and whose memorial is in Swillington Church. A
set of designs signed J. Carr, one dated June 1777,
survives, although they are not inscribed with the name of
the house or owner. However, a tablet on the side of the
house gives Carr's name and the date 1774.

The house was of two storeys and seven bays with a
central canted bay on the entrance front, which led to a
circular hall, and a pair of canted bays on the garden front.
These lit the dining and drawing rooms, one of which had
semi-circular ends, the other canted ends. Services were in
attached wings similar to those at Thornes House and
Basildon Park. These have been demolished and the
interior stripped.

Four architectural drawings in the possession of Mrs Brian
    Wragg
Elizabeth Chivers's diary cited in H. M. Colvin, *Biographical
    Dictionary of British Architects* (New Haven and London, 1995),
    224
Thomas Whitaker, *Loidis et Elmete* (Leeds, 1816), 258
BE/WR/351

Lincoln, County Gaol, Lincoln Castle

Lincolnshire magistrates
Unexecuted plan for a new gaol, 1775

Davies includes the County Hall and Prison, Lincoln
Castle, 1786–88, in his list of Carr's commissions. In
August 1774 the Grand Jury commissioned William
Burrell-Massingberd (who employed Carr to make designs
for Ormsby Hall) 'to write to Mr Carr of York to take a
View of the Castle of Lincoln and make a Plan for
Erecting a New Gaol'. Carr's plan and estimate was
discussed at the Grand Jury in March 1775, when it was
decided that it should be further considered at the Assizes
in the summer. When nothing had happened by March
1779 Carr put in a bill for £97 5s. In July 1780 the

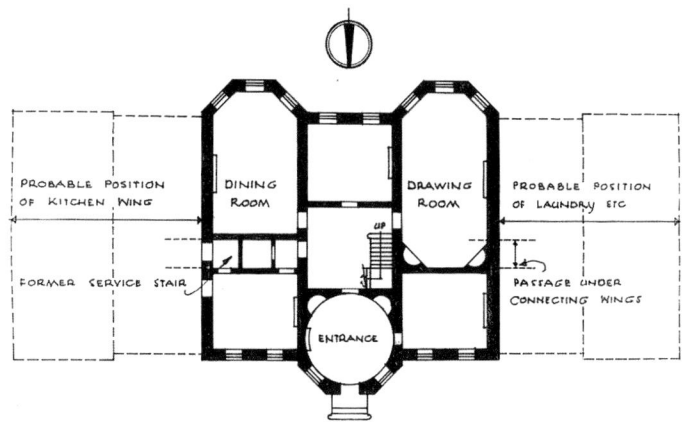

182 Leventhorpe Hall, garden front
183 Leventhorpe Hall, plan of ground floor

committee resolved to pay Carr £50 on account as 'this
Plan may in a short time be adopted when the Mode of
Paying the whole will then be discharged in the usual
manner of so much per cent upon the Building'. When
nothing more had happened by July 1781, Carr's bill was
again considered and he was paid the remaining £47 5s.
No reference was made to Carr's plan when William Legg,
John Langwith and William Lumby submitted designs for
the gaol in 1785. Lumby's scheme was accepted and
carried into effect in 1786–88.

Lincolnshire Archives, CO.C.2/1, pp. 156, 158, 171–75, 180,
    184–85
Lincolnshire County Record Office, Minute Book of the Grand
    Jury; Minute and Order Book (Sleaford)

184 Lincoln Hospital

R. Davies, 'A Memoir of John Carr', *Yorkshire Archaeological Journal*, 4 (1877), 205
Archaeological Journal, 103 (1946), 158
H. M. Colvin, *Biographical Dictionary of British Architects* (New Haven and London, 1995), 628
BE/Lincs/506

The County Hospital, Wordsworth Street, Lincoln
(Fig. 184)

New hospital, 1776–81

In January 1776 Christopher Nevile was authorized to discuss the requirements of a proposed hospital with Carr, who was working at the time for two of the Lincolnshire gentry, John Harrison, at Norton Place, and Edmund Turnor, at Panton Hall. On 30 March it was minuted 'That the plan for a new Hospital generously given by Mr Carr be accepted and that the thanks of this Board be transmitted to him for the same with a request that he will accept the compliment of becoming a Governor for Life of the said Hospital.'

The comprehensive nature of the accommodation provided, must have reflected Carr's previous experience of hospital design: '4 wards to contain 20 men and 20 women patients besides eight small rooms for accidental patients with a Fire place in each room with separate back staircase to each ward, a Committee room, physicians room, outpatients room, Surgery or apothecarys siting room, apothecarys Shop, Matrons room, Kitchen, back kitchen, hot and cold Baths, Cellar pantries etc. Bed

Chambers for apothecary, Matron, four nurses, four Women and one Man servants, an operation room with Skylight a Cell or dead House with proper conveniences in each ward for Close stools or water closets.'

Advertisements were inserted in the Lincoln, York and Cambridge newspapers asking for sealed tenders from tradesmen by May 1776. Work started in the same month and on 19 October 1777 a sermon was preached in the Cathedral to mark the opening of the hospital. William Lumby, the Lincoln architect and builder, superintended the erection for 60 guineas. The total cost, according to a note in the Willson Collection at the Society of Antiquaries, came to £2,668 15s 2d. Despite having almost as much accommodation as Bootham Asylum — room for forty-eight patients as compared with fifty-four — it cost less than half the money and took half the time to construct.

Planned very simply on three storeys, the County Hospital is a rectangular block with staircases at each end connected by a corridor. It is a plain building, 80 ft long, of brick, three storeys with a nine-bay centre, three-bay pediment and projecting wings, and was extended in the nineteenth century. A new hospital was built in 1860 and the building is now used by the Lincoln Theological College.

Lincolnshire Archives, HOSP/1 fols 44–45
Thomas Sympson, *A Short Account of the Old and of the New Lincoln County Hospitals* (Lincoln, 1878), 3–5, 15, 60
BE/Lincs/510

185 Lismore Sessions House

Lismore, Co. Waterford (Fig. 185)
5th Duke of Devonshire
Design for Sessions House, 1799

Carr provided designs for a new Sessions House on the
Duke of Devonshire's Irish estate at Lismore in 1799. The
building was to include a market hall on the ground floor
for the weighing of corn and potatoes, as well as a couple
of small rooms for men and women prisoners and proper
accommodation for the clerk of the peace and the
jurymen. The building, which was to be of stone, was to
cost about £1,000.

It is not clear if Carr's design was executed but the
existing building, which resembles one of his park lodges
blown up on a much larger scale, could be by Carr. The
building is of stone, of two storeys with a central
pedimented pavilion and lower wings. The sessions hall is
lit by a round-headed window in a shallow receiving arch.
The Italianate clocktower is a later addition. The Old
Sessions House is now used by the Lismore Heritage
Centre.

Chatsworth House Archives, letter from Carr to John Heaton
dated 23 August 1799

Burlington House, Piccadilly, London
3rd Duke of Portland
Alterations, 1771–76, 1786–87

The Duke of Portland rented Burlington House from his
brother-in-law the Duke of Devonshire in October 1770.
By then Lord Burlington's decoration must have seemed
old fashioned and the house neglected as it had not been
lived in since the death of Lady Burlington in 1758. Carr
was called in to modernize and restore the interiors. In
October 1771 Carr wrote to Portland that work would be
complete by Christmas, but a series of bills show
considerable activity between March 1774 and September
1776.

Christopher Dixon of Pimlico appears to have been the
Clerk of Works. He was owed £500 in May 1772, £300 in
March 1774 and £300 in January 1775. The principal
craftsmen were the carver and gilder Solomon Hudson,
the bricklayer Henry Holland, the plasterer Thomas
Collins and the monumental mason John Devall.

Much of the work was simple repair, particularly in the
saloon and main staircase, whose sumptuous decoration
probably spared it the radical alterations made elsewhere

in the house. The most significant changes were the addition of a canted bay to the ballroom on the east side of the house (removed during Samuel Ware's alterations of 1815–19) and the creation of an Anti-Room from a huddle of small rooms behind it. New chimneypieces were commissioned for most of the rooms from John Devall. That in the centre room of the north front was an impressive affair of statuary and Sienna marble with goats' heads and festoons. Only two believed to be by Carr survive, in the Reynolds Room and Secretary's Room, although it is unlikely that either is in its original position. Carr also hung new mahogany doors.

More work may have been carried out in 1786–87, when the Duke of Portland reacquired the lease having surrendered it to Lord George Cavendish in 1782. In 1786 Carr wrote to Portland discussing chimneypieces, apparently for Burlington House, suggesting that he look at those in Mr Devall's or Mr Mail's shops. In 1787 eight and a half tons of lead were used to repair the flat roof at the west end of the house.

Nottingham University Library, Portland Papers, PwF 2,539, 2,546, 2,550, 5,670, 3,369-71; Pl F5/h/232
Survey of London (London, 1963), xxxii, 406
Tim Knox, 'The Decorative History of the Private Rooms of Burlington House', report for the Royal Academy, May 1998

Cleveland House, London
2nd Earl of Darlington
Design for a dining room, after 1774

The earl, for whom Carr worked at Raby Castle, inherited Cleveland House from his uncle the Duke of Cleveland in 1774. Carr's plan for finishing the sides of the great dining room has Ionic screens at each end. It is not known if it was executed. The house was remodelled by James Lewis in 1795–97 and demolished in 1840.

Alistair Rowan, 'Gothick Restoration at Raby Castle', *Architectural History*, 15 (1972), 46–47

Grosvenor Square, London
4th Earl Fitzwilliam
Alterations, 1781–83
Demolished

Carr examined the whole of Lord Fitzwilliam's house in Grosvenor Square in May 1781, which had been built in about 1728, and altered by Flitcroft in 1743. Two years later he spent two days settling the alterations and improvements necessary for the house. Substantial sums were spent by the earl on the house, £3,986 in 1785.

Sheffield Archives, Wwm Stw P6 (ii) 142, (iii) 21; A 1294–96
Survey of London, vol. XL, *The Grosvenor Estate* (London, 1980), 120

Low Bourn, Masham, Yorkshire (NR/NY) (Fig. 186)
North Riding magistrates
New bridge, 1775

The new bridge over the River Burn near Masham, with three 23 ft spans, was built in 1775.

North Yorkshire County Record Office, Book of Bridges, 1772–1803, 57

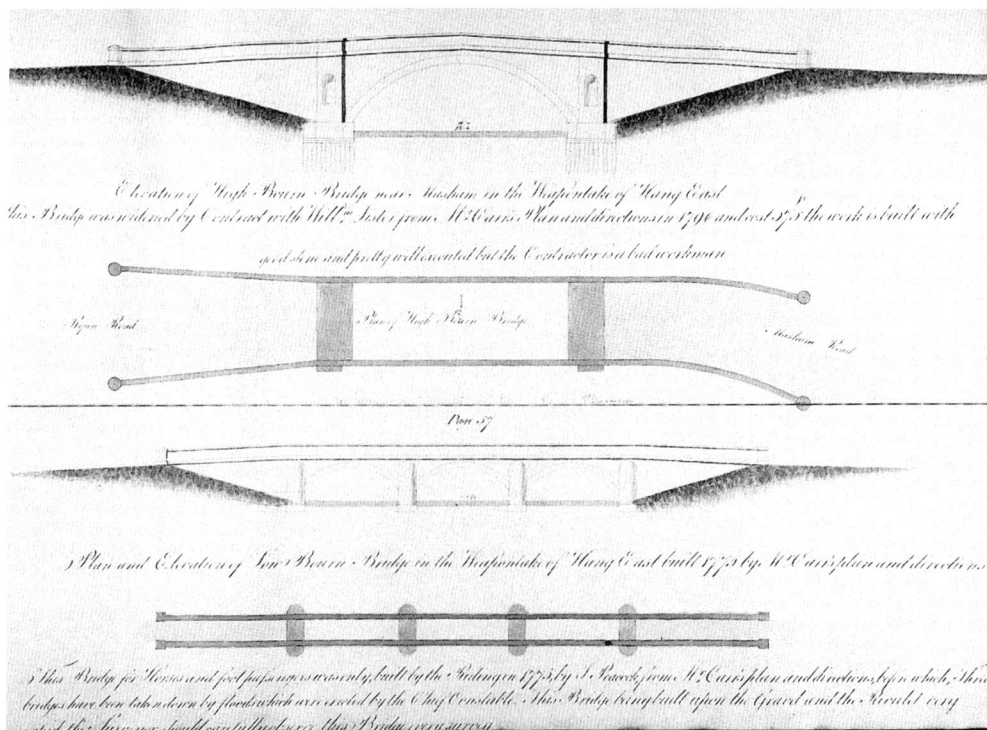

186 Drawing of Low Bourn bridge

187 *above* Lytham Hall, entrance front
188 *right* Lytham Hall, plan of ground, first and attic floors

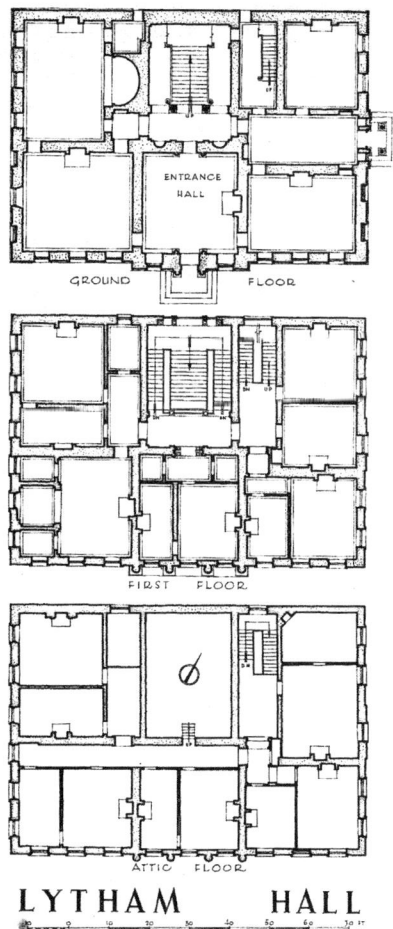

LYTHAM HALL

Lytham Hall, Lytham St Annes, Lancashire

(Figs 20, 187, 188)
Thomas Clifton
New house, 1757–64

Thomas Clifton inherited Clifton, which his family had bought in 1606, aged ten, in 1737. Twenty years later, although he had no obvious Yorkshire connections, he called in Carr to rebuild the house, which lies on flat pasturelands a mile from the estuary of the River Ribble.

Most of the building accounts, bills, plans and drawings have disappeared, but a labourers' account book first mentions building work in 1757 and in 1759 mentions 'Door Casing & Stoothing of grand Staircases Etc'. The 1757-64 account book of the steward, Raymond Watt, shows that the house was complete in 1764, when on 17 March Carr was paid £189 14*s*, the balance of his account. At the same time Mr Cortese was paid £56 18*s* 6*d*. Fitting up of the house continued well into the 1760s. Part of the old house was retained as offices round a low court to the rear of the house. A dovecote and stables was added in 1757 and 1758.

Care and money were lavished on the elevations, with an attached Ionic portico on the south elevation. The main rooms are on the ground floor, and the entrance hall, with a handsome Rococo ceiling, has a heavy Kentian

CATALOGUE

177

fireplace. The imperial staircase, one of Carr's finest creations, is particularly grand and may have been inspired by that by Paine at Doncaster Mansion House of 1745–48. The walls are decorated with cartouches, flowers, fruit along with a hunting bag, a gun, water bottle and a rabbit; or, a fiddle and bow, a flute, a mask, some sheet music and foliage. The ceiling is coved and coffered with flowers and foliage and a central allegorical figure, Jupiter clasping a fork of lightning surrounded by billowing clouds. The dining room shows the influence of Adam and must have been completed later. The house is now offices.

Lancashire County Record Office, A/c Book 'Ra Watt' 1757-64
Mark Girouard, 'Lytham Hall, Lancashire', *Country Life*, 21, 28
    July 1960
BE/N. Lancs 174

Marle Bridge, Darfield, Yorkshire (WR/SY)
West Riding magistrates
Rebuilt bridge, 1766

The bridge over the River Dearne on the Brampton-Houghton road near Darfield was rebuilt in 1766.

West Yorkshire Archive Service, Wakefield, Book of Bridges
    1752–1770

Marske, Yorkshire (NR/NY) (Fig. 189)
North Riding magistrates
New bridge, 1773

The three arch-bridge (also known as Downholme Bridge) with spans of 70 ft, 40 ft and 30 ft over the River Swale was built by King and Peacock for £1,200.

North Yorkshire County Record Office, Book of Bridges,
    1772–1803, 69
BE/NR/139

Methley Hall, Rothwell, Yorkshire (WR/WY)
Sir John Savile MP, 1st Earl of Mexborough
Alterations, before 1768
Demolished, 1963
Attributed

Arthur Young, visiting in 1768, noted that Methley was 'fitted up and furnished in so rich a manner, as to attract the attraction of visitors'. The house was an ancient one, although largely rebuilt around the turn of the sixteenth century, and the new work must have been carried out by Sir John Savile who succeeded in 1741. He was created Baron Pollington in 1753 and Earl of Mexborough in 1766, and died in 1778.

Wheater wrote in 1885, that 'an old engraving, which I have before me of Methley Hall, dated 1788, shows Carr's front then brand new' and Darbyshire and Lumb in 1888 state that 'the hall was remodelled for an earl by Carr of York'. Their comments were probably based on the statement in *Picturesque Views* in 1788 that the new front was 'said to have been executed by Carr of York'. However, the front, with its broken based pediment, central blind arch and projecting Gothic bays is not characteristic of Carr's work and would be more plausibly attributed to Daniel Garrett.

The interiors described by Young were clearly recent and Palladian in style. They included a vestibule, dining room and drawing room on the ground floor and three apartments on the first floor. Young commented that 'the articles of carving and gilding are done throughout the house with much elegance; and the doors, door-cases, window-frames, pannels, &c. are ornamented in this manner; the ceilings are in general very elegantly executed,

the scrolls of gilding, not crowded, but light and neat as well as rich, and the furniture equally well chose. The house, you doubtless observe, is not a large one, but it is, upon the whole, much better finished than most of its size in the kingdom, and than many more capital ones'. It may be that this was Carr's work.

The house was remodelled by A. Salvin in 1830–37.

Arthur Young, *A Six Month Tour through the North of England* (London, 1770), 387

Anon, *Picturesque Views of the Principal Seats of the Nobility and Gentry in England and Wales* (London, 1788), np

John Preston Neale, *Views of the Seats of Noblemen and Gentlemen* (London, 1818–25), v, pl. 45

W. Wheater, *Old Yorkshire* (London, 1885), 287

H. S. Darbyshire and G. D. Lumb, *The History of Methley*, Publications of the Thoresby Society, 35 (1934), 111

Edward Waterson and Peter Meadows, *Lost Houses of the West Riding* (Welburn, 1998), 24–25, figs

BE/WR/365–66

Middleton Lodge, Middleton Tyas, Yorkshire

(NR/NY) (Fig. 190)
George Hartley
New house and stables, 1777–c. 1780

The Hartleys, described as yeomen in the seventeenth century, rose to considerable wealth in the mid-eighteenth century thanks to the exploitation of lead and copper on their land. George Hartley succeeded his father Leonard in 1774 and in 1777 signed an agreement with the Richmond mason John Foss to build a new house 'according to the plans and under the Inspection and Direction of Mr John Carr of the City of York, Architect'. Carving, including chimneypieces, in the drawing room, dining room, octagon room and breakfast room was carried out by John

Dunn. Marble chimneypieces were provided by Foss and the stone for the project came from Hartley's own quarries. Hartley died before the house was complete. The house, of well-cut ashlar, is a particularly fine example of Carr's smaller house manner and is sited on a slight ridge to take advantage of views east and west. Of five bays and two storeys, with a central three-bay pediment and hipped roof, it has a modillion cornice, plat band, running cill, balusters under the first-floor windows and a pedimented Doric porch. The central curved central staircase is especially fine. The side and rear elevations both have canted bays and there is an attached office wing.

North Yorkshire County Record Office, ZKU III 4/1–13

T. R. Hornshaw, *Copper Mining in Middleton Tyas*, North Yorkshire Record Office Publications, no. 6 (1975)

BE/NR/255

Milton House, Soke of Peterborough

(Northamptonshire) (Fig. 75)
4th Earl Fitzwilliam
Alterations, 1792, 1803–05

After Wentworth Woodhouse became his main seat Earl Fitzwilliam continued regularly to visit his family home at Milton, principally in the winter for hunting. Milton had been modernized by Henry Flitcroft and Sir William Chambers in 1750–51 and 1771–73, but Fitzwilliam brought in Carr to do further work in the 1790s and 1800s. This probably included extending the south side of the service range east and filling in a yard to create two libraries, one now used as a dining room. The decoration of these rooms, compared by Hussey to the work of Henry Holland or Charles Tatham, is exceptionally restrained and the chimneypieces very advanced.

191 Morton-on-Swale bridge

Work seems to have begun with the library in 1792, for which John Fisher provided a chimneypiece identical to that for the dining room at Wentworth Woodhouse. This was delayed by Fisher's emprisonment for debt in February. Ill health prevented a visit by Carr in 1794 when Fitzwilliam wanted to discuss alterations and 'a great scheme' was being planned in February 1795. It is not clear if this was executed but a plan in Carr's hand watermarked 1802 survives in the Milton papers and work was probably in hand in March 1803, when Carr noted that he was much wanted at Milton but unable to move. He was there for at least a week in August and in July 1805 passed on Crabtree's account of work done at Milton to the steward at Wentworth Woodhouse.

Northamptonshire Record Office, Fitzwilliam Papers, plan no. 126
Sheffield Archives, WWM Stw P6 (iv) 116, 1794, (v) 112, 127, 132, Stw P7 (i) 13
Christopher Hussey, 'Milton, Northamptonshire', *Country Life*, 1 June 1961
BE/Northants/292–94

Monkwearmouth Rectory, Monkwearmouth, County Durham

Archdeacon Henry Egerton
Alterations, 1788

In 1788 Carr wrote to Egerton, brother of John Egerton, Bishop of Durham, who had employed him at Auckland Castle, with advice on buying and laying slates to repair the roof of his prebendal house at Monkwearmouth.

Hertfordshire County Record Office, AH 2311, 2321
William Hutchinson, *The History and Antiquities of the County Palatine of Durham* (Carlisle, 1787), II, 179

Morton-on-Swale, Yorkshire (NR/NY) (Fig. 191)

North Riding magistrates
New bridge, 1800–03

The old bridge, though built only forty years earlier, was in a very dangerous and ruinous state when the order was given by the Quarter Sessions to rebuild it in 1800. The new bridge was properly founded on strong oak piles which had to be driven 18 ft below the bed of the river. The bridge was built of good Rainton stone and was well executed to Carr's design and directions by workmen employed by the North Riding. Building took three years and the cost of the 275 ft bridge was high, £8,240 10s, the great part of the expense being due to the great quantity of the stonework and timber needed to obtain a secure footing.

North Yorkshire County Record Office, Book of Bridges, 1772–1803, 71
BE/NR/335

Town Hall, Newark, Nottinghamshire

(Figs 54, 192–94)
Mayor and aldermen of Newark
New town hall, assembly rooms and market, 1773–76

On 26 January 1773 the mayor and aldermen agreed to sell land to erect a multi-purpose building in the main square. That December an advertisement seeking tenders appeared in the *York Courant* and the *Nottingham Advertiser*, and noting that 'A Plan and Elevation of the intended Hall may be seen at Mr Brough's in Newark, and at Mr Carr's in York who will answer all Letters post paid.'

The building, which was faced in Mansfield stone, cost more than £17,000 and was supervised by William Matthews of Newark. The other craftsmen were largely local men with masonry by William Mew of Newark; brickwork by Mr Palmer Sheppard of Newark; joinery and carpentry, Robert Baker of Retford; slating by M. Lewis of Nottingham; plasterwork by Moses Kilminster of Derby; carving by George Barrett of Newark and Thickstone of Derby; plumbing and glazing by J. Smalley of Newark, S. Watson of Newark and J. Holmes of Newark; and painting by J. Smith of Newark.

At the front the ground floor was reserved for the sale of corn. The large paved and colonnaded hall behind with closely spaced Tuscan columns was a market for butter. The open space at the rear was intended as a shambles or stalls for butchers. On the first floor was the handsome Hall of the Corporation, used for council meetings and the borough petty session, 35 ft long and 16 ft high opening onto the loggia. Behind it was the tall Assembly Room, used for public meetings, balls, concerts and the borough quarter sessions. This has screened apsidal ends and paired Corinthian pilasters. The walls and coved ceiling are gracefully decorated in low relief and in an act

192 Newark
Town Hall
Assembly Room

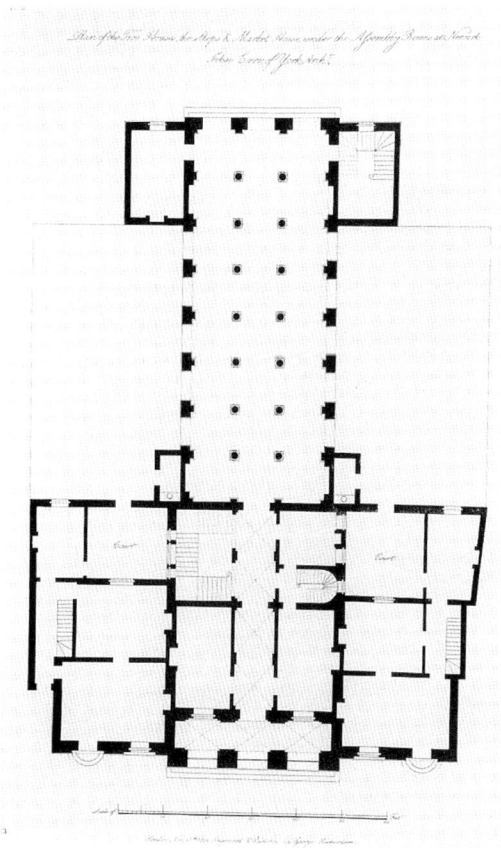

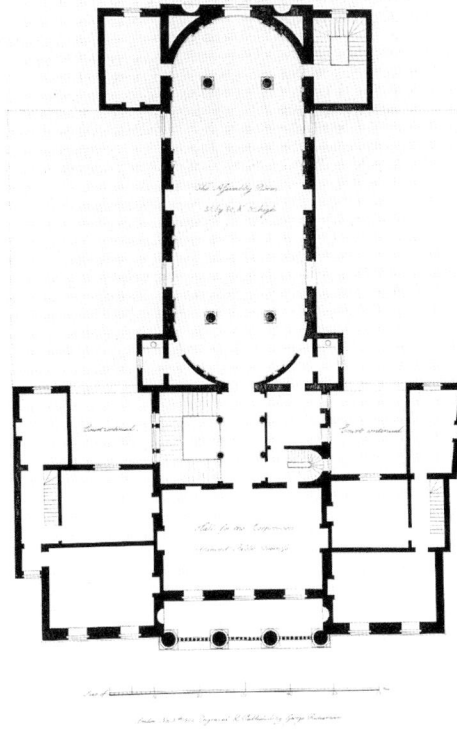

193 *left* Newark
Town Hall, plan of
ground floor

194 *right* Newark
Town Hall, plan of
first floor

of technical bravura the chimneypieces are placed under the windows. Flanking the building, but part of the composition, were two houses intended for rent.

Nottingham Record Office, DDT 134/7, contract 1774, amended 1776
Newark Museum 54.34, drawing dated 1774, signed J.C.
Richard Shilton, *A History of the Town of Newark upon Trent* (Newark, 1820), 366–73
Cornelius Brown, *The Annals of Newark-upon-Trent* (London, 1879), 221–22
George Richardson, *New Vitruvius Britannicus* (London, 1808), II, pls 11–14
Ivan Hall, 'Newark Town Hall', *Georgian Group Journal*, 1 (1991), 54–56
BE/Notts/190

Newby Hall, Yorkshire (NR/NY)
William Weddell MP
Alterations, *c.* 1764

Weddell, a keen collector and dilettante, owed his seat as Member of Parliament for Hull to the 2nd Marquis of Rockingham. He appears to have employed Carr to remodel the late seventeenth-century house some time before 1765. Accounts survive for work carried out from January to August 1764. Carr turned the house round making the east front the entrance. He rebuilt the central three bays so that they project rather than recede, and added single-storey wings — one of them intended as a gallery. There are also signs of his hand on the north floor of the main block.

After Weddell returned from his Grand Tour in 1766 he consulted James Stuart and Sir William Chambers before employing Robert Adam, whose earliest plans are dated 1767, to fit out the house. Carr produced designs for the stables but these were built by William Belwood, who raised the wings on the house a storey after 1776.

Drawings at Newby Hall
Diary of Miss Elizabeth Chivers — H. M. Colvin, *Biographical Dictionary of British Architects* (New Haven and London, 1995), 221
John Cornforth, 'Newby Hall, North Yorkshire', *Country Life*, 7, 14, 21 June 1979
Hugh Pagan Limited, Architecture Catalogue, 31 (London, 1998), 51–52
BE/WR/375–76

New Lodge, Wakefield Road, Barnsley, Yorkshire
(WR/SY) (Figs 67, 68)
For himself
New house and lodges, 1795

Carr bought the estate of New Laithes, about two miles north of Barnsley and four and a half miles south of Wakefield, in 1769. He subsequently rebuilt the house, which can be dated to 1795. In July that year Carr's niece Harriet Clark, explaining that 'New Lodge is a beautiful

195 Northallerton Gaol

place which belongs to my uncle Carr', recorded in her diary that she 'dined for the first time in the new house'. Carr still occupied the house in 1798 when Amelia made another visit, staying for two months, but when Elizabeth Chivers visited in 1803, she noted that although owned by Carr it was then occupied by his nephew John Clark. She described New Lodge as 'a charming new house lately built by Mr Carr' and mentions that it was formerly called Abbey Grange.

The house is very plain, stone, three bays wide, but with an elegant porch with Doric columns and pediment. The substantial octagonal gate lodges, perhaps inspired by the Temple of the Winds in Athens, were demolished by Barnsley Corporation 1956 and the house is an old persons' home surrounded by a housing estate.

York Minster Library, MSS Add. 328/1, fol. 25, 328/2, fol. 17
Diary of Miss Elizabeth Chivers — H. M. Colvin, *Biographical Dictionary of British Architects* (New Haven and London, 1995), 221
Joseph Hunter, *South Yorkshire* (London, 1831), II, 397
BE/WR/94–95

196 Norton Hall stables

84 High Street, Northallerton, Yorkshire (NR/NY)
(Fig. 9)
Daniel Mitford
New house, c. 1755–58

A commission for D. Mitford Esq. in Northallerton is included in the list of Carr's commissions in the A.P.S.D. Daniel Mitford, a chemist, signed a lease on land in Northallerton's main street with his cousins Edwin and Daniel Lascelles on 18 October 1754. The lease ran from 1 May 1755 and the house was described as newly erected, currently empty, but shortly to be occupied by Mr Mitford in a legal document of November 1758.

The design fits well with Carr's early work. The house is an elegant five bays and two and a half storeys, of stone, with a pyramidal roof. The ground floor had alternating segmental and triangular pediments over the windows, but these have been replaced by plate-glass shop windows.

North Yorkshire County Record Office, ZBM543, 545
Wyatt Papworth (ed.), *The Dictionary of Architecture issued by the Architectural Publications Society* (London, 1877), II, 36
BE/NR/272

Court House and County Gaol, Northallerton, Yorkshire (NR/NY) (Fig. 195)
North Riding Magistrates
New court house and gaol, 1784–92

In 1783 the North Riding Magistrates commissioned a search for a suitable site for a Court House and the House of Correction. Carr prepared a scheme, and when the land was subsequently bought (for £80) he was asked to adjust his design to the situation. Contractors were advertised for in the *York Courant* in April 1784 and work started the same year. On 2 October 1787 the Treasurer was ordered to pay John Carr £200 'for planning and effecting the Design of the New Court House and House of Correction'. Work is likely to have drifted on as an additional payment of £20 2s 6d was made to Carr in 1788 for designing 'the last work'. The Treasurer's accounts show that the total cost of the whole project came to £5,217 9s 2d.

The court house was a plain, lofty, rectangular box, built of brick laid in Flemish bond and with a hipped roof. Two storeyed, its floors were lit with simple arched windows. The main entrance, centred in one of the short sides, was through two widely spaced Doric columns supporting entablature and pediment. Decoration of the courtroom was sparse, with Doric cornice and frieze. Alongside it Carr built the gaol, complete with yard, which is now engulfed in the present prison.

The prison was much enlarged and altered in 1848–52. The court house was demolished in 1972.

North Yorkshire County Record Office, North Riding Quarter Sessions Order Books 1782–87, pp. 105, 342 and QFA (A) North Riding Treasurer's Accounts 1765–83
BE/NR/272

Register House, Northallerton, Yorkshire (NR/NY)
North Riding Magistrates
Repairs and alterations, 1775–77

The Register House is a plain, four-square building off Northallerton's main street which was built in 1736–40 to house the public register of wills and the registrar. In 1774 George Crowe was appointed Registrar and in April 1775 Messrs Wallis and Marshall received their first payment for repairing the Register House. Work dragged on until May 1777 when Carr was paid £27 7s 6d for repairing and viewing the Register House. Carr's work must have included an addition as Wallis and Marshall were paid for building an additional part to the Register House as well as for unforeseen foundations they were obliged to make.

North Yorkshire County Record Office, QFA (A), North Riding Treasurer's Accounts 1765–83

Norton Hall, Sheffield, Derbyshire (Yorks/SY)
(Fig. 196)
Samuel Shore
Alterations, c. 1768–69

Samuel Shore, a Sheffield banker, married Urith, daughter and heir of Joseph Offley of Norton Hall in 1759. Offley had died in 1751. In November 1768 he recommended Carr as architect for the Hollis Hospital, explaining that 'Mr Carr is the architect I have employed. He is a very ingenious man, has good taste and I have always found him consult convenience and economy.' He added that he expected to see him soon. Carr accompanied plans for the hospital in February 1769 with drawings for Shore, presumably for Norton Hall. Carr's copy of Morris's *Select Architecture* includes a design for a lodge and gateway labelled 'Mr Shores', presumably for Norton Hall. Shore's two sisters Esther and Mary had previously married Robert and John Milnes of Wakefield, close clients of Carr.

Norton Hall was a Jacobean house whose west wing had been rebuilt by Joseph Offley before 1751. What work Carr carried out at the house is uncertain as the house was rebuilt by Shore's son Samuel in 1815 and no accounts survived the loss of all family papers on the failure of Parker and Shore's bank in the nineteenth century. A drawing by Thomas Malton of 1793 shows no sign of any intervention by Carr. However, the stables, with pediments over the second and sixth bays of a seven-bay front, are characteristically Carr and can be compared with his stables at Arncliffe Hall. A symmetrical farm building adjacent to the stables may also be by Carr.

Sheffield Archives, LD 1164/23
Sir John Soane's Museum, Roger Morris, *Select Architecture* (London, 1755), drawing on flyleaf
Harold Armitage, *Chantrey Land, being an account of the North Derbyshire village of Norton* (Sheffield, 1910), 138–39
BE/WR/479–80

Norton Place, Bishop Norton, Lincolnshire
(Figs 33, 197)
John Harrison MP
New house, stables, coach house, bridge and entrance lodges, 1776

Harrison (1738–1811) was a keen agricultural and landscape improver and a political associate of the Marquis of Rockingham. He replaced the old house on a different site and landscaped the grounds at the same time. Britton notes that Carr was the architect and dates the work to 1776.

The house is of finely finished ashlar with elaborate window surrounds. It has two equal storeys under a balustrade and is seven bays wide with a three-bay pediment and central Venetian window. The end elevations have canted bays. To the rear the stables make a courtyard.

The entrance hall is only a single bay wide and is lit by side lights in the porch. It is flanked by a library and drawing room, and there are octagonal rooms on each of the side elevations. The rear section of the house was given over to service accommodation. The entrance hall opens on to a central oval staircase, one of the most beautiful of any by Carr. The stair, of cantilevered stone steps supporting curved wrought iron balusters and slim mahogany handrails, reminiscent of that at Constable Burton, is lit by a dome. The balustrading, with 'S' bars alternating with pairs of waving ones is based on the Tulip staircase at the Queen's House, Greenwich. The main room has elegant plastered ceilings and fine chimneypieces. Carr was probably also responsible for the elegantly curving bridge in the park (Fig. 30).

John Britton, *Beauties of England and Wales* (London, 1807), IX, 670
Marcus Binney, 'Norton Place, Lincolnshire', *Country Life*, 30 September 1976
BE/Lincs/148

197 Norton Place, entrance front

Assembly Rooms, Low Pavement, Nottingham
New assembly rooms, 1776–78
Alterations, 1790
Demolished, 1836

A meeting of the subscribers to the race stand and assembly rooms moved on 20 December 1776 'that application be made to the corporation for leave to build an assembly rooms, upon their premises, on a plan to be produced by Mr Carr'. A committee of noblemen and gentlemen led by Lord Edward Bentinck, brother of the Duke of Portland, was established on 8 January 1777 when the plan for an assembly room at the New Change was approved. However, on 9 September it was agreed to purchase Mr Taylor's house on Low Pavement for £600 when it was decided that the plan of the assembly room was to be carried into execution. The total cost of purchase and rebuilding was £1,389 11s 7d. Carr was responsible for further improvements in 1790, which were carried out by Samuel Stretton.

James Orange, *The History and Antiquities of Nottingham* (London, 1840), II, 940–41
G. C. Robertson (ed.), *The Stretton Manuscripts* (Nottingham, 1910), 181

Nottingham, Grandstand on the Racecourse (Fig. 198)
New grandstand, 1777
Demolished, 1910

The Nottingham grandstand was an exact copy of that at York with tea and card rooms, vestibule and kitchens and offices on the ground floor, 'geometrical stairs', and on the upper floor a 'genteel room' 61 ft long, with a 'miranda' from which the race could be watched.

Lord Edward Bentinck, brother of the Duke of Portland, headed the trustees to whom the city corporation granted the lease of the land, which included John Musters of Colwick Hall. The subscription list was opened on 21 October 1776 and the foundation stone laid on 1 February 1777. The cost was £1,701 19s 9d and the builder Samuel Stretton.

Thomas Bailey, *The Annals of Nottinghamshire* (London, 1853), IV, 57–58
G. C. Robertson (ed.), *The Stretton Manuscripts* (Nottingham, 1910), ii
Robert Thoroton, *History of Nottinghamshire*, ed. by John Throsby, (London, 1797), II, 68
Tessa Gibson, 'The Designs for the Knavesmire Grandstand, York', *Georgian Group Journal*, 8 (1998), 76–87

198 Nottingham racestand

Nuneham Park, Nuneham Courtenay, Oxfordshire

(Fig. 44)

2nd Earl Harcourt

Unexecuted proposals for alterations, 1778

Lord Harcourt succeeded his father in 1777. The following year, on the advice of his friend William Mason whose rectory Carr had designed at Aston, Harcourt commissioned drawings for extending Nuneham from Carr. These survive at Stanton Harcourt.

Carr proposed turning Stiff Leadbetter's villa of 1756 into a more convenient seat by removing the external entrance stairs and increasing the number of rooms. This house was to be brought forward by two bays (reusing the stone), creating a new entrance front with a portico-in-antis with internal stairs similar to those at nearby Basildon which he had just designed. The entrance hall would have been increased in size and two new rooms added beside it on each floor. The kitchen would have been moved out of the basement, although this remained dedicated to the servants, and a new bedroom suite for Lord and Lady Harcourt created in the north wing, with a bathroom on the ground floor.

In view of the American War Harcourt decided it was untimely to undertake such work. Lancelot Brown and Henry Holland later remodelled the house on a less ambitious scale in 1781.

E. W. Harcourt (ed.), *The Harcourt Papers* (Oxford, n.d.), 7, 49–52

Giles Worsley, 'Nuneham Park Revisted II', *Country Life*, 10

    January 1985

199 Oporto Hospital chapel, drawing after Carr

Hospital de Santo Antonio do Porto, Oporto, Portugal (Figs 24, 199)
Misericordia of the Santa Casa
New hospital, 1769–1843

In 1766–67 the Misericordia of the Santa Casa in Oporto decided to build a new hospital outside the city walls to cope with the growing population. Carr was asked to provide designs and in 1769 sent detailed drawings to the President of the Santa Casa, Don Antonio do Lancastre, for which he sought £500. Although the originals do not survive careful copies were made. There is no evidence that Carr visited Portugal but he remained in contact with the project and in 1777 criticized alterations made by local builders. The scheme received considerable attention in England and was presented to George III.

The foundation stone was laid on 10 June 1770 and work began at the southern angle of the building, continuing until 1780 when it was suspended for lack of funds. Work recommenced in 1791 and patients were finally transferred from the old hospital in 1799. After a series of further stoppages work finally halted in 1843, by which time only the main front and half the side elevations had been completed.

The building, executed in granite, was the largest Carr ever designed, a vast rectangle 540 ft wide and 520 ft deep with a hexastyle Doric portico on the entrance front and an immense interior court. In the middle was to have been a domed chapel with porticoes on four sides, an intepretation of Palladio's Villa Capra. Carr gave considerable thought to ventilation, which would have been achieved by shafts up to the roof, and drainage, with a great arched sewer running the length of the building. Each storey had its own water supply, with pumps being used to raise water to the upper floors.

British commercial influence in Oporto was strong, and the British Consul John Whitehead was a close friend of General Joao de Almada e Melo, the Military Governor of the city, but it remains unclear why Carr received the commission and why it went to a York rather than a London or Bristol architect. One link may have been Carr's friend William Mellish, whose family had traded with Oporto, another the chaplain to the English Factory at Oporto, Dr Wood, a Yorkshireman for whose family Carr subsequently worked at Bolling Hall and who acted as intermediary between architect and client. Carr may also have been recommended because he was currently designing the Leeds Infirmary. Despite some refenestration the hospital is little altered, although many of the wards have been adapted

Records of Santa Casa da Misericordia do Porto, Seccao D, Banco 8 — Livro No. 7, Folhas, 289–94, 306 et seq.
R. B. and M. Wragg, 'Carr in Portugal', *Architectural Review*, February 1959

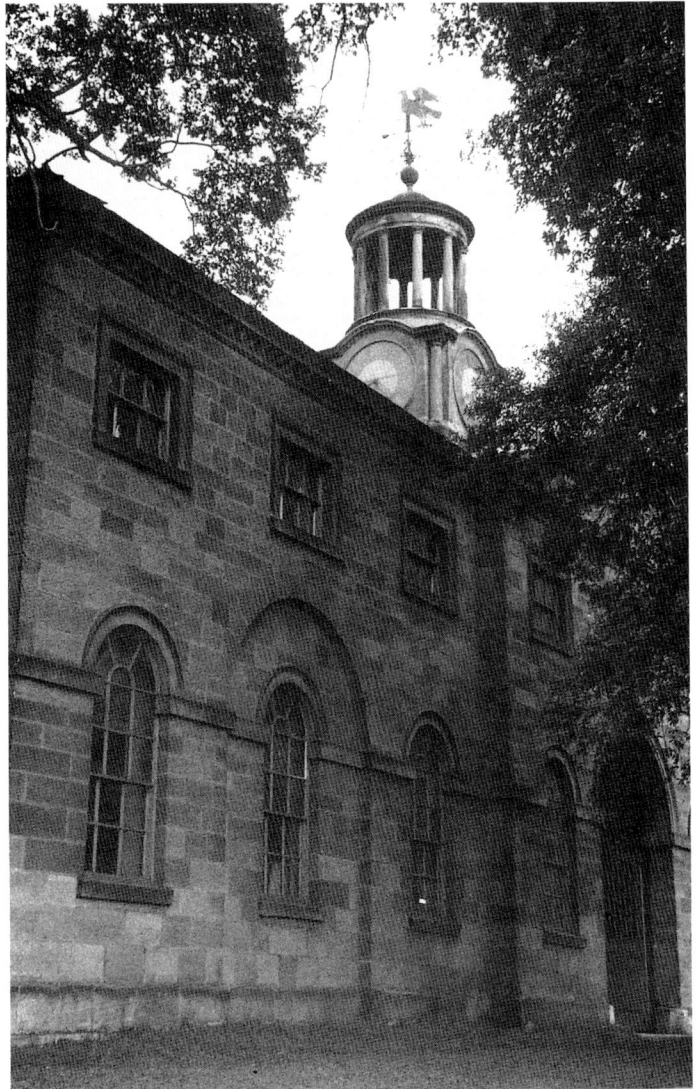

200 Ormesby Hall stables

Rene Taylor, 'John Carr e O Hospital de Santo Antonio Do Porto', *Belas Artes*, no. 15, 1960
Rene Taylor, 'The Architecture of Port Wine', *Architectural Review*, June 1961

Ormesby Hall, Eston, Yorkshire (NR/Cleveland)
(Figs 62, 200, 201)
Sir James Pennyman, Bt, MP
Alterations, stables and lodges, c. 1772
Attributed

The building history of Ormesby remains obscure. It would appear that the current house was begun by James Pennyman during the lifetime of his father Sir James Pennyman, who lived nearby at Thornton. Pennyman had married Dorothy Wake, daughter and co-heiress of William Wake, Archbishop of Canterbury. The house was

201 Ormesby Hall, 'Adam' room

incomplete at his death in 1743 but his widow continued the building and lived there until her death in 1754. It then remained unoccupied, with some of the rooms probably not fitted up, until James Pennyman's nephew Sir James Pennyman succeeded in 1770. He was notoriously extravagant, spent £47,500 buying back part of the estate and must have expended considerable sums building.

Pennyman's work included substantial stables, convincingly attributed to Carr and probably completed in 1772, the date on the bell in the cupola. These can be compared to Carr's stables at Castle Howard, Escrick Park, Ravenfield Hall and Ribston Park. This suggests that Carr may have been responsible for the elegant Adam-inspired dining and drawing rooms and for the screen at the top of the stairs with capitals taken from the Tower of the Winds published in Stuart and Revett's *Antiquities of Athens* published in 1762. The chimneypiece in the 'Adam' Room can be compared to examples at Norton Place, Wiganthorpe Hall and Hawkesworth Hall. The handsome lodges are an elaborate version of Carr's lodge designs.

Pennyman ran heavily into debt and it was reported that when he died in 1808 the house had been shut up for thirty years. It is now owned by the National Trust and the stables used by the Cleveland mounted police.

Arthur Oswald, 'Ormesby Hall, Yorkshire' *Country Life*, 26 February 1959
BE/NR/276–77

Ormsby Hall, South Ormsby, Nr Louth, Lincolnshire
William Burrell-Massingberd
Unexecuted alterations, n.d.

James Paine built Ormsby Hall in 1752–55. Paine's house was small and a plan in the Massingberd-Mundy archives inscribed 'Pane's plans for Ormsby House with Carr's additions' and two further plans in Carr's hand (4/13/5–6) show Carr proposed doubling the size of the house. Peter Atkinson added wings in 1803.

Lincolnshire Archives Committee, Massingberd-Mundy MSS, MM4/13/1–9
BE/Lincs/666

Church of the Holy Rood, Ossington, Nottinghamshire (Figs 48, 49, 202)

Robert Denison

New church and mausoleum, 1782–84

Denison commissioned a new church and mausoleum from Carr as a memorial to his brother William, who had left him the Ossington estate. According to William Denison's obituary in the *Leeds Intelligencer* of 30 April 1782 he was 'interred with great funeral pomp in the church there, previous to his being removed to a superb mausoleum, which is intended to be built to perpetuate his memory', having left 'the immense fortune of £700,000'. Robert Denison's executors accounts show that Carr was paid £104 14s 'In full for his plans attendance etc, at Ossington in 1782, 1783, 1784'. Detailed drawings survive in the Nottingham University Library.

Carr had already been commissioned by William Denison to design a temple at Ossington, although nothing had come of it. After Horbury Ossington, with its colonnaded tower, was Carr's most elaborate new church. It was entered through a Doric porch in the centre of the side elevation, which was flanked by pairs of round-headed windows in relieving arches. The body of the church is rectangular and has no aisles.

A domed octagonal mausoleum, topped with a vase and housing statues of William and Robert Denison by Joseph Nollekens, was attached to the east end of the church. It was demolished in 1838 because the failure of its structure threatened the church.

Nottingham University Library, Denison of Ossington papers, De H 47; De 2P/11–16; Robert Denison's Memo Book, and Account Book 1769–85; information from Dr Terry Friedman

R. G. Wilson, 'Denisons and Milnses: Eighteenth-Century Merchant Landowners', in J. T. Ward and R. G. Wilson, *Land and Industry: The Landed Estate and the Industrial Revolution* (Newton Abbot, 1971), 145–72

H. A. Johnson 'The Architecture of Ossington Hall, c. 1728–1963', *Transactions of the Thoroton Society*, 84 (1980), 51, pl. 5

BE/Notts/284–85

Ossington Hall, Ossington, Nottinghamshire

William Denison

Unexecuted design for a circular temple, 1780

Robert Denison

Unexecuted designs for a circular temple, 1782–86

The Leeds-based Denison family was Yorkshire's leading cloth exporter, the family's large fortune having established in the first half of the century when it gave up cloth manufacture for export. William Denison bought the Ossington and Sutton-on-Trent estates from the heirs of George Cartwright in 1768 for £34,000 as part of a large-scale transfer of much of his capital into landed property in Lincolnshire, Yorkshire, Durham and Nottinghamshire. Ossington was his favourite estate, but he spent little time there, devoting most of his energy to his business in Leeds. In 1779 he wrote that he had only spent fourteen days in Nottinghamshire that year.

Denison spent large sums improving the estate, including repairing and extending farm buildings, but did little if anything to Ossington Hall, which was extensively altered by William Lindley for John Denison in 1788–90 and 1805–06. In 1780 he commissioned Carr to design an impressive garden temple, a circular building on two floors with a freestanding Roman Doric colonnade, similar in design to the circular temple at the Rievaulx Terraces in Yorkshire but with Adamesque decoration on the frieze and an urn on the top. This was not executed and Denison died in 1782. He was succeeded by his brother Robert, for whom Carr produced five more circular temple designs between 1782 and 1786. These did not progress beyond laying the foundations.

R. G. Wilson, 'Denisons and Milneses: Eighteenth-Century Merchant Landowners', in J. T. Ward and R. G. Wilson, *Land and Industry: The Landed Estate and the Industrial Revolution* (Newton Abbot, 1971), 145–72

H. A. Johnson 'The Architecture of Ossington Hall, *c.*1728–1963', *Transactions of the Thoroton Society*, 84 (1980), 51, pl. 4

Nottingham University Library, De 2P/6–10; De B/35–39

Otterington Bridge, South Otterington, Yorkshire (NR/NY) (Fig. 203)
North Riding magistrates
New bridge, 1776

The new, five-arch bridge over the River Wiske was built by John Peacock for £680.

North Yorkshire County Record Office, Book of Bridges, 1772–1803, 74

Painthorpe House, Barnsley, Yorkshire (WR/WY)
Mrs Heaton
Alterations, *c.*1806
Demolished

Carr was friendly in his old age with the Heatons, who lived at Painthorpe, near New Lodge. In a letter of 7 October 1805 to Mrs Chivers Carr describes the house as lying a mile from Barnsley. In fact Painthorpe House, in the small hamlet of Painthorpe near Chapelthorpe, lay about five miles north of Barnsley. It was described when advertised for sale in the *York Courant* in 1787 as 'a handsome modern-built mansion house with stables, barns … and 43 acres in a ring fence lying in front of the house and very suitable for the residence of a gentleman's family'. It is not known when it was bought by the Heatons.

Two of the Miss Heatons accompanied Carr to the Lake District and Scotland in 1805 but this did not prevent a falling out in 1806 when Carr carried out work for the Heatons. As Mrs Heaton complained to another of Carr's travelling companions Elizabeth Chivers: 'John Carr who has done some business for us lately, but nothing for which we thought he could possible charge us more than

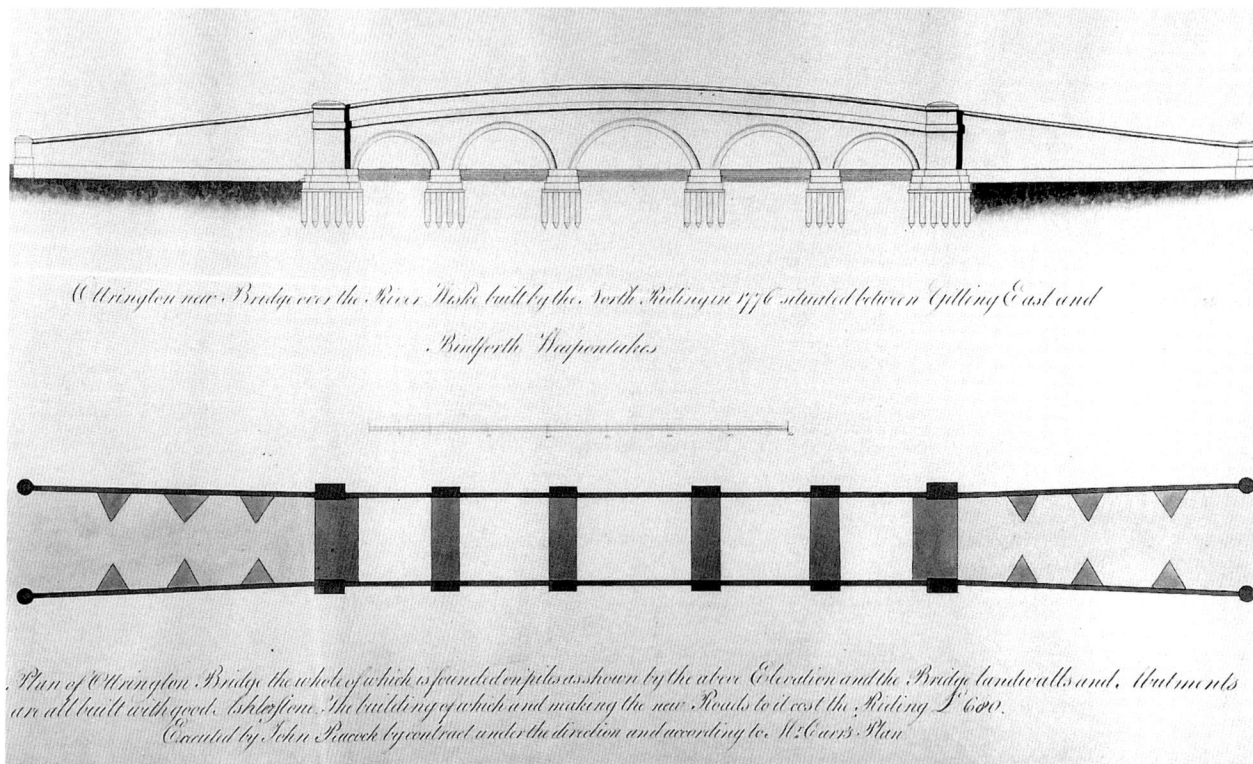

203 Drawing of Otterington bridge

CATALOGUE

204 Panton Hall

6 or 8 pounds & today he has sent us a bill for 20 pounds & some shillings.'

Painthorpe is not to be confused, as it is in the Y.G.S., with Painsthorpe Hall in the East Riding.

North Yorkshire County Record Office, Worsley Bower Docs, ZON/3/1/37
York Courant, 31 July 1787
York Georgian Society, *The Works in Architecture of John Carr* (York, 1973), 26

Panton Hall, Nr Wragby, Lincolnshire (Fig. 204)
Edmund Turnor
Alterations, 1774–76
Demolished 1960

The A.P.S.D. and Davies both record that Carr made additions to Panton Hall, which was built by Nicholas Hawksmoor in about 1720. According to Angus Panton was bought by Turnor in 1775. However, Turnor's bank account shows that Carr was paid £48 6s on 22 January 1774, £83 16s 5d on 25 February 1775 and £115 10s on 13 March 1776, which suggests that Turnor had already purchased Panton by that date. Carr added wings, with canted bays, sympathetically modelled on the original design. The large stables were the work of William Legg,

not Carr. After the house was demolished the interior fittings were reused at Basildon Park.

Barclays Bank Archives, Goslings Bank Ledgers, 49/192, 53/210
William Angus, *The Seats of the Nobility and Gentry in Great Britain and Wales in a Collection of Select Views* (London, 1787), 1, pl. xxx
T. Allen, *History of Lincolnshire* (1834), 11, 70
Wyatt Papworth (ed.), *The Dictionary of Architecture issued by the Architectural Publications Society* (London, 1877), 11, 36
R. Davies, 'A Memoir of John Carr', *Yorkshire Archaeological Journal*, 4 (1877), 205
H. M. Colvin, *Lincolnshire Historian*, 7 (1951), 287–90
BE/Lincs/599

Parlington Hall, Yorkshire (WR/WY) (Figs 46, 47)
Sir Thomas Gascoigne, Bt, MP
Unexecuted designs for a mansion, and chapel and chaplain's house, 1772; attributed estate buildings including the Home Farm and Aberford Road cottages

The Gascoignes moved to Parlington about 1721 but it was not until the marriage of Thomas Gascoigne in 1772 that improvements were considered to the house. For the next thirty-eight years he, his son Thomas and stepson-in-law Richard Oliver Gascoigne considered numerous schemes for alterations, for which drawings survive in the Gascoigne papers. Carr provided plans in 1772, Thomas

Atkinson in 1774, Thomas Leverton in 1781 and William Pilkington in 1810. All proved abortive.

Carr put forward four schemes. One, for a compact house with a portico-in-antis with internal stairs, a canted bay on the garden front and low pavilion wings, was similar to Basildon, built a few years later. A second would have retained the portico-in-antis but with a pair of canted bays on the garden front. The other two were for grander houses, eleven bays long with attached porticos and wings.

One of Carr or Atkinson's plans must have been accepted as stone was ordered and delivered, but the scheme had been abandoned by 1778 when a visitor commented that 'I saw there pyramids of a very fine stone which I understand were designed to build a house for Sir Thomas Gascoigne's son'.

Carr also produced designs for the Home Farm, although the Home Farm as built does not follow these. It is a larger building, quadrangular, red brick, with the barn on the north and farmhouse on the south and probably by Carr. Carr may also have been responsible for the Aberford Road cottages. His unexecuted Gothic design of 1772 for a chapel and chaplain's house of 1772 is particularly charming.

West Yorkshire Archives Service, Leeds, Gascoigne Papers, GC/MA 55 and 56

Terry Friedman, 'Romanticism and Neoclassicism for Parlington: The Tastes of Sir Thomas Gascoigne' *Leeds Arts Calendar*, no. 66 (1970), 16–24

John Martin Robinson, *Georgian Model Farms* (Oxford, 1983), 134, pl. 10

Platt Hall, Nr Manchester, Lancashire

John Lees (later Worsley)
Unexecuted designs for a new house, 1761

William Jupp produced a scheme for Lees in 1760. Carr provided a much more competent design the following year, seven bays wide with a projecting pedimented centrepiece, and three storeys high with a *piano nobile* over a rustic, and with the entrance on the ground floor. This formed the basis for the executed scheme by Thomas Lightoler.

Manchester City Art Gallery, drawings
Ivan Hall, 'John Carr: A New Approach', *York Georgian Society Report*, 1972, 25–26, plates

Plompton Hall, Plompton, Yorkshire (WR/NY)

(Figs 14, 15)
Daniel Lascelles MP
Alterations to the old house, new house (unfinished), stables, farmhouse Gothic farm, estate buildings, gate lodges and dam head, 1755–65

Daniel Lascelles acquired the Plompton estate, near Harewood, in the mid-1750s for £28,000. He immediately set about modernizing and improving the estate, setting out farms, creating an elaborate park and building farmhouses, workers' cottages and a stable block. Plans for planting were underway by May 1755 and that year Carr presented a remarkable scheme, worthy of Vanbrugh, for the dam head, with heavy rusticated piers and a pyramid. A simplified version with rusticated arches and massive piers crowned with ball finials was being built, with difficulty, that winter. On 30 November 1756 James Sanderson, Benjamin Child and John Newland agreed to build two farmhouses 'agreeable to any of the plans now drawn by Mr Carr of York'. They were to be finished by 25 December 1757. Carr also proposed a Gothic farmhouse in 1760, on a long ridge facing the proposed site of Plompton Hall. Lascelles questioned the design as extravagant but was persuaded to accept it.

Progress on the house proved slow, the steward, Samuel Popplewell complaining that 'so much pulling down and making up ... in old houses are monstrously tedious'. At first Carr was asked to modernize the old house, but this was abandoned in favour of a new house, for which a design survives dated May 1761. This in its turn was abandoned and demolished when Lascelles bought the adjoining Goldsborough estate in 1762.

In the meantime handsome stone stables had been built with blind arcading, a rusticated central arch with open pediment and substantial octagonal cupola, with a haybarn behind. Later, the details suggest the 1770s or 1780s, what was probably a tea-room was created in the south range with Venetian window and elaborate chimneypiece set in a deep niche. This subsequently became Plompton Hall.

Carr was also responsible for the unusual farmhouse immediately north of the stable courtyard, with a tall, two-storeyed central block with pyramidal roof and central Diocletian window on the ground floor, flanked by lower wings. Among the farm buildings the square butcher's shop with pyramidal roof, blind arch, ashlar facing and fine Classical detail is particularly handsome.

West Yorkshire Archives Service, Leeds, Stewards Correspondence 1754–61

Drawing of 'Plompton, S. front as it is executed for Daniel Lascelles 11 May 1761. J.C.' formerly in the collection of Sir Albert Richardson

Royal Commission on the Historical Monuments of England, Report on Farm buildings north of Plompton Hall Farmhouse, nd

R. B. Wragg, 'John Carr: Gothic Revivalist', in *Studies in Architectural History*, ed. by W. A. Singleton (London and York, 1956), II, 14–15

Catherine Thompson-McCausland, 'Separated by Nature', *Country Life*, 13 February 1992

BE/WR/392

Pavilion for the Preston Guild, Preston, Lancashire
Preston Guild
1760–62

The Preston Guild meets once every twenty years or so to entertain the town to great festivities, often building a temporary Guildhall to house the event. Hardwick quotes what was evidently a contemporary statement that the 1762 Guildhall was 'an elegant structure, designed by Mr Carr, an eminent architect, in York'. His building is often confused with the Town Hall, built by Mr Johnson in 1760–61, which collapsed in 1780 and was rebuilt by an unrecorded architect and subsequently demolished in 1862.

Harris Public Library, Preston, Council Minutes and Orders, May, June, 1760; information from Sir Howard Colvin
C. Hardwick , *History of Preston* (Preston, 1857), 295
Peter Whittle, *History of Preston* (Preston, 1837), II, 59
A. Crosby, *The History of the Preston Guild* (Preston, 1991)

Pye Nest, Halifax, Yorkshire (WR/WY) (Fig. 205)
John Edwards
New house, *c.* 1771
Demolished, 1935

John Edwards, who came from Birmingham, married Elizabeth Lees in 1762 and shortly afterwards became a partner in Edwards, Lees and Lees, which manufactured worsted yarn and shipped it principally to South America and West Africa. According to Kendall, Edwards built Pye Nest in 1768, but Kendall also states that the Pye Nest estate was bought by Revd William Wainhouse on 21 February 1770, who sold it on to Edwards in May 1771.

The A.P.S.D. and Davies confirm that the house was designed by Carr. It was an elegant, compact two-storey, five-bay house with a central pediment and flanking pavilions linked by quadrant. Sales particulars of 1887 give a detailed description of the interior and mention that the entrance hall was lit by a central dome. Nearby Crow Nest, designed by Thomas Bradley and started in 1778, was a close copy of Pye Nest, though with the detail simplified and an extra two bays.

Bernard Burke, *A Visitation of Seats and Arms* (London, 1855), 210, plate
Wyatt Papworth (ed.), *The Dictionary of Architecture issued by the Architectural Publications Society* (London, 1877), II, 36
R. Davies, 'A Memoir of John Carr', *Yorkshire Archaeological Journal*, 4 (1877), 205
Edward Waterson and Peter Meadows, *Lost Houses of the West Riding* (Welburn, 1998), 54, figs

Raby Castle, County Durham (Fig. 63)
2nd Earl of Darlington
Alterations, stables, lodges, and farmhouses (attributed), 1768–71, 1780–88

The great medieval castle at Raby was subject to major restoration in the middle and late years of the eighteenth century by the 1st and 2nd Earls of Darlington employing successively Daniel Garrett, James Paine and John Carr. The 2nd Earl (1726–92), who succeeded in 1758, is first known to have employed Carr in 1768. Paine, who had worked there up to 1756, was employed as a consultant and commented, favourably, upon Carr's proposals in 1771 to restore the great hall, create a new south front and add new buildings in the south-east corner of the castle. Extensive drawings survive but no ledgers or account books.

Much of Carr's work was restoration, for which his approach was pragmatic. He dictated the general alterations on plan and left the specifics of the exact position of new doors and windows and the construction of passages to the masons. The executant mason under Carr was Mr Wing. For details Carr generally made the masons copy existing models at the castle. He also reused medieval elements such as coping stones, moved when the kitchen louvre was heightened.

Carr's earliest work was alterations to Clifford's tower in 1768. In 1770 the old stables were turned into a servants' hall which was linked to the kitchen with a passage that ran east across the court, off which were a new steward's room, sculleries and necessary houses. The same year an extra floor was added to Joan's tower and in 1771 the details of the interior of the attic floor were completed. Although a design was made in 1771, the lower hall was not rebuilt until 1780–85, when it was transformed into a grand carriage entrance. At the same time the ground floor of the round tower, the oval drawing room immediately to the east and the Gothic bedroom above were built. The round tower was never completed and in 1785 a 'temporary roof' was put over the drawing room. However, part of the Gothic carpet for the room survives. Work on the grand staircase began in 1788 but was halted that year and never completed. Four years later the earl died.

Carr's Gothic designs developed with greater experience of the severe, workmanlike detail of the castle. His earliest scheme for the great hall was an elegant Rococo Gothic design but the executed lower hall was far more archaeological, a robust, almost austere design inspired by the existing architecture with authentic Gothic mouldings copied from Staindrop church. It is one of the most impressive Gothic interiors of the eighteenth century. Carr also designed a court of castellated stables, a variety of lodges, bridges and a D-shaped menagerie. Few of his proposals were executed according to existing designs. The menagerie was never built. In 1770 Carr enlarged the battlemented garden house in the walled garden with single-bay, single-storey wings. He was probably also responsible for Grass Hill Farm and Henderson's Farm (a Gothic design), both of c. 1774.

Raby Castle Muniments, numerous drawings by Carr
Alistair Rowan, 'Raby Castle, Co. Durham', *Country Life*, 1, 8, 22 January 1970
Alistair Rowan, 'Gothic Restoration at Raby Castle', *Architectural History*, 15 (1972), 23–50
John Cornforth, 'Architects' Carpets at Raby', *Country Life*, 31 May 1990

206 St James's Church, Ravenfield

John Martin Robinson, *Georgian Model Farms* (Oxford, 1983), 135
BE/Durham/382–89

Flannel Hall, Rathdrum, County Wicklow, Ireland
4th Earl Fitzwilliam
Design for the Flannel Hall, 1789; design for alterations 1802
Demolished

The centre of Rathdrum, owned by Lord Fitzwilliam, was damaged by fire in July 1789. It was suggested that the damaged buildings be removed to improve the centre of the town and provide a better site for the proposed market house. The Flannel Merchants forwarded a plan for their hall to Lord Fitzwilliam on 29 October 1789 and on 24 November William Wainwright wrote to Lord Fitzwilliam asking 'Whether your Lordship would wish to adopt such a plan or that I must prepare for carrying Mr Carr's sketch into execution'. He wrote again on 5 January 1790 enclosing the sketch 'given me by Mr Carr which is all I have seen of his'. In 1792 Enoch Johnston provided a design which was criticized by William Wainwright, the steward, who put forward an alternative by Samuel Hayes of Avondale. However, this does not seem to have been executed as the cover of Wainwright's letter is endorsed 'not executed'.

It is thus possible that the new Flannel Hall, built on the summit of Rathdrum Hill by Lord Fitzwilliam in 1793 at a cost of £3,500, was designed by Carr. It was a plain building, 200 ft long and two storeys high over a basement, with a cupola. Built around a central courtyard, it had a long hall on the upper floor which was carried round three sides of the building.

In 1800 the Flannel Hall was occupied as barracks during the Irish disturbances. It was not handed back until

June 1802, by which time it needed significant repair. It was in connection with these that Carr wrote to Wainwright in May 1802 enclosing detailed designs for alterations including a new central staircase and skylight.

By 1837 the flannel trade had ceased and the market had been converted to a court house, Roman Catholic chapel and schools. It was used as an auxiliary workhouse during the potato famine and subsequently demolished.

Sheffield Archives, Fitzwilliam Papers, WWM MP 22, F 89/141, 231, 283, 286, 298
Irish Architectural Archive, photocopy of letter from Carr to William Wainwright, 20 May 1802; information from Ann Martha Rowan
Samuel Lewis, *A Topographical Dictionary of Ireland* (1837), II, 495

St James's Church, Ravenfield, Yorkshire (WR/SY)
(Fig. 206)
Elizabeth Parkin
New church, 1755–56

Elizabeth Parkin, described by Joseph Hunter as 'a pious and benevolent lady', submitted a petition for a faculty 'to pull down & Rebuild the … Chapel at Ranfield at her own Expense agreeable to a plan thereto annexed' on 19 April 1755. The plan is missing, however a copy of the licence in the Rotherham Archives does include a plan and two elevations. The drawings are relatively crude, but would appear to be in Carr's hand. According to Hunter the church was erected to a design of Carr's and opened in 1756.

The three-bay Gothic church with its narrower flat polygonal apse is set in fields near Ravenfield Hall. The top of the tower has a curious concave-sided spirelet and quatrefoils below the bell openings.

York Minster Library, Chapter Acts from 1747–1756 (H9/1), fol. 116ᵛ; information from Dr Terry Friedman
Rotherham Archives, 63/B, uncatalogued collection; information from Anthony Munford
Joseph Hunter, *South Yorkshire* (1831), I, 398
BE/WR/398

Ravenfield Hall, Nr Hooton Roberts, Yorkshire (WR)
(Figs 207, 208)
Walter Oborne
Alterations, stables, gate piers, 1767–74
William Parkin Bosvile
Alterations, after 1788
House demolished, 1963

Walter Oborne inherited Ravenfield in 1766 from his cousin Mrs Elizabeth Parkin, a wealthy unmarried lady whose family had grown rich through hardware manufacture in Sheffield and mercantile connections in London and Bristol, who had bought the house. Surviving accounts show that it was substantially altered for Oborne by Carr who refenestrated the house and added a canted

207 Ravenfield Hall
208 Ravenfield Hall gates and stables

bay on the north side enclosing a drawing room. Carr was paid £428 18s between 13 March 1767 and 2 June 1771. Of this, £146 18s was for marble chimneypieces, including a black and gold marble slab for the drawing room, and £12 for two glass lustres for the drawing room chimneypieces. The remaining £270 was paid on account. The stable is a typical Carr design, as are the gate piers.

Including Carr's payments, £6,573 10s 10½d was spent between 1767 and 1778, most of it by 1774. The craftsmen employed were the masons Henry and George Downes, the quarry master Thomas Whitehouse, Jo Johnson, William Thompson, the painter Francis Fenton, Richard Bolar and George Cox, Charles Roberts and John Shaw, the carver Christopher Richardson, the plasterer James Henderson and the joiner John Pitt. Carr was responsible for measuring and settling the bills. A further £345 was paid to John Foster in 1776–77 for building Brampton Farm.

209 Redbourne Hall gates

Oborne died in 1778. As he had no children Ravenfield was left to Matthew Morgan who preferred to live near Bath. After his death in 1788 it passed to William Parkin Bosvile who lived there until his death in 1811. This is presumably the Col. Bosvile for whom the A.P.S.D. records 'a mansion at Ravenfield near Rotherham', suggesting that Carr carried out further work at Ravenfield after 1788.

Joseph Hunter, *South Yorkshire* (London, 1828), I, 398
Wyatt Papworth (ed.), *The Dictionary of Architecture issued by the Architectural Publications Society* (London, 1877), II, 36
Sheffield Archives, Oborne Record, OR 11
Edward Waterson and Peter Meadows, *Lost Houses of the West Riding* (Welburn, 1998), 10–11, figs
BE/WR/398

Redbourne Hall, Lincolnshire (Fig. 209)
Revd Robert Carter Thelwell
Alterations, 1773

A payment of £25 is recorded to 'Mr Carr Architect for several Plans' in August 1773 and a further payment of £10 was made in June 1784 to 'Mr Carr for Alteration of a Plan'. What Carr did is unclear, but a drawing attributed to him in the RIBA is very similar to the castellated boundary wall and gateway as built in 1776. There is also a drawing of a Gothic porch for 'Mr Carter' in the manuscript copy of Batty Langley's *Ancient Architecture* in the Sir John Soane Museum. The west wing of the house dates from the second half of the eighteenth century and is five bays wide with a broad bow at the south end lighting the elegantly plastered drawing room. It is not clear if this is Carr but it is possible that a range of Gothic outbuildings at the back of the Hall was built to his design.

The Y.G.S. suggests that Carr's work was carried out for the Duke of St Albans, but the estate only passed to this family after the marriage of Lord William Beauclerk to Charlotte, daughter and heiress of the Revd Robert Carter Thelwell, in 1791. Thelwell died in 1787.

Lincolnshire Record Office, Red 3/1/4/6/2ff 30, 116
British Architectural Library, K 3/13
Sir John Soane's Museum, Anonymous architect, copy of Batty and Thomas Langley, *Ancient Architecture Restored* (1741), drawing on pl. 48 verso
Thomas Allen, *The History of the County of Lincoln* (London, 1834), II, 218
GEC, *The Complete Peerage* (London, 1949), XI, 292
York Georgian Society, *The Works in Architecture of John Carr* (York, 1973), 28
BE/Lincs/608–09

210 Ribston Hall stables

Reeth Bridge, Yorkshire (NR/NY) (Fig. 26)
North Riding magistrates
New bridge, 1773

The three-arch bridge over Arkle Beck on the Richmond-Kirkby Stephen road was built by John Peacock at a cost of £1,300 after the earlier bridge was destroyed in a flood.

North Yorkshire County Record Office, Book of Bridges, 1772–1803, 30

Ribston Hall, Little Ribston, Yorkshire (WR/NY)
(Figs 36, 210, 211)
Sir John Goodricke, Bt, MP
Alterations, stables and lodges, c. 1773

Sir John Goodricke is believed to have remodelled his great-grandfather's seventeenth-century house, carving an immense saloon out of the centre in about 1773. Although he succeeded his grandfather in 1738 he spent most of the years from 1750 to 1773 as a diplomat in Brussels, the Hague, Copenhagen and Stockholm. In the latter year he inherited a fortune from his wife, the illegitimate daughter of 2nd Lord Bingley, who also left them Bramham Park for life.

Details of Carr's involvement at Ribston are unclear, although John Carr was paid £15 5s in Goodricke's

account at Hoare's Bank on 22 June 1781 and Elizabeth Chivers refers to the house as by Carr. The alterations to the interior of the house and the new stables and lodges all display features identical with other, documented Carr designs. The military and musical trophies, for instance, reappear exactly in the dining room at Thirsk Hall and at Lairgate in Beverley. Carr was probably also responsible for the dining room and drawing room, for replacing the French-inspired steep roofline of the original house with a continuous shallow roof and for two pairs of lodges and the stable block.

The saloon, once attributed to James Wyatt, is one of Carr's masterpieces. It was probably created by throwing two rooms into one and takes in much of the upper floor. The inspiration may have been Adam's Spanish Library at Harewood, completed in 1768. The design reveals a complete unity of design from the marble chimneypieces to the carved wooden doorcases and plasterwork picture-frames. This extends to the four semi-circular pier tables whose frieze is a continuation of the moulding of the dado rail. The two chimneypieces have reliefs of Cleopatra and Aphrodite, symbolizing the contrast between Profane and Sacred love. The source for these was Volfmann's new and enlarged edition of Joachim von Sandart's *Deutsche*

211 Painting of Ribston Hall stables

Academie, published in 1768. The vibrant paint scheme was added in 1846.

Worsley papers, Hovingham, Elizabeth Chivers, Diary 1805
Hoare's Bank Archives, 10/299
Gervase Jackson-Stops, 'Ribston Hall, Yorkshire', *Country Life*,
    11, 18 October 1973
BE/WR/399–400

Riccall, Helmsley, Yorkshire (NR/NY) (Fig. 212)

North Riding magistrates
New bridge, 1803

The two-arch bridge over the River Riccall on the Scarborough-Thirsk road near Helmsley was built in 1803.

North Yorkshire County Record Office, Book of Bridges,
    1772–1803, 83

Richmond, Yorkshire (NR/NY) (Fig. 29)

North Riding magistrates
New bridge, 1789

The new bridge with three arches of 48 ft over the River Swale was built by T. Parkin at a cost of £899. The cost was shared with Richmond Corporation.

North Yorkshire County Record Office, Book of Bridges,
    1772–1803, 76
BE/NR/296

St Mary's Church, Rokeby, Yorkshire (NR/County Durham)

John Sawrey Morritt
Completed church, 1775–78

The church, designed, largely built and paid for by Sir Thomas Robinson, was unfinished when Robinson sold the Rokeby estate to J. S. Morritt in 1769. Robinson contracted to complete the building within six months as part of the terms of sale but had failed to do so when he died in 1777. In 1775 Morritt agreed to complete the work and the church was consecrated in 1778. Morritt sued Robinson's executors to recover the cost of completing the church and for the value of various pieces of furniture which had been removed from Rokeby Park, a total of £121 10s, suggesting that the amount of work that needed to be done was relatively limited. The design is very similar to Carr's standard small church design seen at Farnley Chapel and elsewhere. The plain rectory built at the same time as the church may also be by Carr.

Ripon Diocesan Registry, Leeds, Records of the Archdeaconry
    of Richmond, Correction Book
Notebook of 'J.T' (thought to be John Tuke) dated 1805,
    transcript formerly in the possession of Revd W. Oliver,
    Rector of Rokeby
Rokeby Park, title deeds; information from Andrew Morritt
BE/NR/310

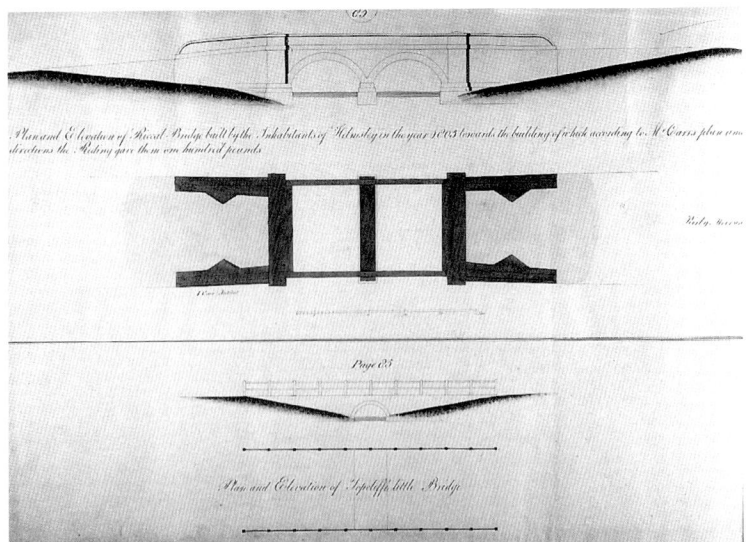

212 Drawing of Riccall bridge

213 Rokeby Park, dining room

Rokeby Park, Yorkshire (NR/County Durham)
(Fig. 213)
John Sawrey Morritt
Alterations, *c.* 1776
Attributed

Morritt acquired Rokeby Park, which had been built by Sir Thomas Robinson in the 1720s and 1730s, in 1769. He removed the stables to a separate block and remodelled the floor above the former stables as a dining room, with a large elaborately plastered niche, approached through an elegant Ionic columned lobby. Dr Ivan Hall attributes this work to Carr, whom Morritt employed in 1775–78 at Rokeby Church and who was also responsible for Greta Bridge, on the edge of the estate in 1773. The form of the broad niche and chimneypiece parallels the much simpler

niche in Plompton Hall and there is a similar niche at Lytham Hall. Many of the decorative details in the niche, frieze and ceiling can be paralleled at Bretton Park and there were similar putti in the frieze at Wiganthorpe Hall.

Giles Worsley, 'Rokeby Park, Yorkshire III', *Country Life*, 2 April 1987
BE/NR/309

Rotherham, Yorkshire (WR/SY)
West Riding magistrates
Bridge widened, 1768

The bridge over the Don was widened by 9 ft on the south.

West Yorkshire Archive Service, Wakefield, Book of Bridges 1752–1770
BE/WR/420

214 Sand Hutton Hall

Rutherford Bridge, Scargill, Yorkshire (NR/County Durham) (Fig. 27)
North Riding magistrates
New bridge, 1773

The 82 ft span bridge over the River Greta was built at a cost of £400 by Robert Shout, Jnr of Helmsley.

North Yorkshire County Record Office, Book of Bridges, 1772–1803, 68
BE/NR/333

Sandbeck West Bridge, Yorkshire (NR/NY)
North Riding magistrates
Bridge improved, 1796

The one-arch bridge over Sand Beck was improved in 1796.

North Yorkshire County Record Office, Book of Bridges, 1772–1803, 77

Sand Hutton Park, Sand Hutton, York (NR/NY)
(Fig. 214)
William Read
New house, 1786
Demolished 1971

The A.P.S.D. records a house for 'William Reede, esq at Sandhutton', Davies 'Sand Hutton near York for William Read, Esq'. Carr designed a square two-storey house in white brick with a large three-bay projecting bow in 1786 for William Read, whose family had held land at Sand Hutton since at least the beginning of the century. In 1839 and 1851 Anthony Salvin greatly increased the house, which was further extended in 1885–87. Carr's house formed the south wing of the larger house, although disguised by later embellishments.

In 1955 the southern half of the house was auctioned for its materials. The remainder of the house was demolished in 1971. Small stables remain.

Wyatt Papworth (ed.), *The Dictionary of Architecture issued by the Architectural Publications Society* (London, 1877), ii, 36
R. Davies, 'A Memoir of John Carr', *Yorkshire Archaeological Journal*, 4 (1877), 205
York Central Library, T. P. Cooper, York Miscellaneous Notes (MSS)
Edward Waterson and Peter Meadows, *Lost Houses of York and the North Riding* (Welburn, 1998), 10–11, figs
BE/NR/318

Deer Park House, Scampston, Yorkshire (ER/NY)
Sir William St Quintin
New house, *c.* 1768
Attributed

St Quintin built the Gothic teahouse as an eyecatcher. It has a castellated façade with a canted two-storey bay, flanking single-storey wings, pointed windows with hoodmoulds and a pretty stucco ceiling within. The style of the building and the employment of two of Carr's closest craftsmen, the carver Daniel Shillito and the plasterer James Henderston suggests the attribution to Carr could be plausible.

BE/ER/671

Sedbury Park, Gilling with Hartforth and Sedbury, Yorkshire (NR/NY)

Robert Darcy Hildyard
Alterations, 1771
Demolished, 1927

Sedbury, a part-medieval, part-seventeenth-century house, was left by Henry Darcy to his grandson Robert Hildyard, son of Sir Robert Hildyard of Winestead. In a letter dated 12 October 1771 to John Grimston Sir Robert Hildyard mentions that 'Carr has indeed shown great skill in the Alterations of the old house at Sedbury, the Dining Room is 34ft by 19 taken off by columns, the Drawing room above has a handsome ceiling and cornice and is elegantly furnished. My son has six good bed chambers, besides one of the most convenient Apartments for himself and Mrs Hildyard that I know of in an old house, but he has a great (deal) still to do. Must build new Stables and a kitchen garden but as he is now well lodged, I hope he will go on with the other improvements gently.' Hildyard's bank account at Drummond's shows that Carr was paid £119 7s 6d in December that year, and a further £21 in May 1774. William Bromwich the carpet manufacturer was paid £38 19s in April 1771 and Joseph Rose, with whom Carr worked at Harewood House, £59 15s in May.

The house was subsequently altered by John Foss in the 1790s and demolished in 1927. The stables, embattled cottages and a lodge, which remain are probably by Carr. The suggestion in the Y.G.S. that Carr built a house at Ledbury, Herefordshire, is a misreading of Sedbury.

East Riding of Yorkshire Archives, Grimston Papers, DDGR 42/21/134
Drummond's Bank, DR 427/62/485, 47/68/485
York Georgian Society, *The Works in Architecture of John Carr* (York, 1973), 19
Edward Waterson and Peter Meadows, *Lost Houses of York and the North Riding* (Welburn, 1998), 42–43, figs
BE/NR/170

Selby, Yorkshire (WR/NY)

Advice on new bridge, 1791

By the Selby Bridge Act of 1791 Carr was one of the engineers on whose advice the proprietors of the new bridge, a wooden structure, were bound to act.

B. F. Duckham, *The Yorkshire Ouse* (1967), 168
BE/WR/443

Serlby Hall, Nr Blyth, Nottinghamshire

3rd Viscount Galway
Estate buildings and possibly work in Serlby Hall, *c.* 1774

A book of building prices 'allow'd at Serlby by John Carr and James Paine Esqs' dated 1774 shows that Carr was employed at Serlby. James Paine had built Serlby Hall in 1754 for the 2nd Viscount Galway, and he subsequently redecorated the dining room and added the west wing in 1771. Carr's account at Goslings Bank records a payment from Lord Galway of £42 on 21 January 1772. The only building mentioned in the book of prices is 'Whiteaker's Building at Haworth', but the prices listed include decorative plasterwork which suggests he worked on Serlby Hall, perhaps fitting up the wing which is referred to in Paine's building accounts as a carcass.

Nottingham University Library, Galway MSS 12,415, 12,558, 12,200/24
Barclay's Bank Archives, Goslings Bank, 46/482

Seven Bridge, Appleton-le-Moors, Yorkshire (NR/NY)

North Riding magistrates
Bridge widened, 1783

The 43 ft bridge over the River Seven was widened in 1783.

North Yorkshire County Record Office, Book of Bridges, 1772–1803, 64

The Shay, Halifax, Yorkshire (WR/WY)

Sir James Ibbetson, Bt
Alterations or new house, after 1787
Demolished, 1903

The list of Carr's commissions in the A.P.S.D. includes 'The Shay, in that city [Halifax], for the Ibbetson family'. The Shay had been the home of John Caygill, an immensely rich Halifax merchant whose daughter and sole heiress Jenny married Sir James Ibbetson in 1768. The Ibbetson clothier's business in Leeds had been sold on the death of Sir James's father in 1761 and in 1770 the family house in Kirkgate was offered for sale. Sir James settled principally at Denton Park in Wharfedale, which Carr rebuilt from about 1772, but presumably retained and either improved or rebuilt the Shay following Caygill's death in 1787. It would appear to have been lived in by John Caygill's widow and after her death in 1806 was advertised to be let in 1807.

Nathaniel Priestley, Some Brief Memoirs of the family of Priestley written in 1779', *Surtees Society*, 77 (1883), 38–39
GEC, *Complete Baronetage* (Exeter, 1906), v, 96
Halifax Guardian Almanack 1921, illustration
R. Bretton, 'The Square and the Piece Hall, Halifax', *Halifax Antiquarian Society* (1961), 59

215 Hollis Hospital, Sheffield

R. G. Wilson, 'Merchants of Land: The Ibbetsons of Leeds and
   Denton 1650–1850', *Northern History*, 24 (1988), 92
Peter Thornborrow, 'John Carr's West Yorkshire Buildings',
   York Georgian Society Report, 1992, 29

Sheffield, Yorkshire (WR/SY)
West Riding magistrates
Bridge widened, 1760

The bridge over the River Don was widened 9 ft on the
west.

West Yorkshire Archive Service, Wakefield, Book of Bridges
   1752–1770

Hollis Hospital, Sheffield (Fig. 215)
Trustees of the Hollis Hospital
New hospital, master's house and school, designed
1769–71, built 1774–76
Demolished 1901

The Hollis Hospital, at the bottom of Snighill, facing
Millsands, was founded in 1703 as almshouses for sixteen
old people and a school for fifty children. In November
1768 Samuel Shore, for whom Carr was working nearby at
Norton Hall, suggested Carr be asked to give his opinion
on the buildings and sketch a design for rebuilding them.
'Mr Carr will draw as plain and simple a design as is
wished for but in a better form and proportion and with
more taste than any other person we have about
Sheffield.' The following month William Fairbank, a local
Sheffield surveyor, surveyed the site and in February Carr
presented Shore with plans, elevations and estimate for
sixteen almshouses, the school and master's house: 'The

whole of which design is particularly delineated, and the
dimensions of every part figured, and in the Estimate of
the expence I have put down the prices of almost every
article the quantity of materials wanted, and the Trustees
inform'd how to make Contracts with them without being
imposed upon.' It was not expected that the scheme
would be built at one go so Carr calculated his estimate by
the square.

   Lengthy correspondence reveals the indecision of the
trustees. Thomas Hollis, who lived in London, considered
getting a surveyor of his acquaintance to draw up a plan,
but nothing came of this. A gentleman amateur, Thomas
Bernard, son of Sir Francis Bernard, who had been
educated at Harvard, also presented plans which were
rejected as pretty but impractical. In 1770 more land was
acquired and in February 1771 Carr submitted further
plans 'upon a new Idea which I hope will be approved of'.
Eventually in 1774 the decision was taken to rebuild the
hospital at once 'agreeable to the plans Mr Shore has been
so good to procure', that is Carr's. Carr was paid 10
guineas for his designs and took no part in the building
process which was measured by Fairbank.

   The buildings were of red brick in a plain Georgian
style and roofed with stone slates. There were two
detached blocks, each with eight almshouses, four
upstairs, four downstairs comprising a single room, small
pantry and coal place. The master's house had two small
rooms and a kitchen on the ground floor and three
bedrooms above. Hollis Hospital was demolished in 1901
to make way for the widening of Newhall Street and

Bridge Street. A photograph of about 1890 survives in the Sheffield City Library and shows it to have been a very plain building.

Sheffield Archives, LD 1160, 1164/23–102; FB 35, pp. 64–67
Report by the Charity Commissioners to the House of Commons, *Endowed Charities, administrative county of West Riding of York and the county borough of Sheffield* (London, 1897), 596–604
Robert Leader, *Sheffield in the Eighteenth Century* (Sheffield, 1905), 318

St Peter's Church, Sheffield (Fig. 41)
The Duke of Norfolk and Burgesses of Sheffield
Restoration, 1772–74

Worried about the state of the church, the town burgesses and Duke of Norfolk (who as Lord of the Manor was responsible for part of the costs) sought advice from Carr in 1771. His report of 1 June was damning. The outside stonework on the south, east and north fronts was exceedingly decayed, particularly on the south front where it could only be repaired by rebuilding the side of the church or by casing it with new stone. Many parts of the battlements, pinnacles, windows and the wall of the upper transept above the roof on the south side needed repair, the steps to the foot of the spire were ruinous and lead pipes were needed to convey water from the tower. Repairs would cost at least £620. The same year Carr prepared drawings for repairs.

In July 1772 Carr was instructed to carry out the work and place an advertisement for workmen. A contract between the builder, John Bishop of Sheffield, the Duke of Norfolk and the Sheffield burgesses was signed on 29 September 1772. Work was to be carried out to Carr's designs and under his supervision. It included repairing and refacing the south and east sides of the chancel and renewing battlements and pinnacles where necessary. Carr replaced the existing south window on the east front with a new window copied from the adjacent east window. His sympathetic work could easily be accepted as authentic Decorated work but for the plain necking at the top of the mullions and the return of the hood moulds on to Classical imposts.

Bishop submitted his invoice for £321 5s 2d on 18 August 1774 which Carr countersigned and passed on, noting that the work had been 'perform'd in a workmanlike manner according to his contract … I have added such allowances as I thought reasonable for doing such extra work as was unforseen when the contract was made'.

Carr also submitted his own invoice for £42. He had made four journeys, the first to survey the building, the second to present his designs and estimate, the third to contract the workmen and the fourth to examine the execution of the work. Carr also charged for making drawings for the new designs for the south and east sides of the church, calling at the church three times to examine work and measuring it on completion. He charged a further £12 12s on 7 May 1774 for a journey to Sheffield to consider a plan for a new vestry at the north-east corner of the church, four drawings for which survive. Carr also added a Gothic clock turret which was removed in the nineteenth century.

Norfolk Estates Office, Sheffield, Account Book of Geo. Townsend
Sheffield Archives, ACM, Ebu 252/1–7, CB 598/2, PR Box 7, nos 3–8
R. B. Wragg, 'John Carr: Gothic Revivalist', in *Studies in Architectural History*, ed. W. A. Singleton (London and York, 1956), II, 21–22
BE/WR/450

Skeeby, Yorkshire (NR/NY)
North Riding magistrates
Bridge improved, 1782

The one-arch bridge over Skeeby Beck on the Richmond Road was improved at a cost of £205.

North Yorkshire County Record Office, Book of Bridges, 1772–1803, 80

Skip Bridge, Wilstrop, Yorkshire (Ainsty/NY)
Wardens of Micklegate Ward, York
Bridge rebuilt, 1787

The River Nidd marked the boundary between the Ainsty and the West Riding and responsibility for maintaining the bridge on the York-Knaresborough road was divided between the two counties. In 1787 the wardens of Micklegate Ward, of whom Carr was one, contracted with John Peacock and Henry King to rebuild the south-east section of the bridge. The wardens had been authorized to enter into the contract at the York Quarter Sessions the previous April.

According to the surviving deed, dated 16 February 1787, Peacock and King were to follow the 'Elevation thereof designed by the said John Carr and hereunder Drawn and delineated'. The drawing survives. Peacock and King were to be paid £630 in instalments and detailed instructions were given for building a temporary bridge and putting in wood piling. The bridge had three spans of 31 ft.

York Archives, Acc. 203.2.10
York Archives, F24/94

Skipton-on-Swale, Yorkshire (NR/NY) (Fig. 216)
North Riding Magistrates
New bridge, 1781

The eight-arch bridge over the River Swale was built by John Peacock for £1,715.

North Yorkshire County Record Office, Book of Bridges, 1772–1803, 79
BE/NR/346

216 Skipton-on-Swale bridge

Sledmere House, Sledmere, Yorkshire

(ER/Humberside) (Figs 217, 218)

Sir Christopher Sykes, Bt, MP

The Castle, 1778; designs for alterations to Sledmere House, suggested, *c.* 1782; ice house (dem.), 1784–85; unexecuted designs for Sledmere House, 1787

Christopher Sykes became tenant for life of Sledmere in 1770 when he married Elizabeth Egerton of Tatton but he was not to live in the house built by his uncle in 1751 until after the death of his father, the Revd Mark Sykes in 1783. Despite this Sykes was closely involved in running and improving the estate, employing Lancelot Brown on the landscape in 1777–78. Most of the farmsteads were designed and supervised by Sykes. Castle Farm, designed by Carr as a Gothic gateway and built in 1778, was the exception. Its pavilions remained unexecuted.

Sykes had probably been considering improving Sledmere House before his father died in September 1783. On 21 May 1782 Carr 'dined and stayed' with him and although there are no records to show what Carr was designing at the time he was paid £18 3s later that month. New offices were begun in 1784 and that year Carr provided a design for an ice house which was filled in January 1785.

Sykes began work on his remodelling in 1787. Carr's designs for a seven-bay pedimented front with an attached Ionic portico were rejected and Sykes acted as his own architect. Joseph Rose executed the interiors from 1789. Sykes continued to turn to Carr for technical advice. In 1791 he wrote to the architect asking about the method of measuring staircases. Elizabeth Chivers, in her diary of a tour in 1806, wrote 'the inside is one of the many specimens of Mr Carr's superiour and much approved taste in architecture'.

Sledmere House, drawings
A memorandum of Elizabeth Chivers's Journey with her Parents in the year 1806; information from Sir Howard Colvin
John Popham, 'Sir Christopher Sykes at Sledmere', *Country Life*, 16, 23 January 1986
BE/ER/693, 698

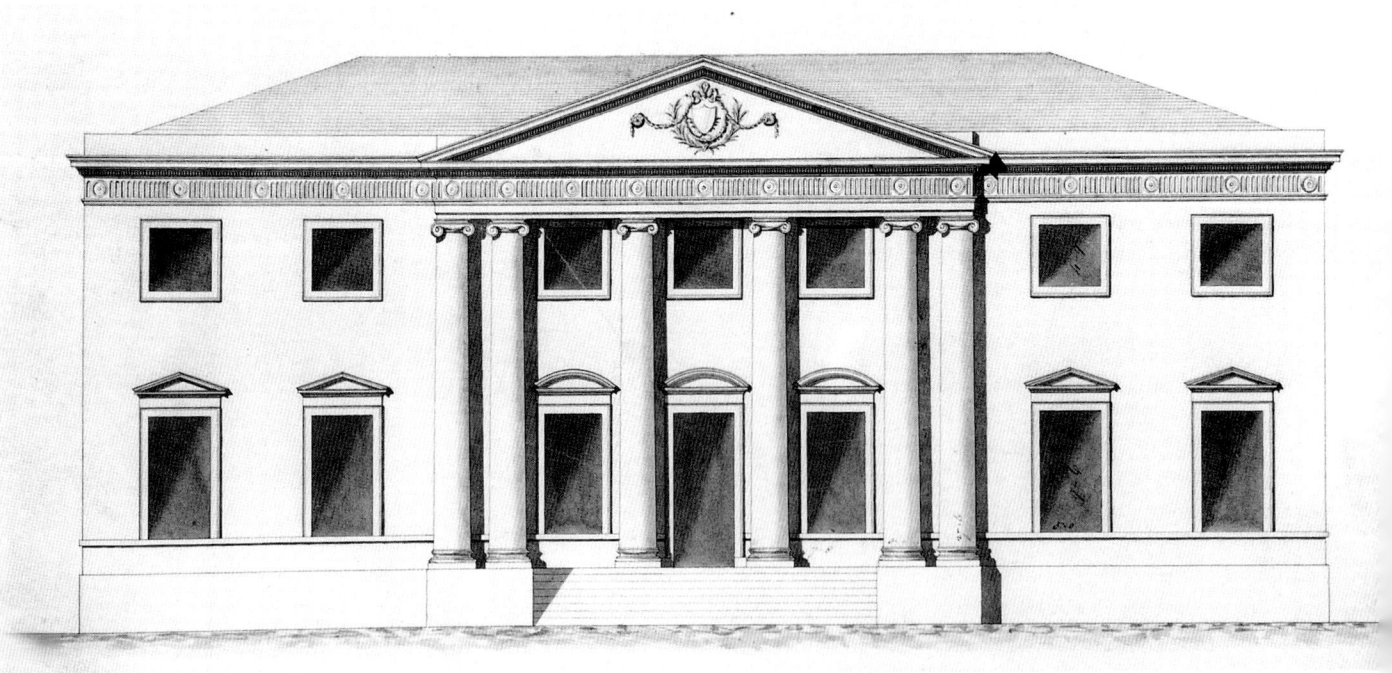

217 Design for Sledmere Hall

CATALOGUE

218 The Castle, Sledmere

Somerby Hall, Nr Caister, Lincolnshire
Edward Weston
Possible alterations, 1768
Demolished, by 1848

Somerby, a mid-seventeenth-century house, was bought
by Edward Weston (1703–70) in 1750. His second wife
Ann, whom he married in 1741, was daughter of John
Fontaine of Melton, York. Carr made survey drawings,
one initialled JC, of the ground plan and elevation which
are dated November 1768. The house had not been
altered when it was drawn by J. C. Nattes in 1796, so any
alterations made by Carr must have been internal. The
house was replaced in the nineteenth century. In the park
is a column with an urn, erected in 1770 by Edward and
Ann Weston to celebrate twenty-one happy years of
marriage. Grange Farm, south east of the house, is dated
1764.

British Architectural Library, K 3/10 (1–2)
Terence R. Leach and Robert Pacey, *The Lost Lincolnshire Country
    Houses* (Burgh-le-Marsh, 1992), II, 56–63, figs 27, 28
BE/Lincs/659

The Residence, Southwell, Nottinghamshire
The Chapter of Southwell Minster
Unexecuted design for alterations, 1783

Carr was paid 15 guineas in 1783 for surveying the
Residence in Vicar's Court and making plans for additions.

The work as carried out in 1785 is in Carr's manner but
was by William Lumby, surveyor and clerk of works at
Lincoln Cathedral.

Southwell Minster Library, Decree Book, 24 July, 1783
BE/Notts/332

Staindrop Church, Staindrop, County Durham
2nd Earl of Darlington
Unexecuted design for a family pew, nd

Carr designed a Gothic family pew for the Earl of
Darlington, for whom he carried it out extensive work at
Raby Castle. It was not built.

Alistair Rowan, 'Gothic Restoration at Raby Castle', *Architectural
    History*, 15 (1972), 23–50, fig. 20a

Stapleton Park, Darrington, Yorkshire (WR/WY)
(Fig. 219)
Edward Lascelles MP, 1st Earl of Harewood
Alterations, *c.* 1762–64
Demolished, *c.* 1930

The architectural history of Stapleton Park has not been
sufficiently established. The estate was bought in 1762 by
Edward Lascelles, cousin of Edwin and Daniel Lascelles
of Harewood and Plompton, and the following year Carr
arranged the supply of 19 tons of slate. Letters to Bacon
Frank show Carr at work there in 1762–64, using William
Moxon as mason and his friend Daniel Shillito as carver,

219 Stapleton Park stables

220 Streetthorpe

for which he was paid £20. Carr was certainly responsible for the staircase, which so impressed Frank that it was used as the model for that at Campsall Hall. In 1789, the Hall was sold to 16th Baron Stourton who seemingly was in occupation at an earlier date for in 1784 Carr was doing work, including the estate walling, for Lord Stourton at 'Stourton House near Doncaster'.

Though it is assumed that Carr rebuilt the house, photographs taken before its demolition show that it was not characteristic of his work and it appears to have a late eighteenth or early nineteenth-century date. It may be that more work was carried out by William Cleave about 1820 than has been assumed. The stables are characteristically Carr with round-headed windows linked by running cills.

West Yorkshire Archive Service, Leeds, Harewood Archives,
    Stewards accounts and correspondence
Sheffield Archives, Wentworth Woodhouse Muniments,
    Stewards correspondence
Sheffield Archives, BFM 1314/67, 1316/6 and 22
J. P. Neale, *Views of the Seats of Noblemen and Gentlemen in England,*
    Wales, Scotland and Ireland (London, 1822), v, 51
John Fletcher, *Memorials of a Yorkshire Parish* (London, 1917), 131
Edward Waterson and Peter Meadows, *Lost Houses of the West*
    Riding (Welburn, 1998), 67, figs

Staunton Hall, Staunton-in-the-Vale, Nottinghamshire
Anne Charlton
Alterations, 1778–80

Staunton belonged to the two unmarried daughters of Job Staunton Charlton who died in 1777. According to Throsby, writing in 1797, the house had a pleasing appearance 'from the late improvements in and about it'. These are recorded in Anne Charlton's accounts for alterations to Staunton Hall in 1778–80. The work was substantial and by 4 December 1780 £2,184 13s 4d had

been spent, including £70 on stuccoing the outside. The illustration of the house in the *Beauties of England* — which describes the house as handsome with many excellent rooms — shows a Tudor H-shaped house with eighteenth-century canted bays added to the ends of the wings. This suggests that Carr may have added the canted bays as well as remodelling the interior of the house. Carr was not paid until 27 December 1785, when he received £43 1s, and the account of Matthew Sheppard, the builder, was not settled until 24 January 1786.

Nottinghamshire County Record Office, Staunton papers,
    43/13–29
BE/Notts/336

Streetthorpe, Kirk Sandall, Yorkshire (WR/SY)
(Fig. 220)
George Cooke
New house, *c.* 1769
Attributed
Demolished, 1920s

George Cooke, son of a younger son of the Cookes of Wheatley Hall, Yorkshire, bought Streetthorpe in 1769. Hunter notes that he built 'a handsome house at Streetthorpe for his own residence and much improved the estate by cultivation and planting'. This is confirmed by Miller who in 1804 recorded that Cooke had built the new house about thirty years ago and that he had converted the barren common into rich pasture and arable land.

Streetthorpe was a plain, five-bay, two and a half storey house with a hipped roof and wings that is very similar in design to John Milnes's house in Wakefield, attributed to Carr, and to nearby Campsmount, with service wings extending parallel to the house as at Thornes House, Gledstone Hall and Basildon Park. As Campsmount was

CATALOGUE

designed by Carr for Cooke's uncle Thomas Yarborough (whose estate Cooke inherited in 1802) an attribution of Streetthorpe to Carr seems plausible. The house was subsequently renamed Edenthorpe and was demolished in the 1920s.

Edward Miller, *The History and Antiquities of Doncaster and its Vicinity* (Doncaster, 1804)
Joseph Hunter, *South Yorkshire* (London, 1828), I, 207
Edward Waterson and Peter Meadows, *Lost Houses of the West Riding* (Welburn, 1998), 63, figs

Strensall Bridge, Yorkshire (NR/NY) (Fig. 221)
North Riding magistrates
New bridge, 1798

The one-arch bridge over the River Foss on the Sheriff Hutton road was built to Carr's designs at a cost of £1,363 3s 2d. The whole of the bridge and the landwalls were built of good Rainton stone and the whole structure was well executed and well founded on a bed of strong clay.

North Yorkshire County Record Office, Book of Bridges, 1772–1803, 82

222 Swarland Hall

Swarland Hall, Nr Felton, Northumberland (Fig. 222)
Davidson Richard Grieve
Design of a house, *c.* 1765
Demolished, 1934
Attributed

Among the sketches in Carr's copy of Roger Morris's *Select Architecture* in Sir John Soane's Museum is 'a house for Mr Grieve Northumberland'. This may be an early design for Swarland Hall, west of Alnwick, which was built by Davidson Richard Grieve in 1765. Grieve's father had bought the estate in 1735 and he had succeeded in 1760.

The elevation of the house did not correspond with this plan but the design could have been by Carr. It was of one and a half storeys over a rustic and had a Doric portico-in-antis flanked on either side by two bays. The design can be compared with Constable Burton, built in 1762–68, although the treatment of the Doric portico does not appear so well resolved as in the Ionic portico at Constable Burton. The Duchess of Northumberland, who visited in 1773, was much impressed by the house which she described as modern and built of stone by Mr Grieve, but felt the portico was too high for the width.

Alnwick Castle, Duchess of Northumberland's diaries, 121/51
Sir John Soane's Museum, Roger Morris, *Select Architecture* (London, 1955), drawing opposite pl. 4
John Crawford Hodgson, *A History of Northumberland* (Newcastle, 1904), VII, 399, 403
John Summerson, *The Architect and Building News*, 15 June 1934, 304
Thomas Faulkner and Pheobe Lowery, *Lost Houses of Newcastle and Northumberland* (Welburn, 1996), 60
BE/Northumberland/581

221 Strensall bridge

223 Tabley Hall, entrance front

Swinton Park, Swinton-with-Wathermarske, Yorkshire (NR/NY)
William Danby
Alterations, 1764–71

William Danby inherited Swinton from his father in 1750. After building new stables in 1752–53 he turned to Carr to remodel the plain, square late seventeenth-century house built by Sir Abstrupus Danby. Considerable sums were spent in 1764 and in 1765 with Carr adding canted bays to the north and south façades and remodelling the interiors. Neither façades nor interiors survived remodelling by Danby's son William after 1781.

Carr was paid £30 5s for two chimneypieces for the parlour and best bedchamber on 2 June 1764, £20 'in further part for his assistance in the buildings and alterations at Swinton' on 28 April 1765, and £47 11s 6d for 'marble work, for his advice and Directions as an Architect etc' on 10 April 1767. Small payments to Carr occur until April 1771. John Fisher of York was responsible for the carving and James Henderson for the plasterwork.

Bradford Art Gallery, Cunlifee-Lister Manuscripts, Bundle 13; information from Sir Howard Colvin
John Cornforth, 'Swinton, Yorkshire', *Country Life*, 7 April, 1966
BE/NR/363

Tabley Hall, Nr Knutsford, Cheshire
(Figs 38, 53, 223–25)
Sir Peter Leicester, Bt, MP
New house, stables and lodges, 1760–67

Sir Peter Byrne inherited Tabley through his grandfather. His father, Sir John Byrne, Bt, was the descendant of a rich Irish army clothier and his mother the heiress of the Cheshire family of Warren. On inheriting in 1742 Byrne assumed the name of Leicester, sold his Irish estates and bought Over Tabley with the intention of building a new house looking down on Old Tabley Hall and Nether Tabley Mere.

Carr was commissioned to build one of his most substantial new houses, nine bays wide with a Doric portico, perron, rustic, *piano nobile* and pavilions, one of which held the kitchen, linked by quadrants. The rustic included a billiard room and a family entrance but was

CATALOGUE

208

224 Tabley Hall, plan of ground floor
225 Tabley Hall, plan of basement

largely given over to offices. The entrance hall was on the *piano nobile* on the south front, flanked by dining and drawing rooms with an apsidal ended library on the west front. A suite of bedrooms and dressing rooms lay along the north front and an octagonal common parlour on the east front, connected to a family staircase. An unusually extensive staircase filled the centre of the house. The decoration marks the transition from Palladian to Adamesque with restraint as the keynote. The exuberance of Rococo motifs is replaced by the sober Doric of the plain, rectangular entrance hall.

Work began in 1760, with the chief mason, James Oates, sent from Yorkshire. Thomas Oliver was the plasterer and Daniel Shillito and Matthew Bertram carvers. Carr procured marble chimneypieces and iron grates in Yorkshire although William Atkinson of Hyde Park Corner in London may have provided the principal chimneypieces.

Thomas Harrison of Chester created a tripartite picture gallery out of the drawing room, library and two bedrooms in about 1810. The house is now an old peoples' home. It was originally known as Oakland House.

Tabley Hall, estate accounts
James Woolfe and John Gandon, *Vitruvius Britannicus* (London, 1771), v, pls 16–19
Christopher Hussey, *English Country Houses 1760–1800* (London, 1956), 55–60
BE/Ches/349–50

Tadcaster, Yorkshire (WR/NY)
North and West Riding magistrates
Bridge widened, 1791

The bridge over the River Wharfe was widened following an advertisement in the *York Courant*. As the bridge linked the Ainsty of York and the West Riding estimates for the two halves of the bridge were to be submitted separately to Mr Gott, surveyor of bridges for the West Riding, and to Mr Carr in his office in York. Plans for the additions to the bridge could be seen at Carr's office, but not Gott's, suggesting that Carr designed the new work.

York Courant, 4 October, 1791

CATALOGUE

Tanfield Hall, Yorkshire (NR/NY)
2nd Lord Bruce
Repairs and alterations, 1765
Demolished 1816

Tanfield was a subsidiary estate of Lord Bruce, whose principal seat was at Tottenham in Wiltshire. Sir William Chambers presented Bruce with a design for an elegant casino before 1759, but this was not executed. It is not known exactly what Carr's work entailed, but it seems to have been principally repairs, improvements such as new hearths, minor alterations such as reordering the closets and the addition of a new room for the upper servants. By June 1765 work on the house and offices was partly finished, although it had been discovered that the back buildings were so decayed that they needed reroofing. A survey of 1804 shows the building had a rectangular plan with a projection on the north front.

North Yorkshire County Record Office, ZJX 7/2/9,10,13
John Harris, *Sir William Chambers* (London, 1970), 248–49

Tankersley Park, Yorkshire (WR/SY)
2nd Marquis of Rockingham
'Temple', presumably the 'Lady's Folly, *c.* 1763
Demolished

Harriet Clark's journal of 1795 refers to a visit to 'the Temple in Tankersley Park, the views from which are the most beautiful and extensive in the kingdom, design'd by my uncle Carr'. This was presumably the building whose masonry John Platt contracted to complete for £80 'in Tankersley Park ... according to the plan showd me and directions given by Mr Carr'. Tankersley Park lies three miles north-west of Wentworth Woodhouse. The Lady's Folly, now demolished, was a two-storey building, with a pyramid roof and three arches on the north and south façades of the upper storey separated by attached Tuscan columns.

Sheffield Archives, WWM Stw P6 (i) 34
York Minster Library, MS 328/1, fol. 3
BE/WR/508–09

Temple Newsam House, Nr Leeds, Yorkshire
(WR/WY)
9th Viscount Irwin
Plans and alterations to mansion house, 1762–68; estimate for barn, stable and cow-house, 1772

Carr made numerous proposals for alterations at Temple Newsam for Lord and Lady Irwin and was paid substantial sums in the 1760s and 1770s, but it is unclear how many of his suggestions were carried out. Lord and Lady Irwin's account at Drummond's Bank first records a payment of £58 3s to Mr Carr on 12 June 1759, with another one of £65 10s 9d on 1 February 1762. Further payments are recorded to Carr and Co. of £18 on 18 January 1768, £38

on 25 April 1769, £16 12s 3d on 3 March 1770, £84 on 10 October 1770 and £46 12s on 1 February 1772.

A bill 'for attendance at Templenewsam, & Various drawings made since Octbr. 5th 1764 the Time he was last paid, to decemr. 30: 1768' of £38 17s shows that on 18 September 1765 he visited Temple Newsam 'with a drawing for finishing the Hall, and planned the alteration of the Great Stair Case, sketch'd the manner of altering the Cupola, made a plan of the Old Rooms as they are at present on the south front and a Drawing for the Keeper's Lodge &c'. On 20 December 1768 he visited again 'about altering the disposition of the whole South Front, took dimensions of the Elevation &c., and made rough drawings of the intended alterations on that side of the House'. On 7 March 1767 he 'Made fair drawings of the Ground Plan, Chamber plan & Elevation of the South Front'. This bill was was paid on 25 April 1769, tying in with the Drummond's account. Carr also provided an estimate of £100 18s 1¼d for building a barn, stable and cow-house in 1772. The Keeper's Lodge was presumably that on the East Avenue, demolished in 1946. It was formed of two matching, single-storey dodecahedral Gothic buildings.

Although it has been suggested that Carr's staircase was executed, Lady Irwin's account at Drummond's records a payment of £300 to James Wyatt. Since the original balustrade (removed to the north-west staircase *c.* 1890) is a Wyatt pattern it is probable that Wyatt was responsible. Drawings for the south wing were also supplied by Lancelot Brown in 1766 and Robert Adam.

West Yorkshire Archives Service, Leeds, two receipted bills. TN Green Index Book, Vol. 1; information from Mr James Lomax
Drummond's Bank, London, DR/427/34 359; information from Mr James Lomax
Derek Linstrum, *West Yorkshire Architects and Architecture* (London, 1978), 32
David Hill, 'Archives and Archaeology at Temple Newsam House', *Leeds Arts Calendar*, 89 (1981), 30–31
Brett Harrison, 'The East Lodge at Temple Newsam', *Georgian Group Journal*, 7 (1997), 105–06, fig. 1

Thirkleby, Yorkshire (NR/NY) (Fig. 226)
North Riding magistrates
New bridge, 1799
Rebuilt, 1931

The 18 ft 6 in span bridge over New Beck on the York–Thirsk road was rebuilt at a cost of £231 10s 0d.

North Yorkshire County Record Office, Book of Bridges, 1772–1803, 19

School Building, Thirsk, Yorkshire (NR/NY)
Ralph Bell
Unexecuted design for a school, 1770

Carr was paid £8 8s for a design for a school and house for the master 'the plans and elevations thereof particularly delineated'. Nothing apparently came of them.

North Yorkshire County Record Office, Bell of Thirsk papers, ZAG 22

The Hall, Thirsk, Yorkshire (NR/NY) (Fig. 227)
Ralph Bell
Addition of a third storey and wings and internal alterations, 1771–74

Ralph Bell succeeded his father in 1770 and employed Carr to add an extra storey and two-bay and three-bay wings to the earlier house. In 1775 Carr invoiced for making 'the plans of the old house and the new wings and all the parts thereof at large for the workmen and making all the drawings for the chimneybases, bases and surbases, plaisterers &c and measuring their several works and giving all the necessary directions for the proper execution of the work for 3½ years from 8 June 1771, the whole designs, drawings and directions included at 30 guineas a year, £110 5s'.

Masons' work was by John Peacock, James Henderson was responsible for the plasterer's work (particularly in the great room) and Robert Blakesley the carver's work, charging £30 8s 3d for carving in the great room. Carr provided numerous marble chimneypieces for the bedrooms, for which he was paid £170 6s 8d.

North Yorkshire County Record Office, ZAG 22
BE/NR/366–67

227 *top* Thirsk Hall | **228** *below* Thirsk bridge

Thirsk Mill, Thirsk, Yorkshire (NR/NY) (Fig. 228)
North Riding magistrates
New bridge, 1789

The three-arch bridge in Millgate over Cod Beck was built at a cost of £621 12s 7d.

North Yorkshire County Record Office, Book of Bridges, 1772–1803
BE/NR/367

Thoresby Lodge, Perlethorpe-cum-Budby, Nottinghamshire (Figs 32, 229, 230)
2nd Duke of Kingston
New house, stables, garden buildings and possibly landscape buildings, 1767–71
Charles Pierrepont, 1st Earl Manvers
Alterations, lodges and Castle William, c. 1788–c. 1803

Thoresby House was burnt down in 1745 or 1746. It was not till twenty years later that it was rebuilt, perhaps inspired by the duke's intended marriage to his notorious

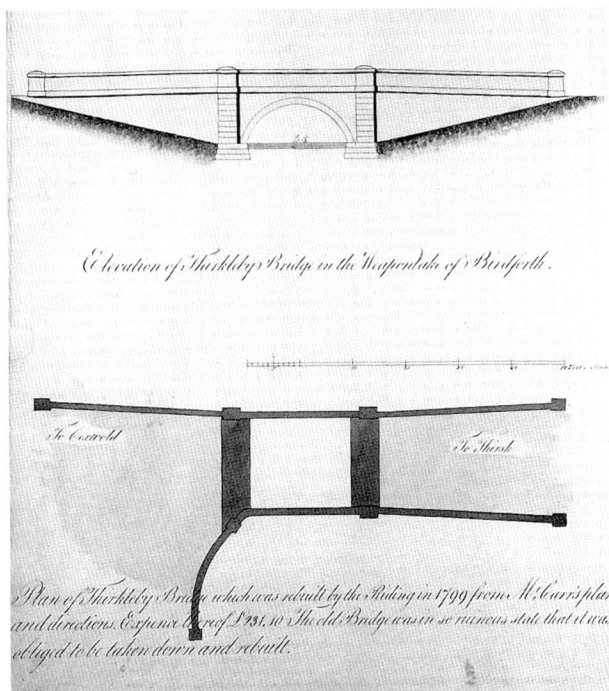

226 Drawing of Thirkleby bridge

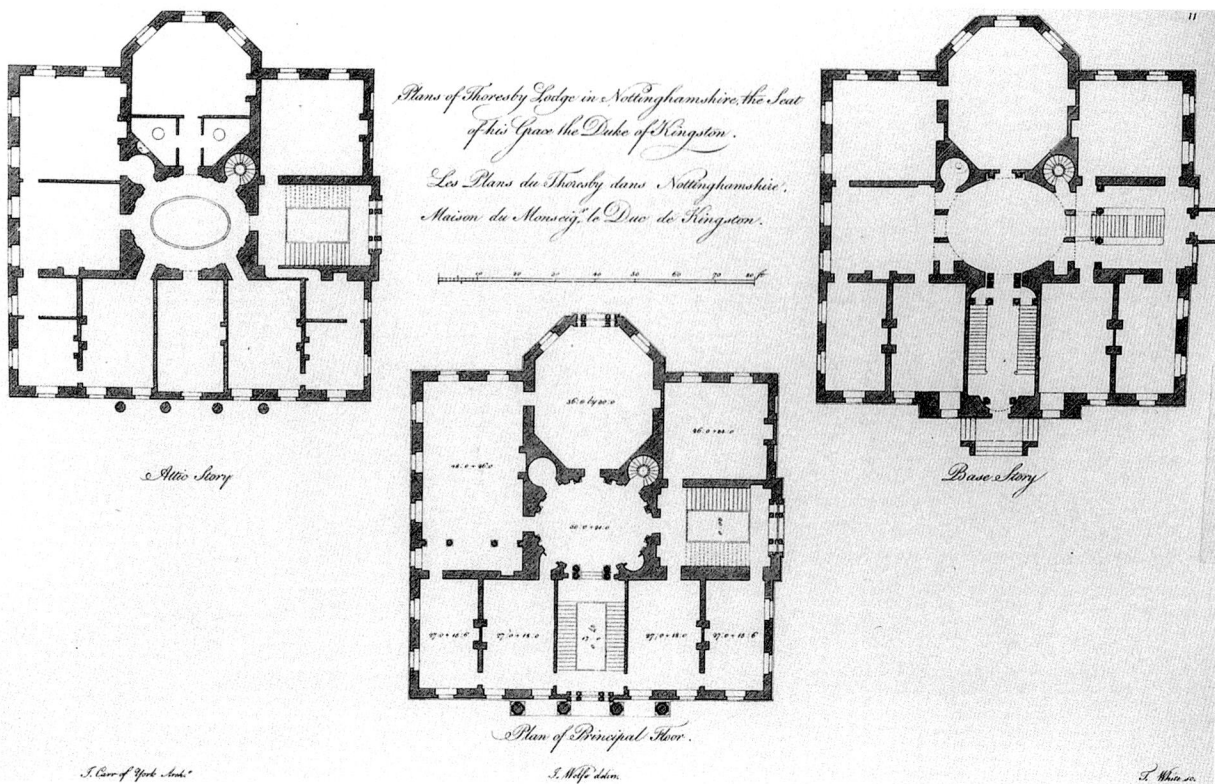

229 Thoresby Lodge, plans of ground, first and bedroom floors

mistress, Elizabeth Chudleigh, which took place in 1769. Carr's estimate for the new house — his grandest new-built house — was £11,000 although the actual expense totalled £17,000. A further £13,000 was spent on the stables, greenhouse, engine house, engine works and other alterations. It was described by Bray as a comfortable rather than a magnificent seat.

Entrance was into the rustic where there were breakfast, dining and drawing rooms. Handsome imperial stairs led to the saloon, a skylit room commonly called the Dome, in the centre of the house. The walls, floor and fourteen columns of this room, which cost £1,000, were of yellow and white scagliola similar to that in the hall at Wentworth Woodhouse. The saloon led to two further drawing rooms and a small library.

Carr was paid £850, 5 per cent of the cost of the house, for his drawings, attendances and his clerk coming over twice to assist in measuring. £300 was paid through the duke's account at Hoare's Bank on 3 January 1769 and a further £302 10s on 17 December 1771. The offices, alterations and repairs were supervised by John Simpson, clerk of works on the Thoresby estate, so Carr made no charge. Clerici and Vassalli were paid for marble work from July 1769 to August 1771.

Charles Pierrepont, created Viscount Newark in 1796

and Earl Manvers in 1806, inherited in 1788 and moved to Thoresby in 1789. An account drawn up by the steward in 1805 shows that he spent £22,500 improving Thoresby between 1788 and 1803. Carr returned and rectified a settlement in the centre of the house on the south side. He altered the dog kennels, reduced the stables, added coach houses and a laundry and demolished the great room he had earlier built over the greenhouse. He also built Castle William, a towered and castellated house on the estate, and was responsible for Clarke's Lodge and the Shepherd's Lodge which Lord Newark built, and alterations to Freeman's Lodge and Wordsworth's Lodge. The greater part of this work was executed between 1790 and 1794.

Carr's house was burnt down in 1868. The present mansion is by Salvin.

Nottingham University Library, Manvers Deposit, Ma 2 X 2/1–2
Hoare's Bank Archives, D/224, E94
James Woolfe and John Gandon, *Vitruvius Britannicus* (London, 1771), v, pls 11–13
William Bray, *Sketch of a Tour into Derbyshire and Yorkshire* (London, 1783), 348
J. H. Hodson, 'The Building and Alteration of the Second Thoresby House, 1767–1804', *Thoroton Society Record Series*, 21 (1962), 16–20
BE/Notts/84, 348–50

CATALOGUE

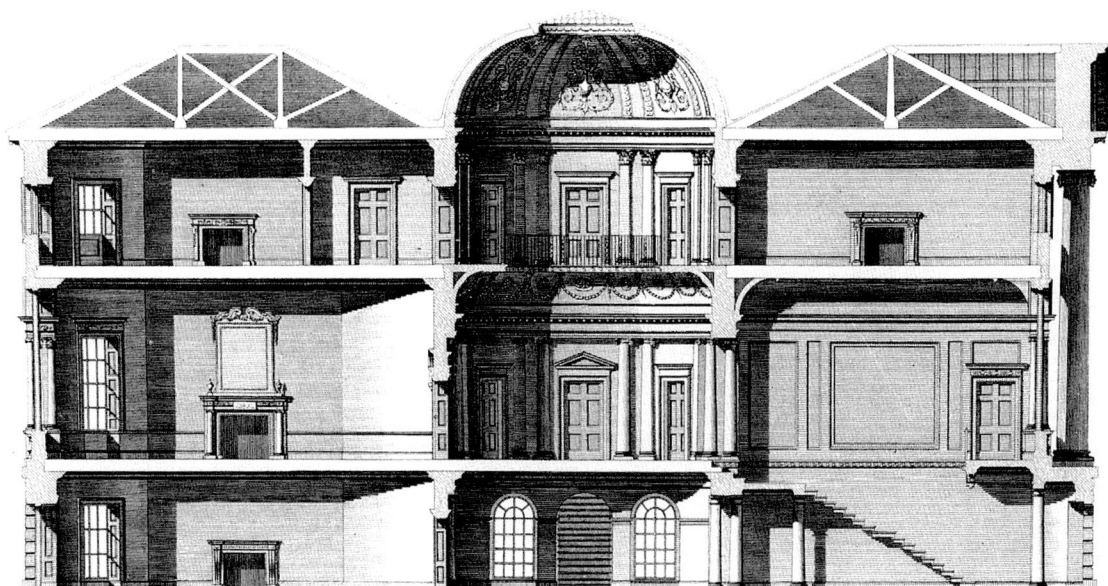

Section of Thoresby Lodge.
Profile de la Maison de Thoresby.
J. Carr of York.   J. Wolfe del.   T. White sculp.

230 Thoresby Lodge, section

Thornes House, Wakefield, Yorkshire (WR/WY)
(Figs 231, 232)
James Milnes
New house, 1779–81
Demolished, *c.* 1951

By 1778 the Milnes family of Wakefield was the closest
rival to the Denisons of Leeds in the claim to be the
largest cloth exporters in Yorkshire. James Milnes added
to his substantial fortune by marrying one of the two co-
heiresses of Hans Buck, a prosperous Leeds cloth
merchant, in 1778, reputedly gaining a dowry of over
£100,000. Presumably with the proceeds, Milnes
commissioned Carr to design Thornes House on an
elevated site with a fine view overlooking Wakefield.

According to Richardson, Thornes House was one of
Carr's favourite designs. The entrance front, of stone, was
seven bays wide and two and a half storeys high with an
attached Ionic portico with pilasters, an unusual feature
for Carr. The garden front, of brick, is shown by
Richardson with a central bow window but the house as
executed had a canted bay on the garden front. Several
other features reveal Carr 'purifying' the design for
publication: decorative swags on the pedestals of the
pilasters, fluting on the architrave of the porch and
keystones over the windows were all removed. Later

alterations make it impossible to know if the pavilions and
the unusual flanking doors were executed or were another
'improvement' by Carr.

The rooms had delicate Adamesque plasterwork. The
house was demolished after a fire in 1951.

George Richardson, *New Vitruvius Britannicus* (London, 1802), I,
    pls 51–53
J. W. Walker, *Wakefield, its History and People* (Wakefield, 1934),
    528
R. G. Wilson, 'Denisons and Milnses: Eighteenth-Century
    Merchant Landowners', in *Land and Industry: The Landed Estate
    and the Industrial Revolution*, J. T. Ward and R. G. Wilson
    (Newton Abbot, 1971), 145–72
Edward Waterson and Peter Meadows, *Lost Houses of the West
    Riding* (Welburn, 1998), 48, fig.

Thorp Arch Hall, Thorp Arch, Yorkshire (WR/WY)
(Fig. 4)
William Gossip
New house, 1750–56

The genesis of Thorp Arch Hall is particularly well
documented thanks to the survival of numerous
contemporary letters as well as a notebook of floor plans,
sketches and elevations which passed between Carr and
Gossip as the house was designed, along with Gossip's
own plan and memorandum book and relevant accounts.

231 Thornes House
232 *opposite* Thornes House
engraving

Gossip, son of a West Riding mercer, inherited estates in Hatfield, York and Beverley in 1733, but from 1742 was merely tenant of Skelton Hall, near York. In 1748 he bought the manor of Thorp Arch with the aim of building a seat. Gossip was a friend of Stephen Thompson, for whom Carr was then building Kirby Hall, and sought his advice. He was also a friend of Edmund Garforth who employed Carr on Gossip's advice at Askham Hall in about 1750.

At first Gossip sought designs for a new house from James Paine, but Paine was busy and failed to respond adequately. Instead Gossip turned to Carr who visited with his father in August 1749 and finalized plans that month. Carr visited Thorp Arch twenty-six times between 8 August 1749 and 14 September 1750.

Foundations were laid in August 1749 for a plain, square, two-storey house with flanking wings. Cellars were turned in February 1750 and the house was roofed in August 1751. After that Carr's direct involvement reduced and between 5 December 1751 and 31 August 1752 he only made eleven visits. His last visit was in May 1753 to measure up the work of the mason Joseph Taite and settle his account. By the end of 1753 construction was nearly complete, apart from a staircase, and work was concentrated on finishing the interior. Carr provided hearths and mantelpieces, not without some difficulties. In 1754 Gossip complained that the drawing room chimneypiece was too low. To resolve the problem an extra band of grecian key pattern was added. The house was largely finished by the end of 1756. Gossip estimated his expenses at £2,035 15s 6¼d, although this did not include all costs.

Some of the same craftsmen were employed at Thorp Arch that had been employed at Kirby Hall. The carpenter was Richard Allott of West Bretton and the carver W. Sone from Wakefield. Thomas Perritt provided the plasterers and Charles Mitley some of the mantelpieces.

West Yorkshire Archives Service, Leeds, Thorp Arch Estate
  Records, acc. 4337, TA 3/3, 7/6, 7/10, 11/4, 19/4, 21/10,
  21/11, 23/2,
Brett Harrison, 'Thorp Arch Hall, 1749–1756: "dabbling a little
  in Mortar"', *Thoresby Society*, 2nd ser., 4 (1994 for 1993), 1–39

Topcliffe, Yorkshire (NR/NY)

North Riding magistrates
Bridge widened, 1786
Parapet altered 1954

The old bridge of 1622 over the River Swale on the Thirsk–Ripon road was widened at a cost of £994.

North Yorkshire County Record Office, Book of Bridges,
  1772–1803, 73

Towneley Hall, Burnley, Lancashire

Charles Towneley
Repairs and alterations, 1766–67

In March 1766 Carr visited Towneley Hall, a medieval house which had been extensively remodelled in the early eighteenth century. He provided his opinion over repairs to the roof of the great hall and designed two drawings rooms at the end of the south wing, one with a large coved alcove similar to that at Rokeby Park. The drawings were provided in December and the work was carried out by Mr Butler and Mr Atkinson, who provided an estimate of £313 18s 6d, with occasional supervision by one of Carr's brothers. However, Carr's fee for the designs and

North Elevation of Thornes House, in Yorkshire, the Seat of James Milnes Esq. John Carr, of York, Architect.

visit of 20 guineas had still not been paid in 1775 when Carr wrote plaintively that 'I shall be very glad if you can put me into a method of being paid, as I have not been very pressing for my recompense'. Carr's interiors were swept away by Jeffry Wyatville 1814.

Lancashire Record Office, DDTO Box 2
Susan Bourne, *An Introduction to the Architectural History of Towneley Hall* (Burnley, 1979), 19–20

Upleatham Hall, Guisborough, Yorkshire
(NR/Cleveland)
Sir Thomas Dundas MP, 1st Baron Dundas
Alterations, n.d.
Demolished, 1897

Sir Lawrence Dundas purchased Upleatham in 1762, which was occupied during his lifetime by his son Thomas. Carr was commissioned to enlarge the house, perhaps after Dundas's marriage in 1764. The extent of Carr's work is unknown as the house was altered by Sir Robert Smirke in 1810 and again by Ignatius Bonomi *c.* 1836–40. Photographs do not show any obvious work by Carr although the service wing to the east is perhaps closest to his manner.

York Central Library, YO 40, John Knowles, *York Artists*
North Yorkshire County Record Office, Zetland Archives
Edward Waterson and Peter Meadows, *Lost Houses of York and the North Riding* (Welburn, 1998), 26–27, figs

County House of Correction, Wakefield, Yorkshire
(WR/WY) (Figs 233, 234)
West Riding Magistrates
New gaol, 1766–68
Demolished

In 1766 it was ordered that the West Riding Surveyor of Bridges — John Carr — should draw up plan for a new House of Correction in the county town of Wakefield. The scheme was presented to the Grand Jury at York and Carr and his fellow surveyor John Watson were ordered to advertise for building tenders. On 6 August Robert Carr and Luke Holt, a carpenter who also lived in Horbury, contracted to build the new jail for £2,650. The final cost for what was one of the largest provincial jails in England was £2,772.

The prison was formed by two main buildings. The entrance block, a plain, five-bay, two-storey hipped-roofed building with an arched and rusticated central entrance, included the Sessions Room and Committee Room but was mainly given over to the Governor's House. Behind it was the cell block, which was H-shaped, with a projecting chapel range at the rear, underneath which was the turnkey's house. Apart from two day-rooms the building was otherwise largely given over to the eighty cells. In 1776 the prison held 186 prisoners.

A women's prison was added in 1770 and the infirmary was built to Robert Carr's designs in 1774. Additional wings with solitary cells and enclosing walls were built between 1788 and 1795 and the jail was extensively enlarged and improved in 1819–24 and 1837. The new prison opened in 1847.

West Yorkshire Archives Service, Wakefield, QD1/382/1–12, QD1/697
J. Horsfall Turner, *The Annals of the Wakefield House of Correction* (Bingley, 1904), 88, 91
Kevin Grady, *The Georgian Buildings of Leeds and the West Riding*, Publications of the Thoresby Society, 62 (1987), 16, 20, 38, 179

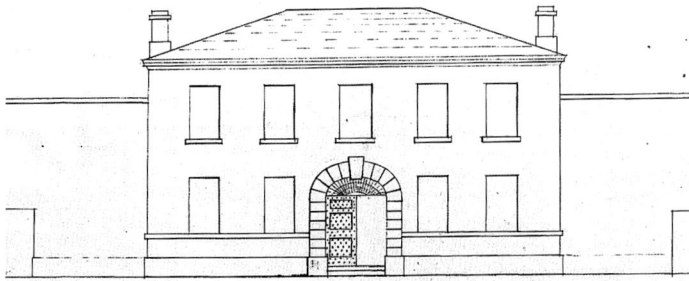

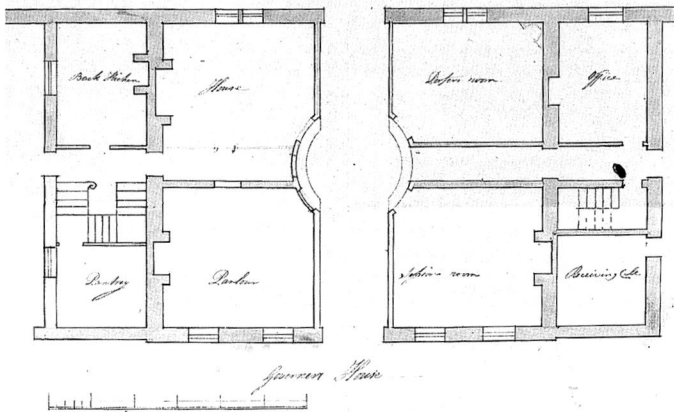

233 Design for Wakefield Prison elevation

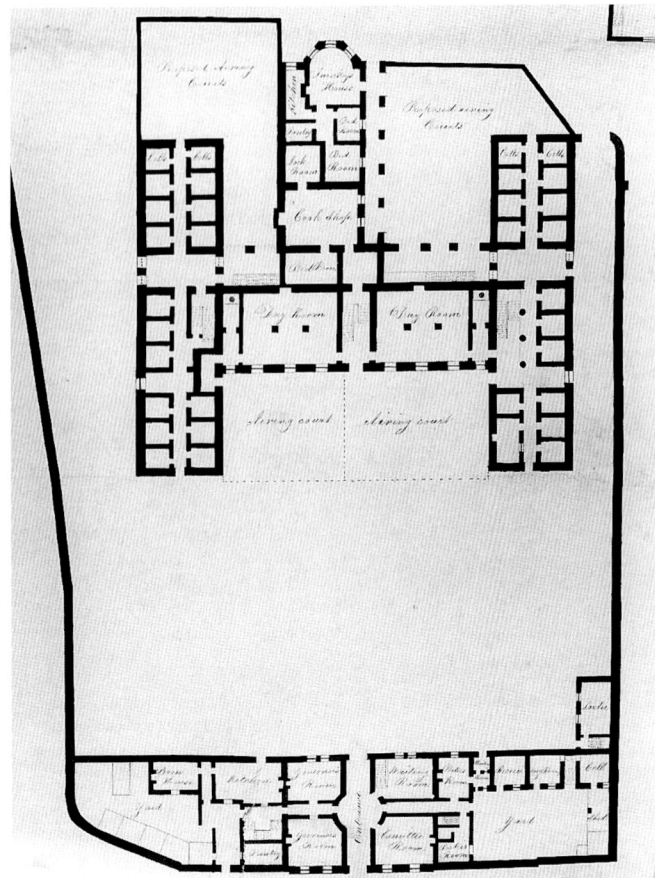

234 Wakefield Prison, plan of ground floor

R. S. Duncan, 'Here we go round the Mulberry Bush': the House of
Correction 1595, the West Riding House of Correction, HM Prison
Wakefield 1995 (Wakefield, 1994), 10–11

Houses in Westgate, Wakefield (Figs 235, 236)
Milnes family
New houses, c. 1750–53 and 1773
Attributed
Demolished

According to Kitson, Carr 'is responsible for some of
those great plain comfortable-looking brick houses in
Westgate'. It is not clear on what evidence this is based,
but Carr was close to the Milnes family, the leading
merchants in the town, four of whose members had
houses in Westgate. In February 1750 William Gossip sent
two letters to be left for Carr at Messrs Richard and John
Milnes, merchants at Wakefield, suggesting that he may
have been working for them at that time. The family had
grown rich on trade with Russia and rivalled the claim of
the Denisons of Leeds to be the largest export house in
the Yorkshire cloth trade.

The founders of the dynasty were Robert (d. 1734) and
John (d. 1742). Robert had four sons, Richard (d. 1755),
Joseph, Robert (who moved to Leeds and died in 1729)
and John (who married Mary, sister of Carr's client Samuel
Shore, and died in 1771). Both Robert and his sister
Hannah married into the Priestley family, which employed
Carr at White Windows. Richard (d. 1755) had two sons,
Robert (who married Esther, sister of Carr's client Samuel
Shore, and died in 1771) and Pemberton (d. 1795). John
(d. 1771) had two sons, Sir Robert Shore Milnes (d. 1831)
and John (born 1751). The elder John Milnes had three
sons, John (d. 1769), Richard (d. 1741) and James (d.
1792). James's son, James (d. 1805) employed Carr at
nearby Thornes House in 1779–81.

All the Milnes's houses in Westgate have been
demolished and it is not clear for which, if any, of these
houses Carr was responsible. Robert Milnes had an older,
gabled house on the north side which was altered in the
1750s. James Milnes's house on the south side of Westgate
was built about 1750 and Pemberton Milnes's house,

235 *above* John Milnes house, Wakefield
236 *left* John Milnes house, plan of
ground floor

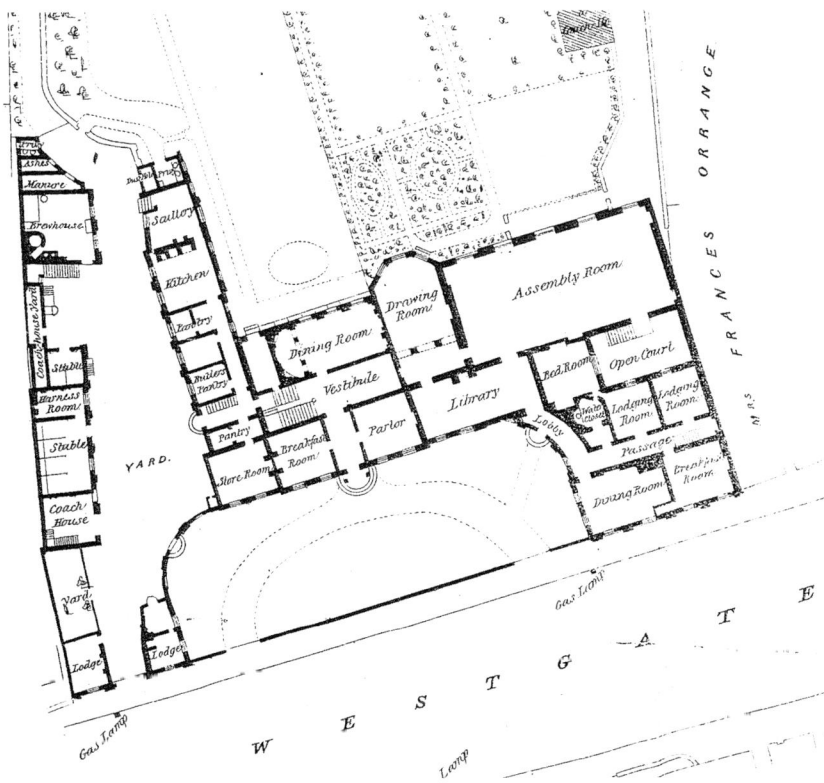

which was rich in carving and plasterwork, was built in 1752–53 in preparation for his marriage.

The largest and finest of the houses was that built for John Milnes in 1773, soon after his father's death in 1771. A plain, five-bay, two-and-a-half-storeyed villa with a pyramidal roof, this is the most plausible attribution to Carr given its close similarity to Campsmount. The house had extensive gardens and was extended in 1790 with quadrant wings containing a ballroom and kitchen. A plan and elevation of the house can be found in the original sale particulars in the John Goodchild collection in Wakefield.

West Yorkshire Archives Service, Leeds, Thorp Arch Papers, TA 19/4, 10 February 1750, 21 February 1750

Sidney Kitson, 'Carr of York', *RIBA Journal*, 3rd ser., 17 (1910), 254

J. W. Walker, *Wakefield: its History and People* (Wakefield, 1934), 397, 463, 538

R. G. Wilson, 'Denisons and Milnses: Eighteenth-Century Merchant Landowners', in *Land and Industry: The Landed Estate and the Industrial Revolution*, J. T. Ward and R. G. Wilson (Newton Abbot, 1971), 162–65

Derek Linstrum, *West Yorkshire Architects and Architecture* (London, 1978), 99

Edward Waterson and Peter Meadows, *Lost Houses of the West Riding* (Welburn, 1998), 48, fig.

CATALOGUE

237 Well Head House

erected to Carr's designs, who was paid £160 'in full for his Attendance at Welbeck & Drawing Designs &c: to this day' on 8 December 1764. Carr also modernized the chapel and the monastic refectory. Payments were made in 1764 to Christopher Richardson, the Doncaster carver, for ornamenting the cupola over the chapel clock.

Welbeck was criticized for its indeterminate character and John Byng described it as 'mean, ugly and ill-built', but Portland's financial problems prevented major rebuilding. Nevertheless, stables were added in about 1774 and the suite of reception rooms on east front — ante room, drawing room, dining room and library — in 1775–77. The only external embellishments added by Carr were a battlemented parapet and central entrance porch on the west front. The work was not without its problems. In 1791 Carr reported to the steward at Wentworth Woodhouse that a beam over the dining room had had to be replaced after three years.

Carr's stables were demolished by the 5th Duke of Portland, who succeeded in 1854. The east wing was remodelled by George and Yeats in 1900–02 but Mr Pete Smith suggests that more may survive of Carr's work than has been realized.

Nottingham University Library, Portland Papers, PwF2 2, 536–50
Nottinghamshire Record Office, Portland Papers, DD5P 6/1-17, DD5P 6/2/2; P6/7/2/17–27
Sheffield Archives, Wwm, Stw P6 102 5/12/1791
A. S. Turberville, *Welbeck Abbey and its Owners* (London, 1939), II, 454
BE/Notts/368

Welbeck Abbey, Welbeck, Nottinghamshire
3rd Duke of Portland
Alterations, including chapel and kitchen offices, 1763–65, stables, *c.* 1774, east wing, 1775–77

The Duke of Portland inherited Welbeck through his mother, daughter of the Countess of Oxford. On succeeding to the dukedom in 1762 he allowed her the family seat at Bulstrode in exchange for Welbeck. In 1766 the duke married Lady Dorothy Cavendish, daughter of the 4th Duke of Devonshire.

The great rambling house, originally an abbey, had been much enlarged by the Duke of Newcastle in the seventeenth century and extensively altered by the Countess of Oxford, who had died in 1755.

Work was soon underway. The 'Improvement Account Book' shows that 'the old offices East of the Chappel', which belonged to the south cloister range of the monastery, were pulled down in the spring of 1763. New buildings, including a kitchen, scullery and offices, were

Well Head House, Halifax, Yorkshire (WR/WY)
(Fig. 237)
John Waterhouse
New house, *c.* 1767
Demolished
Attributed

Well Head House, a few hundred yards from the centre of Halifax, was built following the marriage of John and Elizabeth Waterhouse in 1767. Waterhouse, younger son of John Waterhouse of Lower Range, Halifax, was a prosperous textile merchant. His wife was the daughter and co-heiress of Charles Beaty of Louth. The house was a five-bay, two-and-a-half-storey house with single-bay, single-storey wings. The entrance elevation was handsomely finished in ashlar with a Doric porch. Although documentary evidence is lacking, the house has been attributed to Carr, and a comparison of details with his other houses make the attribution acceptable.

The façade is characteristic of his work (Langford Hall and Fangfoss Hall are variations on the same theme) but it is the detail of the decoration that is most telling. In

238 Wentworth Woodhouse stables

particular, the frieze of the ground-floor south-east room is identical to decoration on the doorcase into the council room at Newark Town Hall, on the door on the landing of the Assembly Room at Buxton and to that in one of the rooms at Langford Hall. The dado rail and skirting board in the ground-floor central south-west room repeats that in the room at Langford Hall and the detail of the frieze over the door can also be found in the frieze in the Green Drawing Room at Basildon Park and at Denton Park. Well Head House was demolished in 1976.

Edward Waterson and Peter Meadows, *Lost Houses of the West Riding* (Welburn, 1998), 57

Wentbridge, Yorkshire (WR/WY)

West Riding magistrates
Bridge widened, 1764

The two-arch bridge over the River Went on the Great North Road was widened in 1764.

West Yorkshire Archive Service, Wakefield, Book of Bridges 1752–1770

Wentworth Castle, Yorkshire (WR/SY)

2nd Earl of Strafford
Alterations, *c.* 1770

Davies notes the east front of Wentworth Castle for the Earl of Strafford, 1770, as a commission of Carr's. Davies is usually accurate but Carr was clearly not responsible for the design of the east wing as it was built in *c.* 1710–20 to the designs of Johann von Bodt. Nor could this be a mistake for the south wing, which was built in 1759–64 to the designs of the 2nd Earl of Strafford, with John Platt as master mason and Charles Ross as executant architect. However, a reference in a letter of 1799 to Strickland Fawley to designs for a sash rail which would be as strong as that at Wentworth Castle but lighter and more elegant suggests that Carr was responsible for alterations including refenestration of the south wing. Certainly the round-headed ground-floor sash windows of the south front are a later alteration and could be Carr's work. They are very similar to those at Farnley Hall.

Gloucester County Record Office, Strickland of Apperley Papers, FF38, D 1245/C/4; information from Dr Eileen Harris

R. Davies, 'A Memoir of John Carr', *Yorkshire Archaeological Journal*, 4 (1877), 205

H. M. Colvin, *Biographical Dictionary of British Architects* (New Haven and London, 1995), 1038

Wentworth Woodhouse, Wentworth, Yorkshire

(WR/SY) (Figs 31, 71, 81, 238, 239)
2nd Marquis of Rockingham (d. 1782)
Alterations, 1762–82; stables 1766–83; Keppel's Column, 1776–81
4th Earl Fitzwilliam
Alterations, 1782–1807; Rockingham Mausoleum 1785–91; North Lodge, 1793; Rainborough Lodge, 1798; Lion Gate, 1804

The Marquis of Rockingham and his successor, his nephew, Earl Fitzwilliam, were Carr's most important

239 Keppel's Column, Wentworth Woodhouse

constructed a room in the south tower for Lady Rockingham; and from 1776 to 1783 he built grand new stables, including a large riding house with elaborate plasterwork, just to the north of the house. In the park Carr erected Keppel's Column in 1776–81, a giant Tuscan column.

The arrival of Earl Fitzwilliam in 1782 saw a new wave of activity. The state rooms were redecorated in 1783–84, with Carr preparing drawings of the window wall of the Great Dining Room so that new curtains could be made and presenting alternative designs for curtain cornices. Tunnicliffe's service wings were heightened and given attached Doric porticos and the kitchen rebuilt in 1785-86. Fitzwilliam also commissioned Carr to design an imposing mausoleum to his uncle. First designs dated 1783 were for an obelisk on a colonnaded plinth, the obelisk being the Egyptian symbol of immortality, but these were rejected in favour of a design apparently based on the Tomb of the Julii at St Remy in Provence. The mausoleum contained a full-length statue of Rockingham, surrounded by busts of his friends, all by Joseph Nollekens. Work continued from 1785 to 1791 and the total cost was £3,208 3s 4¼d. In 1793 obelisks were moved from behind the house and set around the mausoleum.

Work continued on a regular basis with significant alterations to the family rooms on the west front in 1792–93 and 1800–01, including remodelling the dining room (with a chimneypiece by John Fisher) and alterations to the gallery including adding a French window and external stairs. The most important late alteration was the creation of a semi-circular stair from the hall to the saloon, discussed in 1800 but not complete until 1806. At the same time Carr was rebuilding the south wing and adding an extra storey and attached portico, work beginning in 1803.

In the park Carr was responsible in his old age for a series of lodges, the North Lodge in 1793, the Rainborough Lodge in 1798 and the Lion Gate in 1804. His last known letter, dated 7 December 1806 to Joshua Biram, the steward at Wentworth, shows that he was still closely involved in the interior design of the house. Just over two months later he was dead.

The house and stables were used as Lady Mabel College of Physical Education with part retained by Earl Fitzwilliam before being sold as a private house. Most of the park buildings are owned by a charitable trust and have recently been restored.

Sheffield Archives, Wentworth Woodhouse Muniments
William Bray, *Sketch of a Tour into Derbyshire and Yorkshire* (London, 1783), 223–24
C. L. Stieglitz, *Plans et Dessins Tirés de la Belle Architecture* (Paris, 1801), pl. LXI
R. Warner, *A Tour through Northern Counties* (Bath, 1802), I

patrons. For over fifty years from about 1760 until his death Carr worked almost continually at Wentworth Woodhouse, being paid his first annual salary of £80 in August 1763, a practice which continued until his death. He replaced Henry Flitcroft, who had been the house's architect since about 1735, although Flitcroft was consulted as late as 1764. Carr's work included minor alterations such as painting the underside of the portico and setting up a watercloset in the garden together with major remodelling and extensive work in the park and estate. It is well, if sometimes confusedly, documented in letters and accounts, although few drawings survive. Carr was still working on the house when he died.

Carr's first known involvement at Wentworth Woodhouse, then known as Wentworth House, was in 1760 when he submitted a design for a substantial bridge in the park. Although a further design was submitted in 1763 neither was erected. In 1762 he rebuilt Clifford's Lodging, at the north-west corner of the house; in 1778 he

240 Wetherby Grange

H. Avray Tipping, 'Wentworth Woodhouse, Yorkshire', *Country Life*, 20, 27 September, 4, 11 October 1924

A. A. Booth, 'The Architects of Wentworth Castle and Wentworth Woodhouse', *RIBA Journal*, 3rd ser., 41 (1933), 61–72

M. and R. B. Wragg, 'Admiral Keppel's Column', *Country Life*, 27 December 1956

R. B. Wragg, 'Stables Worthy of Stately Homes', *Country Life*, 1 November 1962

R. B. Wragg, 'The Rockingham Mausoleum', *Yorkshire Archaeological Journal*, 52 (1980), 157–66

Juliet Allan, 'Wentworth Woodhouse', *Archaeological Journal*, 137 (1980), 393–96.

Marcus Binney, 'Wentworth Woodhouse Revisited', *Country Life*, 24 March 1983

Marcus Binney, 'Wentworth Woodhouse, Yorks', *Country Life*, 24 January 1991

BE/WR/539–45

Wentworth Estate, Yorkshire (WR/SY)

2nd Marquis of Rockingham
Additions to a farmhouse at Swinton, 1775
Farmhouse, 1779
4th Earl Fitzwilliam
Terrace of ten miners cottages at Elsecar, 1796
Terrace of four cottages at Skiers Hill, 1797

Occasional references in letters together with drawings show that Carr designed a number of farmhouses and estate cottages during his long involvement with the Wentworth estate. He is known to have made additions to a house, apparently a farmhouse, at Swinton in 1775 and another farmhouse was measured by Peter Atkinson in 1779. In 1796 he sent a series of designs for cottages for miners at Elsecar to Lord Fitzwilliam for one, two and three families, costing respectively £100, £190 and £270 each. The intention was that the cottages should be as economical as possible. Carr also provided alternative plans for a row of ten houses with estimates of £731 4s 6d and £617 12s 6d.

Two terraces at Elsecar, a terrace of ten on Wath Road and a terrace of four at Skiers Hill, can be identified as by Carr. Both have been heavily refenestrated but use the same vocabulary of symmetry, simple detail and contrasting taller and lower elements to create an economical visual effect. Carr's cottages at Aston follow the same pattern.

Sheffield Archives, Wwm 7, (23/3/1775) Wwm 24, (26/2/1779) Wwm 121, (25/1/1796), MP 16, 30 (d)

John Martin Robinson, *Georgian Model Farms* (Oxford, 1983), 143

Weston Park, Staffordshire

Sir Henry Bridgeman, MP
Survey, 1784

Sir Henry Bridgeman succeeded his uncle to the Weston estate in 1762, when he commissioned James Paine to carry out alterations and design garden buildings. He subsequently employed Carr who presented a 'report into the state of the buildings at Weston' on 8 November 1784.

Carr pointed out that the lead on the roofs was perished, the parapet balustrade and its coping ruinous, the chimneys were ruinous, the window cornices were broken and decayed, the pediments at each end of the house in need of repair, the ends of the main tie-beams probably rotten and that the laundry and brewhouse needed retiling. He suggested that the chimneys, balustrade, window cornices and giant pediments should be repointed, the window cornices be remade of single pieces of stone and that all should be leaded. He also recommended a brick drain be made below the second joist of the flags all around the house, carrying water away from the walls into a cesspool.

There are no complementary documents and Carr may not have done anything. The roofs are still double-pitched and covered in lead rather than Westmorland slate. But his report does suggest that he had some executive responsibility as he states that he had 'given directions to the Mason in what manner he shoud repair [the chimneys], the stone for which he will immediately prepare.'

Staffordshire is outside Carr's usual circuit but Bridgeman was a Whig MP, which may explain his connection with Carr.

Staffordshire Record Office, Bradford Mss, E/180; information from Richard Hewlings

Wetherby Grange (formerly Micklethwaite Grange), Yorkshire (WR/WY) (Fig. 240)

Beilby Thompson
Unexecuted plans for a new house and gateway, 1764; unexecuted scheme for a house, 1783; altered James Wyatt's plans to suit Thompson, 1784
Demolished, 1964

Wetherby Grange (formerly known as Micklethwaite Grange) near Wetherby, had been the seat of the Beilby family and was a secondary estate of Beilby Thompson of Escrick. In 1764 Carr was paid £21 for 'a design for a new House at the Grange with all the Plans and Elevations particularly figured & described, a drawing for the Gateway into the Park & measuring the work thereof'. Thompson's energies were concentrated on Escrick and nothing came of the scheme.

Further plans were made in 1783 when Carr presented two drawings, one signed and dated November 1783, for a house very similar in appearance to Norton Place and reminiscent of the earlier, rejected design for Busby Hall. Carr's plan was not accepted and instead in 1784 he adapted a scheme by James Wyatt (referred to by Thompson as 'the great Mr Wyatt's plan'). This includes a bowed centrepiece rising to a central oval tower flanked by two-storey, three-bay wings.

East Riding of Yorkshire Record Office, DDFA/37/28
West Yorkshire Archives Department, Leeds, Lane-Fox papers CXVIII/18
Beilby Thompson diary, 1764, in the possession of Mr Nigel Forbes-Adam of Skipwith Hall; information from Mr Sam Taylor
Harry Speight, *Lower Wharfedale* (London, 1902), 439
Edward Waterson and Peter Meadows, *Lost Houses of the West Riding* (Welburn, 1998), 16, fig.
J. P. G. Taylor, *Escrick: A Village History* (York, 1999), 51
BE/WR/550

Whitby, Yorkshire (NR/NY)

North Riding Magistrates
Repairs, 1780

Tenders were sought for repairs to the bridge over the Esk at Whitby 'according to plans in the Hands of Mr Carr in York, Surveyor of the Bridges within the same Riding' in May 1780.

York Courant, 9 May 1780

The Rectory, Whitchurch, Shropshire

Francis Henry Egerton
Designs for a new house, 1789

Francis Henry Egerton, nephew of Carr's patrons John Egerton, Bishop of Durham, succeeded his uncle Henry Egerton, another patron of Carr, as rector of Whitchurch in 1779. The rectory had been rebuilt as a modest five-bay house by Richard Newcome in 1749. Egerton sought designs for additions from Carr, as well as plans from Mr Wallace in June 1785, and Willey Reveley in October 1789. It is not known whose designs, if any, were executed.

Shropshire Records and Research Centre, Shrewsbury 3127/9, 11–14, 16–18, 21–43; information from Dr Terry Friedman
George Eyre Evans, *Whitchurch of Long Ago* (Oswestry, 1893), 11

White Windows, Sowerby Bridge, Yorkshire (WR)
(Figs 37, 241, 242)
John Priestley
New house, 1767–68

John Priestley, a prosperous clothier, bought the White Windows estate, which his family had rented for three generations, in 1765 and according to his cousin Nathaniel Priestley rebuilt it in 1767–68 so that there were 'not many better (if any) in the parish of Halifax'. This is confirmed by the date 1768 on the plaster decoration of the hall. The A.P.S.D. and Davies record that Carr was the architect.

The house is a rectangular pile with a narrow entrance hall, a pair of large rooms on either side, a corridor running across the centre of the house and a staircase lit by a Venetian windows on axis with the hall. The slope of the hill allows the west door to open at ground level but leaves the basement above ground level to the south, the most elaborate façade which has ashlar facing as against the plain coursed masonry on the other elevations. The roof is pyramidal, truncated to end in a balustrade. The unusual feature of the corner quoins being replaced by an incised panel in the attic above the string course may be a local detail. It could also be found on Bradford Manor House, built in 1705 and demolished in the 1860s, which White Windows closely resembles in appearance. Little of the original internal detail survives except in the staircase hall and unfortunate alterations have been made to the west elevation. It is now a Cheshire Home.

John Watson, *The History and Antiquities of the Parish of Halifax* (London, 1775), 299

Wyatt Papworth (ed.), *The Dictionary of Architecture issued by the Architectural Publications Society* (London, 1877), 11, 36

R. Davies, 'A Memoir of John Carr', *Yorkshire Archaeological Journal*, 4 (1877), 205

Nathaniel Priestley, 'Some Brief Memoirs of the Family of Priestley Written in 1779', *Surtees Society*, 77 (1883), 38–39

H. P. Kendall, 'White Windows', *Halifax Antiquarian Society Transactions*, 3 (1906), 109

Edward Waterson and Peter Meadows, *Lost Houses of the West Riding* (Welburn, 1998), 37

St Mary's Church, Whitkirk, Yorkshire (WR/WY)

9th Viscount Irwin
Repairs to monument, 1772

Carr was paid £11 15s 7d on 26 September 1772 by Lord Irwin for repairs to the Irwin monument in Whitkirk church. This included payment for two masons working for fifteen days cleaning, repairing and putting up the monument, new marble used in the repairs, Mr Muson for painting the arms and figures, William Fentiman, bricklayer, for building a new brick wall against the window to receive the monument and James Henderson for plastering the wall and repairing the figures.

Leeds Archives 1938–1988: An Illustrated Guide to Leeds District Archives, 1988, 71; information from Dr Terry Friedman

Wiganthorpe Hall, Terrington, Yorkshire (NR/NY)

(Figs 43, 243, 244)
William Garforth
New house, *c.* 1778
Demolished, 1955

The Garforths rose to prominence and substantial wealth as York merchants and bankers in the eighteenth century. William Garforth's father Edmund employed Carr at Askham Hall and (probably) at Garforth House in York in the 1750s. After his death in 1761 his son William turned again to Carr to design Wiganthorpe Hall, fifteen miles north of York. The dating is uncertain but may follow Garforth's marriage in 1778. As his father's widow Elizabeth, sister of 5th Lord Middleton, survived until 1799 it is likely she continued to occupy Askham Hall and that this was why her son rebuilt Wiganthorpe Hall. This had been owned by the Garforths since at least the early part of the century.

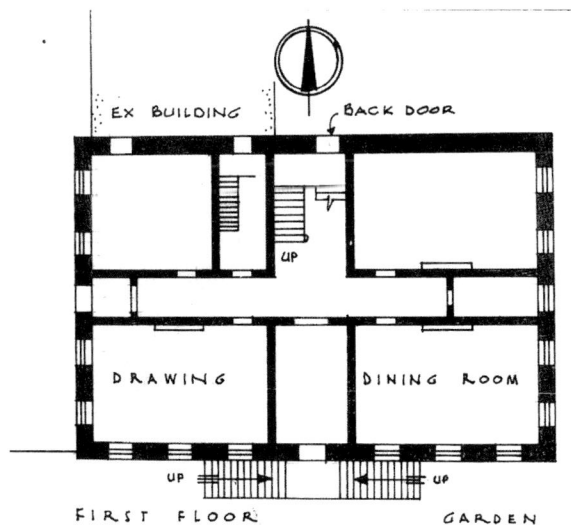

241 *top* White Windows, staircase
242 *below* White Windows, plan of ground floor

243 Wiganthorpe Hall exterior

244 Wiganthorpe Hall, saloon

Drawings by Carr, acquired by Dr Wragg at the demolition of Wiganthorpe, show the house had a complicated genesis. Two alternative designs survive, both for a new block of similar dimensions to that built and with a canted bay on the south front, but of three storeys and approached from the north between flanking service wings. One, distinctly grander than the other, suggested a *piano nobile* approached through a portico-in-antis with internal stairs similar to that at Basildon Park. The rustic would have been given over to office accommodation and the *piano nobile* linked to the chamber floor by a central oval staircase. The other, slightly narrower, was less ambitious, with the main reception rooms on the ground floor, no central staircase and an attached portico.

In the event the courtyard entrance was abandoned. The old house was retained as offices attached to the north of the new house and the new house was of two storeys and five bays, with a three-bay pediment, canted bay on the south front, plat band, running cill and balusters under the first-floor windows. Unusually for a

245 Winestead Hall stables

house by Carr of this scale and date it was of brick and had quoins at the corners. Nineteenth-century alterations make the site of the original entrance uncertain.

The intended entrance hall of the second scheme became an imperial staircase supported by Ionic columns with timber balusters and a vaulted corridor running round it on the first floor. The interior was one of Carr's best, with fine plasterwork, particularly in the staircase and saloon. A drawing for the dining room ceiling survives in the Victoria and Albert Museum. The house was demolished in 1955 when the staircase was moved to Sharow Hall near Ripon.

Victoria and Albert Museum Print Room, 8241.7v, 8
Six drawings acquired from Wiganthorpe Hall, in possession of Mrs Brian Wragg
Roy Strong et al., *The Destruction of the Country House* (London, 1974), figs 282, 310
Edward Waterson and Peter Meadows, *Lost Houses of York and the North Riding* (Welburn, 1998), 14–15, figs
Hugh Murray, 'Rainwater Heads and Fall Pipe Brackets: Part 2', *Yorkshire Archaeological Society Family History and Population Studies Newsletter*, 4, no. 6, December 1978

Winestead Hall, Patrington, Yorkshire

(ER/Humberside) (Fig. 245)
Sir Robert Hildyard, Bt
Stables, 1762
Attributed

We know from the Harewood steward's correspondence that Carr visited Winestead in February 1762, and from the Bacon Frank correspondence that he was probably there again in November. He was probably supervising the erection of the stables which are dated 1762 on the keystone. These are of seven bays, built of brick with blank arches and a clock turret with cupola and fit with Carr's style, the façade of the stables at Gledstone being particularly close. According to a letter to John Grimston Carr visited Winestead again in September 1769. He also worked for Hildyard son at Sedbury Park in 1771.

Winestead Hall was demolished in 1936 but the stable block was retained by Winestead Hospital which took over the site and a boiler and large chimney was added to its rear.

Sheffield Archives, BFM 1314/67
West Yorkshire Archives Service, Leeds, Harewood Papers, Stewards Corres., 5 Feb, 1762
East Riding Record Office, DDGR 42/19/102
David Neave and Edward Waterson, *Lost Houses of East Yorkshire* (Bridlington, 1988), 67
BE/ER/758

Wood Hall, Collingham, Yorkshire (WR/WY)

(Fig. 246)
Fenton Scott
New house, c. 1790

Elizabeth Chivers referred in 1805 to a 'new house built by Fenton Scott' as having been designed by Carr. William Fenton Scott, inherited a large fortune in 1790 through his grandfather, William Fenton, his father Henry Scott having married Fenton's only daughter. With this money he founded the Commercial Bank in 1792, which for a

246 Wood Hall

time rivalled Beckett's as the leading Leeds bank, and also presumably built Wood Hall. The staircase balustrade is similar to that at Clifton House, Rotherham, of about 1786, and Pevsner compared the arrangement of the entrance hall and staircase to that at Farnley Hall, Yorkshire, of 1786–92. Part of the old house was retained as offices and kitchens. The bowed centre appears to be an addition and alterations occurred in about 1910, removing original detail.

R. G. Wilson, *Gentlemen Merchants* (Manchester, 1971), 137, 156, 243, 247

Giles Worsley, 'Crediting Carr', *Country Life*, 5 May 1988

BE/WR/557

Workington Hall, Cumberland (Cumbria) (Fig. 247)

Henry Curwen
Alterations, *c.* 1778
John Christian Curwen
Alterations, 1783–95
Demolished, *c.* 1972

Henry Curwen, who was a supporter of Carr's patron the Duke of Portland against Sir James Lowther and Member of Parliament for Cumberland, actively developed his estates, especially the coastal coalfields at Workington and Harrington. He also owned shares in several ships trading from Harrington and Workington. By the time he died in 1778 the collieries brought in an annual profit of £5,000, on top of the £2,000 rental of the estate. He also had personal estate worth £15,000.

Flush with funds, Curwen set about improving Workington Hall, a medieval fortified manor house, to Carr's designs. He had pulled part of it down and was ready to roof some of the new work when he died. His executors were faced with a dilemma as his daughter and heiress Isabella was only thirteen. They resolved to cover in what had been begun but do no more.

In 1782 Isabella married her cousin John Christian Curwen who completed the work. It is uncertain exactly what Henry Curwen had already done but most of the alterations seem to have been carried out by John Christian Curwen. The massive walls of the pele tower were demolished, except the wall between the solar and the library, and an elegant suite of reception rooms created with particularly fine chimneypieces in the salon, library and dining room. A new entrance hall was created, together with a generous semi-circular stone staircase and a suite of bedrooms over the great hall. The north wing was raised to three storeys, passages were added on the inner sides of the courtyard and a new kitchen built. Photographs show that the house had Georgian battlements and windows and that a canted bay had been added to the library. Work was probably still continuing in 1796 when Amelia Clark's diary notes that Carr left her for a couple of days during their tour of the Lake District to go to Mr Curwen's house at Workington.

York Minster Library, MS Add. 328/2, fol. 18
Cumbria County Record Office, Curwen's General Ledgers 1770–1792

247 *left* Workington Hall
248 *above* House in Potter Street, Worksop

D & S Lysons, *Magna Britannia, Cumberland* (London, 1816), IV, 173

J. F. Curwen, *Workington Hall* (Kendal, 1899), including plan

J. F. Curwen, *A History of the Ancient House of Curwen* (Kendal, 1928), 174–88

BE/Cumb/209–10

House in Potter Street, Worksop, Nottinghamshire
(Fig. 248)
George Donston
Alterations, 1768–69

A letter from Carr, dated 23 January 1769, with detailed instructions about alterations to a house survives among papers relating to the Donston family of Worksop. Although it has no addressee it is presumed to have been sent to George Donston and to relate to alterations to his house in Potter Street, Worksop. The letter discusses the design of the main rooms and the bedrooms as well as a drain and when linked to a contemporary account for stone from 28 May 1768 to 29 December 1769 totalling nearly £1,800, suggests that the work was substantial. Carr recommended that Donston buy a marble chimneypiece for the best room in London from Walsh's in South Street, Berkeley Square.

Carr must have remodelled the garden front, which is of stone. It is two storeys high, with two central bays flanked by a pair of canted bays and attached wings. In characteristic Carr fashion the windows are linked by running cills and a plat band and there are balusters set under the first-floor windows. The design is very close to the central block of Leventhorpe Hall and to Monk Fryston Lodge, which has been attributed to Carr.

Nottingham County Record Office, Huthwaite Papers, M 5935/2, 5936

Wortley Hall, Wortley, Yorkshire (WR/SY)
James Archibald Stuart-Wortley
Design for alterations, probably unexecuted, *c.* 1797

Wortley Hall was extensively rebuilt in the eighteenth century first by Giacomo Leoni in 1742–46 and Matthew Brettingham in 1757–61 for Edward Wortley-Montagu and then in 1784–88 by John Platt for James Archibald Stuart-Wortley. In 1797 Peter Atkinson submitted an estimate for completing work undone in the north and west ranges and for adding stables and a farm. That August Carr left directions for preparing ground for the 'new building in the Hall Green' and taking surplus earth round to the east front. This may have been done, but no more. In 1800 the house was described as being without stables and surrounded by rubble.

Sheffield Archives, Wh M 142

Richard Hewlings, 'Wortley Hall', *Archaeological Journal*, 137 (1980), 397–99

Wynyard Hall, County Durham
Sir John Tempest MP
Alterations, 1777–79
Attributed
Rebuilt, 1820s

In July 1777 Carr wrote a letter explaining that he was on a northern tour and addressing it from Brancepeth Castle,

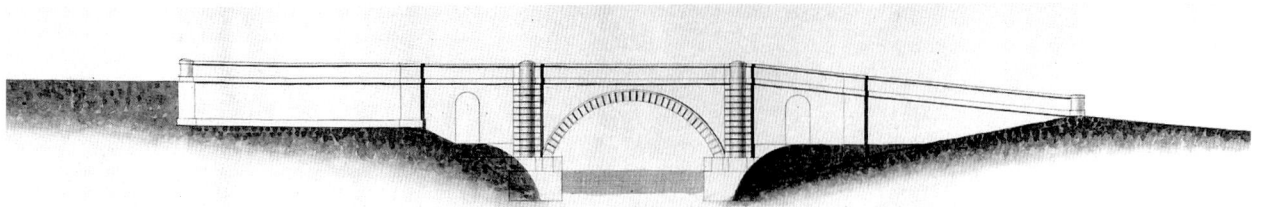

Plan and Elevation of Yearsley Bridge over the River Fojs near the City of York in the Weapentake of Bulmer

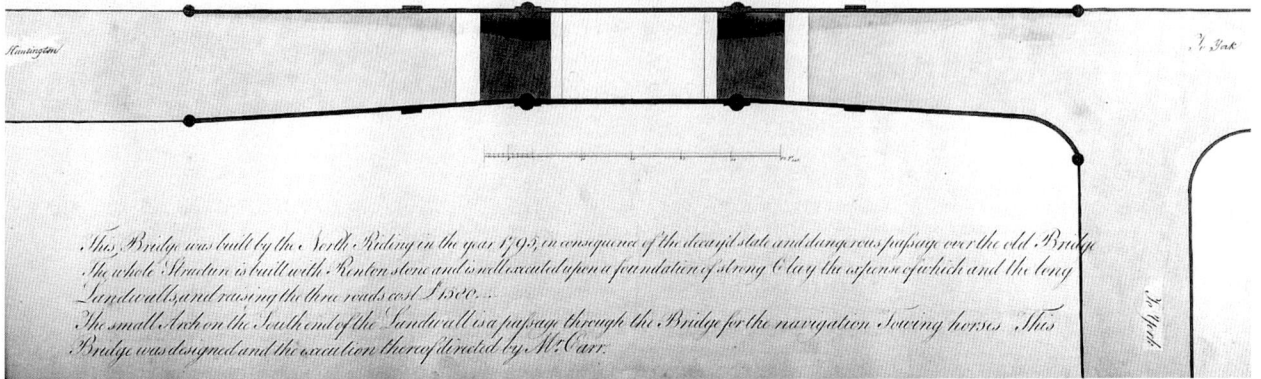

This Bridge was built by the North Riding in the year 1793, in consequence of the decayed state and dangerous passage over the old Bridge. The whole Structure is built with Renton stone and is well executed upon a foundation of strong Clay the expense of which and the long Landwalls, and raising the three roads cost £1500.
The small Arch on the South end of the Landwall is a passage through the Bridge for the navigation Towing horses. This Bridge was designed and the execution thereof directed by Mr Carr.

249 Drawing of Yearsley bridge

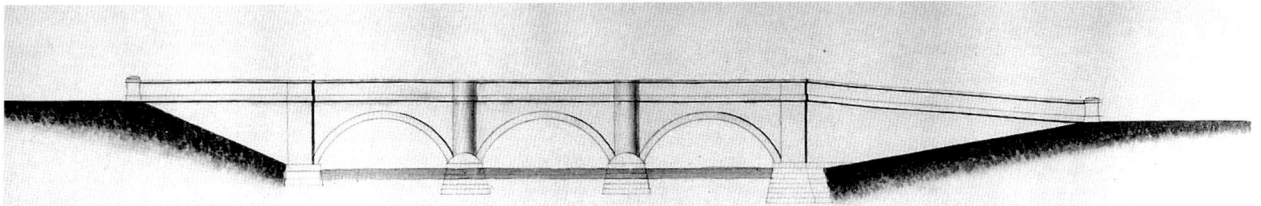

Elevation of Yore near Bridge built over the River Yore or Ure by the North Riding 1793 In the Weapentake of Hang West

Plan of the new Bridge over the Yore near Bainbridge; The foundation of which, the Piers, the Arches and fascia Courses are built with good Ashler from all the other parts thereof and Landwalls are built with Common Hammer scapled small stones, the expense of which to the Riding was only £ ...4.0 This Bridge was designed by Mr Carr and executed under his directions by the deputy Surveyor I. Peacock

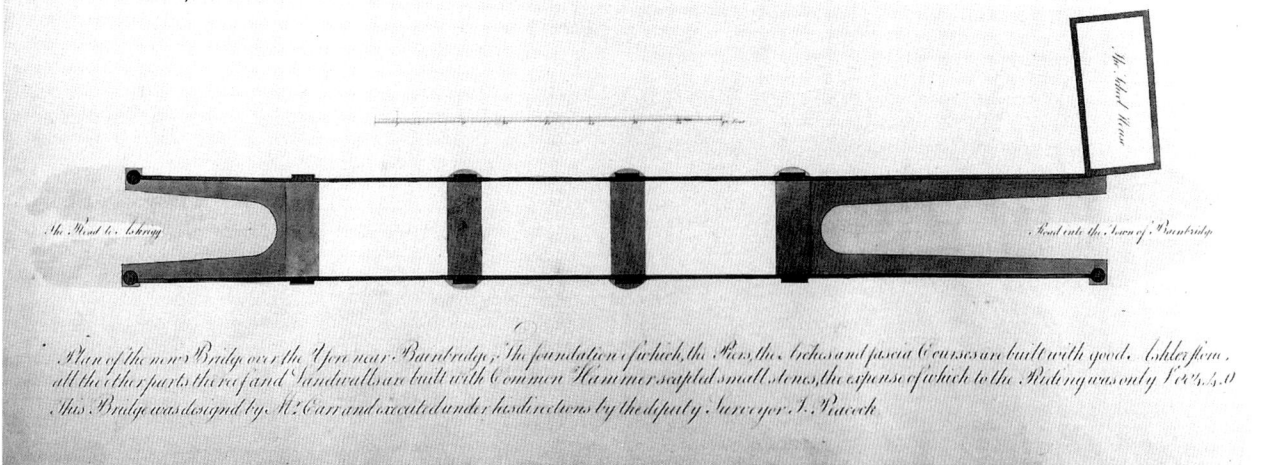

250 Drawing of Yore bridge

CATALOGUE

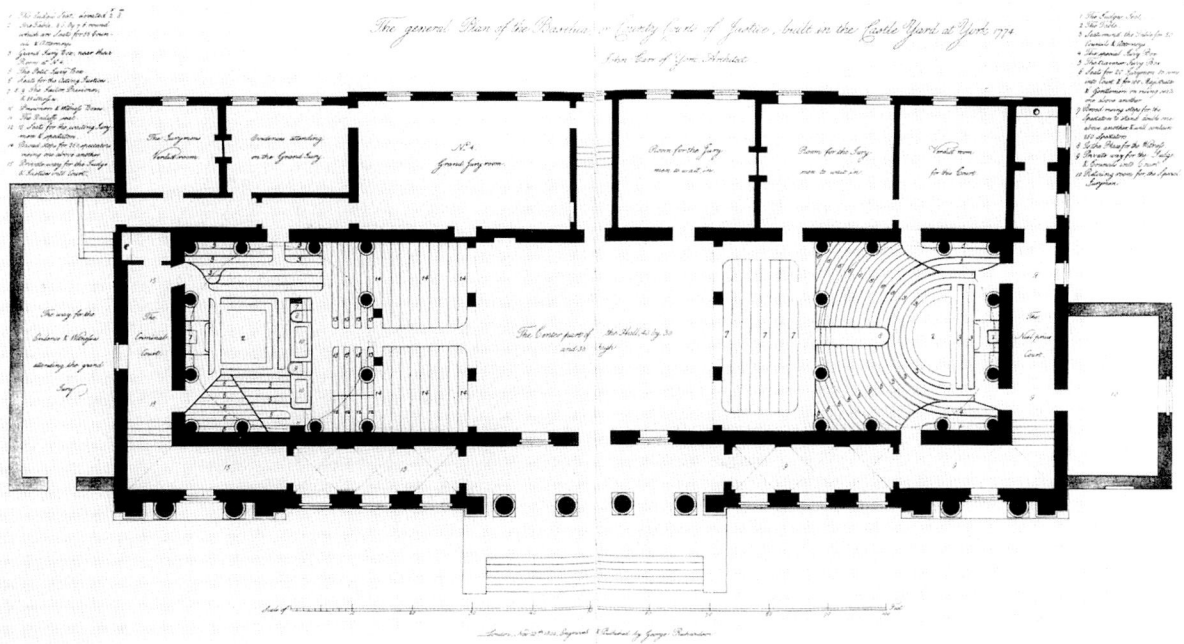

251 Assize Courts, York, plan

County Durham. Given the intensity of Carr's working tours it is hard to imagine him staying at Brancepeth unless he had business there. The castle had been bought by John Tempest, Member of Parliament for Durham, in 1773. It was completely remodelled by John Paterson in 1818–21 and any evidence of what Carr might have done there has been lost.

However, in 1779 Edward Elwick, who provided furniture for many of Carr's houses, reported to John Grimston that he was furnishing a house near Hartlepool, the property of Mr Tempest of Brancepeth Castle. This is clearly Wynyard, to which Tempest succeeded on the death of his father in 1777. The commission was sumptuous (the Tempests were immensely rich from coal) with 'many different pieces of needlework and tapestry in the drawing room, the ornaments about the chimney glass and girondelles … are from the Vatican gallery'.

Wynyard was also completely remodelled in the nineteenth century and very few accounts survive from the eighteenth century, but a pastel drawing of the house before alteration shows that it was a three-storey, nine-bay mid-eighteenth-century house with two-storey canted bay wings added at each end. A surviving plan shows one of the end rooms to have semi-circular ends with niches and the other angled bays. Such canted bays and rooms are typical of Carr's work and their appearance, coupled with Carr's connection with Tempest and the employment of Elwick suggest that Carr may have been employed at Wynyard, although documentary proof is lacking.

East Riding of Yorkshire Record Office, Grimston Papers GR 42/29/14
E. W. Short, *The Story of Brancepeth Castle*, nd, 16
Giles Worsley, 'Wynyard Park, County Durham', *Country Life*, 28 August and 4 September 1986

Yarm, Yorkshire (NR/NY) (Fig. 80)
North Riding magistrates
Bridge widened, 1806–10

A new iron structure widening the bridge over the Tees collapsed in 1806. Carr designed its replacement in stone. Work was finished in 1810, three years after his death.

North Yorkshire County Record Office, correspondence, Yarm Bridge

Yearsley, Yorkshire (NR/NY) (Fig. 249)
North Riding magistrates
New bridge, 1795
Replaced

The 30 ft span bridge over the River Foss, near York, was built at a cost of £1,580.

North Yorkshire County Record Office, Book of Bridges, 1772–1803

Yore Bridge, Bainbridge, Yorkshire (NR/NY) (Fig. 250)
North Riding magistrates
New bridge, 1793

The bridge over the River Ure on the Richmond–Lancaster turnpike road was rebuilt with three spans of 30 ft to Carr's design under the direction of J. Peacock. Foundations, piers, arches and fascia courses were built of good ashlar, the other parts were built of common hammer-scapled small stones, as a result the cost was only £884.

North Yorkshire County Record Office, Book of Bridges, 1772–1803, 56
BE/NR/69

The Assembly Rooms, York
The Subscribers
Alterations, 1752–54, minor works, 1775, 1776, 1779 and 1782

Carr regularly carried out minor alterations and repairs to the Assembly Rooms.

York Archives, M23/1,2,4

Assize Courts, York Castle, York (Figs 60, 61, 251)
Yorkshire Magistrates
New lawcourts, 1772–76

The castle came within the jurisdiction of the county and the construction of a 'more commodious building' for the law courts was sanctioned in 1765, but it was not until May 1772 that Robert Hildyard remarked to John Grimston that the new courts and grand jury room at York were to be built to 'a plan of Carr's approv'd by so many good Judges'.

Carr not only designed the building, he was also the person to whom the treasurers of the various ridings made their payments (as was also to be the case at Bootham Park Hospital). In October 1772 the treasurers were authorized to pay sums totalling £1,767 to Mr John Carr as 'the first payment of the sum contracted for, for Rebuilding the new Courts'. The West Riding contributed £820 18s 4d, the North Riding £548 10s 1d and the East Riding £397 11s 6d. A further payment of £929 3s 4d from the West Riding, £620 16s 8d from the North Riding and £450 from the East Riding was approved in 1773. No further authorizations have been found but the account book of Christopher Goulton, Treasurer of the North Riding, (whose accounts are the only ones available) reveal further payments not approved in the Order Books. On 16 April 1775 Carr was paid £596 2s 6d for the North Ridings Quota for New Building York Castle and in April 1776 he was paid a further £892 3s 9¼d 'on compleatg the new buildg called Basilica at York Castle'. Assuming that the other Ridings paid proportionally, the three quotas would add up to £4,723, making a total of nearly £8,500. Ward's *York Guide* notes that the building was opened at the Summer Assizes of 1777.

The building is 150 ft wide and 45 ft deep and contains a criminal and civil court, separated by an entrance hall. Each court was lit by lofty dome with a circular skylight — a feature which Carr also used at Thoresby Park (1768), Norton Place (1776) and Denton Hall (1778) — supported by twelve scagliola Corinthian columns. Both are elegantly plastered. Carr followed tradition in leaving the courts open to the central vestibule but this caused problems. On 18 July 1782 the Justices asked Carr to arrange for the whole ground floor to be matted and curtains hung 'to prevent the sound of voices going from one court to another' and dividing walls have subsequently been erected

Later extensions c. 1803 were by Peter Atkinson and Son. The building is still in use as lawcourts.

East Riding of Yorkshire Record Office, Grimston Papers, DDGR/42/22/65
Anon, *The York Guide* (York, 1787), 24
George Richardson, *New Vitruvius Britannicus* (London, 1808), II, pls 1–4
Royal Commission on Historical Monuments, *City of York* (London, 1972), I, 82–85
BE/ER/191–2

47 Bootham, York (Fig. 11)
Mrs Mary Thompson
New house, 1752

The A.P.S.D. records a house for Mr Thompson in Bootham among Carr's commissions. The client was in fact Mrs Mary Thompson, widow of Edward Thompson MP, of Oswaldkirk. Mrs Thompson first paid rates in 1752 and her initials appear on a rainwater head. The house is three storeys and four bays with a pyramidal roof. It was well fitted out and the interior is little altered.

Wyatt Papworth (ed.), *The Dictionary of Architecture issued by the Architectural Publications Society* (London, 1877), II, 36
Royal Commission on Historical Monuments, *City of York* (London, 1975), IV, 58

Castlegate House, Castlegate, York (Fig. 252)
Peter Johnson
New house, 1762–65

Castlegate House was one of Carr's finest York mansions. It was built for Peter Johnson, recorder of York from 1759 to 1789. The rainwater head is dated 1763 and Johnson advertised his old house for sale in Coney Street in the *York Courant* in 1765. The five-bay, three-storey house is of brick with stone dressings. The first-floor windows are set in shallow relieving arches and on the garden front two projecting canted bays flank a central Venetian window. The entrance and stair halls are divided by a Corinthian screen. The cantilevered main staircase is lit by the Venetian window and decorated with a Rococo cartouche and festoons. Several excellent richly carved doorcases and chimneypieces are attributed to Daniel Shillito.

252 Castlegate House, York

R. Davies, 'A Memoir of John Carr', *Yorkshire Archaeological Journal*, 4 (1877), 206

Royal Commission on Historical Monuments, *City of York* (London, 1981), v, 114

BE/ER/213

County Lunatic Asylum, York (Fig. 55)

New hospital, 1774–77

The County Lunatic Asylum, now Bootham Park Hospital, was one of the first purpose-built lunatic asylums in the country. In 1772 Robert Hay Drummond, Archbishop of York, and twenty-four Yorkshire gentlemen decided to establish an asylum. A committee was set up, to which Carr was co-opted, and £2,500 was immediately subscribed. The Marquis of Rockingham pledged 100 guineas, Carr 25 guineas. By July 1773 £5,000 had been promised and on 25 August Carr's scheme to accommodate fifty-four patients was approved. Bricklayers, joiners, carpenters and masons were asked to submit sealed tenders in December and the following May the foundation stone was laid.

A list of payments shows that the majority were made directly to Carr. The first payments, of £300, were made in April 1774. This was followed by £460 in July, £400 in

September, £1,200 in December, £300 the following September, £100 in December, £350 in January 1776, £300 in June, £145 7s 6d in October and £240 in February 1777. Of the £5,080 16s 11d paid out by June 1777 Carr received £3,795 7s 6d. The only other substantial payment was £800 to William Meeke in April 1774. However, this is unlikely to be all Carr received as there was a financial crisis in May 1777 when it was reported that the building could not be completed without more funds. In August it was stated that no more than £2,000 was needed. Enough was raised to open the hospital on 1 November that year, the total subscriptions coming to £6,252 18s.

A tall, red brick building with stone dressings, the building is similar in design to the Leeds Infirmary but with an extra floor and therefore no corner turrets and with the addition of an attached Doric portico. The extra cost of the building is not surprising as the finish is expensive and the quality of workmanship exceptional for a utilitarian building. This can be seen particularly in the brickwork, in the use of stone dressings, the presence of a portico and the Doric detailing of the cornice. Clearly the subscribers were determined that the building should reflect well on York, the county capital. As at Constable

Burton, Carr eliminated the architrave in the entablature of the portico. The hospital originally had a dome and turret but these were removed in 1939 and 1951.

The plan was 'simple and convenient consisting only of a corradore, extending from end of the building, and has on each side of it, on the two upper floors, rooms very commodiously and securely finished for the reception of lunatics'. The ground floor had accommodation for patients and provision for the physician and apothecary and for a committee room. The kitchen and other offices were placed in a separate building at the rear. The Committee Room retains its original fireplace and cornice. The building is still used as a hospital.

Borthwick Institute, York, BOO 3/10/2/2,3
York Courant, August, November 1772, July, September, December, 1773, May, July, August 1777
Jonathan Gray, *History of the York Lunatic Asylum* (York, 1815)
Charles Gaskell, *Passages on the History of the York Lunatic Asylum 1777–1901* (Wakefield, 1902)
Victoria County History, *City of York* (London, 1961), 469
Royal Commission on Historical Monuments, *City of York* (London, 1975), IV, 47–48
BE/ER/200

Fairfax House, Castlegate, York (Fig. 22)

Charles, 9th Viscount Fairfax
Extensive internal alterations within a recently completed shell, 1761–65

Fairfax House was built, not by Carr, for Joseph Marsh about 1755–56. In 1760/61 it was acquired for Anne Fairfax, second daughter and only surviving child of 9th Viscount Fairfax, whose second wife and other children had all died. Fairfax House was intended to brighten his daughter's life after the collapse of her marriage plans and to provide her with somewhere to live after his death, which occurred in 1772.

In October 1762 Fairfax refers in a letter to 'my daughter's house, which is just finished and paid for, draining me of all my money' and the following spring gave an opening ball on his birthday for 'over 200 Gentlemen and ladies to an elegant entertainment in his magnificent House on Castle Hill, newly completed'.

Carr worked within Marsh's shell, but the saloon and drawing room were new. What impresses are the richness of the materials and the elaboration of the decoration, particularly in the staircase. James Henderson was paid 30 guineas in 1762 for plastering the drawing room ceiling. Maurice Tobin executed the balustrade of the main staircase between June 1762 and April 1763. Painting work was still progressing in 1765 when Carr was finally paid 50 guineas for 'attending and designing his building' and he was writing to his patron about the house even after that.

After years of decay and use as a cinema and dance hall Fairfax House was bought and restored by the York Civic Trust with the help of Francis Johnson. It now houses the Noel Terry collection of English furniture.

North Yorkshire Country Record Office, Fairfax Papers, Vouchers
R. Davies, 'A Memoir of John Carr', *Yorkshire Archaeological Journal*, 4 (1877), 206
John Cornforth, 'Fairfax House, York', *Country Life*, 7, 14 March 1985
Royal Commission on Historical Monuments, *City of York* (London, 1981), V, 112
BE/ER/211–13

Female Prison, York Castle, York (Fig. 56)

Yorkshire magistrates
New prison, 1779–83

With the assize courts complete the magistrates proposed further improvements to the castle. The old courts were demolished in 1779 and in October John Gott, the West Riding Surveyor, presented a report at the Barnsley Sessions and was given the authority with Carr to contract for the building 'according to the Plan and Estimate' for the sum of £1,850. (Although in the East Riding Order Book £1,540 is given.) The builders were Messrs Wilkinson and Prince of York who received their first payment on 1 May 1779 and their ninth and final one on 22 April 1783. Carr was requested to superintend the works for a fee of not more than £50 a year and when the building was complete, was paid 'for his trouble in designing and Conducting the Building in the Castle Yard'. According to the *York Guide* for 1796 the new building contained on one side offices for the clerk of assize, a depository for county records and cells for petty criminals, and on the other accommodation for female prisoners, with a spacious yard, and an infirmary. The roof of this part of the building was flat and palisaded so that convalescents could take the air. A simple rectangle with two wings at each end extending backwards to enclose prison courts, the façade replicated that of the Law Courts facing it, although the end bays were not added until 1803, to the design of Peter Atkinson. The building is now the Castle Museum.

East Riding of Yorkshire Record Office, Order Book E 1771–82, 1779, 400; Grimston Papers, DDGR/42/28
North Yorkshire County Record Office, North Riding Quarter Sessions Order Books; accounts of County Treasurer 1770–78; Christopher Gouldon's accounts
Victoria County History, *City of York* (London, 1961), 526
Royal Commission on Historical Monuments, *City of York* (London, 1972), II, 85–86
BE/ER/192

Garforth House, 54 Micklegate, York (Fig. 12)

Revd Edmund Garforth
New house, *c.* 1753–57
Attributed

Edmund Garforth, born Dring, inherited money from his uncle William Garforth, a York merchant, in 1746 on the condition that he changed his name to Garforth. In 1750 he married Elizabeth, daughter of the Hon. Thomas Willoughby of Birdsall and Garforth House was built soon after. A rainwater head dated 1757 probably marks the completion of the building. According to Knowles's *York Artists* the house was built by Carr and as Carr is known to have worked for Garforth at Askham Hall the attribution is considered strong. Built of brick with stone details, the house is five bays wide and three storeys high with a slight projecting three-bay centrepiece and pediment. The interior, which has an unusual plan, has excellent Rococo plasterwork both on the staircase and in the first-floor saloon.

York Central Library, YO 40, John Knowles, *York Artists*, I, 104
West Yorkshire Archive Service, Leeds, Letters of William Gossip
Royal Commission on Historical Monuments, *City of York* (London, 1972), III, 76–77

Knavesmire Grandstand, York (Fig. 13)
Under the patronage of 2nd Marquis of Rockingham
New racestand, 1754–57

In December 1753 the York Corporation granted a 99-year lease and leave to erect a stand on the racecourse at Knavesmire. Four architects submitted designs, two amateurs, Sir Thomas Robinson and Robert Dingley, and James Paine and John Carr. Robinson had already made a design for the grandstand in October. Carr and Paine's schemes were submitted in 1754.

Carr's proposal draws on that of Sir Thomas Robinson but was two bays wider and had a balcony or 'miranda' which freed the principal room from its dual role as a reception room and viewing area. 'Miranda' presumably comes from the Latin *mirandus*, meaning wonderful, suggesting something about the quality of the view.

The cost of the building, which was completed for the August 1756 races, was £1,896 0s 7¼d. The bricklayers were paid £769, the joiners £260, the plumbers and glaziers £330, the plasterer, Richard Ward, £20, and John Carr, his fees of £160 10s. The final payment to Carr was made on 27 August 1760. Carr capitalized on his success with the publication in 1755 of an engraving by Fourdrinier and of a perspective by his assistant William Lindley in about 1760. Many of the subscribers were to become Carr patrons, including the Marquis of Rockingham, the Earl of Carlisle, Lord Irwin, Daniel Lascelles, Edwin Lascelles and Viscount Fairfax.

The building established a precedent in grandstand design and was followed by a series of grandstands in the North modelled upon it over the next thirty years. The stand was removed before 1925 and the groundfloor was re-erected in the paddock.

Sheffield Archives, WWM A1395, Grandstand at York Subscription Book 1755
R. B. Wragg, 'The Stand House on the Knavesmire', *York Georgian Society Report*, 1965/66, 3–9
Royal Commission on Historical Monuments, *City of York* (London, 1972), III, 50–51
Tessa Gibson, 'The Designs for the Knavesmire Grandstand, York', *Georgian Group Journal*, 8 (1998), 76–87
BE/ER/201

Micklegate Bar, York
Corporation of York
Alterations, 1753–54

In 1753 the corporation paid £96 for work on Micklegate Bar in which Carr created two arches in the wall adjacent to the Bar, and also made repairs to ramparts.

York Archives, B43/422, CB38/18–18ᵛ
Victoria County History, *The City of York* (London, 1961), 209

House in Oglethorpe, York
William Gossip
Alterations, 1757
Demolished, late nineteenth century

In 1757 William Gossip, Carr's patron at Thorp Arch, was negotiating with Lady Legard to lease her his house in York. Lady Legard proved a demanding tenant, insisting on extensive alterations before she took on the house. William Fleming was in charge of the bricklayers, but Carr supplied masons and new marble chimneypieces in some of the rooms.

Brett Harrison, 'William Gossip's House in Oglethorpe. York, 1733–1808', *York Historian*, 15 (1998), 53–59

Petergate House, Petergate, York
J. Mitchell
New house, 1755

The A.P.S.D. records a house for J. Mitchell in Petergate of 1755 among Carr's commissions. It was probably demolished on the creation of Duncombe Place in 1862–63.

Wyatt Papworth (ed.), *The Dictionary of Architecture issued by the Architectural Publications Society* (London, 1877), II, 36

Pikeing Well, New Walk, York (Fig. 10)
Corporation of York
New building enclosing a medicinal spring, 1752–56

Carr was commissioned to build a new structure to form a decorated well-head over the Pikeing Well, York's answer to a spa, in 1752. His design, which seems to reuse medieval masonry and has a rusticated doorway, was inspired by grotto designs.

York Archives, B43/318, 394, 417, B44/18, CB39/6, 12
Royal Commission on Historical Monuments, *City of York* (London, 1975), IV, 53

253 Skeldergate House, York, porch

St Leonard's Landings, York
Theophilus Garenciers
New stable and offices, 1774

In 1774 a stable, coach house, kitchen and offices near St Leonard's Landings leased by Theophilus Garenciers from the city corporation burnt down. A new lease was granted on the provision that Garenciers rebuild the buildings 'according to Mr Alderman Carr's plan' and at a cost of at least £150.

York Archives, B44/348–49

St Saviour Gate, York
Corporation of York
Alterations to the street line, 1756

Two drawings in the City House Books for 1756, concerning a revision of the building line in St Saviour Gate near its junction with Peasholme Green and the siting of a proposed house for Mr Dawson in Bishophill, though not signed, are apparently in Carr's hand.

York Archives, B44/1, 29

Skeldergate House, Skeldergate, York (Figs 18, 253)
John Carr
New house, 1765–66

The A.P.S.D. list of Carr's commissions includes a house for himself in York. This was in Skeldergate where he bought a house in 1751. In 1764–65 he bought two adjoining properties and redeveloped the site. Work was probably complete by October 1766 when a lease of a garden facing the river which Carr took from the city corporation referred to his 'new house'. The house, which was substantial and handsomely fitted out, is described in the sale particulars published in the *York Courant* in 1813. After Carr's death it was left to his nephew William Carr. Albion Street was built on the site of the house's gardens in 1815. The house was demolished in 1945.

York Archives, E93/268-9, E94/58ᵛ–59, 75, 86; B44/215
York Courant, 30 August 1813, 18 October, 1813, 11 April, 1814
R. Davies, 'A Memoir of John Carr', *Yorkshire Archaeological Journal*, 4 (1877), 206
Sidney Kitson, 'Carr of York', *RIBA Journal*, 3rd ser., 17 (1910), 248, plate

York Minster, York
Dean and Chapter
Survey and repairs, 1770–73; repairs, 1794–97

In 1770 Carr submitted a detailed nineteen-page survey of the condition of the minster, which survives with annotations noting whether suggested repairs had been executed. The nave roof was condemned as 'exceeding bad [and previously] much injudiciously repaired', with some principal wooden beams 'so much sunk by the weight of the Roof, that they are incapable of being properly repaired'. Carr recommended supporting the failing structures 'as soon as Possible' by adding a system of 'new Beams' and 'Horizontal Collar Beams under the King Posts, and oblique Braces from the Foot of the ... Ceiling to the several Prince Posts'. Some of the beams required 'Straps of Iron to secure the Joints of the Ribs'. The south transept roof 'wants Splicing and Straping with a Plate of Iron'. The leads of one roof were 'so misplaced that the Rain runs into the Roof'. 'Several holes in the ceiling' also needed repairing. The estimated cost 'upon a moderate Valuation' was around £4,200. For this Carr was paid £21 10s 6d in 1771. Some, but not all, of his recommendations were carried out as the fabric fund was worth a mere £200 a year and only £697 was raised by a subscription.

In February 1794 Carr was called in again when further problems were found in the nave roof. He served until 1797 as consultant architect to the dean and chapter at a salary of £100 a year. A further survey was produced of 'the canopy of the middle aisle' in which he reported that the lead on the south side of the middle aisle of the nave had totally perished. At his suggestion the lead was replaced by Westmorland slates. Browne records that the decision was taken to clean the whole interior, in the course of which the gilded bosses in the vaults, the gilded ribs and all the decoration of the vaults and walls were either painted or coated with lime and ochre and all the remnants of the former embellishments were lost.

However, the opportunity of the extensive scaffolding was taken by Joseph Halfpenny to record details of the building which he published in 1795–1800 as *Gothic Ornaments in the Cathedral Church of York drawn and Etched by Joseph Halfpenny*, a volume to which Carr subscribed.

York Minster Library, A4/1/a1, 'A Report of the State of the Minster at York. Made by Jno. Carr. 1770. Then Lord Mayor of York', with a note of the work done, dated 22 February 1773; H 9/3, 'Acts of Chapter Beginning 11th: Novr. 1784 and ending 16th: Septr. 1807 inclusive'; E4a, 'The Fabrick Book of Rents & Accounts' 1661–1827, fols 68, 71ᵛ; information from Dr Terry Friedman

John Browne, *History of the Metropolitan Church of St Peter, York* (London, 1847), 317–18

J. Wylson 'York Minster: its Fires and Restorations', *Builder*, 3 (1845), 158

G. E. Aylmer and Reginald Cant, *A History of York Minster* (Oxford, 1977), 249–50

Terry Friedman, 'Church Architecture in Leeds 1700–1799', *Thoresby Society* 2nd ser., 7 (1996), 35

JOHN CARR'S COMMISSIONS ARRANGED BY DATE

T HE EXTENT of John Carr's architectural career means that a study of his buildings by date has considerable interest in gauging the volume of work executed by his practice. Inevitably such a list can only be indicative. Although we have firm building dates for many of his projects, for others we have only a single date, perhaps indicating the completion of a building. Where the date for the start of the project is known this has been used, otherwise the firmest known date has been taken. Where no plausible date is known the house has not been included.

No account has been made for the significance of a commission, which might be a minor alteration or a complete building. No distinction is made between bridges and other buildings. Bridges are particularly significant from the 1780s.

Where there are distinct building projects at the same house these are distinguished. However, where Carr was involved in continuous building work for the same patron over many years only one date is recorded. This means that Harewood and Wentworth Woodhouse, where Carr worked extensively on a number of projects over many years, have only been counted once. Unexecuted projects have not been included.

What is noticeable is the escalation of Carr's career in the 1760s, its peaking in the mid-1770s and a marked drop during the American War of Independence.

1748	2	1763	8	1778	3	1793	2
1749	0	1764	8	1779	3	1794	2
1750	4	1765	7	1780	3	1795	6
1751	1	1766	6	1781	7	1796	2
1752	4	1767	5	1782	5	1797	4
1753	2	1768	8	1783	3	1798	1
1754	5	1769	5	1784	2	1799	2
1755	4	1770	5	1785	5	1800	3
1756	5	1771	8	1786	5	1801	0
1757	3	1772	7	1787	3	1802	2
1758	1	1773	10	1788	2	1803	3
1759	3	1774	13	1789	4	1804	0
1760	5	1775	5	1790	1	1805	0
1761	4	1776	10	1791	4	1806	3
1762	9	1777	4	1792	2	1807	0

NOTES

INTRODUCTION

1 E. W. Harcourt (ed.), *The Harcourt Papers* (Oxford, n.d.), VII, 49–52.

2 R. A. Davies, 'A Memoir of John Carr', *Yorkshire Archaeological Journal*, 4 (1877), 202.

3 On 14 July 1804 Carr wrote to Benjamin Hall asking him to pay his salary direct to the bank. According to L. S. Pressnell and John Orbell, *British Banking*, Aldershot, 1985, no records survive of this bank. Barclays Bank Archives, Goslings Bank, ledgers 43/182; 46/482; 49/192; 53/210.

4 West Yorkshire Archive Service, Leeds, Harewood Papers, SC 1/1/65.

5 Leeds General Infirmary Letter Book, 7 June 1768.

CHAPTER 1: YOUTH

1 *Gentleman's Magazine*, 77 (1807), 1, 202.

2 Thomas Whitaker, *Loidis and Elmete* (Leeds, 1816), II, 1816.

3 John Charlesworth (ed.), *The Registers of the Chapel at Horbury*, Yorkshire Parish Register Society, 1900.

4 Lancashire Record Office, DDB acc. 6685.

5 John Charlesworth (ed.), *The Registers of the Chapel at Horbury*, Yorkshire Parish Register Society, 1900, 151, 184.

6 Yorkshire Archaeological Society, Radcliffe Correspondence, Lot 112.

7 Lancashire Record Office, DDB acc. 6685, box 189, bundle 2.

8 Lancashire Record Office, DDB acc. 6685, box 189, bundle 2.

9 Now in the North Yorkshire County Record Office.

10 Horbury Book of Accounts, I, 32.

11 West Riding Yorkshire Archive Service, Wakefield, County Clerk Order Books, 13 January 1742.

12 *Idem.*, 12 April 1743.

13 York Central Library. However, it should be noted that the document varies in several details from the Horbury Parish Records.

14 The relevant entry in the Church Register reads, 'Robert Carr of Wakefield & Rose Lascels of Cundal married with a Licence November 13, 1721.'

15 Yorkshire Archaeological Society, Radcliffe Corr., Lot 112.

16 A further suggestion of Northumbrian gentry origins comes in a paper at Browsholme Hall, Lancashire, 'The Genealogy of the Clark Family', written in 1889 by C. F. G. Clark. This suggests that the first Carr of Horbury, who arrived in the township in the first half of the seventeenth century, might have been a younger son of the Carrs of Southey 'but that as lesser gentry of the North about that time were miserably poor a younger son moving to a new locality would not be likely to take a high rank unless by a good marriage; and his children again would have to take to a trade to earn a livelihood'. Clark did not explain why the Carrs of Southey should have been particularly singled out. The connection has proved impossible to trace, and it would appear that Clark, a descendant of the Carrs on the female side, was putting the rosiest complexion on his own ancestry.

17 South Kilvington Parish Register; information from the Revd Dudley Hill.

18 He was elected to a Cave Scholarship at Clare College, Cambridge, in 1754, became Sixth Wrangler and a Fellow of his College in 1758, M.A. in 1761 and D.D. in 1782. Eventually he was made Prebendary of St Paul's Cathedral, London. He was Rector of the united parishes of St Andrew Undershaft and St Mary Axe, and Rector of St Mary, Finchley. He married Elizabeth Jackson, daughter of a York linen draper at St Clements in the Strand in 1768. Buried Abbey Church, Bath, 1794.

19 East Riding of Yorkshire Record Office, Grimston Papers, DD GR43/5/37. Also, on 17 June 1786 'never in my 49 years experience ...' Sheffield Archives, WWM, Stw P.6 (ii) 157.

20 R. A. Davies, 'A Memoir of John Carr', *Yorkshire Archaeological Journal*, 4 (1877), 207–08.

21 *Ibid.*, 210.

22 *Ibid.*, 203.

23 *Ibid.*, 203.

24 Peter Thornborrow, 'John Carr's West Yorkshire Buildings', *York Georgian Society Report*, 1992, 29.

25 St Peter's, Felkirk Parish Registers.

26 *Ibid.*, baptized 11 December 1712.

27 R. A. Davies, 'A Memoir of John Carr', *Yorkshire Archaeological Journal*, 4 (1877), 202.

28 Yorkshire Archaeological Society, Leeds. Radcliffe Corr., Lot 112, Letter 103.

29 West Yorkshire Archive Service, Leeds, Harewood Papers, SC 2/2/220, 3/3/204.

30 C. F. G Clark, 'The Genealogy of the Clark Family'. Harriet married Thomas Swann, Banker, York in 1796; Amelia, William Rayner, Cloth Merchant, Horbury in 1804 and Caroline, Robert Ogden, Cotton Spinner of 'The Oaks', Manchester, in 1815.

31 J. B. Atkinson, *Dictionary of Architecture* (London, 1877), II, 36.

32 C. R. Andrews, *Story of Wortley Ironworks* (Nottingham, 1956), 45.

33 Giles Worsley, *Classical Architecture in Britain: The Heroic Age* (New Haven and London, 1995), 223–26. Other architects who established themselves at this time include James Paine, William Hiorn, Thomas Wright, Stephen Wright, Sir Robert Taylor and Stiff Leadbetter.

34 East Riding of Yorkshire Record Office, Grimston Papers, DD GR41/4/44.

35 East Riding of Yorkshire Record Office, Grimston Papers, DD GR 41/5/13, 41/6/18.

36 East Riding of Yorkshire Record Office, Grimston Papers, DD GR/41.

37 R. A. Davies, 'A Memoir of John Carr', *Yorkshire Archaeological Journal*, 4 (1877), 212.

38 Sidney Kitson, 'Carr of York', *RIBA Journal*, 17 (1910), 241–66.

39 York Archives, E93/268–69.

40 York Archives, B43/394.

41 York Archives, CB39/6, 12ᵛ.

42 York Archives, B43/422.

43 York Archives, CB38/18–18ᵛ.

44 York Archives, M23/1.

45 West Yorkshire Archive Service, Wakefield, Book of Bridges, 1752–70.

46 Brett Harrison, 'Thorp Hall 1749–1756: "dabling a little in Mortar"', *Thoresby Society*, 2nd ser., 4 (1994 for 1993), 28, 39.

47 West Yorkshire Archive Service, Leeds, Harewood Papers, SC 1/1/65.

48 The editor is indebted to Mr Andrew Martindale for this observation.

49 Wakefield City Art Gallery, Gott Collection, vol. x, fol. 7., discovered by Derek Linstrum. 1748 is presumably an error for 1758 when work on the Harewood stables was largely complete.

50 Incidental work continued until 1759.

51 West Yorkshire Archive Service, Leeds, Harewood papers, Ledger for the New House and Stables.

52 Possibly William Jones who designed the Rotunda at Ranelagh Gardens, or Richard Jones who worked on Prior Park, Bath.

53 Drawings are now distributed between Harewood Stables, Leeds City Archives and the Borthwick Institute, York.

54 Royal Institute of British Architects Library, CHA/2/3, John Hall Stevenson to William Chambers, November 1755.

55 Dorothy Stroud, *Capability Brown* (London, 1975), 105.

56 British Library, Add. MSS 41135, 35b; 41136, 19–21, 35.

57 This could refer to a house for Popplewell himself, although this was not finished until 1767.

58 Scottish Record Office, Penicuik Muniments, GD 18/4848.

CHAPTER 2: MATURITY

1 York City Archives, B 44/1, 9.

2 West Yorkshire Archive Service, Leeds, Harewood papers, SC 2/2/7.

3 York Archives, E93/268–69.

4 York Archives, E94/58ᵛ–59, 75, 86.

5

		Self	House or Land	Total
Aldm. Carr	Houses (lateNewton's)	1¼		1¼
Ditto	Self and Ho	2	1¼	3¼
Ditto	Rodwells Ho	1½		1½
Ditto	Atkinsons Ho	1¼		?1½
Ditto	Kiplings Ho		1½	1½
Ditto	Duke's Hall and Yard	1		1
Ditto	New House		3½	3½
Dittolate	Harrison's	3		3
Ditto	Fairfax Close	1		1

6 *York Courant*, 30 August 1813, 18 October 1813, 11 April 1814.

7 York Archives, B44/215.

8 Jeffrey (1792); Francis White (1785).

9 York Archives, B44/207.

10 Francis Drake, *Eboracum* (London, 1736), 183.

11 York Archives, B44/253.

12 York Archives, B44/258.

13 East Riding of Yorkshire Record Office, Grimston Papers, DDGR/42/20/35.

14 York Archives, B44/349.

15 York Archives, B44/444.

16 York Archives, B45/206.

17 Sheffield Archives, WWM, Stw P 6 (ii) 134.

18 Sheffield Archives, LD1164/52.

19 York Archives, B46/180.

20 A large centrepiece has the inscription 'Presented to the Corporation of York by Alderman John Carr with great respect, 1796'.

21 York Archives, B47/9.

22 Sheffield Archives, WWM, Stw P6 (vii) 70.

23 York Central Library, City House Books

24 For a comprehensive study of York and Yorkshire politics at this time see Sir Lewis Namier and John Brooke, *The History of Parliament: The House of Commons 1754–90* (London, 1964), on which this account is largely based.

25 W. S. Lewis, *The Correspondence of Horace Walpole* (London, 1955), XXVIII, 362.

26 Sheffield Archives, WWM, Stw P6 (ii) 2.

27 Sheffield Archives, WWM, Stw P6 (ii) 237.

28 Sheffield Archives, WWM, F34/59.

29 Sheffield Archives, WWM, Bundle E18–21, election 1784.

30 Sheffield Archives, WWM, Stw P6 (v) 17.

31 *York Courant*, 15 May 1797.

32 North Yorkshire County Record Office, ZFW 7/2/108/3.

33 Sheffield Archives, BFM 1316/22.

34 Records of Santa Casa da Misericordia do Porto.

35 East Riding of Yorkshire Record Office, DDGR 42/21/127.

36 North Yorkshire County Record Office, Book of Bridges.

37 West Riding Yorkshire Archive Service, Wakefield, County Clerk Order Books Order Books, 27 April 1761.

38 Sheffield Archives, BFM 1326/44.

39 Sheffield Archives, WWM, Stw P6 (ii) 17.

40 Sheffield Archives, WWM, MP8.

41 Nottingham University Library, Portland Papers, PwF 2,536.

42 A. E. Richardson, *Robert Milne* (London, 1955), 67.

43 William Bray, *Sketch of a Tour into Derbyshire and Yorkshire* (London, 1783), 344.

44 T. Connor, 'The Building of Campsmount', *Yorkshire Archaeological Journal*, 47 (1975), 121–32.

45 West Yorkshire Archive Service, Leeds, Lane Fox 118/18.

46 West Yorkshire Archive Service, Leeds, Thorp Arch, TA 19/4, 21 May 1751.

47 West Yorkshire Archive Service, Leeds, Harewood papers, SC 2/2/50.

48 Leeds General Infirmary Letter Book, 7 June 1768.

49 We know from his letters, that he was in London in 1777, 1778, 1781, 1783, 1784, 1785, 1786, 1788, 1789, 1791, 1792, twice in 1793 and once in 1796.

50 Sheffield Archives, WWM, Stw P6 (iii) 53.

51 Sheffield Archives, WWM, Stw P6 (v) 84.

52 Sheffield Archives, WWM, Stw P6 (i) 93.

53 Sheffield Archives, WWM, Stw P6 (iv) 72.

54 East Riding of Yorkshire Record Office, DDGR 42/21/38.

55 Sheffield Archives, LD 1164/52; East Riding Record Office, DDGR 42/21/127.

56 York Archives, M23/1,2,4.

57 Sheffield Archives, WWM, Stw P6 (iii) 116.

58 York Minster Library, MSS Add. 328/1, fol. 11, 328/2.

59 York Minster Library, MS Add. 328/2, fol. 38.

60 Nottingham University Library, Portland papers, PwF 2,549.

61 R. A. Davies, 'A Memoir of John Carr' *Yorkshire Archaeological Journal*, 4 (1877), 210.

CHAPTER 3: THE PRACTICE

1 The document once encouraged the idea that it was the original draft of the much maligned book and that Langley was really Carr in disguise.

2 York City Art Gallery.

3 East Riding of Yorkshire Record Office, DDGR 42/19/70 3/7/1769.

4 Angus Taylor, 'William Lindley of Doncaster', *Georgian Group Journal*, 4 (1994).

5 Sheffield Archives, WWM Stw P6 (ii) 6.

6 Sheffield Archives, WWM Stw P6 (ii) 133; Lancashire Record Office, Parker of Browsholme Papers DDB acc. 6685, box 33, bundle 7.

7 Sheffield Archives, WWM Stw P6 (iv) 75.

8 Lancashire Record Office, Parker of Browsholme Papers DDB acc. 6685, box 33, bundle 7, box 189, bundle 2.

NOTES

9 Lancashire Record Office, DDTO Box 2.

10 Leeds General Infirmary 13/1, building committee minutes, 29 May 1769.

11 Sheffield Archives, WWM Stw P6 (iii) 194.

12 Barclays Bank Archives, Goslings Bank Ledgers.

13 Sheffield Archives, WWM Stw P6 (i) 188.

14 Lancashire County Record Office, DDCA 22/9/9.

15 Sheffield Archives, WWM Stw P6 (ii) 49.

16 Sheffield Archives, WWM Stw P6 (iii) 61.

17 York Archives, Register of Apprentices' Indentures, 20 July 1757.

18 Temple Newsam Museum, Leeds, Abstract of Accounts of Denton Park.

19 Nottinghamshire County Record Office, Huthwaite papers, M5936.

20 Nottingham University Library, Portland Papers, PwF 2,539.

21 West Yorkshire Archives Service, Leeds, Harewood Papers, SC 1/1/65 22/9/54.

22 Sheffield Archives, CB 598/2, PR Box 7.

23 Sheffield Archives, BFM 1314/60.

24 Sheffield Archives, BFM 1314/67.

25 West Yorkshire Archives Service, Leeds, Harewood Papers, SC 3/3/204.

26 West Yorkshire Archives Service, Leeds, Harewood Papers, SC 4/1/51.

27 West Yorkshire Archives Service, Leeds, Harewood Papers, SC 4/1/87.

28 Sheffield Archives, BFM 1316/22.

29 Nottinghamshire County Record Office, Huthwaite Papers, M 5936.

30 Sheffield Archives, WWM Stw P6 (ii) 17.

31 Sheffield Archives, WWM Stw P6 (iii) 192, (iv) 150, (vii) 70.

32 E. W. Harcourt (ed.), The Harcourt Papers (Oxford, n.d.), VII, 49–52.

33 East Riding of Yorkshire Record Office, DDGR 43/7/37.

34 Sheffield Archives, WWM Stw P6 (i) 159.

35 Sheffield Archives, WWM Stw P6 (iii) 51.

36 Sheffield Archives, WWM Stw P6 (i) 128.

37 West Yorkshire Archives Service, Leeds, Harewood Papers, SC 1/1/1.

38 The rejected design for Platt Hall is signed 'Jno Carr, 1761'.

39 Sheffield Archives, BFM 1326/44.

40 Sheffield Archives, LD 1164/52.

41 Sheffield Archives, BFM 1316/1.

42 Leeds General Infirmary Book of Letters 1767–73, 2 March 1769.

43 Sheffield Archives, WWM Stw P6 (ii) 133.

44 Sheffield Archives, BFM 1316/6.

45 Sheffield Archives, WWM Stw P6 (iii) 49.

46 Sheffield Archives, WWM Stw P6 (iii) 57.

47 Sheffield Archives, WWM Stw P6 (iii) 76.

48 John Bradshaw and Ivan Hall, John Carr of York: Architect 1723–1807, catalogue of the 1973 Ferens Art Gallery Exhibition, Hull, no. 29.

49 Sheffield Archives, Spencer-Stanhope papers, 60633/21.

50 Sheffield Archives, WWM Stw P6 (i) 81.

51 Sheffield Archives, WWM Stw P6 (ii) 50.

52 Chatsworth Archives, Buxton MSS, C42.

53 Sheffield Archives, LD 1164/29.

54 In the possession of Mrs R. B. Wragg.

55 York Minster Library, Fabric Rolls.

56 Sheffield Archives, LD 1164/29.

57 E. W. Harcourt, The Harcourt Papers (Oxford, n.d.), vii, 52.

58 In 1783, for instance, prior to negotiating for the building of Northallerton Court House, the North Riding magistrates were busily arranging for the supply of bricks ('at a sum not exceeding Eight Shillings per thousand …').

59 Nottingham University Library, Galway MSS, 12415.

60 Sheffield Archives, WWM Stw P6 (iii) 157.

61 East Riding of Yorkshire, DDGR 43/7/33.

62 Nottinghamshire County Record Office, Staunton papers, 43/22a.

63 Nottingham University Library, Manvers papers, Ma 2X 2(i).

64 Sheffield Archives, WWM Stw P6 (v) 17.

65 North Yorkshire County Record Office, ZAG 22.

66 Sheffield Archives, WWM Stw P6 (iii) 199.

67 J. H. Hodson, 'The Building and Alteration of the Second Thoresby House, 1767–1804', Thoroton Society Record Series, 21 (1962), 16–20.

68 Archaeological Journal, 103 (1946), 158.

69 North Yorkshire County Record Office, QFA (A) North Riding Treasurer's Accounts, 1765–83.

70 North Yorkshire County Record Office, ZK 6628.

71 In June 1768 a payment of 50 guineas was made to Carr through his brother, the Revd Samuel Carr.

72 Barclays Bank Archives, Goslings Bank, 56/99,102, 60/112, 60/114, 64/107, 64/273, 68/525, 72/124, 72/125, 72/126, 72/127.

73 Information from Mr J. P. G. Taylor.

74 Barclays Bank Archives, Goslings Bank, 44/272, 274, 51/147, 55/179.

75 North Yorkshire County Record Office, ZAG 22.

76 R. B. Wragg, 'Scagliola: A Substitute for Marble', Country Life, 21 October 1957; R. B. Wragg, 'Charles Clerici: Craftsman in Scagliola', Architectural Review, 7 December, 1959.

77 Sheffield Archives, WWM, Stw P6 (iii) 57.

78 Sheffield Archives, WWM, Stw P6 (iv) 158, (v) 6.

79 Sheffield Archives, WWM, Stw P6 (iv) 116, (v) 6.

80 Sheffield Archives, LD 1164/23.

81 E. W. Harcourt (ed.), The Harcourt Papers (Oxford, n.d.), VII, 52.

82 T. D. Whitaker, Loidis and Elmete (Leeds, 1816), 295.

83 Peter Leach, James Paine (London, 1988), 144.

CHAPTER 4: OLD AGE

1 Ellen Wilson, 'Beilby Porteus, Occasional Memorandums & Reflexions on Several Subjects. Vol. 4 MS 2103, Lambeth Palace Library', York Georgian Society Report, 1978, 56.

2 Sheffield Archives, WWM Stw P6 (iv) 259.

3 Sheffield Archives, WWM Stw P6 (v) 17.

4 They could have been relatives of Carr's wife for they came from Carlton not far from Sarah's birthplace.

5 York Archives, B47/9.

6 Sheffield Archives, WWM Stw P6 (iv) 175.

7 Sheffield Archives, WWM Stw P6 (v) 55.

8 Sheffield Archives, WWM Stw P6 (vii) 199.

9 Lancashire Record Office, Parker of Browsholme Papers DDB acc. 6685, box 189, bundle 2; box 33, bundle 7; Public Record Office, IR 27/93.

10 Lancashire Record Office, Parker of Browsholme Papers DDB acc. 6685, box 189, bundle 2.

11 Joseph Hunter, South Yorkshire (London, 1831), II, 397.

12 Lancashire Record Office, Parker of Browsholme Papers DDB acc. 6685, box 133, bundle 4.

13 Sheffield Archives, WWM Stw P6 (v) 88, 89.

14 Lancashire Record Office, Parker of Browsholme Papers DDB acc. 6685, Box 189, bundle 4.

15 York Minster Library, MS Add. 328/1, fol. 25.

16 Diary of Miss Elizabeth Chivers; quoted in H. M. Colvin, Biographical Dictionary of British Architects (New Haven and London, 1995), 221.

17 British Architectural Library OS 5/8; Lancashire Record Office, Parker of Browsholme Papers, DDB acc. 6685, box 178, bundle 3.

18 British Architectural Library OS 5/8.

19 The younger John Carr was described as being 'of Carr Lodge' in 1790, Lancashire Record Office, Parker of Browsholme Papers DDB acc. 6685, box 178, bundle 4; York Minster Library, MS Add. 328/2; 'A memorandum of Elizabeth Chivers's Journey made with her Parents in the year 1803', information from Sir Howard Colvin.

20 Sheffield Archives, WWM Stw P6 (vii) 139.

21 British Architectural Library OS 5/8.

22 *York Courant*, 31 July 1787.

23 Unfortunately, the Bank of England Archives have been in storage for the past three years so it has not been possible to trace Carr's investments there in any greater detail.

24 West Yorkshire Archives Service, Leeds, Harewood Papers, SC 1/3/140.

25 West Yorkshire Archives Service, Leeds, Harewood Papers, SC 3/3/1 2/1/1761.

26 Sheffield Archives, Spencer-Stanhope papers, 60633/21.

27 Sheffield Archives, WWM Stw P6 (ii) 49.

28 Nottingham University Library, Middleton papers Mi Da 153/1.

29 Julia Ionides, *Thomas Farnolls Pritchard of Shrewsbury* (Ludlow, 1999), 215.

30 Nottingham University Library, Portland Papers, PwF 2,541.

31 Nottingham University Library, Portland Papers, PwF 2,542.

32 Nottingham University Library, Portland Papers, PwF 2,543.

33 Sheffield Archives, WWM Stw P6 (ii) 107.

34 Sheffield Archives, WWM Stw P6 (i) 159.

35 Sheffield Archives, WWM Stw P6 (iii) 51.

36 Sheffield Archives, WWM Stw P6 (iii) 61.

37 Sheffield Archives, WWM Stw P6 (iii) 76.

38 Sheffield Archives, WWM Stw P6 (iii) 181.

39 Sheffield Archives, WWM Stw P6 (iv) 9 August 1789.

40 Sheffield Archives, WWM Stw P6 (iv) 72.

41 Sheffield Archives, WWM Stw P6 (iv) 75.

42 Sheffield Archives, WWM Stw P6 (iv) 114.

43 Sheffield Archives, WWM Stw P6 (iv) 108.

44 Sheffield Archives, WWM Stw P6 (iv) 172, 178.

45 Sheffield Archives, WWM Stw P6 (iv) 181.

46 Sheffield Archives, WWM Stw P6 (iv) 184.

47 Sheffield Archives, WWM Stw P6 (iv) 1794.

48 Sheffield Archives, WWM Stw P6 (v) 6.

49 Sheffield Archives, WWM Stw P6 (v) 17.

50 Sheffield Archives, WWM Stw P6 (vi) 119.

51 Sheffield Archives, WWM Stw P6 (v) 19.

52 Sheffield Archives, WWM, Carr to Fitzwilliam, 22/1/1796.

53 East Riding of Yorkshire Record Office, DDGR 42/21/38.

54 York Minster Library, MS Add. 328/1, 3.

55 Sheffield Archives, WWM, Carr to Fitzwilliam, 9/1/1796.

56 Sheffield Archives, WWM Stw P6 (v) 62.

57 Sheffield Archives, WWM Stw P6 (v) 84.

58 York Minster Library, MS Add. 328/2.

59 Gloucestershire County Record Office, FF38 D1245/C/4.

60 York Minster Archives, MS Add. 328/2.

61 Gloucestershire County Record Office, FF38/D 1245/C.

62 Hovingham Archives, Bower ZON 3, 7 October 1805.

63 Chatsworth Archives, Letter 533, 15 September 1783; quoted in Ivan Hall, 'A Neoclassical Episode at Chatsworth', *Burlington Magazine* (June, 1980), 410.

64 Sheffield Archives, WWM Stw P6 (vi) 110, 112.

65 Sheffield Archives, WWM Stw P6 (vii) 12.

66 R. Davies, 'A Memoir of John Carr', *Yorkshire Archaeological Journal*, 4 (1877), 205.

67 A. Booth, 'Notes on the "New Bridge" at Ferrybridge', *RIBA Journal*, 39 (1931), 55–56; West Riding Yorkshire Archive Service, Wakefield, County Clerk Order Books, 27 January 1797.

68 North Yorkshire County Record Office, Quarter Sessions Order Book of North Riding, 15 April 1806.

69 North Yorkshire County Record Office, Yarm Bridge Archives.

70 Sheffield Archives, WWM Stw P6 (vii) 76.

71 Sheffield Archives, WWM Stw P6 (vii) 110.

72 Sheffield Archives, WWM Stw P6 (vii) 112.

73 Hovingham Archives, Bower ZON 3, c. 1804.

74 Sheffield Archives, WWM Stw P6 (vii) 199.

75 Sheffield Archives, WWM Stw P6 Wwm (vii) 200.

76 Sheffield Archives, WWM Stw P6 Wwm (vii) 214.

77 Sheffield Archives, WWM Stw P6 Wwm (vii) 235.

78 Hovingham Archives, Bower MSS, diary of Elizabeth Chivers, 1805; Giles Worsley, 'John Carr's Last Tour', *Country Life*, 30 April 1987; Giles Worsley, 'Crediting Carr', *Country Life*, 5 May 1988.

79 Gillian Darley, *John Soane: An Accidental Romantic* (New Haven and London, 1999), 115.

80 Hovingham Archives, Bower MSS, ZON 3/1: John Carr, Wentworth House, to Mrs Chivers, Gainsbro, 7 October 1805.

81 Hovingham Archives, Bower MSS, ZON 3/1/1–112.

82 Sheffield Archives, WWM Stw P7 (i) 64.

83 Sheffield Archives, WWM Stw P7 (i) 72.

84 Sheffield Archives, WWM Stw P7 (I) 83.

85 Hovingham Archives, Bower MSS ZON 3/1/37.

86 Sheffield Archives, WWM Stw P7 (i) 88.

87 Sheffield Archives, WWM Stw P7 (i) 89.

88 Sheffield Archives, WWM Stw P7 (i) 194.

89 *Gentleman's Magazine*, 77 (1807), i, 282.

90 Obituary Notice: *Gentleman's Magazine*, 77 (1807), i, 282.

91 Public Record Office, IR 27/93.

92 *York Courant*, 30 August 1813, 18 October 1813, 11 April 1814.

93 Sir John Soane's Museum, Priv. Corr. XVI E4:8.

94 Information from Dr Ivan Hall cited in Gervase Jackson-Stops, 'Ribston Hall, Yorkshire', *Country Life*, 18 October 1973.

95 *Bibliotheca Architectonica*, Priestley and Weale (Bloomsbury, 1825), lots 342–45 and 1540.

96 Harry Speight, *Lower Wharfdale* (London, 1902), 199, 473

97 Lancashire Record Office, Parker of Browsholme Papers DDB acc. 6685, box 128, bundle 1, box 129, bundle 1.

NOTES

SELECT BIBLIOGRAPHY

Anon. 'A Great Yorkshire Architect', *Yorkshire Post*, 25 June 1919

Booth, Alfred, 'Carr of York and the Book of Bridges', *Yorkshire Archaeological Journal*, 38 (1955), 367–72

Bradshaw, John and Ivan Hall, *John Carr of York*, duplicated catalogue of an exhibition held at Ferens Art Gallery (Hull, 1973)

Davies, R., 'A Memoir of John Carr', *Yorkshire Archaeological Journal*, 4 (1877), 202–13

Eden, W. A., *John Carr. An Unpublished Monograph*, University of Liverpool

Eden, W. A. and R. B. Wragg, 'John Carr, Stonecutter Extraordinary, and Architectural Virtuosi', *Transactions of the Ancient Monuments Society*, new ser., 24 (1979–80)

Hall, Ivan, 'John Carr: A New Approach', *York Georgian Society Report*, 1972, 18–28

Harrison, K. L., 'John Carr of York, A Master Builder', *Dalesman*, December 1968, 707–10

Ingamells, John, 'Portraits of John Carr', *City of York Art Gallery Quarterly*, January 1971, 842–47

Ingram, M. E., 'John Carr's Contribution to the Gothic Revival', *Transactions of the Georgian Society for East Yorkshire*, 2 and 3 (1947–48), 43–52

Kitson, S. D., 'Carr of York', *RIBA Journal*, 17 (1910), 241–66

Papworth, Wyatt (ed.), *The Dictionary of Architecture issued by the Architectural Publications Society* (London, 1877), 11, 36

Thornborrow, Peter, 'John Carr's West Yorkshire Buildings', *York Georgian Society*, 1992, 29

Worsley, Giles, 'John Carr's Last Tour', *Country Life*, 30 April 1987

Worsley, Giles, 'Crediting Carr', *Country Life*, 5 May 1988

Wragg, R. B., 'Constable Burton Hall', *York Georgian Society Report*, 1955/56, 46–48

Wragg, R, B., 'Some Notes on 18th Century Craftsmen', *York Georgian Society Report*, 1955/56, 55–65

Wragg, R. B., 'John Carr: Gothic Revivalist', in *Studies in Architectural History*, ed. by W. A. Singleton (London and York, 1956), 11, 9–34

Wragg, R. B., 'John Carr's Crescent', *Derbyshire Countryside*, 26 (October/November 1956), 12-13, 33

Wragg, R. B., 'John Carr: Bridgemaster', *York Georgian Society Report*, 1957, 47–54

Wragg, R. B., 'John Carr: Early Years and the Meeting with Robert Adam', *Journal of the West Riding Society of Architects*, 17, No. 3 (December 1957), 8–12

Wragg, R. B. 'Everingham Park: Carr's Work Authenticated', *Transactions of the Georgian Society for East Yorkshire*, 4.11 (1957), 56–58

Wragg, R. B., 'Scagliola: A Substitute for Marble', *Country Life*, 21 October 1957

Wragg, R. B., 'Two Architects of York', *York Georgian Society Report*, 1957/58, 37–42

Wragg, R. B., 'John Carr of York', *Journal of the West Riding Society of Architects*, 17, no. 3 (December 1957), 8–12; no. 4 (March 1958), 11–16

Wragg, R. B., 'Chesters', *Archaeologia Aeliana*, 34 (1958), 221–26

Wragg, R. B., 'The Architect of Greta Bridge', *York Georgian Society Report*, 1958/59, 30–33

Wragg, R. B., 'Charles Clerici: Craftsman in Scagliola', *Architectural Review*, 7 (December 1959)

Wragg, R. B., 'Hospital de Santo Antonio do Porto and Hospital Design', *York Georgian Society Report*, 1959/60, 37–40

Wragg, R. B., 'The Architects of Greta Bridge', *Yorkshire Life Illustrated*, 14, No. 111 (7 March 1960)

Wragg, R. B., 'Stables Worthy of Stately Homes', *Country Life*, 1 November 1962

Wragg, R. B., 'The Standhouse on the Knavesmire', *York Georgian Society Report*, 1965/66, 1–9

Wragg, R. B., 'Small Beginnings', *York Georgian Society Report*, 1967/68

Wragg, R. B., 'Harewood House', *Archaeological Journal*, 125 (1969), 342–47

Wragg, R. B., *The Works of John Carr of York, 1723–1807*, unpublished Ph.D. thesis, Sheffield University, 1975

Wragg, R. B., 'John Carr, a Georgian Bridge Builder', *Industrial Archaeology*, 11 (1977), 74–83

Wragg, R. B. 'A Bath on the Peak', *Country Life*, 6 July 1978

Wragg, R. B., 'The Houses of Clifton and Eastwood, Rotherham', *York Georgian Society*, 1978, 57–65

Wragg, R. B., 'The Architect of the Harewood Stables', *York Georgian Society*, 1979, 66–73

Wragg, R. B., 'The Rockingham Mausoleum', *Yorkshire Archaeological Journal*, 52 (1980), 157–66

Wragg, R. B., 'The Travels of John Carr', *York Georgian Society*, 1980, 59–65

Wragg, Mary and Robert Brian Wragg, 'Two Houses by Carr of York', *Country Life*, 12 April 1956

Wragg, Mary and Brian Wragg, 'A House for Mr Cockshutt', *Hunterian Society Transactions*, 7.v (1956), 271–75

Wragg, M. and R. B. Wragg, 'Admiral Keppel's Column', *Country Life*, 27 December 1956

Wragg, R. B. and M. Wragg, 'Carr in Portugal', *Architectural Review*, February 1959, 127–28

The Works in Architecture of John Carr, a list prepared by the York Georgian Society, York, 1973

Pevsner, Nikolaus, *The Buildings of England, Derbyshire*, rev. by Elizabeth Williamson (Harmondsworth, 1986)

Pevsner, Nikolaus, *The Buildings of England, Durham*, rev. by Elizabeth Williamson (Harmondsworth, 1983)

Pevsner, Nikolaus, *The Buildings of England, Leicestershire*, rev. by Elizabeth Williamson (Harmondsworth, 1984)

Pevsner, Nikolaus, *The Buildings of England, Nottinghamshire* (Harmondsworth, 1979)

Pevsner, Nikolaus, *The Buildings of England: Yorkshire, North Riding* (Harmondsworth, 1966)

Pevsner, Nikolaus, *The Buildings of England, Yorkshire: West Riding*, rev. by Enid Radcliffe (Harmondsworth, 1967)

Pevsner, Nikolaus, and John Harris, *The Buildings of England, Lincolnshire* (revised by Nicholas Antram), Harmondsworth, 1989

Pevsner, Nikolaus, and Ian Richardson, *The Buildings of England, Northumberland*, rev. by John Grundy, Grace McCombie, Peter Ryder and Humphrey Welfare (Harmondsworth, 1992)

Pevsner, Nikolaus, and David Neave, *The Buildings of England, Yorkshire: York and the East Riding* (Harmondsworth, 1966)

LIST OF ILLUSTRATIONS AND PHOTOGRAPHIC ACKNOWLEDGEMENTS

ILLUSTRATIONS

INDEX

Buildings and bridges in **bold type** are in some measure attributable to Carr.
Figure numbers are given in *italic type*.

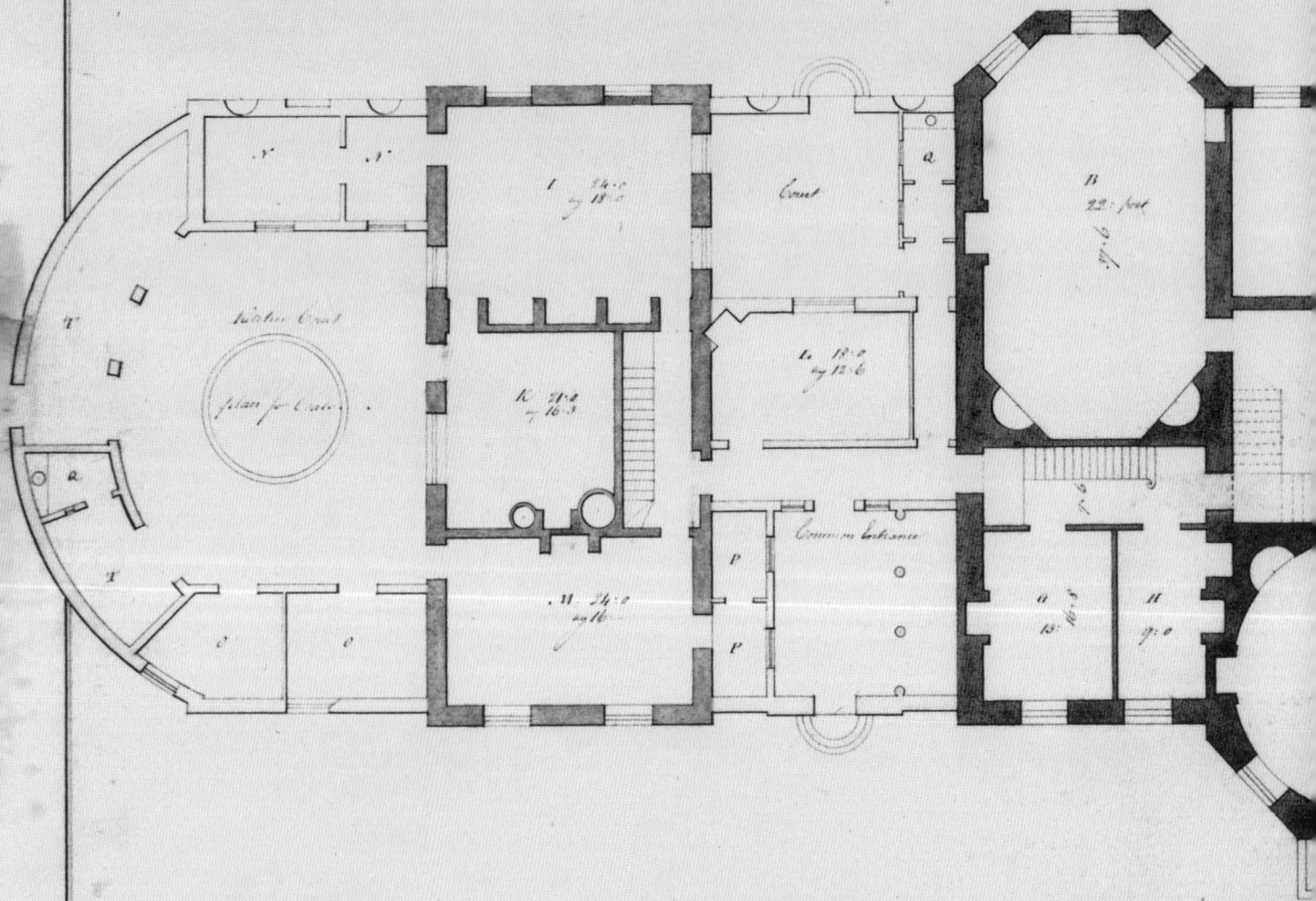

A. The Hall
B. The dining Room
C. The drawing Room
D. The Library & Breakfast Room
E. The Best Stair Case
F. Mr Grysdale's own Room, with four Closets to it
G. The Steward's Room
H. The Butlers Pantry
I. The Kitchen
K. The Back Kitchen
L. The Housekeeper's Room

The Ground Plan of